Ashoka, the Great

ASHOKA THE GREAT

Series Editor
Dr. M.H. Syed

Editor
R.K. Singh **P.K. Choudhry**

Himalaya Books Pvt. Ltd.

'Ramdoot', Dr. Bhalerao Marg, Girgaon, Mumbai - 400 004
Tel : (022) 23863863, Fax : (022) 23877178
Email : himpub@vsnl.com

First Edition : 2011
Edition : 2016

Published by : **H.B.P.L.**
"Pooja Apartment", 4-B, Murari Lal Street, Ansari Road,
Darya Ganj, New Delhi - 110 002.
Phones: 011-23270392, 23278631; Fax: 011-23256286
Email: hphdel@vsnl.com

Sole Distributors : **Himalaya Publishing House Pvt. Ltd.**

Branch Offices :

Mumbai : "Ramdoot", Dr. Bhalerao Marg, Girgaon, Mumbai - 400 004.
Phone: 022-23860170/23863863, Fax: 022-23877178
E-mail: himpub@vsnl.com; Website: www.himpub.com

Nagpur : Kundanlal Chandak Industrial Estate, Ghat Road,
Nagpur - 440 018. Phone: 0712-2738731, 3296733;
Telefax: 0712-2721216

Bengaluru : Plot No. 91-33, 2nd Main Road Seshadripuram,
Behind Nataraja Theatre, Bengaluru-560020.
Phone: 08041138821, 9379847017, 9379847005

Hyderabad : No. 3-4-184, Lingampally, Besides Raghavendra Swamy
Matham, Kachiguda, Hyderabad - 500 027.
Phone: 040-27560041, 27550139

Chennai : New-20, Old-59, Thirumalai Pillai Road, T. Nagar,
Chennai - 600 017. Mobile: 9380460419

Pune : First Floor, "Laksha" Apartment, No. 527, Mehunpura,
Shaniwarpeth (Near Prabhat Theatre), Pune - 411 030.
Phone: 020-24496323/24496333;
Mobile: 09370579333

Lucknow : House No 731, Shekhupura Colony, Near B.D. Convent School,
Aliganj, Lucknow - 226 022. Phone: 0522-4012353;
Mobile: 09307501549

Ahmedabad : 114, "SHAIL", 1st Floor, Opp. Madhu Sudan House, C.G. Road,
Navrang Pura, Ahmedabad - 380 009. Phone: 079-26560126;
Mobile: 09377088847

Ernakulam : 39/176 (New No: 60/251) 1st Floor, Karikkamuri Road, Ernakulam,
Kochi – 682011. Phone: 0484-2378012, 2378016;
Mobile: 09387122121

Bhubaneswar : 5 Station Square, Bhubaneswar - 751 001 (Odisha).
Phone: 0674-2532129, Mobile: 09338746007

Kolkata : 108/4, Beliaghata Main Road, Near ID Hospital, Opp. SBI Bank,
Kolkata - 700 010, Phone: 033-32449649, Mobile: 7439040301

Printed at : M/s. Aditya Offset Process (I) Pvt. Ltd., Hyderabad. On behalf of HPH.

Preface

Biography, is now a form of literature, very much in vogue. In fact, biography is a description or account of someone's life and the times, which is usually published in the form of a book. A biography is more than a mention of personal facts (life, education, work, relationships and death), it also portrays the subject's experience of events. Technically speaking, a work is biographical, if it covers, all of a person's life. Biography writing has a long history. A biography is real. Ancient Greeks developed the biographical tradition, which we have inherited, although until the 5th century AD, when the word 'biographia' first appeared, in Damascius' "Life of Isodorus," biographical pieces were called simply "lives". It is quite likely that the Greeks were drawing on a pre-existing eastern tradition. Certainly Herodotus' "Histories" contains more detailed biographical information on Persian kings and subjects. The earliest surviving pieces, which we would identify as biographical are Isocrates' "Life of Evagoras" and Xenophon's "Life of Agesilaos," both from the fifth century BC. "Parallel Lives" by Plutarch, a Greek writing under the Roman empire, is a series of short biographies of eminent men.

The Golden Age of English biography emerged in late eighteenth century, the century in which the terms "biography" and "autobiography" entered English lexicon. The classic works of the period were Samuel Johnson's "Critical Lives of the Poets" and James Boswell's "Massive Life of Johnson". Generally American biography followed English model. By World War I, cheap hardcover reprints had become popular. The decade of the 1920s witnessed a biographical 'boom'. Later, biographical writings developed a lot and today biographies are written and compiled in the finest form of the genre. In India too, biography, as a form of literature has been evolved, cultivated and polished over the years. Here is an effort to promote this tradition further.

This series of biographies of great men, great women and celebrities in all walks of life is an adventurous academic endeavour, in its own right. A team of researchers and compilers has worked for a good period of time to accomplish the project. For this purpose, hundreds of books by eminent authors and editors have been consulted and referred to. We have benefited from various works, liberally, in order to illustrate and enrich this effort of ours. Present book is devoted to the great personality of Ashoka.

Ashoka, popularly known as Ashoka the Great, was an emperor of the Mauryan Dynasty who ruled almost all of the Indian subcontinent. One of India's greatest emperors, Ashoka reigned over most of present-day India, after a number of military conquests. His empire stretched from present-day Pakistan and Afghanistan in the west, to the present-day Bangladesh and the state of Assam in the east, and as far south as northern Kerala and Andhra. He conquered the kingdom of Kalinga, which no one in his dynasty had conquered. He embraced Buddhism. He was later dedicated to the propagation of Buddhism, across Asia and established monuments, marking several significant sites in the life of Gautama Buddha. Ashoka was a devotee of ahimsa (nonviolence), love, truth, tolerance and vegetarianism. Ashoka is remembered in history as a philanthropic administrator.

This is a compact and comprehensive account of the above mentioned great life, which is bound to attract the attention of scholars, researchers, students and the general readers, alike. Let's hope this humble effort would receive a warm welcome and due applause.

— ***Editors***

Contents

Preface *vii*

1. **An Eventful Life** 1

Introduction • Family Background • Parentage, Brothers and Sisters • Early Life • Physical Form and Personality • Wives and Children • Length of Reign and Last Days

2. **Character and Personality** 51

Ashoka, the King • Refinement and Dignity • Intellectual Faculties • Strength of Will • Idealism and Human Feelings • Moral Traits of Character • People's Friend • Statesmanship and ability for Administration • Discharge of Duties

3. **Ashoka, the Emperor** 63

Star of Mauryan Dynasty • At Taxila • Prince on Throne • Kalinga War • Vanquished Kalinga • Vigilant on All Sides • An Old Age of Sorrow • Dynastic Successors

4. **Empire and Administration** 71

Imperial Administration • System of Governance • The Cabinet • Imperial Secretariat • Main Functionaries • General Administration • Department of Dharma • Judicial Administration • Jail Administration • Provincial Administration • City Administration • Frontier Administration • Royal Domain • Mauryan State • Extent of Empire • The Divisions • Autonomous Regions • Home Provinces • Sphere of Influence • Pataliputra, the Capital • The Population • The Territory • The Sovereignty • The Constitution • The Legislature • Law and Order • Military Strength and War Policy

5. Ashoka, the Conquerer of Hearts **201**

Ashoka's Religious Faith • Cultural Conquest • Change of Heart • The Noblest Victory • Spreading the Message of Dharma • Seeds of Dharma • Religious Conference • Pillar at Sarnath • Ashoka, the Builder of Monuments

6. Ashoka's Religious Role **309**

Ashoka, as a Buddhist • Ashoka's Dhamma • Ashoka, as a Missionary • Imperial Patron of Buddhism • Benevolent Institutions • Missionary Activity • Foundation of Shrines and Cities • Moral Exhortations

7. Golden Words of Ashoka **357**

8. Great Life at a Glance **359**

Bibliography 361

Index 365

1

An Eventful Life

Introduction

Ashoka, one of the greatest rulers of India, stands out in ancient history as the only ruler who had a genuine respect for human life. He was a man of great wisdom and strength of character. He was a great man not only because of what he achieved, but also because of his personal qualities.

Ashoka became an Emperor in 273 BC, about 2250 years ago. He ruled over a vast kingdom which stretched from the Hindu Kush mountains in the west, to the foothills of the Himalayas in the North and Madras in the South. Pataliputra was the capital of Ashoka's Empire.

In the first five years of his reign, Ashoka behaved like the other rulers of the day. He kept a splendid court and ruled like a despot, without bothering about the advice of others or thinking about the effect of his commands on the people. His favourite pastimes were hunting, feasting and war. He killed thousands of beasts during royal hunts and he gave very little thought to the lives of his subjects.

In the ninth year of his reign, Ashoka decided to conquer Kalinga, a kingdom in the region of present-day Orissa. A fierce battle took place and more than 1,00,000 people were killed and

1,50,000 taken prisoners. Ashoka was horrified and shocked by the terrible destruction and death which took place during the battle. Although he won the battle, Ashoka felt very unhappy. This may not seem surprising to you because many conquerors throughout history have felt unhappy over the deaths that have occurred during their conquests. But Ashoka was the only one who had the courage to publicly admit his mistake. Not only did he announce his feelings of grief and regret, he vowed that he would never go to war again.

Soon after the Kalinga War, Ashoka became a Buddhist. He obeyed the rules of conduct laid down in the Noble Eightfold Path, which were to use right vision, right thoughts, right speech, right action, right livelihood, right efforts, right mindfulness and right concentration to achieve true salvation and liberty. He also followed the rules of 'dharma' preached by Lord Buddha, such as obedience to one's father and mother, respect for life and avoidance of violence.

Ashoka's greatness lies in not only setting a personal example for everyone to follow but also in taking practical steps to ensure that the rules he had laid down would benefit the common man throughout his vast Empire.

Ashoka stopped killing of certain animals for food such as parrots, porcupines and tortoises. Besides, he prohibited killing for sport, which was the favourite pastime of the nobility of that time. He stopped the killing of peacocks and deer for his own kitchen.

Ashoka took practical steps to see that the rules of 'dharma' were observed by all his people and that they understood its meaning. He appointed officers to discuss and explain the principles of 'dharma' to the people. Not only did he insist that his subjects follow these principles, he personally set an example for all to follow.

One of the important steps Ashoka took to announce his new way of life was to send missionaries to preach Buddhism to far corners of his Empire. They were sent to Kashmir, Ceylon, Nepal and even Egypt. He had many inscriptions carved on pillars and rocks across his kingdom to explain and lay down rules of behaviour. Ashoka's teachings inscribed on rocks and pillars can be seen even to this day. And India has adopted Ashoka's wheel as an emblem in our national flag. Where other great Kings sent generals to conquer men's bodies, Ashoka sent monks to conquer men's minds.

Ashoka reigned for about forty years. Apart from the Kalinga War, they were years of peace for India. Ashoka governed by kindness rather than by force. Throughout his immense kingdom there was prosperity, contentment and happiness. Not even the Mughal Emperors like Akbar or Aurangzeb controlled such a large part of India, nor have conditions of life ever been as good as in Ashoka's day.

Ashoka worked hard for the benefit of the people. He set up roads, planted shady banyan trees by the side of the roads, dug wells, constructed free rest-houses and hospitals in his vast Empire.

Before Ashoka's reign Buddha's teachings had not spread beyond India. Ashoka was responsible for spreading Buddhism throughout the eastern world. He sent missionaries to other countries and he himself showed how Buddhism could be applied in everyday affairs and the affairs of a large Empire.

It is surprising that such a powerful King decided to give up wars of conquest. He devoted all his energy towards making his people happy. Herein lies the greatness of Ashoka. He was a man of character who lived by all he preached and did not expect others to do what he did not do himself.

In the annals of kingship there is scarcely any record comparable to that of Ashoka, both as a man and as a ruler. To bring out the chief features of his greatness, historians have instituted comparisons between him and other distinguished monarchs in history, eastern and western, ancient and modern, Pagan, Muslim, and Christian. In his efforts to establish a kingdom of righteousness after the highest ideals of a theocracy, he has been likened to David and Solomon of Israel in the days of its greatest glory; in his patronage of Buddhism, which helped to transform a local into a world religion, he has been compared to Constantine in relation to Christianity; in his philosophy and piety he recalls Marcus Aurelius; he was a Charlemagne in the extent of his Empire and, to some extent, in the methods of his administration, too, while his Edicts, "rugged, uncouth, involved, full of repetitions," read like the speeches of Oliver Cromwell in their mannerisms. Lastly, he has been compared to Khalifa Omar and Emperor Akbar, whom also he resembles in certain respects. As in the case of great characters like King Arthur and his Knights of the Round Table, the good King Alfred, or King St. Louis of France, a mass of tradition has gathered round the name of Ashoka. Myths and legends have freely and luxuriantly grown round it, especially in the tropical climate of Ceylon, and it would have been very difficult to recover his true history, were it not for the fact that he has himself left us a sort of autobiography in his messages to his people, written on rocky surfaces or exquisitely finished and polished pillars of stone. In these sermons-on stone we find his true self revealed and expressed, his philosophy of life, his conception of an Emperor's duties and responsibilities, and the extent to which he lived to realise the high ideals and principles he professed and preached. This kind of evidence, which is not only a contemporary but a personal record, too, is unique in Indian history, and, whether suggested by indigenous or foreign precedents, it is fortunate we have it for one of our greatest men. "O that my words were written! That they were graven with an iron pen and lead in the rock for ever!" This pious wish of Job was more than realised in the case of Ashoka in a series of thirty-five inscriptions published on rock or pillar, of which some are located at the extremities of his Empire.

Family Background

Of the two sources of his history, the legends (whether Ceylonese or Indian) rather hover over his early life and stand to retreat before the light of the edicts thrown upon his later life, his career as Emperor. The two sources are, again, sometimes in agreement, but oftener in conflict, in which case the inscriptions, as personal and contemporary documents, will have to be preferred. Moreover, the legends are themselves at conflict with one another in many places, and thus betray themselves all the more.

Ceylon tradition (as narrated in the *Dipavamsa* and the *Mahavamsa)* makes Bindusara the husband of sixteen wives and father of 101 sons, of whom only three are named, viz., Sumana

(Susima according to the northern legends), the eldest, Ashoka, and Tisya (uterine brother of Ashoka), the youngest son. The mother of Ashoka in the northern tradition is Subhadrangi, the beautiful daughter of a Brahmin of Champa, who bore Bindusara another son named Vigatashoka (Vitashoka), and not Tisya of the Ceylon books. In the southern tradition she is called Dharma, the principal Queen *(aggamahesi)*, the preceptor of whose family was an Ajivika saint named Janasana—a fact which may explain Ashoka's patronage of the Ajivika Sect. Dharma came of the Kshatriya clan of the Moriyas.

According to established constitutional usage, Ashoka as Prince served as Viceroy in one of the remoter provinces of the Empire. This was the province of Western India called Avantirattham *(Mahabodhivamsa)* with headquarters (Rajadhani) at Ujjain in the Ceylon tradition, but in the Indian legends it is the kingdom of the Svasas in Uttarapatha with headquarters at Taxila, where Ashoka was temporarily sent to supersede Prince Susima and quell the revolt against his maladministration. There was a second rebellion at Taxila which Prince Susima failed to quell, when the throne at Pataliputra fell vacant and was promptly seized by Ashoka with the aid of the minister, Radhagupta, and subsequently held deliberately against the eldest brother who was killed in the attempt to dethrone the usurper (*Divyavadana*). But the story of the accession is somewhat differently told in the Ceylonese legends, which make Ashoka seize the throne from Ujjain, where he had been throughout serving as viceroy, by making a short work of all his brothers except Tisya.

The northern and southern legends, however, agree as regards the disputed succession, which may therefore be taken as a fact. The southern legends are far wide of the truth in making Ashoka a fratricide, the murderer of 99 brothers for the sake of the throne, for which he is dubbed Chandashoka. Senart has well shown how the legends themselves are not at one in their account of Ashoka's career of cruelty, Taranath makes Ashoka kill only six brothers. Other authorities do not attribute to him any murder at all, but other forms of cruelty. The *Ashoka-avadana* represents him as killing his officers and wives, and setting up a hell where some innocent people are subjected to the most refined tortures. The *Mahavamsa* also relates how his minister under his instructions decapitates some false monks till he is stopped by his brother. In the *Ashoka-avadana,* he *sets* a price upon the heads of Brahmin ascetics who insulted the statue of the Buddha till he is checked by his brother, Vitashoka. Yuan Chwang records the tradition of "Ashoka and his Queen, in succession, making determined efforts to destroy the Bodhi Chinese traveller, I-tsing, according to which Ashoka's sovereignty was propnesied by the Buddha himself. The tradition relates that King Bimbisara once saw in a dream that a piece of cloth and a gold stick were both divided up into eighteen fragments which, as explained by the Buddha, symbolised the eighteen schools into which his teaching would be split "more than a hundred years after his nirvana, when there will arise a King named Ashoka, who will rule over the whole of Jambudvipa". The Buddha's prophecy about Ashoka as a righteous King who will enshrine his bodily relics in 84,000 "dharmarajikas" occurs in the *Divyavadana*, tree," and when each attempt failed and the tree grew up each time, "Ashoka surrounded it with a stone wall". According to Fa-hien, the Queen tried to destroy the Bo-tree out of jealousy when Ashoka, already a zealous Buddhist, was always to be found under that tree for worship. The fact is that these legends were out to emphasise the contrast between the criminal career of Ashoka prior to his conversion and his virtuous conduct that followed it. They were interested in blackening his character to glorify the religion which could transmute base metal into gold, convert Chandashoka into Dharmashoka, and make of a monster of cruelty the simplest of men!

The epithet Chandashoka suggested by Ashoka's earlier cruelties does not, however, seem to be justified, if we limit his cruelties only to the murder of a single brother in the contest for the throne, while it may be that the brothers referred to as being alive well on in his reign might be only his uterine brothers, of whom the legends give the name of one, viz., Tisya. The number of brothers slain according to the legends may be an exaggeration which marks legends, and even the edicts of Ashoka. It may be well assumed, too, that the brothers slain might have been his stepbrothers. According to the *Mahabodhivamsa*, as already stated, these 98 brothers with their leader, Yuvaraja Sumana, were slain in the course of the war of succession they had forced on Ashoka, whom they regarded as the usurper. Thus Ashoka could not be held responsible for their death under such circumstances.

"Sons and grandsons", who were all maintained at royal expense. Pillar Edict VII contains the expression: "In all my female establishments, both here (at the capital) and in the outlying towns". Besides the evidence showing the existence of the harems of his brothers at different provincial towns, we have also the evidence of such brothers (called *kumaras* and *aryaputras)* serving as his Viceroys at headquarters named, viz., Taxila, Tosali Ujjaini and Suvarnagiri. These Viceroys could not be his Sons. Lastly, his affection for his children, too, expresses itself in the Kalinga Edict I: "I desire for my children that they may enjoy every kind of prosperity and happiness both in this world and in the next" A man with such tender solicitude for the welfare of all his relations could not be a monster of cruelty, as the legends represent him to be.

The relations between Ashoka and his younger brother appear to be quite friendly and natural in the legends, but they give different accounts of these relations. Yuan Chwang, calling him Mahendra, relates that he used his high birth to violate the laws, lead a dissolute life, and oppress the people, till the matter was reported to Ashoka by his high ministers and old statesmen. Then Ashoka in tears explained to his brother how awkward was his position due to his conduct. Mahendra, confessing guilt, asked for a reprieve of seven days, during which, by the practice of contemplation in a dark chamber, he became an arhat and was granted cave-dwellings at Pataliputra for his residence. According to Fa-hien, Ashoka's brother, whose name he does not mention, had retired to the solitude on a hill which he was loath to leave, though "the King sincerely reverenced him and wished and begged him to come and live in his family where he could supply all his wants." In the end, the King constructed for him a hill inside the city of Pataliputra to live closer to him. A different story is, however, given in other works. The Pali works call him *Tisya*, the *Divyavadana Vitashoka,* and some Chinese works *Sudatta* and *Sugatra.* These works also specify his offence to be that, as a Tirthika, he had slandered the professed Buddhists as living in luxury and subject to passions. To convince him of his error, Ashoka conspired with his chief minister to place him on the throne, and then appeared suddenly to accuse him as a usurper, whom he condemned to die after seven days. During this time he was treated to all pleasures and luxuries for which, however, he had no taste, with death facing him. By this example, Ashoka wanted to show that no Buddhist with his dread of death and birth could ever give himself to pleasures. He then set free Vitashoka, who, however, went away to a frontier land, became an arhat, saw Ashoka at Pataliputra, but soon left for another district where he was beheaded, being taken for one of the Nirgranthas upon whose heads the local King set a price. In the *Mahavamsa,* Ashoka appoints his brother Tisya as *uparaja,* his Vice-regent, but he retired as a religious devotee under the influence of the Yonaka preacher, Mahadharmaraksita; and was known by the name of 'Ekaviharika, a vihara being excavated for him at enormous expense in the rock called Bhojakagiri by Ashoka according to the story given in Dhammapala's comment on the verses composed by Ekaviharika in the *Theragatha Commentary.* The same work refers to the youngest brother of Ashoka, called Vitashoka, whom it treats evidently as not the same brother as—Tissa Ekaviharika. It relates how he grew up, mastering all the *vidyas* and *silpas,* arts and sciences, prescribed for the study of Kshatriyakumaras; then he became a householder, and, under his teacher, Giridatta Thera, mastered the Sutra Pitaka and Abhidhamma Pitaka, until one day, while at shaving *(massu-kamma),* he noticed in his mirror his grey hairs, which set him a-thinking of the decay of life, and he at once embraced monkhood under Giridatta and soon became an arhat. This particular text thus distinguishes between the two brothers of Ashoka by their different teachers, and attributes to them different *gathas.*

Some of the Edicts mention the names of his closer relations. Thus the second Queen Karuvaki is mentioned, together with her son, Prince Tivara. A later inscription mentions Ashoka's grandson Dasharatha. Both legends and inscriptions are at one in making Ashoka a polygamist. The chronicles make his first wife the daughter of a merchant of Vedisagiri, Devi by name, whom Ashoka had married when he was Viceroy at Ujjain. The *Mahabodhivamsa* calls her Vedisa-mahadevi and a Shakyani or a Shakya-kumari, as being the daughter of a clan of the Shakyas who had immigrated to *"Vedisam nagaram"* out of fear of Vidudabha menacing their mother-country *(Vidudabhabh-ayagatanam Sakiyanam avasam Vedisam)*. Thus the first wife of Ashoka was related to the Buddha's family or clan. She is also described as having caused the construction of the Great Vihara of Vedisagiri, probably the first of the monuments of Sanchi and Bhilsa *(taya karapitam Vedisa-girimahaviharam)*. This explains why Ashoka selected Sanchi and its beautiful neighbourhood for his architectural activities. Vedisa also figures as an important Buddhist place in earlier literature (*Sutra Nipata*). Of Devi were born the son, Mahendra, and the daughter, Sanghamitra, who was married to Ashoka's nephew, Agnibrahma, and gave birth to a son named Sumana, According to *Mahavamsa,* Devi did not follow Ashoka as sovereign to Pataliputra, for there his Chief Queen *(agramahisi)* then was Asandhimitra. The *Divyavadana* knows of a third wife of Ashoka, Padmavati by name, them other of Dharmavivardhana, who was afterwards called Kunala. Both *Mahavamsa* and *Divyavadana* agree in mentioning Tissarakkha or Tisya-raksita as the last Chief Queen of Ashoka. The *Divyavadana* mentions Samprati as Kunala's son. The Kashmir Chronicle mentions Jalauka as another son of Ashoka, Fa-hien mentions Dharmavivardhana as a son of Ashoka, whom he appointed as the Viceroy of Gandhara.

Thus, taking the legends and Edicts together we find the following relations of Ashoka:

Father: Bindusara, who had many wives.

Mother: Subhadrangi, as named in the northern tradition; also called Dharma in the southern tradition.

Brothers: (1) Sumana or Susima, eldest, but stepbrother; (2) Tisya, uterine and youngest brother; also called Vitashoka or Vigatashoka in the northern legends, Mahendra by Yuan Chwang, and Sudatta and Sugatra in some Chinese works; (3) Vitashoka, according to *Theragatha Commentary*.

Wives: (1) Devi, with her full name, "Vedisa-Mahadevi Shakyakumari"; (2) Karuvaki, called *"Dvitiya devi Tivalamata,"* "second Queen, mother of Tivara" in the Edict; (3) Asandhimitra, designated as *agramahisi,* Chief Queen; (4) Padmavati; (5) Tisyaraksita.

Sons—(1) Mahendra, son of Devi; (2) Tivara, son of Karuvaki; (3) Kunala, son of Padmavati, also known by the name of Dharmavivardhana, as mentioned in *Divyavadana*, and by Fa-hien; (4) Jalauka, mentioned in the Kashmir Chronicle. The Edicts tell of four Princes serving as Viceroys in four different, and remote, provinces, and designated as *Kumaras* or *Aryaputras*, as distinguished from the sons of a lower status called *dalakas* from the status of their mothers.

Daughters—(1) Sanghamitra, whose mother was Devi; (2) Charumati.

Sons-in-law—(1) Agnibrahma, husband of Sanghamitra; (2) Devapala Ksatriya, married to Charumati

Grandsons—(1) Dasharatha, who became King; (2) Samprati, son of Kunala; (3) Sumana, son of Sanghamitra.

On the basis of the texts to which we owe most of these names, it is also possible to ascertain some dates in the domestic life of Ashoka. For instance, we are told in the *Mahavamsa* that Ashoka's eldest son and daughter, Mahendra and Sanghamitra, were both ordained in the sixth year of his coronation when they were respectively twenty and eighteen years old. Taking the date of Ashoka's coronation to be 270 BC, we get 284 BC and 282 BC as the dates of the birth of Mahendra and his sister respectively. If we take the father's age at the birth of his eldest child as twenty years, then Ashoka must have been born in 304 BC and was thus seen by his august grandfather, Chandragupta Maurya, who died in 299 BC It is also stated that Ashoka's son-in-law, Agnibrahma, was ordained in the fourth year of his coronation, i.e., in 266 BC, before which a son was born to him. Thus Sanghamitra must have been married in 268 BC at the latest, i.e., at the age of fourteen.

Parentage, Brothers and Sisters

The inscriptions of Ashoka throw no light on his early life and parentage. His brothers and sisters along with other kith and kin find mention in R. E. V in connection with the distribution of charities from their households by the Dharmamahamatras. Ashoka introduces them in such a manner as to suggest that they were persons who ranked with him in family relationship, and that they had their family establishments in Pataliputra and outlying towns.

The Pali tradition speaks of just one sister of Ashoka to whose son, Prince Agnibrahma, was married his daughter Sanghamitra and to whom she bore a son called Sumana.

The Pali Chronicles expressly tell us that King Bindusara married sixteen wives by whom he had one hundred and one sons. Amongst *them, Ashoka was second to none but Sumana, the eldest of all The Divyavadhana* names the eldest son of Bindusara as Susima.

Ashoka's only uterine brother was Tishya who is called Vigatashoka or Vitashoka in the Divyavadhana, and Sudatta or Sugatra in some Chinese works. The Theragatha contains two psalms, one attributed to the Thera Ekavihariya and the other to another Thera named Vitashoka. The scholiast Dhammapala identifies Ekavihariya with Ashoka's brother Tishya and the second Thera with Ashoka's another brother Vitashoka, and represents them as two different individuals. This identification is not at all borne out by the earlier Canonical legends in the book of Apadana, and may therefore be dismissed as pure invention.

According to the Pali narrative, when Ashoka seized the throne of Magadha, taking advantage of his father's old age and illness, his ninety-nine stepbrothers made a common cause with Sumana Susima who was the rightful heir to the throne and were all slain with him. The Tibetan historian Taranatha "makes Ashoka kill only six brothers" while in the Divyavadhana the fratricidal battle is described as one fought only between Susima-Sumana and Ashoka. Susima's defeat was mainly due to the lack of support from the ministers of his father who were all up against him. The substance of truth in these legends seems to be that Ashoka's succession was a disputed one, which, however, has no corroboration from his records.

The evidence of Ashoka's inscriptions may be construed in a sense to run counter to the trend of the Buddhist stories. In R. E. V, engraved not later than the 13th or 14th year of abhisheka, Ashoka mentions their brothers as having their family establishments in Pataliputra and outlying towns. On the other hand, in P. E. VII, engraved in the 27th year of abhisheka, he replaces his brothers by other Princes of the blood royal ranking with his sons in family relationship. The inference which may reasonably be drawn from this is that in the course of thirteen years his brothers either died or retired from the world.

According to Pali legends, Ashoka appointed his uterine brother Tishya-Vitashoka as uparaja or vice-regent. After Tishya had joined the Buddhist Order, the offer went to Ashoka's nephew and son-in-law Agnibrahma, and when he too joined forthwith the Buddhist Order in the fourth year of Ashoka's abhisheka, the office of the vice-regent went a begging.

If reliance be placed upon the Pali account, there was no brother of Ashoka left after the 4th year of his abhisheka to function as his viceroy. But the preamble or forwarding note of the three Isila or Northern Mysore versions of M. R. E., probably engraved not earlier than the 26th year of abhisheka, seems to suggest that the fact was otherwise. The Isila copy of the edict in question was to be forwarded to the Mahamatras of the place under the authority of the Aryaputra and the Mahamatras stationed at Suvanjagiri, which was evidently the headquarters of the southern viceroy. If the forwarding note of the Isila versions were despatched by Ashoka, as seems more probable, by Aryaputra (Ayaputa) Ashoka could not but have meant a brother of his. If locally drafted at Suvarnagiri, as would seem less likely, by Aryaputra one must understand just a son of Ashoka.

As for Ashoka's early life, the Buddhist story as narrated in the Dipavamsa has nothing to say beyond the fact that he was the second son of Bindusara and a grandson of Chandragupta of the Maurya family, or that his personal name was Priyadarshana, meaning "one of amiable mien", "one whose handsome appearance was comparable to that of the moon". According to the same authority, Ashoka and Priyadarshin were the names or titles assumed by Priyadarshana at the time of his two consecrations. The Divyavadhana story, on the contrary, says that Ashoka was the name of the Prince given him by his father at the instance of his mother. Furthermore, the Sanskrit legend goes to represent him as a person of ugly appearance and fierce nature evidently to build thereupon the grotesque and repulsive story of how he came to pass as Ashoka the Wicked.

The earlier Pali account, met with whether in the Dipavamsa or in the Samanta-pasadika and Mahavamsa, is silent on Ashoka's mother. The Mahavamsatika introduces us for the first time to his mother Dharma (Pali Dhamma) who was a princess from the Maurya clan of Kshatriyas (Moriyavavamsaji) and whose family preceptor was an Ajivika named Janasana, Jarasana or Jarasona. She is represented as the chief Queen of Bindusara. She is called Subhadrangi in the Avadanamala. The Divyavadhana story does not name her but certainly represents her as "the beautiful daughter of a Brahman of *Champa." Jealous of her excessive beauty, the Queens of Bindusara made her do the work of a female barber. Highly pleased with her* work, the King granted her a boon, which she availed of by asking him to marry her. Satisfied with her social position which she disclosed, the King made her his chief Queen. The Divyavadhana legend, too, associates an Ajivaka named Pingalavatsa with Ashoka's mother. Precisely as in the Pali story, Ashoka received him with due honour when his prediction about his succession came true.

In the Mahavamsa-tika, Bindusara's mother is said to have been Chandragupta's eldest maternal uncle's daughter whom he married.

The tradition is a late one and of a very doubtful character. It is very strange indeed that none of the Indian legends says anything of the daughter of Seleucus Nikator who gave her in marriage to Chandragupta to make a matrimonial alliance with him. It would have been a more interesting fact, if Bindusara were represented as a son of Chandragupta by his Greek wife.

Predecessors and Pedigree: Ashoka, in his P. E. VII, speaks of the former Kings who had reigned in the long past and during several centuries, who too were the sincere well-wishers of their subjects, and by whom too various public works of a philanthropic nature were done. He introduces them, however, just to throw into bold relief the ineffectiveness of the means and methods adopted by them, the insufficiency of the results obtained, and the lesser value of the works done as compared and contrasted with those adopted, obtained and done by him.

Whom did he mean by these predecessors? Such expressions of his as atikamtam (in the long past), bhutapuve (formerly) and bahuni vasa-satani (during many hundred years) correspond to such introductory Jataka phrases as atite (in the past) and bhutapubbam. (bhutapurvam, "formerly"). Going by this correspondence, one cannot but take it that Ashoka had within his mental purview rather the legendary monarchs noted for their righteous rule and noble deeds, such as those extolled in the Brahmanas, Aranyakas and Upanishads, the Sanskrit Epics, and the Canonical texts of the Jainas and Buddhists.

Ashoka's predecessors in the Magadha line of Kings belonged to five royal dynasties, to wit, (1) the Barhadratha or Brihadratha, *(2) the Haryanka, (3) the Saisunaga or Shishunaga, (4) the Nanda, and (5) the Maurya (Pali Moriya).*

The Barhadratha dynasty founded by Brihadratha, son of Vasu Uparichara of the Chedi race and father of Jarasandha of the Great Epic fame, came to an end in the 6th century B. C., prior to the rise of Buddhism. The founding of the hill-girt city of Girivraja or Rajagriha is the notable work of this dynasty.

The Barhadratha dynasty was followed at about the rise of Buddhism by the Haryanka, which latter is said to have come to an end seventy two years after the Buddha's demise. Bimbisara, Ajatashatru and Udaya are the three successive rulers of this dynasty who are noted in history. Amongst them, Bimbisara deserves to be honoured not only as the real founder of the Haryanka dynasty but also as that of the imperial power of Magadha. The Pali Nikayas credit him with the creation of some permanent land-endowments and royal fiefs in favour of certain Vedic colleges in his dominions. He is also known as the builder and donor of the Venuvana monastery at Rajagriha dedicated to the Buddha and his followers which was the first Buddhist monastery in India. He lent the service of his court-physician, Jivaka, to the Sangha and befriended the Buddha and his followers in various ways. He allowed his talented Queen Kshema to become a bhikshuni. It was indeed during his reign and in his dominions that many new movements of religious thought were started and fostered. In these respects, the name of his great contemporary, Prasenajit of Kosala, is equally noteworthy.

Ajatashatru paved really the way for a further extension of the *supremacy of Magadha in Northern India. It is evident from the Samannaphala Sutra that he occasionally met the well-known religious* teachers and leading thinkers of the time to discuss the problem of importance. Later Buddhist traditions credit him with the extension of patronage to the Buddhist Theras when they met at Rajagriha to hold the First Buddhist Council, as well as with the erection of a memorable stupa at a suburb of Rajagriha for the preservation of the bodily remains of the Buddha collected from the stupas erected by others. The Jainas claim that he greatly honoured Mahavira and his doctrine.

Ajatashatru's son and successor, Udayi, is said to have transferred his capital from Rajagriha to Pataliputra, definitely in the fourth year of his reign, according to the Puranas.

The Manjusri-mulakalpa would in vain have us believe that he committed the Words of Buddha to writing, though it may be true, as suggested, that he was able to effect a further extension of the supremacy of Magadha.

Even as regards Udayi's grandson, Munda, it is stated in the Anguttara Nikaya and its Commentary that deeply grieved at the death of his beloved Queen, Bhadra, he sought solace through instructions from the Buddhist Thera, Narada, a fact which goes to indicate that in the matter of meeting holy persons of wisdom he followed in the footsteps of his forefathers.

Ajatashatru and his successors earned, according to the Pali Chronicles, the notoriety of being patricides, and sick of it, the citizens deposed the last King of their line and replaced him by his popular minister Shishunaga. Thus the Haryanka dynasty was supplanted by the Shishunaga.

The Shishunagas ceased to rule one hundred and forty years after the Buddha's demise (c. 348 or 347 BC). The only King of this family, worthy of mention, is Kalashoka (Ashoka the Blackie), apparently the same person as Bana's Kakavarna Shishunaga. The Pali Chronicles relate that during his reign, just a century after the Buddha's demise, and under his royal patronage was held the Second Buddhist Council at Vaishali, which is not improbable. It may be noted here that the confusion made between Dbarmashoka and the crow-black Kalashoka was accountable for the Divyavadhana description of the former as a man of ugly appearance.

Even the Mahabodhivamsa records nothing noteworthy of the reign of Kalashoka's ten sons and successors whom it names. According to this later Pali Chronicle, his eldest son and immediate successor was Bhadrasena. His ninth son, Nandivardhana, may be identified with his namesake in the Puranas, in which case his tenth or last son, Panchamaka, will figure as the same person as Mahanandi, the last King of the Shishunaga dynasty, according to the Puranas.

The Mulakalpa praises Visoka as a good King who worshipped Buddha's relics for 76 years, and his successor, Shurasena, who reigned for 17 years as a monarch who "caused stupas to be put up to the confines of the sea," which is evidently a baseless exaggeration.

The Shishunaga dynasty came to an end with the rise of the Nandas into power one hundred and forty years after the Buddha's demise (c. 348 or 347 BC). Both the Pali Chronicles and the Puranas speak of nine Nandas, but they differ when the former represent them as nine brothers with a short reign of 22 years and the latter represent them as father and eight sons with a much longer reign of 40 (28 + 12) or 100 (88 + 12) years. The first King of this dynasty is Ugrasenananda according to the Mahabodhivamsa, and the last King Dhanananda. The Puranas name the first King as Mahapadmananda but leave his sons unnamed. The Greek writer Curtius speaks only of two Nandas, namely, Agrammes who was a contemporary of Alexander the Great, and whose father was a usurper of the throne, while the Mulakalpa speaks only of one Nanda who is said to have died at the age of 66.

The traditional accounts differ as to how the Nandas came to replace the Shishunagas. According to the Mahavamsa-tika, the founder King of this dynasty accidentally fell into the hands of a gang of thieves and freebooters (chora) who used Malaya as their hiding place. He was a warrior-like man (yodhasadiso puriso). After the death of their leader he managed to secure their leadership and went on as theretofore to plunder villages and kingdoms. Pricked by conscience that such a life as this did not behove a warrior like him, he made up his mind to take a kingdom. He declared himself under the name of Nanda, and getting his brothers and people to side with him, seized a frontier town, the citizens whereof made an alliance with him instead of accepting his ultimatum. In this very manner he gained the support of a large number of the inhabitants of Jambudvipa, and ultimately marched into Pataliputra. Thus he seized the kingdom of Magadha. But he was destined to die shortly after that.

According to the Mulakalpa story, on the other hand, Nanda rose into power and gained the throne from a position of the Prime Minister, as though by a magical process. He was surrounded in his capital by the Brahman controversialists with false pride and big claims. Though pious and a man of judgement, the King gave them riches and did not deny them his patronage. But he had a Buddhist saint for his good spiritual guide under whose influence he became a believer in Buddha, honoured his sacred relics, and built 24 viharas. Vararuchi is represented as his Prime Minister, and Panini as his friend, a tradition to which Jayaswal attaches undue importance. The Puranas extol Mahapadmananda as an "extirpator of all kshatriyas" and as a "sole monarch bringing all under his sway". The historical justification of this praise has been fully discussed by Raychaudhary. It may suffice here to add that the epithet Mahapadma is a numerical term, which is expressive of the enormous wealth of the founder of the Nanda dynasty. The signification of the Pali name, Dhanananda, of the last King of the family is the same. Raychaudhary rightly observes indeed when he says, "'The first Nanda left to his sons not only a big Empire but a large army and a full exchequer as well." None need be surprised, therefore, that Indian literature preserves the tradition of fabulous riches of a Nanda King.

As for the last King, we read in the Mahavamsa-tika, "The youngest brother was called Dhanananda for his passion for hoarding wealth. He collected riches to the amount of eighty crores... Levying taxes even on skins, gums, trees and stones, he amassed further treasures which he disposed of similarly." The same authority also relates that Dhanananda built a danasala at Pataliputra, from which he gave away abundant riches to the Brahmans according to their seniority and ranks, a fact which finds mention also in the Mulakalpa account of King Nanda. The Mulakalpa has evidently mixed up the two accounts, namely, that of the first Nanda and that of the last.

With regard to the fall of the last Nanda King 140 years after the Buddha's demise, c. 326 or 325 B. C., the Mahavamsa and its tika on the one hand, and the Puranas on the other show a complete agreement in so far as they attribute it to the machination of the "Brahman named Kautilya-Chanakya. The Mulakalpa alone suggests that the fall of the Nanda King was due to the alienation of the *feeling* of the whole body of ministers inadvertently caused by him. *The tradition of extermination of the Nanda dynasty by Vishnu-gupta-Kautilya,* is *met with in the concluding* verse of *the Kautilya* Arthashastra, the opening verses of the Kamandakiya Nitisara, as well as Vishakhadatta's Mudrarakshasa and the Mulakalpa.

In the Mahavamsa and the Mulakalpa, Chanakya, the Prime Minister of Chandragupta Maurya, is described as "full of fierce wrath" (chandakkodhava), "successful in wrath, who was Death (Yamantaka) when angry." The Mahavamsa-tika and the Mudra-rakshasa give us slightly different stories of how Chanakya avenged the humiliation suffered by him at the hands of the last Nanda by using Chandragupta as a tool and established the latter in the throne of Magadha in c. 326 or 325 BC.

In the Mahavamsa-tika Chanakya is described as an erudite, resourceful and tricky Brahman of Takshashila who was well versed in the Vedic lore, and an expert in the principles of polity. But his teeth being all broken, his face became ugly to look at. As a controversialist he came to Pataliputra, and as a Brahman leader he took his seat when King Dhanananda was distributing large gifts among the Brahmans. Disgusted with his uncomely sight, the King ordered his men to turn him out. Enraged by this, Chanakya pronounced his curse, saying, "In this earth bounded by the four seas let there no longer be the prosperity of the Nandas." This being reported, the King became very angry and ordered his men to arrest him forthwith. Whilst trying to escape in the disguise of an Ajivika, he cleverly managed to evade the detection, though still inside the inner court of the royal residence. In the meantime he got hold of Prince Parvata whom he tempted with sovereignty, made good his escape together with the Prince and went to the Vindhya mountain. On looking out for a person who was worthy of sovereignty he chanced to see Prince Chandragupta of the Maurya family who was then being brought up in the family of a cowherd unaware of his royal origin. He took Chandragupta to his retreat in the Vindhya mountain and trained him up. First he employed him to behead Prince Parvata and subsequently to collect treasures by plundering villages and towns. When he was thus able to prove his ability and to raise an army Chanakya set him to march to Pataliputra and seize the throne by putting Dhanananda *to* death.

The connection of Chanakya with Takshashila is interesting. The explanation for the introduction of Parvatakumara in the story lies really in the Mudrarakshasa in which the machinations of Chanakya against Nanda were directed to conciliating Rakshasa, a minister of Nanda, and getting Malayaketu of Parvata as an ally. The early career of Chandragupta it is necessary to watch in the light of the available Greek accounts his activities and position in the Punjab and Northwestern Frontier Provinces at the time of and immediately after Alexander the Great's invasion. And for the same the reader may be referred for the present to Raychaudhary's critical summary.

As for the most notable events of the life and career of Chandragupta mention may be made of the following six:

- The unification of all the states and fighting forces of Northwestern India beyond the Middle Country under his leadership.
- The liberation of India from foreign yoke.
- The overthrow of the Nanda power.
- The defeat of Seleucus Nikator ending in a treaty by which the Greek general and successor of Alexander the Great ceded certain territories to Chandragupta and which was consummated by a matrimonial alliance.
- The foundation of a mighty Indian Empire.
- The coming of Megasthenes as an ambassador of Seleucus

Nikator to Chandragupta's court and capital. The account of India left by Megasthenes in his Indika is invaluable as presenting to us a contemporary picture of Chandragupta's palace, capital, kingdom, country, administrative system, etc.

Chandragupta who is otherwise praised in the Malakalpa as 'a very prosperous lord of the earth', 'true to his word', and 'a man of pious soul' (mahabhogi satyasandhas cha dbarmatma sa mahipatih), is said to have killed many living beings on the advice of a bad spiritual guide (akalyanamitra.)

He died after a successful reign of 24 years and was succeeded by his son Bindusara. According to the Mulakalpa legend, Bindusara was a minor when he was placed on the throne by his father. It is said that 'while a minor he obtained great comfort; when of full manhood he turned out to be bold, eloquent and sweet-tongued. He reigned for 28 years,—25 years according to the Puranas, and 70 years according to the Mulakalpa, which is improbable. Strangely enough, the Mulakalpa represents the wicked Chanakya as his Prime Minister. The royal family in which he was born is called Nandarajakula instead of Maurya.

One may just be amused by the ingenuity of the Mahavamsa-tika in the invention of stories to account for the etymological significance of the names, Chandragupta ("one who was guarded by a bull called Chandra") and Bindusara (one on whose body flowed the blood of she-goats"), both of which are far-fetched. The son and successor of Sandrokottos (Chandragupta) is known to the Greek historian Strabo by the name of Amitrochades, Allitrochades, and to Athenaios by that of Amitrachates equated by Fleet, and subsequently also by Jarl Charpentier, with Amitrakhada (Devourer of enemies) which is traceable in literature as an epithet of Indra. Raychaudhary still sticks to his equation with Amitraghata, a term which is met with in Patanjali's Mahabhashya and corresponds to Amitranam hanta in the Aitareya Brahmana.

The following two facts are really important to be noted: (i) That Ptolemy Philadelphos, King of Egypt, sent Deimachos as his ambassador to Bindusara; and (ii) That, according to the Dipavamsa and Samantapasadika, Bindusara was a votary of the Brahmans and a staunch supporter of the Brahminical sects.

Social Status: The barber story is almost proverbial in the ancient royal tradition of India. When a reigning monarch was found stingy in the payment of rewards or in making gifts, he was taken to be a barber's son. There must have been some such reason at the back of the Brahminical tradition regarding the Shudra origin of the Nandas and Mauryas. The Puranas predict, "As son of Mahanandin (the last Saisunaga) by a Shudra woman will be born a King, Mahapadma (Nanda) who will exterminate all kshatriyas. Thereafter Kings will be of Shudra origin."

The founder of the Nanda family is called 'the leading vile man' (nichamukhyah) in the Mulakalpa (verse 424). In the Mahavamsa-tika the first Nanda, who was a warrior-like man, figures, as we saw, as the powerful leader of a gang of thieves and a band of freebooters. He is not, however, connected by the Pali tradition with the last Saisunaga through blood-relationship The Mulakalpa legend says that originally he was the Prime Minister of the last King of Visoka's family.

Curtius narrates a story from an Indian source, which is devised to account for the Shudra origin of Agrammes (Augrasainya Nanda). According to this story, father of Agrammes was a wretched barber, who could be in love-intrigue with the Queen of the reigning King because of his prepossessing appearance. By her influence he gained so much confidence of the King as to figure ultimately as a trusted adviser. Taking advantage of this privileged position, he treacherously murdered the King, and 'under the pretence of acting as guardian to the royal children, usurped the supreme authority, and having put the royal young Princes to death begot Agrammes. The suggestion is that the Nanda contemporary of Alexander was a barber's son by the Queen dowager of the last Saisunaga. Hemachandra in his Parisishtaparvan, however, represents the first Nanda 'as the son of a courtezan by a barber', while, according to the Puranas, he was 'a son of the last Saisunaga by a Shudra woman.

The process of myth-making did not stop short there; the Shudra or barber story continued. Despite the fact *that neither the Pali* Chronicles nor the Puranas suggest any blood-connection between the Nandas and the Mauryas, Vishakhadatta in his Mudrarakshasa, describes Chandragupta not only as Mauryasuta but also as Nandanvaya (one belonging to the Nanda dynasty). "Kshemendra and Somadeva refer to him as Purvananda-sutra. The commentator on the Vishnu Purana says that Chandragupta was the son of Nanda by a wife called Mura, whence he and his descendants were called Mauryas. Dhundiraja, the commentator on the Mudrarakshasa, informs us on the other hand that Chandragupta was the eldest son of Maurya who was the son of the Nanda King Sarvarthasiddha by Mura, daughter of a Vrishala Shudra. In the Mudrarakshasa itself Chanakya addresses Chandragupta as a Vrishala or Shudra.

Mr. C. D. Chatterjee rightly points out to me that the derivation of the dynastic name Maurya as a matronymic from Mura is grammatically incorrect; it may be treated as a patronymic from Mura. It is untenable also on the ground that according to the Vishnu Purana and the Arthashastra, the child takes the caste of its father, whether born of conjugal wedlock or not.

The force of the story of the barber mother or grandmother of Chandragupta may be counteracted by the Divyavadhana story of the barber-mother of Ashoka himself. His mother was not a woman of the barber caste but a very handsome and accomplished Brahman girl from Champa whom other Queens of Bindusara, jealous of her, employed her in the palace to attend on the King as a female hairdresser. When she disclosed the real fact to the King, she said, "Lord, I am not a barber girl but a daughter of a Brahman by whom I am offered to be your wife.

Hemchandra in his Parisishtaparvan, derives the name Maurya from mayura (peacock) and suggests that Chandragupta came to be styled Maurya from the circumstance that he was "the son of a daughter *of the chief of a village of peacock-tamers. If the Greek writer Justin describes Sandrocottus* as a man "of mean origin", it does not mean much, since he must have based his account on an Indian tradition.

The Pali Chronicles, on the other hand, and Buddhist legends generally represent Chandragupta as a scion of the Moriya clan of kshatriyas, the Moriyas of Pipphalivana. Led, however, by a Shakya-phobia, the Buddhist legends describe the Moriyas as descendants of the Shakyas who fled away from their own territory when it was overrun by the army of Vidudabha-Virudhaka, the usurper King of Kosala, and founded a new territory. The story is guilty of anachronism because, as borne out by the Mahaparinibbana Suttanta, the Moriyas of Pipphalivana were, precisely like the

Shakyas of Kapilavastu, one of the eight rival claimants for the bodily remains of the Buddha.

As for the connection of the Mauryas of Pataliputra with the Moriyas, the Mahavamsa-tika tells us that Chandragupta's mother who was the chief Queen of the then reigning Moriya King fled in disguise from the Moriya capital to Pushpapura (Pataliputra) during her advanced pregnancy, and gave birth to her son there when the Moriya territory was seized by a powerful neighbour (samantaranna). The story built up in this connection reads somehow as a later replica of the earlier legend of the birth of Ashoka's elder stepbrother's son Nyagrodha, and at the root of the ingenuity of the one, precisely as at that of the other, is a fantastic philological justification of the personal name.

Chandragupta does not appear to have been known to Megasthenes, and, for the matter of that, to most of the Greek writers, as a scion of the Maurya family. None need be surprised at all if the connection of the Mauryas with the Moriyas was due to an after-thought on the part of the Buddhists when they wanted to especially honour their Dharmashoka and claim him as their own man. The Buddhist legends concerning the Shakya lineage of the Moriyas or Mauryas would seem accountable also for the representation of the Mauryas in certain late medieval Mysore inscriptions as Kshatriyas who sprang from Mandhatri of the solar race. Hemchandra, as we noted, accounts for the dynastic name Maurya by the tradition that Chandragupta was a son of the daughter of the headman of a village of mayuraposhakas (peacock-tamers). The Mahavamsa-tika which connects Chandragupta with the Moriyas, accounts for their name also by a tradition averring that they built in their capital 'peacock palaces that were filled and resounded with cries of peacocks.

In support of the connection of the Mauryas with peacocks, Raychaudhary notices the following two facts which create but a presumptive evidence:

- That Aelian speaks of tame peacocks that were kept in the parks attached to the Maurya palace at Pataliputra and
- That figures of peacocks were employed to decorate some of the projecting ends of the architraves of the east gateway as Sanchi.

If any light is thrown on this point by Ashoka's R. E. I, it is rather this, namely, that the Mauryas of Pataliputra were inordinately fond of peacock's flesh. All the animals could be dispensed with and exempted from daily slaughter in the royal kitchen for the purpose of curry but not two peafowls. In other words, the Mauryas were rather mayarakhadakas than mayaraposhakas. The figure of a peacock carved on the lower part of Ashoka's pillar at Rampurva does not necessarily indicate that the peacock was the emblem of the Mauryas, It may at the most be interpreted as a cognizance of Pipphalivana which was the fatherland of the Moriya race of kshatriyas.

There is no conclusive evidence as yet to establish Chandragupta's lineal descent from the Shakya-Moriyas or Nandas. Plutarch's remark that "Androkottus himself, who was then a lad, saw Alexander himself and afterwards used to declare that Alexander might easily have occupied the whole country, as the then King was hated by his subjects on account of his mean and wicked disposition" must be taken with a grain of salt. There was nothing in Chandragupta's conversation to enrage Alexander who, according to Justin, 'did not scruple to give orders to kill the intrepid Indian lad for his boldness of speech'. It was quite against the youthful spirit of Chandragupta who in Justin's opinion was the brave hero and military leader to make India free, shaking off 'from its neck the yoke of slavery' since Alexander's death.

To me Chandragupta was a man of the Uttarapatha or Gandhara, if not exactly of Takshashila. His early education, military training, and alliances were all in that part of India. He added the whole of the province of Gandhara and the surrounding tribal states (in the Punjab and N. W. Frontier Provinces) to the growing Magadha Empire together with the territories ceded to him by Seleucus Nikator. The love was never lost between this aparanta and the Mauryas. Some at least of Ashoka's scribes were all persons whose habitual script was Kharoshthi, and a few of his artists were those who were still carrying on the tradition of the architecture of Persepolis. Chandragupta and Ashoka of the Maurya dynasty who could create a glorious history for themselves and their country did not need credentials based upon royal lineage. The Greek writers speak only of one matrimonial alliance by which Seleucus ratified his treaty with Chandragupta.

Early Life

There is hardly any educated person in India who has not heard of Ashoka and his stone inscriptions. Ashoka, he knows, was a Prince of the Maurya dynasty and grandson of Chandragupta, the Sandrakottos of the Greek writers and, for some time, a contemporary of Alexander the Great. The inscriptions of this monarch, he again knows, have been found all over India. But he may not be aware of their contents and may not know what account they furnish of that Maurya King. There are, no doubt, some Buddhist works, which set forth his life and work, but their trustworthy character has been rightly called in question. They mention many stones, which represent him to have been Kalashoka or Black Ashoka before, and Dharmashoka or Pious Ashoka after, his conversion to Buddhism. As the one aim of these works is to eulogise Buddhism by showing how it transformed Ashoka the Ogre into Ashoka the Pious, a suspicion naturally crosses our mind in regard to the correctness of their account. Such is not, however, the case with his epigraphic monuments, which being contemporary records and engraved by his orders, are of undoubted veracity. Nay, as we go through them, we feel as if his voice is still speaking to us and confiding what is passing in the innermostnecesses of his mind. The story of Ashoka that is being narrated is based almost entirely on these monuments, and we can be pretty certain that our account is not fiction, but history.

What kind of records has Ashoka left behind him? Are they sufficiently numerous and important in details? These records, as we know, are all engraved on stone. They have been inscribed either on rocks or pillars or in caves. Ashoka's rock inscriptions, again, are of two kinds: namely, (i) the Fourteen Rock Edicts, and (ii) the Minor Rock Edicts.

The former are called Fourteen Rock Edicts, because they together form a set of fourteen different inscriptions following a serial order, and have been found in seven different localities—all on the confines of India, at any rate, of his Empire. The Minor Rock Edicts consist of two different records. They are inscribed together only in the three copies found in Mysore; in all other places, which are no less than four, Edict I only has been engraved. Ashoka's Pillar Inscriptions also may be distinguished into two classes: (i) Seven Pillar Edicts, and (ii) the Minor Pillar Inscriptions. The former of these constitute a group, but the latter are four different epigraphs. The Cave Inscriptions of Ashoka are, of course, those engraved in caves in the Barabar Hills of Bihar. These are altogether no less than thirty-three different inscriptions throw light on a number of points connected with Ashoka, his administration, his religious faith, his missionary operations, and so on. A careful comparison of these records is just what is needed in order to obtain the maximum that is knowable and historically acceptable about Ashoka.

Those who have studied these epigraphs know full well that they profess to have emanated from a King who calls himself Piyadarshi, that is, Priyadarshin. When they were first being deciphered, now about three-quarters of a century ago, by James Prinsep to whom must go the credit of having unravelled the mystery of the Brahmi lipi, he was very much puzzled by the name Priyadarshin. He did not know who this Priyadarshin was, to what dynasty he belonged, and in what age he flourished. Soon thereafter, however, Tumour, who belonged to the Ceylon Civil Service, and was himself a great Pali scholar, identified Priyadarshin with Ashoka. He pointed out that the Sinhalese chronicle, the Dipavamsa, gave Piyadarshi or Piyadarshana as but another name of Ashoka, grandson of Chandragupta, the founder of the Maurya dynasty. This identification, it is true, has not since then been called in question, but it was definitively demonstrated only nine years ago when the sixth copy of Minor Bock Edict I was discovered at Maski in the Raichur District, Nizam's Dominions. For this inscription mentions the name of Ashoka clearly and in the very first line. It is not therefore possible now to doubt that Priyadarshin and Ashoka are one and the same person, and that the author of these inscriptions is really the grandson of Chandragupta, who founded the Maurya Empire.

We thus see that the author of our epigraphic records was known both as Ashoka and Priyadarshin. It was customary for the Kings of ancient India to have more than one name, of which one was their proper individual name and the others epithets or *birudas* as they are called. One of these two appellations must have been the personal name of the King, and the other his epithet. And it appears that Priyadarshin was his epithet, for we know that Ashoka's grandfather, Chandragupta, has also been styled Priyadarshana like him in one of the Ceylonese chronicles. Nobody can doubt that Chandragupta was his individual name. Priyadarshana or Priyadarshin must, therefore, be taken to be the *biruda* or secondary name. We know that this epithet in the case of Ashoka was Priyadarshin, and it is quite possible that Priyadarshin and not Priyadarshana was the *biruda* of his grandfather also. For in later times we find grandfather and grandson belonging to the same dynasty adopting the same *biruda*. The Ceylonese chronicles style Ashoka not only Priyadarshin but also Priyadarshana, taking the two words apparently in one and the same sense. And as from Ashoka's inscriptions we find that he was known really as Priyadarshin and not Priyadarshana, it is natural to presume that his grandfather also was Priyadarshin, not Priyadarshana. It is curious that this records call him Ashoka, only once, and Priyadarshin, in all other places. But instances are not wanting of Kings being known almost invariably by their epithets. Thus the son of Govinda III of the Rashtrakuta family of Manyakheta is known to us from all the documents so far only by his epithet, Amoghavarsha. We are somewhat better in regard to the author of our inscriptions. For one record at least gives his personal name, Ashoka.

In most of his inscriptions Ashoka styles himself Devanampriya Priyadarshi Raja. This is the fullest appellation of the King. But sometimes the formula is abbreviated by the omission of one or two of these components. Thus we find Ashoka designated also Devanampriya Priyadarshi, Priyadarshi Raja, Devanampriya Raja, or even Devanampriya merely. The second component of Ashoka's full name is Priyadarshin, which we have just considered. Literally it means ' one of amiable look,' and may be freely rendered by one who is of gracious mien.' When and why he adopted this epithet we do not know, but certain it is that he used it almost as his personal name. We had better not, therefore, translate it, but leave it as it is. It is worthy of note that although Ashoka was a supreme ruler, he designates himself simply Raja. The grandiloquent titles, Maharaja and Rajadhiraja, employed singly or conjointly, had not come into use in Ashoka's time. What is more worthy of note is that he calls himself Devanampriya, and one can well understand how the modern students of Grammar *(vyakarana)* may feel inclined to laugh at it. For do not Bhattoji Dikshita, author of the *Siddhantakaumudi,* and Hemachandra, author of the *Abhidhanachintamani,* tell us that Devanampriya means 'a fool' or 'dunce'? They are, therefore, apt to wonder what Ashoka means by calling himself Devanampriya. But it is to be noted that though this word has now a derogatory sense, it was not so originally, and especially in the time of Ashoka. Patanjali, we know, associates this word with *bhavat, dirghayus, and ayushmat.* This shows that like these honorific terms Devanampriya was employed as an auspicious mode of address or characterisation. Now, if we turn to Rock Edict VIII of Ashoka, we shall find that for *Devanampriya* of some versions we have *rajano* of others. This means that Devanampriya was an auspicious mode of address used with reference to Kings. And, as a matter of fact, the Dipavamsa applies the appellation Devanampriya to Tissa, the ruler of Ceylon and contemporary of Ashoka, and often employs it alone to denote that King. Epigraphic records also point to the same conclusion. Thus in the Nagarjuni Hill Cave inscriptions, the term Devanampriya is used to designate a King called Dasharatha, who has been taken to be the grandson of Ashoka. Similarly, an epigraph from Ceylon gives this epithet among other Kings to Vankanasika-Tissa, Gajabahuka-gamini, and Mahallaka-Naga. Devanampriya was thus an auspicious mode of address or honorific characterisation, before the Christian era, confined to the Kings only, and was so used probably to indicate the belief that the rulers were under the protection of the gods *(devas).* The term had therefore be better translated by " dear unto the gods," or " beloved of the gods." Ashoka's full royal style was thus " King Priyadarshin, beloved of the gods."

Many of Ashoka's inscriptions commence with the formula: *Devanampriya Piyadarshi Raja evam aha,* " thus saith King Priyadarshin, beloved of the gods." This has been rightly compared by Senart with the phrase with which the proclamations of the Achaemenides, from Darius to Artaxerxes Ochus, begin. One such instance is that *Darayavaush kshayathiya,* "thus saith the King Darius." In both cases the form of address commences with a phrase in the third person, and what is further worth noticing is that this phrase is immediately followed by the use of the first person. Of course, nobody can now maintain that this formula was imitated by Ashoka directly from Persia, for, as a matter of fact, we know that this was one of the protocols of the royal chancery noticed by Kautilya in his Arthashastra and consequently prevalent before the time of Ashoka. But nothing precludes us from holding with the French savant that the Indians adopted the Persian protocol and that this adoption was due to the Achaemenian conquest and administration of northwest India.

Wherever in his records Ashoka gives any dates, he counts the years from the time of his coronation. This has led scholars to believe the Sinhalese tradition that Ashoka was crowned four years after his accession to the throne. But this tradition also tells us that after the death of his father, Ashoka seized the throne by massacring ninety-nine of his brothers, and spared only one, the youngest, namely Tishya. This story is, however, refuted by his inscriptions which speak, not of one brother, but of several, living and staying again not only in Pataliputra, his capital, but also in various towns of his Empire. And if this is found to be a fiction, it is not intelligible why we should hold fast to that part of the tradition which places his coronation four years after his seizing the throne. In fact, it is not at all clear how his dating certain events of his reign from his coronation is evidence of there having been an interval between his coronation and accession to the throne. Again, in the Nagarjuni Hill caves there are at least three inscriptions which are dated immediately after the coronation of Dasharatha, grandson of Ashoka. Are we to suppose here also that because these records, in their dating, refer to Dasharatha's coronation, this event did not coincide with his coming to the throne and that some period must have elapsed between them? There is therefore no good reason to think that any long interval such as that of four years elapsed between Ashoka's coronation and his assumption of the reins of government.

It appears that Ashoka was in the habit of celebrating the anniversary of his coronation by the release of prisoners. This is inferrible from what he says at the end of Pillar Edict V. "By me, who am consecrated twenty-six years up till now," says he there, " twenty-five jail deliveries have been effected just in that period." As prisoners were released twenty-five times in the space of twenty-six years, it means that the twenty-sixth year of his reign had not elapsed but was running on when the Pillar Edict was promulgated. It thus seems that the dates which he specifies for the incidents of his life are current regnal years, and not expired, as has been taken by scholars.

Kautilya in his Arthashastra lays down that the King shall prohibit castration and destruction of animal fetus on certain days. Among these he includes the days of the *nakshatra* of the King and the country. In Pillar Edict V, Ashoka speaks of castration and branding of animals, and specifies on what days he has prohibited them.

Curiously enough, most of these days agree with those mentioned by Kautilya. And what is noteworthy is that here he specifies only two *nakshatra* days, namely, Tishya and Punarvasu. One of these is most probably the *nakshatra* of the King and the other of the country. And the question must arise: which *nakshatra* is of the King and which of the country? It is worthy of note that the Tishya *nakshatra* has been mentioned also in the two separate Edicts of Dhauli and Jaugada. These edicts, we know, were intended by Ashoka solely for the exhortation and guidance of the officials of the newly conquered province of Kalinga, and he issues the order that they shall be recited every Tishya day for their benefit. Evidently, of the two *nakshatras* greater importance has thus been assigned to Tishya than to Punarvasu. This may be seen also from the fact that although in the usual list of the *nakshatras* Tishya comes after Punarvasu, it is placed prior to the latter, not once but twice, in Pillar Edict V. It is difficult to avoid the conclusion that as so much importance has been given to Tishya, that must be the *nakshatra* of the King. If this inference is correct, Punarvasu becomes the *nakshatra* of the country, by which, we suppose, we have to understand the country of Magadha.

The edicts of Ashoka are concerned with his Dhamma and the means he adopted to disseminate it. They naturally, therefore, throw a flood of light on his life and career after he became a Buddhist. But let us here try and see what little these records tell us about his earlier life, both in his private and public capacity. We have already seen that he had several brothers and sisters living till the thirteenth year of his reign, and that they were residing not only in Pataliputra but also in the mofussil towns. Of course, Ashoka had his *avarodhana* or closed female apartments. How many Queens he actually had we do not know. But he had at least two, for there is reference to his second Queen in one of his inscriptions. And the very fact that she had been designated Second Queen shows that the relative rank of the Queens had in his day been fixed.

The name of this Second Queen was Karuvaki, and his son from her was Tivara. The object of the inscription is to ensure for this Queen the merit of any donation she might be pleased to make. In Pillar Edict VII Ashoka speaks of his having commissioned some of his officers to induce the members of his royal household to make gifts and to see to their proper organisation. It is interesting to note what members of his family he mentions in this connection. Of course, he first speaks of himself and his Queens.

But immediately after his Queens he makes reference to his *avarodhana* and tells us that its inmates were living not only at his capital but also in the provinces. Anybody who reads the passage carefully cannot but think that his Queens were not the only members of his *avarodhana*. Who could then be the other members? They cannot be the wives of his male relatives, for they cannot with propriety be called his *avarodhana*. Were they his left-handed wives? His *avarodhana* would thus comprise not only the Queens but also other *Purdah* ladies of lower status.

This no doubt reminds us of the Sinhalese tradition that when Ashoka during his father's lifetime was viceroy at Ujjain, he formed connection with a lady of the Setthi caste, who resided at Vedisagiri, modern Besnagar near Bhilsa, and continued to reside there even when Ashoka seized the throne and his children by her accompanied him to his capital. This legend clearly confirms the inference deducible from the Pillar Edict that Ashoka had women other than Queens and that his *avarodhana* was not all in Pataliputra, but that some of its members stayed in the mofussil. In the same Pillar Edict and in continuation of the same subject, namely, the distribution of the charities of the Royal Household, Ashoka speaks of his own sons and other *devikumaras*. The sons of Ashoka are thus distinguished from the latter. Who could the ' other *devikumaras* be? Most probably, Ashoka is here referring to the sons not of his own Devis or Queens but the Queens of his father and consequently to his non-couterine brothers. Again, how many sons Ashoka had we do not know. But he must have had at least four sons. In ancient times it was customary for a King to appoint his sons, as far as possible, as viceroys of the outlying provinces. And four such Princes we find mentioned in his epigraphic records, as being in charge of the four viceroyalties of Takshashila, Ujjaini, Suvarnagiri, and Tosali. Ashoka had at least four sons. To sum up, Ashoka had a very large family. He had several brothers and sisters staying not only at Pataliputra but also outside in the Empire. Some of them were certainly his couterine brothers, but there were also some, sprung, no doubt, from his father, but by different mothers. Ashoka had also his *avarodhana* or closed female apartments, not only in his capital but also in the provinces. They were occupied not only by his Queens but also other women with whom he had connection. He had at least two Queens, one of whom was named Karuvaki, and at least four sons. But whether Tivara, son of Karuvaki, was one of them it is not possible to determine.

We know very little of Ashoka's private life. His records shed very little light upon it. There is, however, one passage in Rock Edict VI which is interesting. This edict describes how often and at what different places be dispatched the business of his people. Here he tells us that he has arranged to dispose of it at all places and at all times so that no King prior to him ever did it. Naturally, therefore, he specifies the places where he formerly whiled away his time but where now he attends to their affairs. " This therefore, I have done," says he, "namely that at all hours and in all places—whether I am eating or I am in the closed female apartments, in the inner chamber *(garbhagriha)*, with the stud *(vraja)*, on horseback *(vinita)* or in pleasure orchards, the Reporters may report people's business to me."

Evidently, therefore, when Ashoka had no business to dispose of and, of course, was not asleep, he was to be found at his capital either regaling in the dining hall, engaged with the inmates of his harem, chatting in his retiring cabin, or inspecting the royal stud, enjoying a horse ride, or beguiling his time in the orchards. What special tastes and fascinations he had developed or evinced in these matters we do not know, but we do know what articles of food gratified his palate. Even when he was rigorously carrying out his programme of stopping the slaughter and injury to living beings, he made certain reservations in regard to his royal table. But even now when this document of Dhamma was written," says he in Rock Edict I, "only three animals were killed for curry, namely, two peacocks and only one deer, but even that deer not regularly. Even these three animals will not afterwards be killed." Ashoka here admits that although he has stopped the butchering of all other animals, he has allowed the killing of peacocks and deer to serve him with meat. Evidently, he was fond of the flesh of these animals. And as he says that the animal that was regularly butchered for his table was not the deer, but the peacock, it appears that he was inordinately fond of the peafowl. In this connection what Buddhaghosha says in his commentary on the *Samyuttanikaya* is worth noting. "To the people of the frontier provinces, *ganduppadas* are delicious, but they are abominable to those of the Middle Country. To the latter the flesh of a peafowl is delicious. It is, however, abominable to others." It is, therefore, no wonder if Ashoka, who was a native of the Middle Country, could not for a long time give up the eating of the peafowl flesh. We need not, however, harbour any doubt as to his having ultimately eschewed it, as promised in his edict, and thus turned a staunch vegetarian.

In another inscription Ashoka gives us another glimpse into his private life. Rock Edict VIII informs us that for a long time past Kings were in the habit of going out on *vihara-yatras* or pleasure tours, where they enjoyed chase and other similar diversions but that he has replaced these by *Dhammayatras* or tours for Dhamma since the tenth year of his reign when he visited Sambodhi, that is, the place where Buddha obtained enlightenment. What Ashoka gives us here to understand is that until the tenth year he, like all other Kings, used to go out on pleasure excursions, where he indulged in manifold diversions, the most pre-eminent of which, however, was hunting. We cannot have any clear idea of this *vihara-yatra*, as Ashoka gives us no details and as no account of it is also forthcoming from any work of literature. The Ashramavasika Parvan of the Mahabharata, no doubt, contains a reference to the *vihara-yatras* which Yudhishthira organised for enabling Dhritarashtra to forget the grief caused by the death of his hundred sons. But only one verse it gives to show what items constituted these *vihara-yatras.* " There," we are told, " the *aralikas* (jugglers), chefs, and singers of *ragas* and *shadavas* waited on King Dhritarashtra as in town." The programme of Dhritarashtra's pleasure trip thus consisted of music, dainties, and conjurer's tricks. There is no mention of chase here, because an old and blind man like Dhritarashtra cannot be expected to take delight in chase. But as Ashoka speaks of chase only and tells us nothing of the other diversions when he adverts to *vihara-yatras*, it appears that hunting formed the most important feature of a pleasure excursion in his time. In fact, hunting was so much indulged in by the Kings that it was considered by some ancient writers on Hindu polity to be a vice which they were exhorted to avoid. Pisuna, for instance, condemns chase, because danger from robbers, enemies, wild animals, forest conflagration, fear of stumbling, inability to distinguish the cardinal points, and so on, are the evils associated with it. Kautilya, on the other hand, strongly recommends it, because according to him exercise, reduction of fat and bile, skill in aiming at stationary and moving bodies, knowledge of the minds of animals and of their ever-changing movements when they are enraged are the good points of chase. Some of these good points, we involved any kind of brutality or butchery to life.

We shall now try to see what Ashoka was like in his capacity as King before he became a staunch missionary of Buddhism. Very little about him even in this capacity is known, and what little we know is from Rock Edict I. From it, it appears that like all other Kings Ashoka was in the habit of feasting and amusing his subjects, —probably a diplomatic move to keep his people pleased and satisfied. One mode of public entertainment that he practised was the celebration of the *samaja.* The *samaja* was of two kinds. In one the people were treated to dainty dishes in which meat played the most important part. In the other they were treated to dancing, music, wrestling, and other performances. The former was obviously a convivial melee. The latter was intended for the amusement of the people, and in this sense the *samaja* was synonymous with *ranga* or *prekshagara,* that is, the amphitheatre, and sometimes denoted ' the concourse of the people,' assembled there. All the instances of the *samaja* described in the Brahminical and the Buddhist literature show that they were intended to feast the palate or the eye and the ear of the people. There can be no doubt that the ancient Kings of India were in the habit of holding *samajas.* Thus in the celebrated Hathigumpha inscription we are told that Kharavela, King of Kalinga, amused his capital-town by celebrating *utsavas* and *samajas.* Precisely the same thing is reported in a Nasik cave inscription to have been done by Gautamiputra Satakarni, a King of the Dekkan. And, in fact, Kautilya himself lays down that a King " shall imitate (the people's) attachment to the *samaja, utsava,* and *vihara* of their country or divinity." Both the kinds of the *samajas* seem to have been celebrated by Ashoka. But when he began to preach Dhamma, he naturally tabooed those where animals were slain to serve meat, as we may infer from Rock Edict I. As there was nothing in the other *samajas* for him to object to, he retained them, but slightly changed the character of the exhibition of the public spectacles. He no doubt must have provided such spectacles as would not only cause amusement to his subjects but also generate, develop and disseminate Dhamma amongst them.

Reasons of state may also have dictated his taking another step in the same direction. In the same record Ashoka tells us that the slaughter of hundreds of thousands of animals was daily going on in the royal kitchen before the edict was promulgated. The case is precisely like that narrated in the Vanaparvan of the Mahabharata where we are informed that two thousand cattle and two thousand kine were slain every day in the kitchen of a King called Rantideva and that by doling out meat to his people he attained to incomparable fame. And, in fact, the practice of daily doling out food to hundreds of people is still found in the Native States of India. Like Rantideva, Ashoka must have been in the habit of distributing meat among his subjects, and that his object in doing so must have been precisely the same, namely, that of making himself popular. But he put a stop to this terrible animal carnage, the moment his conscience was aroused and he commenced teaching Dhamma.

We thus see what Ashoka was as a private individual and also as a King till he embraced Buddhism. The picture we have here is certainly not as lucid and full as we may desire, but we do obtain something which is reliable and not based on mere legend. We see what sort of family he had, what individual tastes and likings he possessed, and in what pursuits he engaged himself when he was free from his routine work as a ruler. We also know what titles he assumed as King, how he began his royal career, and what measures he adopted to entertain his people and enlist their attachment. He also regularly celebrated the anniversary of his coronation by releasing prisoners from jails. This is all we know of him as ruler before he became a Buddhist, that is, till after the eighth year of his reign when he subjugated Kalinga. Whether the earlier part of his reign was uneventful or whether he had made similar conquests or not we do not know.

The earliest event of his reign that we find referred to in inscriptions is his conquest of Kalinga, which roughly corresponds to the tract of land on the coast of the Bay of Bengal between the Vaitarani and Languliya rivers. He vividly describes the horrors and miseries of this war. " 1,50,000," says he, "were carried away (as captives); 1,00,000 were slain, and many times as many died." These are the figures for Kalinga only, and do not include the casualties in the King's army. We thus have to note that even in such a small province as Kalinga, as many as 1,00,000 were killed on the battlefield, many times as many died as the result of burning and sacking, and, what is more, no less than 1,50,000 were seized as slaves.

Surely, these are appalling figures for a tiny district like Kalinga, and indicate the extreme horrors of a war even in that ancient period when the weapons of destruction were not so diabolical and deadly as now. Soon after this war Ashoka was converted to Buddhism and began to preach Dhamma. And the remembrance of this war struck him with extreme and genuine remorse. When an unconquered province, says he, is being conquered slaughter, death and captivity must occur. This is regrettable enough. But what is still more regrettable is that among those who die, are slaughtered or are taken captive, there must be many who are devoted to Dhamma and that such contingencies to these men, again, must spell disaster and affliction to their friends, acquaintances, and relatives, who, though they themselves are safe, yet feel undiminished affection for them. " This is the lot of all men and is considered regrettable by the Beloved of the gods." The language is instinct with personal feeling, and the rocks still echo across the ages the wail of a penitent soul. There can be no doubt that this was genuine remorse. For, when the edict was proclaimed, he had already commenced in that country a zealous protection, longing and teaching of Dhamma. When a territory is newly subjugated and is in an unsettled condition, the officers who are charged with proper administration and maintenance of peace there are apt to transgress the bounds of justice and mercy.

Such transgressions did actually occur on the part of his officers, and we know from one of his inscriptions how severely he chastised them and what steps he took to prevent such excesses in the future. Nay, the inhuman and iniquitous nature of the war so much haunted his mind that he was even ashamed of engraving this edict in the Kalinga country.

There are two places in Kalinga where his Rock Edicts have been inscribed. But while the edict which describes his conquest of this province has been incised along with other Rock Edicts at all other places this alone has been omitted from the copies coming from Kalinga. Surely, remorse and sense of shame cannot further go.

We may be pretty certain that Ashoka made no further conquests. But why he conquered and annexed Kalinga to his Empire, which was already very extensive, is not quite clear. It seems, however, that Kalinga was a thorn in the body politic of his dominions. From Rock Edict XIII we know that the provinces of Andhra and Parimda were included in his kingdom.

Of these Andhra denoted roughly the country comprising the Kistna and Godavari Districts. As the capital of his Empire was Pataliputra, it is not unreasonable to suppose that it included the greater portion of modern Bengal. And this receives confirmation if my suggestion is true that Parimda was somewhere on the eastern outskirts of the Mauryan Empire, possibly in Bengal. Kalinga was thus a sort of wedge driven into the body politic and might at any time conspire with the foreign Choda kingdoms which were to the south. For the safety and consolidation of his state it was thus absolutely necessary to conquer Kalinga and make his Empire one compact mass; and this he did.

A year after his conquest of Kalinga he became a Buddhist. For one year he was lukewarm, but thereafter he became very strenuous in his exertions for the Dhamma, and the idea of becoming a Chakravarti Dharmika Dharmaraja haunted his mind. Supreme ruler of the earth ideal stimulated him to promote the temporal and spiritual good not only of his people but of the subjects of his independent neighbours, and not only of the human race, but of the whole animate world. We will take note of all his manifold activities, but shall first see what he did for his people as a ruler. For this, however, it is necessary to find out what the extent of his Empire was.

Physical Form and Personality

The perfection of bodily form which goes into the make-up of kingly personality is regarded as another contributory factor. The ugly face with grim looks such as that of an owl is held as a positive disqualification. The Brahmans of India developed a popular science by the name of Mahapurusha-lakshanam or 'Characteristic bodily marks of a great man', and the Jainas-and Buddhists availed themselves of it in establishing the personal greatness of Mahavira and Buddha respectively. The Buddhist came to speak of the thirty-two major bodily marks and eighty minor characteristics. They were persuaded to believe along with the Brahman interpreters of the signs that a person endowed with these marks and characteristics is destined to become a righteous King overlord, if he remains in the world, or in the alternative, a perfect type of Buddha, if he renounces the world.

The inscriptions of Ashoka have, however, nothing to say about his complexion and other details of his bodily form. In the Divyavadhana and other Sanskrit legends he is described as an ugly person with a repulsive appearance. This delineation was due, as I sought to show, to confusion made between Ashoka the Pious and Ashoka the Blackie. The brightness and majesty of bodily form may shed lustre on man's personality but is not to be wholly identified with it. Buddha truly said to his disciple Vakkali, "What's the use looking at this rotten body! He who sees the doctrine, sees me, and he who sees me, sees the doctrine." A great man is indeed a great mind, which conceives and cherishes a grand ideal. It is precisely in this light that one should evaluate the greatness of Ashoka the man as well as of Ashoka the King.

Education and Association: The Arthasastra expects the aspirant for kingship to be 'endowed with intelligence (buddhisampannah), possessed of intellect, talent, strong memory and keen mind (prajna-pragalbha-smriti-mati), trained in all sciences and arts (kritasilpah), and waiting upon the wise men of great experience (vriddhadarsi). In the vriddha-samyoga, the same text enjoins that a Prince shall study the sciences and arts and strictly obey the discipline and rules imposed by them under the authority of his teacher. Having undergone the ceremony of tonsure, he shall learn the alphabet (lipi) and arithmetic (samkhyana), and after investiture with sacred thread, he shall study Vedic system (Trayi), and speculative philosophies (Anvikshaki) under the teachers of acknowledged authority (sishtebhyah), the science of wealth (Varta) under the government superintendents (adhyakshebhyah), and the science of government (Dandaniti) under the theoretical as well as practical politicians (vaktri-prayoktyibhyah). To increase his efficiency in learning he shall ever keep up his contact with the experienced professors of sciences (vidyavriddha-samyogah).

In the Lakkhana Suttanta, a righteous King overlord is expected to be a man of great wisdom, unsurpassed by others in the matter of knowledge, which is the ripe result of his waiting upon the eminent religious teachers with eagerness to learn from them the things that are conducive to human good. In the Singalovada Suttanta, every man as a learner is required to serve well his teachers (acharya) by properly receiving the knowledge of the sciences and arts from them.

In the case of King Kharavela, it is claimed in the Hathigumpha inscription that while a Prince, he had learnt the rules of writing, currency, accountancy, and law and become a master of sciences and arts (savavijavadata).

We need not dwell here at length on the education of Indian Princes, sufficient information about which may be gathered from the later prasastis and literary works of all schools of thought. It may suffice for our immediate purpose to observe that the inscriptions of Ashoka indirectly throw some lights on his education and association. That he was familiar with the two main alphabets then prevalent in India, namely, Brahmi and Kharoshthi, is evident not only from the instructions issued as to the places where and the materials on which his inscriptions were to be incised, but also from the fact that he was aware of the errors committed by his scribes. His acquaintance with different local dialects and command over language is borne out by the inscriptions written obviously to his dictation. His long stay in Western India and occasional mission to North Western India must have enabled him to be acquainted with the dialects of those places. From the forms of his inscriptions, it may be easily inferred that he was an adept also in the rules of royal writs.

The inscriptions bear ample evidence to his sound knowledge of the principles of government. These bear a clear testimony also to his first-hand knowledge of the sacred texts and religious views of different sects. E.E. XII goes to prove that he personally met from time to time the exponents of different faiths and discussed various problems with them. In P.E. VI, he has laid due stress on the importance of going personally to wait upon the representatives of all sects. Waiting upon men of experience and wisdom for instructions and discussions looms large in E.E. VIII. In E.E. XII, he figures as a great lover of learning, healthy discussions and helpful debates.

Wives and Children

The Pali Chronicles and Samanta-pasadika tell us that while a Prince Ashoka married Devi, daughter of a banker, at Vidisha on his way to Ujjaini to join the office of the Viceroy (Uparaja) of Avanti. The Mahavamsa-tika describes her as a very handsome and accomplished lady and names her father Deva. It is quite possible that, like Pushyagupta of the Junagarh rock inscription, Deva was a Rashtriya or Rashtrapala. In the Mahabodhivamsa, she is honoured as Vedisa-mahadevi, and represented as a Shakya Princess. It is said that after her marriage, *she was taken to Ujjaini, where she bore him immediately a son called Mahendra, and two years later a daughter named Sanghamitra.* She is said to have built a vihara at Vidisha for her son when he came to see her back *en route* to the island of Tamraparni. Devi stayed back at Vidisha but her children accompanied their father when he came back to

Pataliputra and seized the throne. Sanghamitra was given in marriage to Prince Agnibrahma, a nephew of Ashoka, to whom she bore a son named Sumana. Agnibrahma, Sumana, Mahendra and Sanghamitra joined all the Buddhist Order. The above authorities offer us a systematic chronology of certain important events of Ashoka's reign in terms of the age of Mahendra. The Buddhist mission to Ceylon was led by Mahendra, and his sister, too, went over to the island when her services were needed for the "founding of an order of nuns there.

The story of Devi and her children is conspicuous by its absence from the Sanskrit legends, The inscriptions of Ashoka are lacking in confirmation of its truth. In the edicts promulgated up till the 14th year of Ashoka's abhisheka we have no mention of his sons, his daughters being altogether out of the question. In his R. E. V, promulgated not earlier than the 13th year of abhisheka, he speaks of charities from the households of his brothers, sisters and others ranking with him in family relationship. He speaks indeed also of his different family establishments at Pataliputra and outlying towns. On the other hand, in his P. E. VII, engraved in the 27th year of abhisheka, his brothers, sisters and other kinsmen ranking with him go out of the picture, and his own sons (dalaka) and other Princes of the blood ranking with them are expressly introduced instead. The way in which they are mentioned leave no room for doubt that his sons were then grown up enough to make charities out of their own funds, though not exactly from their own family establishments (orodhas).

His statement in P. E. VII is sufficiently explicit so as to make the meaning of that in E. E. V clear as to his own households. It goes to show that by his households or family establishments (to avoid the word harems) he chiefly meant his Queens (devis). The Queen's Edict contains his direction to the Mahamatras concerned as to how the donations and benefactions of his second Queen (dutiyaye deviye) Kaluvaki (Charuvaki or Kalavinka), mother of Tivala (Tivara), should be recorded or labelled with inscriptions,

Thus the Queen's Edict clearly proves that Ashoka had at least *two Queens at the time of its promulgation. Although the King's orders* were issued to the Mahamatras everywhere (savata mahamata), it was engraved only on the pillar at Kaushambi, a fact which may lead us to think that her residence was at Kaushambi, an outlying town. But Ashoka speaks of outlying towns, and not of one town only. Are we to understand from this that his Queens were not kept in one place, say, in his palace at Pataliputra, but at different towns, each having her separate establishment?

The Pali tradition about the Vidisha residence of Devi favours the idea of there being separate family establishments for individual wives at different towns. But from Ashoka's statement, it does not necessarily follow that each establishment was allotted to one Queen.

If Kaluvaki was his second Queen, who was his first or chief Queen? According to the Pali tradition, his beloved first Queen consort (piya aggamahisi) was Asandhimitta, a name, better title, which I am inclined to equate with Sk. Asandimitra (consort at the time of ascending the throne). She died in the 26th year of Ashoka's abhisheka, and four years later Tishyaraksha was made his Queen consort. The Mahavamsa and Divyavadhana legends make her jealous of the Bo-tree on account of the King's fond attachment to it. The Divyavadhana legend which is unaware of her predecessor Asandimitra goes further to build up a most scandalous story of Tishyarakshita and her wrathful vengeance on Ashoka's favourite son, Kunala, when he was deputed to Takshashila to quell a revolt. The story of Tishyaraksha has no place in the Dipavamsa, nor even in the writings of Buddhaghosa. It must have grown up at a later period. Ashoka, as he appears in his inscriptions, could not have lost his sanity so much as to behave as a religious maniac with regard to the worship of the Bo tree as he has been represented to be.

It is more reasonable to think and say that his wife by his side at the time of his coronation was the wife who accompanied him from Ujjaini, and she may be no other than the Vedisa-mahadevi.

The Divyavadhana legend represents Ashoka's Queen Padmavati as mother of Kunala who was also known by the name of Dharmavardhana or Dharmavivardhana (the promoter of the cause of piety).

The identity of Padmavati and Kaluvaki rests on the identity of their sons, Kunala and Tivala. Both Kunala and Tivala (Tivara) were nicknames. As for the first, Mukherji rightly remarks that Ashoka first gave to Padmavati's newborn babe the name of Dharmavivardhana but on seeing the beauty of his eyes, as his amatyas, or ministers in attendance, pointed out were like those of the Himalayan bird Kunala, Ashoka nicknamed him as Kunala. He was called Dharmavivardhana because he was born when Ashoka had been reigning prosperously with righteousness. According to the Divyavadhana legend, he was born as soon as the 84,000 dharmarajikas were built, the 7th year of Ashoka's abhisheka being mentioned in the Pali Chronicles as the date of completion of the construction of the 84,000 viharas with chaityas. The name Tivala or Tivara, which is met with in a much later Indian inscription as the name of a King of Kosala, signifies a 'keen-eyed' hunter. Prince Tivala, too, was born when Ashoka had been prosperously reigning with righteousness.

Successors: The Pali Chronicles and Samanta-pasadika do not carry the Maurya history beyond Ashoka. They create rather the impression that the whole glory of the dynasty vanished with him. His uterine brother Tishya-Vitashoka, son and daughter Mahendra and Sanghamitra, son-in-law Agnibrahma, and daughter's son Sumana joined the Buddhist Order. Nothing but the Buddhist religious edifices which he had built and the *memory of other pious deeds performed by him remained to keep his name alive to* posterity.

According to the Divyavadhana legend, Ashoka was succeeded by his grandson Sampadi, son of Kunala who was found unfit for the throne. Sampadi's lineal successors were Brihaspati, Vrishasena, Pushya-dharma and Pushyamitra. The last King of the family who began his career as a reactionary in favour of Brahmanism brought an end to himself and the Maurya dynasty by his ruthless act of vandalism directed to the destruction of the Buddhist viharas and stupas built and the killing of the Buddhist monks and nuns entertained by Ashoka.

Jayaswal suggests that the Buddhist tradition of Pushyamitra is preserved also in the Mulakalpa account of the hostile action of Gomin who is said to have destroyed "monasteries with relics" and killed "monks of good conduct."

The Buddhist tradition is misleading and inconclusive. Pushyamitra who, according to the Puranas, was the founder of the next dynasty, is represented as the last Maurya King and the lengths of the reign of Ashoka's successors are not given.

Raychaudhary's critical summary of the history of Ashoka's Maurya successors seeks to build up a cosmos out of a chaos. The Matsya Purana speaks of ten Mauryas whom it enumerates so clumsily as to make it uncertain whether by the" number ten it meant ten or seven successors of Ashoka. Some versions of the Vayu Purana definitely stand for nine successors, and try to reduce ten to the traditional number of nine Mauryas (nava Mauryah) by combining Bandhupalita and his son Indrapalita into one reign. The Vayu and Brahmanda Puranas speak of six successors who, together with the three first Mauryas, make up the traditional total of nine.

In the circumstances one may reasonably question the accuracy of Raychaudhary's statement when he says, "The Matsya Purana gives the following list of Ashoka's successors: Dasharatha, Samprati, Satadhanvan and Brihadratha", inasmuch as their number, even together with that of the first three Mauryas, does not come up to the given total of ten (dasa Mauryah). The lengths of reigns suggested in the Matsya Purana as well as in some versions of the Vayu do not, when joined together, fit in with the traditional total length of 137 years. Better in this respect is the position of the Brahmanda Purana as also of the Vayu, both of which give only 48 years as the total length of the reign of Ashoka's six successors.

The Vishnu Purana list of six successors, viz., Suyasas, Dasharatha, Sangata, Shalisuka, Somasarman Shatadhanvan and Brihadratha may be reconciled to a great extent, as suggested by Raychaudhary, with that in the Matsya, if Suyasas and Sangata of the one be identified with Kunala and Samprati respectively of the other. Other names do not call for comment as these are mere passing shadows without any historical importance so far.

The immediate successors of Ashoka was, according to the Divyavadhana legend, his grandson Sampadi (Samprati), and not his son Kunala, Kunala-Tivala or Kunala-Dharmavardhana whom Fa-hien distinctly mentions as the Viceroy of Gandhara. According to the Divyavadhana narrative, too, Kunala was deputed as his father's Vice-regent to Takshashila, the headquarters of the province of Gandhara. The Jaina author, Jinaprabhasuri claims Samprati, son of Kunala, as a great King who reigned in Pataliputra as an Emperor of India and founded viharas for the Jaina Shramanas 'even in non-Aryan countries.

Regarding Kunala and his immediate successor or successors, Raychaudhary observes: "Tradition is not unanimous regarding the accession of Kunala to the imperial throne. He is reputed to have been blind. His position was, therefore, probably like that of Dhritarashtra of the Great Epic and, though nominally regarded as the sovereign, he was physically unfit to carry on the work of government which was presumably entrusted to his favourite son Samprati, who is described by Jaina and Buddhist writers as the immediate successor of Ashoka. Kunala's son was Bandhupalita according to the Vayu Purana, Sampadi (Samprati) according to the Divyavadhana and the Pataliputra-kalpa of Jinaprabhasuri, and Vigatashoka according to Taranatha. Either these Princes were identical or they were brothers."

In the Gargi Samhita Salisuka is represented as a wicked King who had to abdicate the throne in favour of his virtuous elder brother, Vijaya.

In deciding on the question of Ashoka's successors, the 'flashes of light that may be obtained from the ancient Indian inscriptions are as follows:

- The Queen's Edict which was probably engraved during the second period of Ashoka's vigorous activity, 19th-21st year of abhisheka, mentions Tivala as his young son by his second Queen Kaluvaki.
- In P. E. VII engraved in the 27th year of abhisheka, Ashoka speaks of the charities of his sons.
- M. R. E. (Mysore copies), engraved probably in the 26th year of abhisheka, speaks of the Aryaputra Viceroy of Suvanagiri.
- S. R. E. I, engraved probably in the 32nd year of abhisheka, speaks of three Kumara Viceroys stationed at Tosali, Ujjain and Takasila respectively.

- The Nagarjuni Hill-cave inscriptions record the three cave-dedications made by Dasharatha to the Ajivikas immediately after his consecration (anamtaliyam abhishitena).
- The form of Brahmi letters employed in Dasharatha's inscriptions indicates certain changes to account for which one must allow an interval of time, however short, between Ashoka and Dasharatha.

The question arises—what was the course of action followed by the four Viceroys immediately after Ashoka's death, if they had survived him as would seem most likely? The conflicting traditions, Buddhist, Jaina and Brahminical, serve to make confusion worse confounded instead of returning a satisfactory answer to this question.

According to the Nagarjuni Hill-cave inscriptions, Dasharatha was a duly anointed King. From the situation of the caves dedicated by him, it is easy to infer that he was the sovereign of Magadha, better of Anga-Magadha. Vincent Smith had strong reasons to believe that Samprati's dominions 'included Avanti and Western India. But, as Raychaudhary points out, the Jaina writers represent him 'as ruling over Pataliputra as well as Ujjaini'. The tradition recorded by Jinaprabhasuri, however, describes Samprati as an Emperor of India whose capital, like that of Ashoka, was Pataliputra. The hypothesis that Ashoka was succeeded by his two grandsons, Dasharatha and Samprati, by the first in respect of his eastern and by the second in that of his western dominions is 'little more than a guess' even on Vincent Smith's frank admission.

If at a future date the veil be properly lifted from the history of Ashoka's successors, it will most probably be seen that no sooner had Ashoka passed away, no sooner had his strong hand been withdrawn than his four Viceroys asserted their independence, parcelling out his Empire into as many as four, if not more, separate principalities.

Length of Reign and Last Days

The length of Ashoka's reign since his abhisheka, which is evident from his dated inscriptions, consists of 27 years, while the same consists of 37 years according to the Pali Chronicles, and of 36 years according to the Puranas. Adding to the later 37 the earlier four years during which he reigned as an unanointed King since his accession according to the Pali tradition, we get the total length of his reign as comprising 41 years.

It may be noted here that the Pali Chronicles and the Puranas give the same length of reign, namely, 24 years, to Chandragupta but slightly differ as regards the length of reign of Bindusara which, according to the former, is 28, and, according to the latter, 25 years. Correcting the Purana figure 25 to 28 and adding up the lengths of the three first reigns we get the total of 89. This total being added to the total length of 48 years of the reign of Ashoka's six successors, yields the traditional Purana figure of 137 years representing the duration of the Maurya dynasty of Magadha. If so, one has to discard the tradition of Ashoka's reign of four years as an unanointed King since his accession. This tradition may be maintained if the duration of Bindusara's reign be accepted as 25 years and that of Ashoka's reign since coronation as 36 years, as suggested in the Puranas, in which case the required figure of 89 years may be obtained by adding up 24, 25, 4 and 36 years.

The S.R.E. I and S.R.E. II represent the set of Ashoka's edicts which may be supposed to have been promulgated and engraved in the closing period of his reign. If he had followed the quinquennial system, the date of their promulgation cannot be earlier than the 32nd year of his abhisheka.

S.R.E. I is addressed to the City-judiciaries of Tosali and Samapa. In it, they are taken to task for their failure in fully grasping the meaning and spirit of his instructions to them. They are urged not to cause oppression to his subjects by sudden arrest and coercion as well as summary trial. In it, he proposes to send forth every five years the Mahamatras under him on tours of inspection so as to check the miscarriage of justice. Here he modifies his quinquennial system and insists that the Kumara Viceroys at Tosali, Ujjain and Takasila should send forth on tours within every three years similar officials under them for the very same purpose.

Thus this edict goes to suggest that highhandedness and arbitrary action of the City-judiciaries, particularly in the outlying provinces, served to cause annoyance to the people.

Similarly S.R.E. II, which is addressed to the Viceroy-in-Council at Tosali and the Mahamatras who were Royal Commissioners at Samapa, presupposes hostile attitude and action of some of the 'frontagers' in violation of the terms of treaty or alliance. Whilst he wanted to assure them of his best intentions and friendliness, he did not omit to mention that he would tolerate them as long as their hostilities had not exceeded the limit of his patience.

The state of things as portrayed in these two edicts is faithfully represented in the Divyavadhana legend which, while giving an account of the last days of Ashoka, relates that the highhandedness and arbitrary action on the part of the officers in charge caused the citizens of the Uttarapatha to revolt (viruddha). On the arrival of the Kumara Viceroy, Kunala, at Takshashila, the citizens said, "We have revolted neither against the Kumara nor against King Ashoka, but the wicked ministers indeed come (here) and humiliate us."

The Mahavamsa describes the last days of Ashoka as unhappy, and the Divyavadhana as both unhappy and tragic. The causes of his unhappiness were, according to the Pali Chronicle, the death of his beloved Queen consort Asandimitra in the 26th year and the destruction of the Bo-tree out of jealousy by Tishyaraksha (rakshita) whom he appointed as Queen consort four years later. Over and above her attempt at the destruction of the Bo-tree, Tishyarakshita caused, according to the Divyavadhana legend, deep remorse to the King by her machination in getting the eyes of his beloved son Kunala plucked out after he had been deputed to Takshashila to quell a revolt in Uttarapatha. She is painted in the exaggerated Sanskrit story in the blackest of colours as a wily, passionate and revengeful woman of vilest character. Her story, which has happily no place in the earlier Pali Chronicle, Dipavamsa, was evidently developed, to heighten the glory of the Bo-tree as the living symbol of Buddha's enlightenment and Buddhism and the importance of its worship, as also to throw into bold relief the purity and magnanimity of the character of Kunala by a contrast with the vileness of the character of his stepmother.

The Sanskrit legend on the strength of which Jayaswal placed much reliance goes a step further and introduces a pathetic episode of the virtual abdication of the throne by Ashoka.

It is said that when Ashoka was about to exhaust the royal treasury by his over-extravagant subsidies to the Aryasangha or Sthavira Church, his Amatyas determined to put a stop- to it approached Sampadi, the heir apparent, and said, "King Ashoka, O Prince! who will live for a very short time is sending on this wealth to the Kurkutarama, but the treasury is the real strength to the Kings, so this (wreckless ruinous action of the King) must be stopped." Thereupon the Crown-Prince prevented the Steward (Bhandagarikah) from letting out any money from the treasury on the King's demand and instructed him to exercise a gradually restraining authority on all goods of value, even including metal plates, that might be given away as gifts to the Sangha. Thus the King was reduced to the position of a nominal ruler, although the administration was being carried on in his name until his death. Neither the amatyas nor the citizens, when asked by him, denied that he was all the time the supreme lord of the earth (prithivyam isvarah).

Obviously this episode, too, was added to stress the significance of giving away everything, treasures, worldwide kingdom, wives and households, officers of the State, self and beloved son, by a powerful and benevolent monarch like Ashoka to the Buddhist Church for the sake of religion (kosham sthapayitva mahaprithivim antahpuramatya-ganam atmanam Kunalam charyasamghe niryatayitva). But Ashoka was not so foolishly extravagant in his charities as to behave like that.

Ashoka, however, speaks of his sons who were sufficiently grown up in the 27th year of his abhisheka to be able to distribute charities on their own account. From all the traditional sources, namely, the Pali Chronicles, the Divyavadhana, Kalhana's Rajatarangini and Taranatha's Tibetan history, one can collect names of just four sons of Ashoka, to wit, Mahendra who became a Buddhist monk, Kunala-Tivala who was deputed as a Viceroy to Takshashila, Jalauka who, as suggested in the Rajatarangini, was appointed the Viceroy or Governor of Kasmira, and Virasena who, according to Taranatha, "apparently wrested Gandhara from the hands of the feeble successor of the great Maurya at Pataliputra."

The inscriptions of Ashoka themselves corroborate none of the three traditions regarding Mahendra, Jalauka, and Virasena. The truth of the tradition about Kunala being his father's Viceroy at Takshashila is borne out by the evidence of S. R. E. I, which expressly refers to three Kumaras functioning then as Viceroys at Tosali, Ujjain, and Takasila, As long as any strong evidence is not forthcoming to prove the contrary, these Kumaras must be taken to represent Ashoka's three sons. Probably Tivala-Kunala was one of them.

The problem of identification of the Kumara Viceroy of Gandhara may thus be solved by the legend of Kunala-Dharmavardhana. As regards the remaining two, we have still to grope in the dark, no light coming from traditions. And to add to the difficulty, the forwarding note of the Mysore copies of M. R. E. introduces us to an Aryaputra who was obviously functioning at the time as Viceroy at Suvarnagiri. He was certainly a brother or son of Ashoka. This is also a problem on which no further light can be thrown from any source.

The giving away of the whole of the vast earth (kingdom, Empire) extending as far as to the seas and oceans with all its treasures by Ashoka in the name of religion and culture and their propounders and promulgators was but a formal affair with several ancient Kings of India who aspired to gain renown and popularity in this world.

All that is possible to believe is that Ashoka virtually retired from active work of administration at his ripe old age, handing over its charge to the heir-apparent and ministers who might in the meantime have formed a conspiracy to upset the methods and policies initiated and followed by him.

Proper Reign: The most vigorous period of Ashoka's reign commenced with the conquest of Kalinga in the 8th year of his abhisheka and ended with the promulgation of the two Separate Rock - Edicts probably in the 32nd year. The notable incidents of his reign, as far as these may be gathered from the inscriptions and legends, have been separately tabulated. They give rise to several problems which have been dealt with by previous scholars.

2

Character and Personality

Ashoka, the King

In the political literature of India the King ranks first and foremost among the seven constituent factors on the strength or weakness of which depends the strength or weakness of the state. These are popularly known as the seven elements of sovereignty' (sapta rajyangani). Kautilya rightly emphasises the relative importance of the first element: "It is verily the King who appoints the ministers, chaplains, and other servants including the superintendents of departments, applies remedies against the troubles of his subjects and of his kingdom, adopts progressive measures, and replaces his ministers and officers who fall into troubles by new ones. It is he who rewards the worthy and punishes the wicked. When he is well off, by his welfare and prosperity he pleases his subjects. The character of the King determines the character of the people; for their progress or decline they depend on him. The King is, as it were, the peak of their lives."

To the same effect the Rajovada Jataka teaches that the King is the acknowledged head and leader of men, precisely as the King of bulls is that of a herd of cattle. If he practises impiety and is given to vice, the rest of men forestall him in the same; the whole kingdom prospers when the King is righteous.

Refinement and Dignity

A person entitled to kingship is expected in the Arthashastra to be 'possessed of dignity, making jokes with no loss of dignity or restraint, never browbeating and casting haughty and stern looks', capable of 'talking to others cheerfully with a smiling face', and observing the rules of behaviour as laid down by the learned. In Buddha's opinion, these are the qualities that go to make 'a man of graceful mien, felicitated by many', the reliever of the sorrow of many.

Ashoka in his P.E. I, speaks of the very best kind of fear (aga bhaya), the fear of public opinion, while in E.E. XIII he insists on feeling "ashamed of one's mischievous action. The open expression of regret or repentance (anutapa, anusochana) was certainly the outcome of a prick of conscience. The epithet Tivala mata applied to his second Queen (Queen's Edict) is to be regarded as a respectful way of referring to one's wife after she has become a mother. In addressing the Sangha, he is most careful to follow the established social convention. He highly prized gentle speech, cool temper and winsome cordiality. The principle of toleration as propounded by him, eloquently speaks of his refined manners, self-respect and respect for others' feelings. Seemly behaviour (samyapatipati) towards all was with him the guiding principle of dealings with men. It is in connection with Ashoka the King that one may see better how well he deserved the two titles of Priyadarshin and Ashoka.

Intellectual Faculties

The Arthashastra mentions intelligence, understanding, talent, sharp memory and keen mind as the typical intellectual faculties with which the King as a man may be expected to be endowed. The personal qualities that are helpful to the acquisition of knowledge (prajna-guna) consist of respectful attention, hearing, grasping, retention in memory, knowing, reasoning, drawing the conclusion, and adherence to the truth. The first of these implies four things in Buddha's language, namely, paying due respect to the teacher (utthana), going to meet (pachchupagamana), regular waiting upon the teacher for lessons (upatthana), and personal services (parichariya), while his term sussusa stands for attentive hearing (saddahita-savanam). The rest of the approved modes are comprehended by Buddha's expression 'the proper way of learning the sciences and arts'. These ideas about the approved modes of learning are comprehended by the three words—seva (waiting upon the learned men of experience), pranipata (homage), and pariprichchha (discussion). Buddha speaks of the three kinds of knowledge, namely, sutamaya panna, chintamaya panna and bhavanamaya panna, that develop from the pursuit of the three modes which, in the language of the Upanishads, are sravana (hearing), manana (thinking), and nididhyasana (meditation). Knowing the true nature of things (pajanana), preliminary enquiry (vichaya), thorough enquiry (pavicaya), investigation into the nature of truths (dhammavicaya) definition by general characteristics (sallakkhana), definition by special characteristics (pachchupalakkhana) thinking (chinta), and closer examination (upaparikkha) are, according to Buddha, the various modes of understanding by which intellectual faculties may be exercised.

In many of his edicts Ashoka stresses the need of respectful attention to teachers, learned men of experience, elders and high personages. He equally lays emphasis on waiting on the wise men of experience for instruction and discussion. In the Bhabru Edict he recommends the constant hearing (study) and remembrance of certain sacred texts with the comprehension of their meaning. Here his expression abhikhinam suneyu corresponds with abhikshnya-sravanam in the Arthashastra. He is argumentative throughout and his main method of convincing others is nijhati, i. e., appeal to reason. His instruction to the Yuktas is to set forth the reason or argument in the document meant for publication (hetuto).

Strength of Will

The Arthashastra demands of a person qualified for kingship that he should be 'highly enthusiastic, not addicted to procrastination' (mahotsahab adirghasutrah) and 'of resolute mind' (dridhabuddhih). Valour (sauryam), readiness (amarshah), quickness (Shighrata) and dexterity (dakshyata) are spoken of as the volitional factors that go to constitute enthusiasm (utsaha-guna). Buddha mentions energy (viriya), energetic action (viriya-rambha), promptness (nikkama), strenuous exertion (parakkama), effort (uyyama), purposive activity (vayama), zeal (ussaha), enthusiasm (ussolhi), stamina (thama), and endurance (dhiti) as the mental factors that represent the strength of the will.

These are the main personal qualities and principles of action on which Ashoka has harped in his edicts. The resoluteness of his mind has found its classical expression in the following statement: "I myself instructing you and making my wishes known until my fortitude and promise remain unshaken, will be a server of the land". Parakrama, pakama uyama, usaha and uthana are the keywords of Ashoka's life as well as his government.

Idealism and Human Feelings

The Arthashastra demands, among other qualities, that the King as a man should have large aims'. Large-heartedness goes together with man's true idealism, while human feelings and tender emotions are just the outcome of a large heart a man develops within himself.

Admittedly the largest aim of man's life is 'doing good to the whole world' (sarva-loka-hita), and this was precisely the real aim of Ashoka's life. The world, as we saw, was extended not only beyond the confines of his Empire but also beyond those of the allied territories. It included also the animals as its denizens.

He aspired by all possible means to be a servant of the land (desa-ayutike). All his earnest efforts were to be directed towards the elevation of man's nature and moral state.

These were to be equally directed towards the alleviation of human and animal sufferings. He is just human when he expresses his natural affection for his wives and sons, brothers and sisters, other Princes of the blood, other kith and kin, as also for his neighbours, or when he pleads for respectful attention to parents, teachers, elders and high personages, and seemly behaviour to slaves and servants, the aged and the helpless, the oppressed and the fallen.

Moral Traits of Character

The Arthashastra enjoins that the King as a man should be 'virtuous, truthful, not of a contradictory nature, grateful, and free from passion, anger, greed, obstinacy, fickleness, haste and backbiting habits'. In the Sarabhanga Jataka and the Great Epic, he is expected to be grateful, wise, largehearted, of charitable disposition, and of firm devotion. Buddha lays stress, in the very language of the Arthashastra, on truthfulness and self consistency.

Ashoka himself speaks of restraint, the purity of heart, gratefulness, and firm devotion as the four moral qualities that enhance the: value of charity. Pity, liberality, truthfulness, purity, gentleness and goodness are with him the fundamental principles of piety and human conduct. Non-harming and friendly is his mental attitude towards the whole of life. Sanity and sincerity characterise his thoughts, words and actions. Well-balanced is his mind. He shows throughout the courage of conviction and displays moral courage in stating his own ideas about persons and things.

Religious Faith: A man is known by the religion he professes. Ashoka's religion was Buddhism. Here Buddhism is taken to be a religion in the sense of a form of Doctrine and Discipline (Dhamma-Vinaya) which not only holds before us the higher ideals of life but also cherishes faith in their reality.

There is a substantial agreement, as we saw, between the Pali tradition and Ashoka's own statement regarding his conversion to Buddhism. It is not very material whether the Mysore copies of M.R.E. speak of a period of about three years and the remaining versions of that of four. Since he had become an upasaka, meaning a lay worshipper inclined towards religion, he did not exert himself strenuously until he met the Sangha or the entire congregation of monks available at his capital (samghe upayate). The evidence of the Dipavamsa is decisive as to the meaning of the expression sarpghe upayate. That he had not assumed monastic vows is certain from Ashoka's own statement, the account having been given of his life as an upasaka (am upasake sumi). His conversion to the Buddhist faith is to be dated from the time he approached or came in contact with the Sangha. I abandon my old position that here Ashoka distinguishes between the two stages of his career as a Buddhist lay worshipper, the first when 'he had been only privately cultivating the company and receiving the instruction of an individual Buddhist teacher', and the second 'when he publicly declared himself to be a follower of the Sangha and entered upon a career of direct service to the Sangha.' As I now maintain, the intended distinction is between the earlier stage when he had adhered to other sects and the later stage when he began to follow the guidance of the Buddhist Sangha in matters of religious faith.

The bhikhsugatika theory started by Charan Das Chatterji has found its supporters in Bhandarkar and Mukherji. But Chatterji himself is not sure about it. Buddhaghosa understands by a bhikhsugatika "a person that dwells in the same vihara with the bhikhsus". This does not necessarily mean that the condition of a Bhikhsugatika is intermediate between an Upasaka and the Bhikhsu. About the reading of the word, too, one cannot be sure, its variant in some of the manuscripts being *bhikhsussa bhatika* (one who is of service to a Bhikhsu), which is more appropriate to the Vinaya context.

Whether in the Bhabru, or in the Schism Pillar Edict, or in the Lumbini Pillar Inscription, Ashoka figures as a King and a lay worshipper of Buddha. There is nowhere the slightest suggestion as to his withdrawal from the world.

The question is often raised if the Buddhist faith of Ashoka is conclusively proved by his inscriptions. In the Barabar Hill-cave inscriptions the Ajivikas who were the donees of the caves are simply introduced as Ajivikas, while in the Nagarjuni Hill-cave inscriptions of Dastratha, the epithet Bhadamta is prefixed to their name. In the same Bhabru Edict, like a devout Buddhist, he professes his profound faith in the Three Jewels and firmly believes that 'all that is said by the Blessed One is well said'. Here, moreover, he expresses his sincere solicitude for the long endurance of the Good Faith, and to that noble end in view he selects seven Buddhist texts and commends them confidently to the monks, nuns and laity for their constant study and remembrance.

He is not known to have gone on pilgrimage to places other than those sacred in the Buddhist eye, e.g., Bodhgaya (Sambodhi), the holy spot of Buddha's Enlightenment, Lumbini, the place of Buddha's Nativity, and the Stupa of Konagamana, the shrine erected in honour of a former Buddha. Going to pay homage to the Sangha (Sangha-dassanam), the Bo-tree (Bodhidassanam), and the Shrine (Chetiya-dassanam, Nigali Sagar) on his part was the pious act of a Buddhist upasaka for his growth in piety (dhammavuddhi). In the Schism Pillar Edict he rejoices to state that he had made the Sangha united for all times to come.

The anuposatha (Sarnath Pillar) as a special day set apart for the Buddhist laity to attend religious service at a local vihara, taken in this technical sense, i.e., meaning the eighth day of a lunar half-month, is not a negligible proof of Ashoka's Buddhist faith. Ashoka was not, however, an ordinary convert, he had the first religious vision of truth, good, and duty as a happy result of his own reflections on the aftereffects of his aggressive war against Kalinga. If Buddhism made thereafter a deep appeal to him, it did so only for the reason that its teachings tallied with his own experience and personal conviction.

People's Friend

There have been many Emperors in the history of India but few that ruled over such a vast Empire as Ashoka's. His Empire extended over a large part of India and Afghanistan and Baluchistan beyond the Northwest province and Nepal in the North, as well as the Bengal, Bihar, Andhra Pradesh and a large part of Karnataka of today. The inscriptions discovered in these parts prove this.

Though Pataliputra was the capital of the vast Empire, for the proper administration of his Empire, Ashoka divided his Empire into four provinces. Malava, Punjab, Dakshinapatha and Kalinga. Ujjain was the capital of Punjab, Taxila of Malava, Suvarnagiri of Dakshinapatha and Kosala of Kalinga. He appointed a representative in each province. The representatives were chosen for their ability and not on the basis of birth or high connections. They enjoyed considerable freedom in the administration of their provinces.

To assist the Emperor there was a council of Ministers in the capital. If the Emperor wanted to make changes, he used to consult the Ministers. After the council examined the pros and cons of a proposal it was implemented. Usually the Emperor accepted the decision of the council of ministers.

Chanakya (Kautilya), the Chief Minister of Chandragupta Maurya, has described the daily life of the Kings of that age as follows:

> 'The King gets up at 3 a.m. And till half past four examines various matters relating to the Empire and takes decisions. He then receives the blessings of teachers and priests. Then he meets his doctors and the officials of the kitchen. He then goes to the court hall and considers from 6 a.m. to 7 a.m. the revenue and the expenditure of the previous day. From 7.30 he grants interviews to persons who have come to meet the Emperor on urgent matters, and examines their submissions. He retires to bathe at 9. After bath, prayer and breakfast, the Emperor meets officers of the Empire at 10.30 a.m. and issues instructions on many matters. All noon he meets the council of ministers and discusses matters of state. After rest between 1.30 and 3 p.m. he inspects the various divisions of the army. After this he receives reports from messengers and spies who have come from different parts of his Empire and from other kingdom.'

Ashoka, who continued the ideal and the tradition of his grandfather Chandragupta, practised in letter and spirit, the routine set down by Chanakya. Besides, Ashoka believed that the prosperity of his subjects was his prosperity; so he had appointed officers to report to him on the welfare and sufferings of the people. They were to report to him no matter what the hour was. His own order best shows his concern for the people:

> "Whether I am dining or in my private apartments, asleep or engaged in some work, setting out on a journey or resting; wherever I may be and whatever the time of the day or night the officers must come and report to me about the people and their affairs. Wherever I may be I shall think about the welfare of the people and work for them." These words are enough to show Ashoka's devotion to the welfare of his people.

Statesmanship and ability for Administration

Of the two main criteria for testing the statesmanship and administrative capacity of a ruler, the first is his proficiency in the science of government and the second his ability for timely and effective application of its principles for his own safety, the safety of his territory and subjects, the safety of other elements of sovereignty, and the furtherance of general good and happiness (Arthashastra).

The inscriptions of Ashoka bear ample testimony to his position as an advanced political thinker and as a far sighted and capable administrator. His knowledge of the science of government and the general philosophy of life was deep and profound. The general principles of piety, duty and good conduct advocated by him in his edicts fall all within the scope of the most advanced rajadharma or political thought of India, and had all the regulations of piety.

Discharge of Duties

Ashoka not only kept the Maurya Empire intact but extended it by the annexation of Kalinga. He tried to consolidate his territory and carefully guarded it against internal troubles and foreign invasions. The internal troubles might arise either from the mischiefs caused by the atavis as well as from popular disaffection and revolt. He took proper measures to punish the offenders. The expression of regret and the declaration of might on his part were intended to see that such mischiefs were not repeated. Behind the repentance was the drastic action which had to be taken, and behind the might was the consciousness of his financial resources and striking power, while before them was the strong warning. He strongly warned the inimical or mischievous neighbours against encroachments into his territory along with assuring them of his goodwill towards them and his sincere desire to respect the territorial integrity. In order to remove the cause of popular disaffection and revolt he took his officers to task and deputed higher officers to redress the wrongs done to the people as well as to prevent the miscarriage of justice.

Ashoka did his best to fulfil his obligations to his own people. In order evidently to prevent the hitch among his Queens he had separate family establishments in his capital and outer towns. He provided his wives and sons with funds to distribute charities on their own account. He appointed his own sons as well as other Princes of the blood to responsible offices of the state when they became grown up and fit for work. He took a keen personal interest also in the family affairs of his brothers, sisters and other kith and kin, and tried to assist them in all matters of piety and social importance.

To his own officers Ashoka acted all along as a friend, philosopher and guide. He took them to task when they went wrong, and encouraged them when they were found diffident of success. He issued instructions to them as to how they should carry out his orders to his satisfaction. He did not forget to remind them of their importance as functionaries of the state.

Ashoka cherished the parental feeling towards his own subjects and expected that they should on their part cherish the filial feeling towards him. He aspired to be the servant of the country (desavutike hosami). With him to love the people best was to serve them best; he never felt tired of impressing this fact on the mind of his officers. The supreme task to which he directed all his efforts was the moral elevation of the people and their satisfactory growth in piety. To increase the good and happiness of the people was the normal duty of a good King. He did not apply to others any principle which he would not apply to himself. Thus he tried to stand as a living example of virtue to his own officers and subjects. Led by the altruistic idea of doing good to the whole world, he wanted to cherish similar feelings towards the people of the neighbouring territories.

Ashoka was fully aware of his duties to the needy, the distressed and the fallen. The people in indigent circumstances, the aged, the destitute, the sick, the slaves and servants, and the imprisoned and those condemned to death by court sentence engaged his special attention. To provide the travellers with comforts he planted shade-trees on the roads and dug wells and tanks. The wells and tanks by the roadside must have served also to help the irrigation work.

His private faith did not stand in the way of his honouring the men of all sects with gifts and in various other ways of honouring them. He desired all the Brahminas and the Sramanas to dwell everywhere in his Empire and do their work without fear or molestation. He wished all of them well, and knew their great importance.

The beasts and birds, the fishes and other animals equally engaged his attention. Just as in the case of men, so in that of beasts, he arranged for medical treatment. The shade-trees and the wells and tanks were meant also for their enjoyment. He enacted the game-laws to minimise their slaughter, and prohibited the performance of animal sacrifices.

The keen sense of duty enlivens all his statements. At all times and in all places, even when and where he was supposed to have observed strict privacy, he attended to the business of the people. There was no higher duty to him than doing good to all.

As a man of graceful mien and as one who viewed the world and all with loving eyes he justified the epithet of Priyadarshin. As a ruler devoted to the duty of relieving the sorrow and misery of all, he tried to deserve the name of Ashoka or Soka-nasana. And as a righteous King Emperor who was able to commingle the gods and men in an unprecedented world of piety, he well merited the epithet of Devanampriya or 'Beloved of the gods.'

3

Ashoka, the Emperor

The Wheel, which adorns the flag of free India, has kept His memory green. Lord of a vast Empire,, after a great victory on the battlefield he grew sick of violence and took an oath never to fight again. He was an ideal ruler. He strove to carry to other lands the light he had won in his life. He dedicated himself to the victories of righteousness.

Star of Mauryan Dynasty

Ashoka was the grandson of Chandragupta Maurya. Chandragupta was the first ruler of the Mauryan Empire. He ruled for about twenty-four years, and then, seeking peace of mind, handed over the reigns of his Empire to his son, Bindusara. This Bindusara was the father of Ashoka.

Subhadrangi was the mother of Ashoka. She was the daughter of a poor man of Champakanagar.

As a boy Ashoka was not only active also mischievous. He was a skilful hunter. From the time of Chandragupta Maurya the hunting expedition of the Emperor and the royal family was a splendid sight.

Ashoka was not handsome. But no Prince excelled him in valour, courage, dignity, love of adventure and ability in administration. Therefore even as a Prince Ashoka was loved and respected by his subjects and by his ministers. Bindusara discovered the ability of his son quire early and, when Ashoka was still young, appointed him Governor of Avanti.

At Taxila

Ujjain was the capital of Avanti. It was a beautiful city, and the home of knowledge, wealth and art. Within a few days of taking over the administration of Avanti, Ashoka became an excellent statesman. It was when he was in this city he married Shakya Kumari, the beautiful daughter of a merchant of Vidishanagar. She gave birth to two children, Mahendra and Sanghamitra.

Ashoka's valour, courage and wisdom were soon tested. The citizens of Taxila rose in revolt against the rule of Magadha. Bindusara's eldest son, Susheema (also called could not put down the rebellion. Bindusara sent Ashoka to suppress the revolt. Ashoka to suppress the revolt. Ashoka did not have enough forces but yet moved towards the city boldly.

A surprising thing happened. The citizens of Taxila never thought of fighting against Ashoka. They gave him a grand welcome.

They pleaded, "We do not hate either Bindusara or the royal family. The wicked ministers are responsible for our revolt. We misunderstood you because of their evil advice. We are not rebels. Please forgive us."

Ashoka understood the real situation and punished those responsible for the revolt. He stayed there for some days and gave the people some advice in simple and beautiful words. When complete peace had been established in the city, Ashoka returned to his province.

Days and years passed.

Bindusara grew old. His body became weak. His health declined. Among his ministers one minister by name Radhagupta was prominent. He and the others began to think about the future welfare of the Empire.

Bindusara's eldest son was Susheema. According to custom he should have succeeded to the throne.

But the revolt of Taxila had exposed his weakness.

Besides, he had begun to behave with insolence.

The council of ministers felt that the Empire would suffer and lose peace, and prosperity and that thee would be no justice in the land if Susheema was crowned King. Therefore they sent word to Ashoka that his father was ill and that he should rush to the bed side of his sick father.

Prince on Throne

Emperor Bindusara had won the title 'Amitraghatha' (one who strikes those who are unfriendly). He had annexed the area between the east coast and the west coast in south India and extended his Empire. He ruled over this Empire for twenty-five years and died in 272 BC. Ashoka who had come to Pataliputra from Ujjain at the request of Radhagupta, the Chief Minister, was crowned King of Magadha after the death of his father.

What happened after this is not very clear. Perhaps Susheema heard the news of his father's death and feared that Ashoka might be crowned King; he probably came from Taxila with a large army. He came prepared to fight if necessary. But he was killed even as he was attempting to gain an entrance to the city.

There is a story that Ashoka had all his brothers killed for the sake of the kingdom. There is no historical basis for this story. Ashoka has spoken affectionately about his brothers in his rock inscriptions.

The fifth day of the third month Jyestamasa of the year 268 BC was the auspicious day on which Ashoka was crowned King. Pataliputra was gaily decorated.

The auspicious time fixed for the coronation arrived. Auspicious music Sounded. Young and radiant Ashoka entered the court, surrounded by his bodyguards. The heir to the throne of Magadha bowed to the throne and ascended it. As the priests chanted sacred verses, the heir was adorned with the appropriate symbols of royalty and the crown was placed on his head. The citizens of Pataliputra rejoiced that the Empire was blessed with an able ruler.

Ashoka was a very intelligent statesman. He ruled over Magadha wisely and ably. The council of ministers and officers of state were obedient, dutiful and able. Therefore peace and plenty brightened the land.

Happiness makes man forget how time passes.

Eight years passed without anyone realising it.

Kalinga War

Ashoka became the lord of a vast Empire. But Kalinga, a small state (now called Orissa), remained independent, beyond Ashoka's Empire.

Kalinga was a rich and fertile land between the Godavari and the Mahanadi. The people of Kalinga were patriots and loved freedom. They were ready to fight and die in defence of their motherland.

Vanquished Kalinga

Ashoka defeated Kalinga in war, hadn't he? He then appointed officers to administer the kingdom. How do officers who go from the victorious state to the defeated land usually behave towards the people? They lose all sense of justice and fair play and behave proudly. They insult the defeated people. Ashoka did not want this to happen. He desired that the people of Kalinga should live in peace and honour. This was his order to the officers who were sent to Kalinga:

> "I have put you in charge of thousands of people. Earn the love and affection of all those people. Whatever situation may arise treat all people alike. Be impartial in your actions. Give up rudeness, haste, laziness, and lack of interest and short temper. Nothing can be achieved if we are bored and idle. Therefore be active. If you understand how sacred your work is and behave with a sense of responsibility, you will go to heaven, and you will also repay your debt to

the King who appointed you." Ashoka who treated his subjects as his children, further said, "Like a mother who gives her child to an able nurse, trusting that she would bring up the baby well. I have entrusted my subjects to your care."

Vigilant on All Sides

Ashoka worked hard especially for the spread of education in his land. Nalanda is famous in history; it was the centre of education and the University of Magadha. It is said that university of Magadha. It is said that Ashoka founded it. Students of that university were very much respected. During his time trade with foreign countries was carried on by sea routes. He encouraged agriculture, trade and industries. There were canals to help irrigation. All the money paid into the government treasury was spent for the welfare of the people.

Ashoka has big roads laid to help the growth of business and industries. For the benefit of travellers he had trees planted on both sides of the roads. Wells were dug and guesthouses and rest houses were put up. There was free medical aid both for men and for animals. Ashoka is among the first in the world who built hospitals for the treatment of animals. He got medicinal plants and a variety of fruit-bearing trees from several places and planted them where they were not found. In one inscription he has expressed the wish that even the forest dwellers in his Empire should live happily.

Sandalwood wears itself out to give a cool and fragrant paste to men. Sugarcane gives up its sweet juice to men and reduces itself to mere skin in the process. The candle burns itself out that others may have light. All his life Ashoka lived like the sandalwood, like the sugarcane, like the candle.

He worked hard without rest and taught the people to live a life of truthfulness, Dharma, Justice and morality. There was happiness and peace. There were social gatherings at which people of all castes and creeds gathered and enjoyed themselves without feeling of high and low.

An Old Age of Sorrow

Ashoka who was the embodiment of pity, kindness and love unfortunately had to suffer much in his old age. The reason was this-his sons, Mahendra, Kunala and Teevala were engaged in spreading Buddhism and so his grandsons Dasharatha and Samprati started quarrelling over the right of succession to the throne. Even the Queens quarrelled over the issue. There was one among them, Tishyarakshite who was a wicked woman. Ashoka was a monk among Kings and had given up all pomp and pleasures and lived a very simple life. This did not please Tishyarakshite who loved the life of ease and comfort. All this made Ashoka sad. By this time he had grown old. Not much is known about the last ten years of his life and about his death. Some say, 'The Emperor got disgusted in life and therefore he went on a pilgrimage as a Buddhist monk with his teacher, for the peace of his mind. At last he reached Taxila and stayed there. Ashoka, the beloved of Gods and men, left the earth at the age of seventy-two.'

However it is clear that Ashoka was unhappy in his old age.

Dynastic Successors

The dynastic successors of Ashoka are by the Brahman and Buddhist traditions diversely reported according to the following scheme:

Brahman Sources.	*Buddhist Sources.*
A Pargiter, *Dynasties of the Kali Age*	A.*Divydvaddna*
1. Kunala or Suyashas, reigned 8 years.	1. Kunala.
2. Bandhupalita, son of Kunala, reigned 8 years.	2. Samprati, son of Kunala.
3. Indrapalita.	3. Brihaspati, son of Bandhupalita.
4. Dashona, son of Indrapalita, reigned 7 years.	4. Vrishasena, son of Indrapalita.
5. Dasharatha, son of Dashona, reigned 8 years.	5. Pushyadharma, son of Dashona.
6. Samprati or Saugata, son of Dasharatha, reigned 9 years.	6. Pushyamitra, son of Dasharatha.

Contd...

Brahman Sources.	*Buddhist Sources.*
7. Shalishuka, son of Samprati, reigned 13 years.	
8. Bevadharman or Devavarman or Somasharman, son of Shalishuka, reigned 7 years.	
9. Shatadhanvan or ShaShadharman, son of Bevadharman, reigned 8 years.	
10. Brihadratha, reigned 7 years.	
B.*Rajatarangini*	B.Taranatha, *History of Buddhism*
Jaloka in Kashmir, son of Ashoka.	1. Kunala.
	2. Vigatashoka.
	3. Virasena

These meagre and conflicting lists are evidently no material for history: but they supply certain indications which may hereafter be verified. One of the Buddhist sources includes in the dynasty the name of Pushyamitra, really the founder of the succeeding line of the Shungas: he was commander-in-chief to Brihadratha and he availed himself of a grand review of the army to overthrow and slay his master. Les. this error of the Buddhists should lead us wholly to prefer the Brahman accounts, let us observe that the latter differ in numerous particulars, some naming more Kings than others, and all presenting diversities of spelling: moreover, none of them justifies in detail the total of 137 years which they unanimously ascribe to the whole Maurya dynasty.

The existence of some of the Kings named in the list is avouched by independent evidence. Dasharatha is known by three inscriptions bestowing on the Ajivika sect caves in the Nagarjuni hills: Samprati is mentioned in the Jain tradition as a convert of their patriarch Suhastin. Jaloka is celebrated in the history of Kashmir, as a great propagator of Shaivism and for a time a persecutor of the Buddhists, further as having freed the country from an invasion of Mlecchas, who would be Greeks, and a conqueror who extended his dominions as far as Kanyakubja or Kanauj.

The extreme confusion reigning in the legends is probably, as was indicated long ago, to be explained by a division of the Empire, perhaps beginning after Samprati. The Buddhists will then give the western line, as is indicated by the fact that Virasena is represented as ruling in Gandhara, and further by the fact that Sophagasenus, or Subhagasena, with whom Antiochus the Great renewed an ancestral friendship in 206 BC, is indicated by his name as a member of this line. This series will then have been terminated by the Greek conquest of the Punjab under Euthydemus and his successors. At Pataliputra the second line may have held out a little longer, until about the year 184 BC, when it was overthrown by Pushyamitra, whose power may have centred about Ujjain, and who, as is indicated in the drama of Kalidasa called the *Malavikagnimitra*, succeeded to the struggle with the Greeks. But descendants of Ashoka were as late as the seventh century AD, if we may trust the statement of Hiuen Tsang, still in possession of small dominions in eastern India: for he relates that shortly before his visit Purnavarman, King of Magadha, a descendant of Ashoka, had restored the Bodhi-tree, which had been destroyed by Shashanka, otherwise named Narendragupta, of Karnasuvarna, or Bengal.

4

Empire and Administration

Imperial Administration

The main function of the imperial administration of Ashoka was, as we saw, to unify the provincial governments for the realisation of a grand idea or ideal expressed through the organ voice of the Emperor. As distinguished from them, the imperial government working apparently under the dictatorial power and prerogative of Ashoka reserved to itself certain rights and privileges.

The reservations included *inter alia* the power of legislation, the promulgation of special ordinances, the proclamation of imperial messages, the publication of edicts, the issue of general directions and instructions, the introduction of administrative changes, the initiation of state policy including fiscal, the framing of budget, foreign relations, war and peace, the exercise of general supervision, the appointment and dismissal of provincial heads and other imperial agents, and the creation of new departments. As regards the imperial seat of government, the appointment and dismissal of ministers, councillors, the Emperor's personal and household staffs, the departmental officers, the organisation and maintenance of the imperial army and navy, the construction and maintenance of ports, road and water ways, irrigation, relief work, public health, and the like must have come also within the province of imperial administration.

The imperial administration of Ashoka, which is to say, that of *Magadha, developed on a purely monarchical basis.* Thus to understand its mechanism and actual working the light may be sought from the monarchical model in the Arthashastra. One may also utilise the information, however scanty, from the Classical sources fathered on Megasthenes, particularly that from Strabo, the inscriptions of Ashoka and the collective Indian literary evidence remaining as our main guide.

Sources of and Charges on Imperial Revenue: The important point needing clarification here is the source of income for the imperial exchequer, or, in other words, the financial obligation of the provincial governments to the parent or central body. The real cause of confusion arises from Ashoka's two positions, *viz.*, as the King and administrative head of Magadha and as the Emperor and paramount sovereign of Jambudvipa.

The general economic principle to be followed by a state in India was the same as that prescribed for the Aryan household. As enunciated by the Buddha, in consonance, no doubt, with the accepted view of social economy, it consisted in collecting abundant wealth for strengthening the bond of friendship, just as the bees gather honey or the white ants build up their hill, and dividing it thereafter into four portions, one for household management, two for investment and public works, and the remaining one for reservation against future contingencies. This very domestic principle was at the back of the Arthashastra prescription laying down that one fourth of the total revenue should be spent for the payment of the staff, permanent or temporary, principal or subordinate, including occasional rewards and bonus. This may enable us to say that after making due provision for these four needs in the provincial budget as approved by the imperial government, the surplus was to go to the imperial exchequer as contribution of each provincial government.

The highest office In a monarchical state was held by the King, just as in an imperial state it was held by the Emperor. The Crown Prince (Yuvaraja) stood next to none but the King or the Emperor. Other high offices either in the royal household or in the King's civil and military services were held by Senani (Commander-in-Chief), the Purohita (Royal Chaplain), the Mahishi (Chief Queen), the Suta (Charioteer), the Gramani (Chief Citizen), the Kshatrti (Chamberlain), the Samgrahitri (Treasurer), the Bhagadugha (Collector of the Royal Share), the Akshavapa (the Dice keeper), the Govikartana (the Chase Companion), and the Palagala (Courier). As RayChaudhary rightly suggests, the Kshatri of the Satapatha Brahmana was the precursor of the Antarvamsika of the Arthashastra, the Samgrahitri of the Sannidhatri, the Bhagadugha of the Samahartri, and the Palagala of the Duta.

The list of the high office-holders was somewhat differently made up in the Kurudhamma Jataka, as will appear from the following enumeration: (i) Raja (King), (ii) Mata (Queen Dowager) (iii) Mahesi (Chief Queen), (iv) Uparaja (Crown Prince), (v) Purohita (Royal Chaplain), (vi) Rajjuka (Rein-holder), (vii) Sarathi (Charioteer), (viii) Setthi (Chief Citizen), (ix) Dona (Measurer), (x) Dovarika (Doorkeeper), and (xi) Ganika (Courtezan).

According to the Commentary version of the birth-story, the King's younger brother was entitled to the office of the Crown Prince, the Purohita was the leading Brahmin in the King's service, the Rajjuka was the Land-surveyor (Rajjuggaho amachcho), the Sarathi, the Royal Charioteer, the Setthi, the Regulator of Equitable Transactions, the Dona, the Mahamatra or the Measurer of things, the Dovarika, the Doorkeeper, and the Ganika, the Courtezan.

In the Arthashastra, the Crown Prince is called Yuvaraja instead of Uparaja, and there is no suggestion as to the office going ordinarily to the King's younger brother. It separates the office of the Purohita from those of the Ritvij (Sacrificial Priest) and the Acharya (Royal Teacher). The Rajjuka would seem to be the forerunner of the Samahartri (Collector General) of the Arthashastra just as the Dona that of the Sannidhatri. The Sarathi was no mere Chariot driver but allegorically either, perhaps, the Mantrin (Prime Minister) or the Gananikyadhyaksha (Accountant General) of the Arthashastra. The Setthi probably stood for the Paura vyavaharika. Similarly the Dovarika was no mere the Doorkeeper but the Commander-in-Chief (Senapati), the Chief Constable (Nayaka), and the like. The Ganika may be taken to represent not only the leading dancing girl or songstress but also all professional artists employed to entertain the King. But the whole thing is so vague and veiled in poetic allegory that it is impossible to make all the points clear. Even the Arthashastra cannot be exonerated from this charge in spite of its methodical treatment of the subject.

We can say, however, that the personal and household expenses of the King Emperor was a regular charge on the imperial revenue. Presumably these were included in the one-fourth share of the total revenue of the official year which usually commenced in the month of Ashadha (June-July). Other stipendiaries in the royal or imperial household were, according to the Arthashastra, the Queen Dowager, the Chief Queen, the new born Prince (kumara) and his nurse. The Sacrificial Priest, the Teacher, the Chief Minister (Mantrin), the Chaplain (Purohita) and the Commander-in-Chief (Senapati) were entitled each to the emolument granted to the Queen Dowager, the Chief Queen or the Crown Prince, while the allowance to a young Prince or his nurse equalled the subsistence allowed in the case of such high officers as the Nayaka (Chief Constable), the Paura Vyavaharika (City Judiciary), the Karmantika (Superintendent of Factories), the members of the Council of Ministers (Mantriparishad), the Dandapala (Commissary General), the Durgapala (Fort-keeper), the Antapala (Warden of the Marches), and the Atavipala (Warden of the Wild Tracts).

In between them and those of the first grade (the Queen Dowager, the Chief Queen, etc.) are to be placed the Dauvarika (Doorkeeper), the Antarvamsika (Superintendent of the Seraglio), the Prasastri (Administrator General of Law), the Samahartri (Collector General of Revenue), and the Sannidhatri (the High Treasurer).

The Queen Dowager is altogether out of the picture in Ashoka's inscriptions. His Queens (Devi) and sons (dalaka) who were typical of the Princes of the Blood (Devikumala) not only find respectful mention in P.E. VII but are said to have been persons in the imperial household who, like the Emperor himself, had their private funds to make charities on their own account. In the earlier edict, R.E. V, the households of his brothers, sisters, and other kinsmen are mentioned as rich enough to be capable of charities, while in the later edict, P.E. VII, his brothers and others are replaced by other Princes of the blood royal in a similar connection. The Queen's Edict expressly speaks of the various donations made by his favourite second Queen, Kaluvaki. In P.E. IV, Ashoka speaks by the way of a child being entrusted to the care of a clever nurse. The Buddhist legends tell us that Prince Tishya-Vitashoka, the only uterine brother of Ashoka, was appointed as the Crown Prince, and that the office went a begging since he renounced the world. If by Aryaputra in M.R.E. (Bra) were meant one of the brothers of Ashoka, not to say, the only surviving brother, his position was not different from that of his sons, the Kumaras appointed to the office of Viceroys in three other outlying provinces, and as such, their case may better be considered in connection with provincial administration.

I should think that not only the Chief Queen but also other Queens (not probably exceeding three at the same time), not only the younger brother appointed to the office of a crown Prince but also other brothers besides sisters, not only the King Emperor's own sons but also nephews and nearest agnates were entitled to stipends in coin or kind. The cost of bringing up the Princes and princesses may also have been a charge on the state revenue.

Ashoka's household expenses consisted also in the maintenance of his family establishments, not to say, harems at Pataliputra and a few moffusil towns, in keeping the kitchen (mahanasa) going to daily feed sumptuously all the inmates of the palace and a thousand others from outside, in the maintenance of the royal pleasances (uyana) and the upkeep of the equipages, for which provision had to be made in the budget even in accordance with the prescription in the Arthashastra.

Ashoka tells us that many hundred thousands of lives were being daily killed in the royal kitchen for purposes of curry, and Professor Bhandarkar relevantly cites the ancient instance of King Rantideva from the Great Epic, ii. 207. 8-10, of whom it is said that his Queen caused to be daily killed in the royal kitchen two thousand cattle and that he acquired an unrivalled fame for having offered food with meat by daily killing two thousand cows, and that invariably during the period of chaturmasya.

According to Pali tradition, as we noted, Binduṣara as a votary of the Brahmins (Brahmana-bhatto) daily fed them including the Brahmanical ascetics and recluses other than Buddhists, and Ashoka was doing the same in the earlier part of his reign. From this, it may be inferred that the Ritvig (Brahmin sacrificial priest) and his assistants (purushah) were in the service of Ashoka's imperial household, precisely as in that of his father and grandfather. Even since and after the promulgation of R.E. I one deer and two peafowls continued to be daily killed in his kitchen presumably for meat offerings to the family deity or idol (rajadevata). Thus the office of the Ritvig must have continued along with those of the Brahmin teacher and the Purohita with their assistants.

The Physician (Chikitsaka) figured among the courtiers of an Indian King. Jivaka, for instance, was the court physician of Bimbisara and Ajatashatru. Under him were employed certain medical experts including the veterinary surgeons, all with their assistants. Subsistences to them must also have created a charge on the imperial revenue. The employment of them may be inferred from the arrangements made by Ashoka for two kinds of medical treatment, one suitable for men and the other for animals.

In connection with Ashoka's kitchen (mahanaṣa), eating (bhojana), life in the inner apartments of the palace (orodha), bedchamber (gabhagara), drives (vinita), pleasances (uyana), and the like, his personal and household staffs creating charges on the imperial revenue may be said to have consisted of the officer in charge of the kitchen (Mahanasika), the soup-maker (suda) and the cook (aralika) with their assistants, the bath-attendant (snapaka), the shampooer (samvahaka), the barber (kalpaka), the toilet-maker (prasadaka), the water-supplier (udaka-paricharaka), the troops of women (strigana), the presenter of the coat (kanchuki), the presenter of the headdress (ushnishi), in short, the keeper of the wardrobe, the kubjas (humpbacked persons), dwarfs and pigmies, the artists such as actors, dancers, singers, players on musical instruments, buffoons, jestors, bards and the like.

It was in connection with the Queens and court-ladies, the maids of honour and the maidservants that there were appointed the Stryadhyaksha Mahamatras.

The Divyavadana speaks of the Bhandagarika (i.e., Sannidhatri) of Ashoka, placed in charge of the imperial treasury and storehouse (kosha-koshthagara), who was restrained by the Emperor's grandson Samprati, then in the office of the Crown

Prince, from lavishly supplying Ashoka's demands. This wise step against the depletion of the imperial treasury and store house was taken on the advice of the Ministers. The same authority introduces us also to Ashoka's Prime Minister Radhagupta whom Jayaswal was inclined to regard as the descendant and successor of Kautilya Vishnugupta without, however, any reliable evidence. The same alludes also to other imperial Ministers.

The Arthashastra, on the other hand, distinguishes between the functions and offices of the Samahartri (Collector General of Revenue) the Sannidhatri (High Treasurer) and the Gananikyadhyaksha (Accountant General), which is more to the point. Whatever were their actual designations, these three high officials must have been in the service of Ashoka.

Correspondence between the Amatyas of the Arthashastra and the Purushas of Ashoka: Apart from and below the Mantri or constant personal adviser to the King mainly in matters temporal or secular, the Chaplain or constant personal adviser mainly in matters religious or sacerdotal, and the Crown Prince holding the office of the deputy King, the Arthashastra speaks of the most important functionaries of the state. These functionaries, termed Sachivas, are broadly distinguished as Mati-sachivas and Karma-sachivas in the Junagarh inscription of Rudradaman I, both being endowed with ministerial qualities. The Mati-sachivas, otherwise called Dhi-sachivas, were those Amatyas who possessed the necessary qualifications to serve as Mantrins or Ministers to the King, either jointly or individually, and the Karma-sachivas those who had the competence to serve as different ministerial officers, civil or military. This very functional distinction is sought to be made in the Arthashastra between the Mantrins and the general body of the Amatyas. It was evidently referring to the Amatyas that Megasthenes and with him other Classical writers spoke of the seventh caste or class of the Indian people as consisting of 'the councillors of state' in the language of Arrian, and of 'the councillors and assessors of the king' in that of Diodorus and Strabo. Arrian describes them as those 'who advise the King, or the magistrates of self-governed cities, in the management of public affairs.' In point of numbers, they were a small class, but they were distinguished by superior wisdom and justice, whence they enjoyed 'the prerogative of choosing governors, chiefs of provinces, deputy governors, superintendents of the treasury, generals of the army, admirals of the navy, controllers, and commissioners who superintend agriculture.'

To Diodorus the Councillors and Assessors were those who deliberated on public affairs. Though numerically they were a small minority, they were the most respected, on account of their high character and wisdom, for from their ranks the advisers of the King were taken, and the treasurer of the state, and the arbiters who settled disputes. The generals of the army also and the chief magistrates usually belonged to them.

These are but a faithful echo in foreign writings of what is stated in the Arthashastra regarding qualifications of the Amatyas in general (amatya-sampat) and the appointment of the high state-functionaries out of them: "Native, born of high family, influential, well-trained in arts, possessed of foresight, wise, of strong memory, bold, eloquent, skilful, intelligent, possessed of enthusiasm, dignity and endurance, pure in character, affable, firm in loyal devotion (dridha-bhakti), endowed with excellent conduct, Strength, health and bravery, free from procrastination and ficklemindedness, affectionate, and free from such qualities as excite hatred and enmity." According as they possess all, or one-half, or one-quarter of the qualifications, they are to be broadly classified into three ranks: high, middle and low.

Assisted by his Mantri (Prime Minister) and his Chaplain, the King was to offer temptations to test the character and fitness of the Amatyas appointed at first to minor offices in government departments. Of those tried Amatyas, those tested under religious allurements were to be employed afterwards for the duties of the Judges (Dharmasthas) and Magistrates (Kantakasodhaneshu); those tested under monetary allurements, for those of the Revenue Collectors (Samahartris) and Treasurers (Sannidhatris); those under love allurements, for those of the superintendents of pleasure grounds (vihara), internal and external; those by allurements under threat, for immediate service (asanna-karyesu); those by all allurements, for the duties of the various Ministers (Mantrinah), while those found deficient under one or all of these allurements were to be employed in mines, manufactories, and timber and elephant forests.

The Amarakosha applies the designation of Mahamatra or Pradhana to the chief ministerial officers (Karma-sachivas). According to Buddhaghosa, too, the Mahamatras were just the leading Amatyas (Mahamatra ti Mahamachcha). The Mahamatra figures in the Great Epic as a warrior seated on the back of an elephant, i.e., as a Hastipakadhipa in the terminology of Dharani. As Mukherji observes, "the Mahamatra figures (in the Arthashastra as a minister, and as the chief executive officer of a city under the title Nagarikamahamatra, while his power and influence will be evident from the fact that the seditious Mahamatra is a cause of much concern to the King."

Here Mukherji is evidently guided by Shama Shastri's translation. But from the text of the Arthashastra, it is not clear that by the designation is anywhere meant a Mantrin. "Just as in the Arthashastra, so in the Vinaya Pitaka and the Amarakosha, the Mahamatras are distinguished from the Judges (Dharmasthas, Akshadarsas). According to the Arthashastra, the Dharmasthas and the Mahamatras had their offices in buildings called Dharmasthiya and Mahamatriya respectively". Buddhaghosa defines the Mahamatras as great Amatyas holding different posts, placed in different charges (thanantarappatta), and understands by the designation Magadhama-hamatta either the great functionary vested with a large measure of royal power (mahatiya issariya-mattaya samannagato) in Magadha or the highest officer of the Magadha king'. "In point of fact, Magadhamahamatra is the epithet applied in Pali to Varshakara who was a Brahmin chief minister of King Ajatashatru of Magadha".

The Arthashastra designation of Amatya is nowhere employed in Ashoka's inscriptions. Ashoka speaks instead of the Purushas in P.E. I and divides them broadly into three ranks, viz., the superior (ukasa), the intermediate (majhima) and the inferior (gevaya), precisely in the manner in which the Amatyas are classified in the Arthashastra. Thus the correspondence being established between the Purushas of P.E. I and the Amatyas of the Arthashastra, one must discard Hultzsch's identification of Ashoka's Purushas with the Gudhapurushas in the Arthashastra representing as they do the secret agents or spies, and welcome RayChaudhary's identification with the Rajapurushas or Royal Agents or officers in general.

The ministerial qualifications demanded by Ashoka of the officers deserving to be appointed to higher offices and entrusted with responsible duties are substantially those stated in detail in the Arthashastra and briefly in Classical writings. The Ashokan way of stating them agrees rather with those in the Great Epic and the Pali Nikayas and Jatakas. The strength of character is to be judged by the power of self-control, the purity of sentiment, the feeling of gratitude and the firmness of devotion. The baneful mental distempers to be avoided consist in wrath, conceit, malignity, irascibility, fierceness, cruelty and oppressiveness. Dealings with men to be effective must be enlivened by one's genial temperament avoiding rudeness and fierceness and expressing winsome cordiality. Little sin, much of good deeds, compassion, liberality, truthfulness, moral purity, gentleness and nobleness are the qualities that go to ennoble human character. Moral and physical energy, ardour and enthusiasm, are to be applied to general good avoiding lethargy, inertia and weariness for exertion. The very best kind of longing for piety, self-examination, attentiveness, fear of public opinion and enthusiasm are needed for success in work. The instructions received are to be grasped in their letter and spirit and to be properly and fully carried out.

The noble feeling to be cherished in rendering service is to think that one is just discharging his debt.

System of Governance

We have given an account of the principal events and measures in Ashoka's life and reign. We shall now describe his work as an administrator, religious reformer, and builder. The government of India under Ashoka was an absolute monarchy in the legal and political sense of the term. Nevertheless, autocracy in India was much more limited in many directions than the autocracies of the West. "The Indian King is no Sultan with the sole obligation of satisfying his personal caprice. The origin of royalty is the growth of wickedness and the necessity of chastisement, the virtue of which the Indian writers celebrate with a real enthusiasm. It is as guardian of the social (including domestic and religious) order and defence against anarchial oppression that the King is entitled to his revenue; failing to perform this duty, he takes upon himself a corresponding share of the national sin. Educated in these precepts among a moralising people, he would have been more than human had he escaped the obsession of this conception of his duties. Hence we not seldom hear on royal, as well as on priestly, lips the expression that the King should be the father of his people".

But apart from this living sense of his moral responsibility to his people, there was an important limitation upon his autocracy from the fact that he was not the source of Law, but rather its support Sacred law, according to Manu and other legal authorities, is derived from four sources, viz., (i) the Vedas, (ii) the Smritis, (iii) the practices of the pious *(sistachara)*, and (iv) the opinions of the pious on doubtful points, while the sources of secular law were the manifold groups and communities which legislated for themselves, so that "Whatever may have been practised by the virtuous, and by such twice-born men as are devoted to the law, that only he shall establish as law if it be not opposed to the laws of castes, communities *(janapada)*, guilds and families. It is the quasi-instinctive postulates and conventions of group-life which come to be formulated as *law*, and not the mandate, command, or decree, of a single, central authority in the state.

Law, under these conditions, is not an *arte-fact*, but a natural growth of consensus and communal life. The fact of the matter was that the defects of personal rule were very largely remedied by the King's own submission to the laws which he had no hand in making or annulling, so that the impersonal rules were the real rulers in the country. In Ashoka's case, the sovereign was theoretically only an autocrat, for he proceeded much farther than the law-books to prescribe limitations upon his own authority by adding to his own duties and responsibilities, and emphasising the supremacy of moral laws even in the secular spheres of life. A great emphasis is laid upon the paternal principle of government in his Edicts: "All men are my children; and, just as I desire for my children that they may enjoy every kind of prosperity and happiness both in this world and in the next, so also do I desire the same for all men". He wants the newly-subdued Kalingas "to grasp the truth that 'the King is to us as a father; he loves us even as he loves himself; we are to the King even as his children'". But this abiding sense of parental responsibility for his people was not confined to the King alone. It belonged to his agents, too, to whom he committed the care of his people "as a man would make over his child to a skilful nurse and, feeling confident, says to himself: 'The skilful nurse is eager to care for the happiness of my child'; even so my Governors have been created for the welfare and happiness of the country"

A King with these ideas of his position and responsibility is practically more representative of his people than the so-called representative assembly or legislature in a regular democracy. Here "the Head of the State represents the people directly and primarily in his person, whether, as in the case of the Mikado or of a Hindu Sovereign, as the symbol of the Shinto, the Dharma or the Law, in hereditary succession and transmission,—or, as in the case of the President of the United States, as the elected representative of the people's sovereignty, standing in an even more direct and vital relationship to the people than the members of the Representative Assemblies and Legislatures." His relationship to the people is more natural and primary, more direct and intimate, than the legal, factitious, and consensual relationship of the electorate and the elected in modern democracies. Indeed, the Head of the State and his people are but integral parts of one corporate and constitutional unity. A democracy only seeks to embody the unitary, undivided sovereignty in a body politic and its various limbs and organs, the various political assemblies and organisations, but in practice it has realised its ideals only partially, in different degrees, in even the most democratically advanced countries of the west.

The defects of democracy show that the problem of government cannot be solved by representative or electoral methods alone, but by the processes of organic growth which it can stimulate by encouraging all vital modes of association prevailing among the people concerned. Thus, "one of the characteristics of the present-day political theory is its reaction against the state, and a salient political *fact* today is the increasing amount and power of group-life—trade unions, professional societies, citizens' leagues, neighbourhood associations, etc.". Ancient Hindu monarchy did not aim at centralisation or over-government, but gave full scope to the varieties of group-life to which the people have been used from time immemorial, even prior to the emergence of a centralised government among them. Thus it was an autocracy limited from below by a vast subterranean democracy, so to speak, a complete system of local self-government embodied in various types of institutions.

Ashoka did not spare himself in trying to realise his high conception of imperial duties and responsibilities. He was an ideal public servant, the most hard working of all his officials. He gave himself to public business at all hours and places. Says he in Rock Edict VI: "A long period has elapsed during which in the past administrative business or information was not attended to at all hours. So by me the arrangement has been made that at all times, when I am eating, or in the harem, or in the bedroom, or in my ranches, or even in the place of religious instruction, or in my pleasure-grounds, everywhere the reporting officials should make known to me the people's affairs.

In all places I shall attend to public business." He says further: "I never feel satisfaction in my exertions and dispatch of business. For work I must for the welfare of all the folk; and of that, again, the root is energy and the dispatch of business; for nothing is more essential than the welfare of all the folk." Hardly has a King emphasised more his obligations to his own subjects! The Brahminical sacred texts insist on three debts which every man is born to and which he must discharge, the debts to his religion *(devarina), to* the Risis (i.e., to learning) and to his ancestors (whose race is to be perpetuated), but Ashoka says that a King has a fourth debt to pay: "And whatsoever efforts I make, they are made that I may obtain release from my debt to my fellow-human beings". The sovereign of a large Empire, Ashoka also recognised his duty of touring the country—touring not for sport or pleasure as his predecessors did, but for "the inspection of the country and the people" *(jana-padasya janasya darsanam)*. But his Empire was so extensive that he could not visit all its parts, as is apparent from a passage in the Rock Edict XIV, where he assumes that in some of his Edicts "something has been written incompletely by blunders of the writer," These blunders in his published Edicts are merely supposed by him, he could not have referred to them if he had actually examined them on the spot, for there are hardly any such glaring blunders in so many of his separately executed and located Edicts.

The Empire was divided for administrative purposes into a number of provinces, of which the more remote ones were placed under Viceroys. The Viceroyalties were generally reserved for the Princes called Kumaras or Aryaputras in the Edicts. The Edicts refer to four princely Viceroys, viz., those governing the provinces with headquarters at Taxila, Ujjain, Tosali and Suvarnagiri [Kalinga Edict I; Kalinga Edict II, Dhauli version; Minor Rock Edict I, Brahmagiri version]. Gandhara is mentioned by Fa-hien as another viceroyalty under Prince Dharmavivardhana. Since Dharmavivardhana, according to *Divyavadana,* was another name for Kunala, who was sent out by Ashoka towards the end of his reign as his Viceroy to Taxila for subduing its hostility, we may take it that the province of Gandhara had its headquarters at Taxila. Sometimes, instead of the Princes, we find local chiefs appointed as Viceroys. Thus Pusyagupta, the Vaishya, was Chandragupta's Viceroy *(Rastriya)* of the western provinces with Girnar as headquarters, which, under Ashoka, came under another Viceroy named Raja Tusaspha, the Persian. The more centrally situated provinces were placed under Governors directly appointed from the capital by the King, and are perhaps marked out by the Pillar Inscriptions, while the Rock Inscriptions are to be found in the outlying regions of the Empire.

While the Edicts do not name any Viceroy, the legends name some. When Bindusara was Emperor, he appointed his two sons, Susima (or Sumana) and Ashoka, as his Viceroys at Taxila and Ujjaini respectively. When later, Taxila was in revolt which could not be suppressed by Susima, Ashoka was transferred there as more competent for the purpose. Prince Kunala, as we have already seen, is mentioned as Ashoka's Viceroy at Taxila. The Emperor on his consecration is also said to have appointed as his deputy or Viceregent *(Uparaja)* his younger brother, Tisya, who, on his retirement as a religious devotee, was succeeded by Prince Mahendra, though he remained in office only for a short time prior to his ordination. Probably the Viceregent *(Uparaja)* was something like the Prime Minister and different from *Yuvaaja,* heir-apparent. Bindusara, Ashoka's father, had, as his Prime Minister, *Agramatya,* Khallataka, who is said to have supported Ashoka in his contest for the throne. Tradition gives to Ashoka himself a trusted minister named Radhagupta, who also helped him in gaining the throne and in his administration, and was his *Agramatya* (the term used in the *Divyavadana).*

The Viceroys, too, had their own ministers. The northern books tell us how the people of Taxila during the reign of Bindusara revolted against the oppressive ministers, and not against the princely Viceroy. In the legend of Kunala, the Viceroy of Taxila, it was the ministers who received the spurious dispatch from headquarters, directing that he be blinded. The Kalinga Edict II shows how the Viceroys, like the King, were empowered to appoint their own officers of the status of Mahamatras for periodical inspection and supervision of judicial administration.

That Viceroys were associated with Mahamatras or Ministers is also shown by the Minor Rock Edict I, Brahmagiri text, and the Kalinga Edict I, Dhauli text. In the former the Prince *(Aryaputra),* acting with his Mahamatras, addresses the King's message to the Mahamatras of Isila; in the latter, the King addresses the Prince and the Mahamatras together. Again, the Jaugada text of the Kalinga Rock Edict II mentions a class of Mahamatras who are described as *Lajavachanikas,* i.e., those who were entitled to receive the King's messages directly, and not through the royal Viceroys. Thus these *Mahamatras* might be regarded as Provincial Governors, as they are given independent charge of their province. Samapa (Jaugada) or Isila was the seat of such a governorship, as Tosali was of a viceroyalty. In the same way, the Kaushambi Edict is addressed by the King directly to the Mahamatras of Kaushambi, which must have been, therefore, the headquarters of another province. Perhaps these Mahamatras were distinguished from the other classes of Mahamatras by the designation, *Pradesika Mahamatras.*

The ordinary Provincial Governors were called *Rajukas* who were "set over hundreds of thousands of souls". The office of the

Rajukas had been in existence before Ashoka, but Ashoka invested them with greater authority. They are granted independence in their administration of Law and Justice in order that they may perform their duties confidently and fearlessly, bestow welfare and happiness upon the people of the country, and confer favours upon them. They will also know of their joys and sorrows. As the child is committed confidently to a skilful nurse, the people are committed to the care of these Governors who are created for their welfare and happiness with intent that fearlessly, unselfishly, and cheerfully, they may discharge their duties.

Sometimes, however, these lofty ideals of duty set before the Governors were not realised. Cases of their neglect of duty or indifference to his injunctions called forth vigorous but dignified protests from the Emperor, like the following: "With certain natural dispositions success (in administration) is impossible, to wit, envy, lack of sustained efforts, harshness, haste, want of application, indolence, and lassitude. You must desire that such dispositions be not yours. At the root of the whole matter lie steadiness, and patience. He who is tired in administration will not rise up, but one must needs move, advance, go on. There will be special officers to remind you of your obligations to the King and of his instructions. Fulfilment of these bears great fruit, non-fulfilment brings great calamity. By those who fail, neither heaven nor royal favour can be won. By fulfilling my instructions you will gain heaven and also pay your debt to me". In these we probably hear the very words of Ashoka, still bringing home to us his impassioned exhortations across the centuries. Lest his words be forgotten by those for whom they are meant, the Emperor, besides having them indelibly engraved on the rocks, ordered that they be recited publicly "at the beginning of each season of four months, (i.e., each of the three seasons, hot, rainy and cold) on the Tisya day, (i.e., when the moon is in that constellation)", nay, even once a month on the Tisya day, and in the intervals between the Tisya days, and on fit occasions even to a single person.

Thus, Ashoka's government was from the very nature of the case partly imperial, i.e., directly under the Emperor, and partly local, i.e., under the Viceroys and Governors. The charge of a Viceroy was more extensive than that of a Governor, Details are wanting as regards the extent of the administration which the Emperor took upon himself as his own work. From the Edicts we may infer that the Emperor's first duty was to settle the fundamental principles on which he wanted his government to be based, the policy to be pursued by his administrators, and to issue his notifications for them from time to time as occasion arose. In Ashoka's case, the Imperial Edicts announcing his policy, principles, and the measures to be taken for their realisation remain permanently gazetted on "tables or pillars of stone." Thus the subject of legislation seems also in certain matters to have been imperialised. The laws of the realm passed by Ashoka on his own initiative have been already indicated from the Edicts.

Thirdly, the subject of the public works of utility seems also to have been an imperial concern from the account of the same already given. Fourthly, the Department of Dharma was also under the imperial government. The Ministers of Morals *(Dharma-Mahamatras)* do not appear to be provincial officers, as their work embraced the entire area of the Empire, and even areas outside of it. Fifthly, the Buddhist Church came to be one of the concerns of Ashoka who practically assumed its temporal leadership, as will appear from the several Edicts bearing on the subject [the Bhabru Edict, and the Pillar Edicts of Sarnath, Kaushambi and Sanchi]. These Edicts announce the imperial decree fixing the penalty for those who promote schism in the church and the means of its publication and enforcement Lastly, Ashoka made periodical touring through his Empire as one of his duties, as he insisted it upon all his local officers.

It is apparent that the Emperor could not depend upon himself alone for the satisfactory discharge of these manifold and heavy duties and responsibilities which he had fixed for himself. His general supervision of the work of government was exercised with the aid of a special set of officers—his private secretaries, who were to report to him on the affairs of the people at all hours and places, and were thus called *Pafivedakas*. Next, the Emperor was also assisted in his administrative work by his Privy Council or *Parishad*. The number of the Cabinet is not known. Kautilya makes it depend on the requirements of administration. According to tradition, Bindusara had a Privy Council of 500 members.

The inscriptions indicate how the King's administrative orders were issued. They are called *sasanam* and *anusasanam* or *anusistam*. They were written down *(likhita)* by the *Lipikara* in accordance with the King's words in documents called lipi. When the King's order was proclaimed, it was called *sravanam*. The preamble to the King's orders was of the form, "Thus saith the King" or "thus ordains the King". The first form, according to Kautilya, applies to *prajnapana-lekha*, and the second to *ajna-lekha* i.e., writs of information and command respectively.

As regards the Provincial Governments, some sort of a general scheme is indicated in the Edicts. The head of the administration, the highest local officer, was the *Rajuka*, while a smaller jurisdiction was placed under the *Pradesika*, the divisional commissioner. There were also the Heads of Departments, called *Mukhas*, and also known by the general title of Mahamatras, while the department assigned to them was indicated by its name being prefixed to that title. The Edicts tell us of the *Dharma-Mahamatras* in charge of the Department of Morals, the *Stri-adhyaksa-Mahamatras* in charge of the affairs of women, and the *Anta-Mahamatras* in charge of the frontiers. The Mahamatras in charge of cities were called *Mahamatra-nagarakas* or *Mahamatra-Nagaravyavaharakas* [the Kalinga Edicts]. Where the name Mahamatra is used by itself without any prefix, it denotes the Ministers. This sense is also borne out in a passage in Rock Edict VI, where the King is said to entrust matters of urgency to the Mahamatras for discussion by the Council of Ministers, *Parisat*, of which the Mahamatras are also members. Lastly, the Mahamatras were also deputed abroad to work as the King's *dutas* or ambassadors, not merely in the frontier states among the *Antas*, but also in foreign states, viz., those of the five Greek Kings, the Chodas and Pandyas, and the island of Ceylon.

Thus there was organised a regular Civil Service assisting the Viceroys and Provincial Chiefs. The Civil Servants were called by the general name of *Purusas* and are distinguished as being of high, low, or middle rank. In Pillar Edict IV, the *Purusas* are differentiated from the *Rajukas* as a separate body of officers who were acquainted with the wishes of the King, and whose duty was to exhort the Rajukas into loyal service of the King, while in Edict VII they are spoken of as being "set over the multitude" *(vahune janasi ayata)* contrasted with "the many hundred thousands of souls" under the charge of the Rajukas. Thus the Purusas might have been like the secret agents, the *gudha-pumsas* of Kautilya, or the inspectorate of the government. The Civil Servants of subordinate ranks are called *Yuktas*. The *Yuktas* were like the Secretaries whose duty was to codify royal orders in the office of the Mahamatras or Ministers under the instructions of the Parishad or Council to which they were attached. They had also to accompany their official superiors on tour. The scribe, lipikara, is also mentioned.

There seems to have prevailed the system of tours by government servants, high and low. In the case of the Viceroyalties of Ujjain and Taxila, the rules of service provided for such tours every three years for the Mahamatras, while the usual rule in other provinces was to have them every five years. The officers sent out on such tours included the Yuktas, the Rajukas, and the Pradesikas.

Frontier administration, too, was successfully tackled by the employment of methods suggested by its special circumstances and problems. In general, the paternal principle of government was specially emphasised in dealing with the subdued and "unsubdued borderers" alike, and also with the backward communities, the forest folks (the Kalinga Edicts). The frontiers were in charge of the *Anta-Mahamatras,* whose exact duties are not indicated in the Edicts. But they are mentioned by Kautilya, who calls them *Antapalas.* Their duty was to impose the transit dues *(variant)* on imported goods, and after examining their quality to stamp them with their seals and pass them on to the Superintendent of Tolls. They had also to make good losses to merchants by thefts committed within their jurisdiction.

Lastly, there must have been some officers to look after the public works of utility about which Ashoka was so keen, though but few of them are mentioned in his Edicts. The *Vraja* must have been the charge of the *Vrajabhumika,* who might also have within his purview the public parks, *udyana,* mango-groves, *amravatika,* wells, *kupa* or *udapana* and travellers' rest-houses, *nisadya,* along the public roads, *patha* or *marga.* There must have been horticulturists, too, to look after the botanical gardens for the growth of medicinal plants, and medical officers to arrange for the *chikitsa* or treatment of the diseases of both man and beast, *manusya-chikitsa* and *pasu-chikitsa*. The King's *naga-vana*, elephant forest, must have been under an officer like the *Hastyadhvaksa* of Kautilya, for elephants were "the speci... property of the King," as noted by Megasthenes.

As regards the policy of the Empire, it may be summed up in Ashoka's message: "The chiefest conquest is the conquest of Right and not of Might". First, war was abolished within the Empire by one stroke. The sovereignty of the smaller states and weaker peoples was respected as a matter of principle. To the many "unsubdued borderers" of the Empire went forth the healing message: "The King desires that they should not be afraid of him but should trust him, and would receive from him not sorrow but happiness". Nor was subjection forced on the ruder peoples on the plea of civilizing them: 'Even upon the forest folk in his dominions His Sacred Majesty looks kindly", So rang through the country the message, loud and clear, repeated on rock and pillar, the message of freedom, of peace on earth and goodwill among men. Silenced was the war-drum: the *bherighosa* was drowned in the *dharmaghosa*.

But we must note that Ashoka attached a condition to his gift of freedom. Freedom must go with morality. While anxious "to secure the confidence of the borderers," he was equally anxious "to set them moving on the path of piety". The forest folks are distinctly "bidden to turn from their evil ways that they be not chastised". Secondly, while military conquest was forsworn, the moral conquests of the good King grew apace. These were undertaken as parts of the daily work of administration. And they were spreading not merely among his own peoples, but also in the foreign countries on his borders and beyond. Thus his international relations were governed by principles that still remain to be recognised. The barriers that divide nations could not stand before his sense of universal brotherhood. Thus we find this good King, centuries ahead of his times, carrying on welfare work among the citizens of other states by the expenses borne by his own state.

Administration is the functional or working feature of the Constitution of a State. It implies both the act of management and the agent. Management means the systematic performance of various activities of the State channelled into different departments and under different authorities, such as imperial, provincial, divisional, district, urban and rural. The agent comprises the administrative and departmental heads and the officers under them besides some semi-official personages and leading citizens. The quality and success of an administration depends not only upon the efficiency of the ruling authority but also upon the loyalty and cooperation of the ruled. In the light of these observations, we may proceed to adjudicate on and estimate the importance of the Ashokan system of administration.

The Cabinet

Mantri-mahamatras and Mantri Parishad: The Arthashastra draws a distinction between the Mantrin, the Mantrins and the Mantriparishad. The Mantrin is placed in the same rank with the Chaplain, the Crown Prince, the Chief Queen and others entitled to the highest amount of subsistence. It is with the assistance of the Mantrin and the Chaplain that the King is advised to test capacity and fitness of the Amatyas or officers in general for the higher offices including that of the Mantrins whose salary is not mentioned. But the members of the Mantriparishad rank each with those entitled to one-fourth of the subsistence payable to the Mantrin par excellence. The King is advised to call both his Mantrins and the Mantriparishad when there is any 'work of emergency' to be done, to tell them of the same, and to follow the course of action suggested by the majority. It appears from the Arthashastra that the Ministers passed as Mantrins when they were consulted with individually and not all together, and that they formed the Mantriparishad when they met together to deliberate upon the affairs of administration. If the Mantrins alone were empowered to meet for such deliberations, the Parishad was just a meeting of the Cabinet. If the Mantrins as political advisers and the Karma-sachivas as high ministerial officers were summoned by the King to meet together for joint deliberations and advice in matters of urgency, the Parishad functioned as a Privy Council' having strict secrecy for its motto. With Mukherji one must treat the Mantriparishad, as described in the Arthashastra, as a Privy Council rather than as a Cabinet. The school of Manu restricted the seats in the Mantriparishad to twelve members, that of Brihaspati to sixteen, and that of Usanas to twenty, while the Arthashastra makes the number depend on the needs of administration.

Neither the inscriptions of Ashoka nor the Classical writings, throw any light on the nicer distinction between the Mantrin par excellence and other Mantrins. But Ashoka certainly speaks of the Parisa or Mantriparishad in which his verbal orders and the urgent works entrusted to the Mahamatras were discussed. In his case, the members of the Parishad are left to themselves in the matter of deliberations, and the King shows much concern to know immediately the course and final result of their deliberations from the Reporters (Prativedakas) who watched the proceedings on the King's behalf. The records of Ashoka are, however, silent as to who the members of the Parishad were. Presumably the Mahamatras to whom urgent works were entrusted were privileged to be present and to take part in the deliberations of the Parishad, at least to state and explain the matters. If so, these Mahamatras might be identified with the high functionaries called Mantri mahamatras in the Kosala-Samyutta, III. 5, This class of Mahamatras served as ministers as well as high ministerial officers. That such was the earlier office of the Mantri-mahamatras is evident also from the fact that King Ajatashatru of Magadha entrusted the responsible duty of fortifying the village of Pataligama to his two great ministers known as Magadhamahamatra.

Other Classes of Mahamatras: There were other classes of Mahamatras. In Pali literature, for instance, the Sabbatthaka-mahamatra or Mahamatra in charge of general affairs (i. e., the Chief Minister), the Voharika-mahamatra or Mahamatra as administrator of justice, the Senanayaka-mahamatra or Mahamatra as head of the army, the Ganaka-mahamatra or Mahamatra as accountant; the Antepura-upacharaka mahamatra or Mahamatras in charge of the inner apartments of the royal palace, and the Vinicchaya-mahamatra or Mahamatra as judicial investigator of the cause of action, ranked below the Voharika. It may be shown that the Sabbatthaka-mahamatra stood for general administration and the Voharika for the judicial, while the Senanayaka-mahamatra stood for military administration.

Ashoka defines the duties of the Dharma-mahamatras and differentiates them as a class of high officials from other Mahamatras, the sectarian Mahamatras who were attached specifically to this or that religious sect. Raychaudhary aptly calls attention to the fact that at least in one case Ashoka applies the designation of Mahamatra to a class of Adhyakshas, namely, the Stryadhyakshas.

The sectarian Mahamatras themselves were responsible officers of the State. The Pali Samannaphala Sutra bears a clear testimony to the fact that among the councillors of a King some were admirers of one teacher and some of another. The same may be inferred from the King's direction appended to the Schism pillar Edict (Sarnath) requiring a Mahamatra to go by turn to attend the Buddhist fast-day service invariably on the eighth day of a lunar half month. By implication there were Mahamatras who went to attend the fast-day service of other religions in which they were believers introduces us to the Vrachabhumikas and other classes of officers along with the Dharma and Stryadhyaksha Mahamatras.

In connection with city-administration we are introduced to the Nagara-vyavaharika or Nagaraka Mahamatras corresponding apparently with the Paura-vyavaharika or Nagarika of the Arthashastra.

As regards the home provinces, the Mahamatras were evidently placed in charge of the administration of such places as Banaras, Kaushambi and Vidisha. As for the outlying provinces or frontier districts, P.E.I mentions the Anta mahamatras corresponding to the Antapalas of the Arthashastra and the Pachchantavasino mahamatra of Buddhaghosa.

It is easy *to infer that the* Mahamatras *of Tosali, too,* previously enjoyed the status of Rajavachanikas. The same remark holds true of the Mahamatras of Suvamnagirl, Ujjain and Takshashila who became attached afterwards as Mantri-mahamatras to the Viceroys concerned, while the official position of the Mahamatras of Isila was obviously on a par with that of the Rajavachanikas of Samapa. It seems very likely that the Mahamatras who were to be sent forth every five years by Ashoka on tours of official inspection and those to be sent forth every third year by the Viceroys concerned were all to be regarded as Rajavachanikas or Imperial Commissioners.

Imperial Secretariat

This was the collective official agency, through which the imperial authority of Ashoka was exercised and the communication between the imperial and provincial governments was possible. It is not unlikely that the Arthashastra term Mahamatriya stood for the royal or imperial secretariat.

The imperial authority of Ashoka was issued in the form of sasanas or orders. The Arthashastra applies the term sasana exclusively to the royal writs embodying and conveying the sovereign's command. The sasanas of Ashoka are met with in one of the following forms: (i) that of penal ordinances; (ii) that of proclamations of piety; (iii) that of regulations of piety; (iv) that of instructions in piety; (v) that of official instructions and directions; (vi) that of warning to the turbulent factors within the Empire, such as the Atavis; (vii) that of the messages of good will to the 'frontagers'. The written form of a sasana is called lipi or document; When a sasana was permanently incised on a rock or stone-pillar, it is said to have been caused to be written in the sense of 'engraved' or incised'. The Lipikara was the scribe-engraver employed to incise a sasana either on a rock or monolith. There must have been the Lipikaras also in the imperial secretariat to incise the sasanas on portable materials for despatch to different destinations. Whether at this or the other end, the Lipikara of Ashoka did not fulfil the requirements of the Lekhaka of the Arthashastra. He was just a mechanical engraver of letters, while the latter was expected to be 'possessed of ministerial qualifications, acquainted with all kinds of customs, smart in composition, good in legible writing, and sharp in reading. Chapada the Lipikara employed at Isila to incise the three copies of M.R.E. was a person whose habitual script was Kharoshthi, and hence a dweller of Uttarapatha. Thus the Lipikaras or mechanical scribe-engravers and copyists must have executed their work under the guidance of some officers in the imperial secretariat responsible for the codification of imperial orders or preparation of drafts and at the other end for editing them to suit local needs.

It appears from R.E. III that the Yuktas were the officers in the imperial secretariat expected to codify the orders under instructions from the Purushas (Secretaries) or the Council of

Ministers. These Purushas are represented in P.E. IV as those official agents who were intimately acquainted with Ashoka's real wishes as to how things should be done, and who were therefore required to intimate to the Rajjukas precisely the way in which they were to carry out duties to the King's satisfaction. They were, according to Hultzsch, no other officers than the Gudhapurushas of the Arthashastra denoting as they did the Secret Agents or Spies who were to be appointed by a King with the assistance of the Council of Ministers. They were, in other words, the Overseers of Megasthenes and other Classical writers to whom was assigned, precisely as to the Gudha-purushas, 'the duty of watching all that goes on, and making reports secretly to the King, some being 'entrusted with the inspection of the city, and others that of the army, the ablest and most trustworthy men being 'appointed to fill these offices.' Such may have been the duty of Ashoka's Prativedakas and not necessarily that of the Purushas. The Purushas are broadly distinguished from the Rajjukas as those who were placed over many people, while the latter are said to have been 'placed over many hundred thousands of beings'. It does not necessarily mean that the Purushas were the imperial officers under the Rajjukas. It would rather seem that as regards the imperial secretariat, the Purushas as Ashoka's Secretaries had many Yuktas to work under them.

The services of the Dutas in the sense of Messengers or Conveyers of imperial orders must have been constantly in requisition to maintain the communication between the imperial and provincial governments. In the case of a proclamation of piety, some 256 copies of the imperial message were supplied to various administrative centres, which meant the employment of a messenger or missioner for the despatch of each copy thereof.

Main Functionaries

The functionaries required to go forth on tours of inspection every five years are broadly distinguished as Rajjukas and pradesikas. Their connection with the Yuttas is still open to dispute.

There were Purushas or personal Agents of Ashoka who served as intermediaries between him on the one hand and the Yuttas and the Rajjukas on the other. The Dapaka and the

Sravapaka might be counted among officers entitled to receive orders from the Emperor's mouth. Among the subordinate officers one must include the Lipikaras or Scribes who were not precisely the Lekhakas of the Arthashastra. The Dutas as imperial emissaries to foreign countries and courts must have a very special significance of their own.

Departments: There were Dharmamahamatras (the Mahamatras) and many other departmental heads (bahuka mukha), while the departments themselves were nowhere enumerated. It is certain that some of them were specifically imperial concerns, while the rest belonged to local administration.

It may be readily conceded to Mukherji that the Emperor's first duty consisted in formulating the fundamental principles upon which his government was to be based and run and the policy to be pursued by his administrators, issuing his notifications for them from time to time, and gazetting, on rocks or pillars of stone the Edicts announcing his policy, principles and the measures to be taken for their realisation.

It may also be taken for granted that the subject of legislation was in certain matters imperialised, or that the subject of the public works of utility was also an imperial concern. There is no gainsaying 'the fact that the Department of Dharma, too, was under the imperial government of Ashoka.' The weak point in Mukherji's otherwise weighty observations is that he seems to have mixed up Ashoka's personal concerns with those of his imperial administration.

As for the newly created 'Department of Dharma', the Edicts contain a good deal of information. 'The public works of utility' were undoubtedly an imperial concern, but whether or not there was a separate department created for the purpose, and if so, how was it officered and operated are questions to which no definite answer can be given. The legislating authority was composed of the Emperor and the Council of Ministers. The announcement of the imperial policy and the principles of government and the measures to be adopted, the engraving of the Edicts, the communication with the local administrators, etc. involve the question of the imperial secretariat.

General Administration

To appreciate the Ashokan system of provincial administration, we may assume that like each province or division, even each district was placed in charge of a body of Mahamatras. It is quite possible that in the case of the frontier provinces, divisions and districts, the Mahamatras concerned were known as Anta-mahamatras, and like the Antapalas of the Arthashastra and the Pratyanta-Mahamatras of the Atthasalini, they were required to guard the frontiers and competent to deal with the 'frontagers' including the semi-independent tribal states. The Mahamatras as administrative heads of the provinces or divisions passed as Rajavachanikas or Imperial Commissioners. Since the appointment and deputation of Viceroys as administrative heads of the four outlying provinces, the Imperial Commissioners at the provincial headquarters began to function as Mantri-mahamatras.

We are not to think with Mukherji and others that the remoter provinces were placed under the Viceroys from the beginning. The Pali Chronicles definitely state that Ashoka was appointed the Viceroy of Avanti some eleven years before the death of Bindusara, while the Divyavadana legends affirm that a Prince was deputed to the province of Uttarapatha only when an alarming report was received about the possibility of popular revolt against the government. The same fact is attested also by the inscriptions. The appointment of the Viceroys from among the sons of Ashoka and other Princes of the blood must be assigned to the latter part of Ashoka's reign. It was when P.E. VII was promulgated in the 27th regnal year of Ashoka that his sons and other Princes of the blood were grown up to make charities out of their own funds.

Bhandarkar puts the Viceroys of Ashoka in two categories: (i) those who wielded practically independent authority, and (ii) those who wielded joint and limited authority subject to the control of the King himself. He argues his case thus:

> "In the case of Ujjaini and Takshashila, the Kumaras seem to have been regular viceroys with their power unfettered, but it was not so in the case of Tosali. Thus from Separate Kalinga Edicts it appears that although the Kumaras of Ujjaini and Takshashila were to send

> on tour a Mahamatra of their own every three years to make sure that there was no maladministration of justice, in the case of the Tosali Province, this Mahamatra was to be deputed, not by the Tosali Kumara, but by Ashoka himself. Secondly, in connection with the dispatch of such an officer, the Kumaras of Ujjaini and Takshashila are mentioned by themselves and not associated with any state dignitaries, whereas in Separate Kalinga Edict II (Dh. version) where alone the Kumara of Tosali is referred to; he is mentioned not by himself but associated with the Mahamatras. Again, in regard to the latter Province we find that Ashoka issues admonitions or instructions to the Nagara-Vyavaharikas and others directly and not through the Kumara-Mahamatras."

This argument is apparently cogent and convincing. Its only weak point is that it proceeds on the questionable assumption that S.R.E.I was directly addressed to the City-judiciaries of Tosali and Samapa when the Viceroy-in-Council remained in charge of the province of Kalinga. The evidence of S.R.E. I goes rather to prove that, previous to the appointment of the Viceroy for Kalinga, the province was under the direct rule of Ashoka himself. It states the circumstances under which Ashoka thought it expedient to depute a Rajavachanika Mahamatra to the province for inspection and the prevention of the rule of tyranny and the miscarriage of justice. It must have been in the next stage that the province was placed in charge of a Viceroy-in-Council, while the administration of its southern division remained entrusted to the Rajavachanika Mahamatras.

The argument that 'in connection with the dispatch of such an officer, the Kumaras of Ujjaini and Takshashila are mentioned by themselves, and not associated with any state dignitaries' is not sufficient in itself to establish that they were practically independent rulers without the Mahamatras attached to them. That would be against the general principle of the Ashokan as well as the Maurya administration which was against reposing the full trust in a single person and always thought it safe and wise to provide mutual checks. In incidental references to provincial affairs, such as those in S.R.E. I, the mention of the Viceroys concerned was enough without their association with the Mahamatras. The argument would have been incontestable if it were based upon an independent document issued or forwarded on the sole authority of the Viceroy of Avanti or Uttarapatha.

It is not accordingly correct to say with Bhandarkar that the Aryaputra and Mahamatras stationed at Suvarnagiri communicated 'certain orders of Ashoka to a Mahamatra at Isila. The preamble of the Mysore copies of M.R.E. definitely speaks of the Mahamatras at Isila.

"Just as some provinces were ruled over by Kumaras, there must have been others which were governed by persons not related to the royal family.' This poignant remark of Bhandarkar stands. The questionable part is its sequel where he observes:

> "It is true that no instance of such a provincial governor is known from Ashoka's inscriptions, but one such instance has been supplied by the celebrated Junagadh inscription of Rudradaman. This epigraphic record tells us that the province of Surashtra or Kathiawar was governed by Vaishya Pushyagupta in Chandragupta's time and by the Yavana King Tushaspha when Ashoka was King."

Yuktas: Figuratively they were 'the horses at work', the horses yoked to the royal chariot. Buddhaghosa defines the Rajayuttas or Rajayuttas as 'royal officers carrying on the administrative duties in the districts'. Mukherji treats Yukta as a general term for 'government employees' and cites the authority of the Arthashastra where the Yuktas, the Upayuktas, and their subordinates (tatpurushah) are connected with all the department service.

Bhandarkar, on *the contrary,* observes: "Kautilya speaks of both the Yuktas and their assistants the Upayuktas. The verse quoted about the Yuktas by Dr. F. W. Thomas from the Manava-dharmasastra confirms the Idea. For Manu says that lost property when recovered, should remain in charge of the Yuktas."

If the Yuktas of R.E, III be treated as all government employees, they become identical with Purushas of P.E. I, and Amatyas of the Arthashastra. But E.E. III does certainly accord to them a prominent official position, a fact which has led Mukherji to think that they probably represented the officers of gazetted ranks, although below those of the Rajjukas and the Pradesikas. If we assume with Thomas and Bhandarkar that the Yuktas with their assistants principally figure in the Arthashastra as treasury-officers, the word 'treasury' must be taken in its much wider sense than that in which it is ordinarily understood; it must be taken to mean the state funds and storehouses in the custody of all departments, income-earning or not. In E.E. III, they are connected with ganana or ganana, a term, which Jayaswal took to be the Ashokan equivalent of Kautilya's gananikya or Accounts department. But it has been found that the Ashokan words ganana and ganiyati (Queen's Edict) may be interpreted in the sense of 'codifying', 'recording', counting', 'labelling' or the like. The Yuktas may accordingly be connected with the Secretariat, whether imperial or provincial, as well as the district Cutchery.

Rajjukas and Pradesikas: The difficulty about the relative positions of the Yuktas, on the one hand, and the Rajjukas and Pradesikas, on the other, arise from the fact that the statement concerning them varies in the available versions of E.E. III. According to the Girnar version, the Yuktas are connected by the copulative conjunction *cha* (and) with the Rajjukas and Pradesikas. With Mr. S. N. Mitra one may construe the Dhauli statement as meaning that the Rajjuka and the Pradesika were just two main divisions of the Yuktas. Except on the assumption that the Magadhi form has occurred by mistake in the Girnar statement, Mukherji cannot take the Yuktas, the Rajjukas and the Pradesikas to stand in an ascending order of official ranks. But the Rajjukas and Pradesikas might also be counted among the Yuktas. In the Arthashastra rajju and chora-rajju are mentioned as two sources of revenue, and these imply two classes of subordinate officers, namely, the Rajjukas and the Chorarajjukas, both under the Samahartri or Collector General of Revenue. The Arthashastra incidentally mentions one of the duties of the Chora-rajjuka, which is analogous to that assigned by Manu to the Yukta. Figuratively the Rajjukas were the rein-holders of the royal chariot of administration, i.e., the Samahartri of the Arthashastra, and the

Pradesikas were the watchers of enemies, or mischief-makers, i.e., the Pradeshtries of Kautilya. If so, the Yuktas as 'the horses at work' were to be controlled by the Rajjukas, and by implication, also by the Pradesikas.

In the later prose version of the Kurudhamma Jataka the Rajjuka is represented as a field-measurer or land-surveyor. This may naturally lead one to think that the rajju as a source of revenue was just the symbolical name for survey operations. But the Rajjukas as land-surveyors were officers under the Samahartri of the Arthashastra. The Rajjukas do not appear in this capacity In the edicts of Ashoka. On the other hand, they are represented as the officials with ruling authority exercised over 'many hundred thousands of the populace.' The same statement occurs in a more elaborate form in P.E. IV. In it, Ashoka tells us that he had delegated his full royal authority to the Rajjukas and made them supreme heads of local administration. They are likened to expert nurses to whose sole care was entrusted the welfare of all the children, i.e., of subjects. In matters of the administration of justice and the maintenance of equitable transactions of human affairs they are made free agents so that they might initiate all necessary measures and proceedings on their own authority and responsibility with self-confidence and without any fear of interference.

The Purushas intimately acquainted with Ashoka's desires as to how things should be done were the communicating agents between him and his Rajjukas. As regards criminal justice, they were the Supreme Judges in the sense that they were allowed to function as the final court of appeal, a position, which theretofore belonged to the Emperor himself. Hence we may regard them as Governors or Imperial Commissioners directly responsible to the sovereign. Hence there is no cause of astonishment that communications from the capital were directly addressed to them with instructions for necessary action, they were the same as the Rajavachanika Mahamatras mentioned in S.R.E. I and S.R.E. II, The effective control of the collection and utilisation of revenue under various heads and through different departments which the Arthashastra relegates to the Samahartri was the basic duty of the Rajjukas. It is interesting, therefore, to note that in the Dipavamsa Prince Priyadarsana as his father's Viceroy for Avanti is called karamoli, 'one charged to collect revenue.'

The Pradesikas find mention only in E.E. III. Their designation must be derived from the word pradesa, whatever its meaning. Taking it to mean a province, probably the Pradesikas were the officials in the outlying provinces corresponding to the Rajjukas in the home provinces. But the word may mean a smaller administrative area under any jurisdiction. On the ground that the word pradesa occurs in the Arthashastra in the sense of 'report', the Pradesikas might be regarded as Reporters, but whether or not, on this ground they might be identified with the Pradeshtris is still a disputed question. In the Amarakosha, the word pradesana is taken to mean 'presents (upahara) due to the King.' Going by this, a Pradesika might be regarded as an official who collected such presents, and this might be considered a connecting link between Ashoka's Pradesika and Kautilya's Pradeshtri. According to the Arthashastra, "in those places which are under the jurisdiction of the gopa and sthanika, the commissioners (pradeshtarah) specially deputed by the collector general shall not only inspect the work done and means employed by the village and district officers, but also collect the special religious tax known as ball."

Thus indeed the connection may be established between the two, the Pradesikas and the Pradeshtris, the latter standing 'as intermediaries between the Samahartri on the one hand and the Gopas, Sthanikas and Adhykshas on the other". The main functions of the Pradeshtris 'consisted in the collection of taxes, administration of criminal justice, tracking of thieves, and controlling of the work of the superintendents and their subordinates'. Accordingly the Pradesikas may be regarded as subordinate functionaries under the Rajjukas, and the Yuktas controlled by them as the Adhyakshas with the Upayuktas and the rest as their subordinates.

In connection with the quinquennial anusamyana or official tours of inspection to be undertaken by the Yuktas, the Rajjukas and the Pradesikas, R E. III mentions certain pleasant duties to be done by them in addition to their usual administrative functions. These duties consisted in imparting instructions in the principles of piety and carrying out the public works of utility. By these extra-administrative duties they were to utilise the two additional months at the end of each yuga or period of five calendar years of the age, as well as to render assistance in the provinces to the Dharmamahamatras in the matter of furtherance of the duties specially assigned to them.

In S.R.E. I, the Rajavachanika Mahamatras are required to undertake such tours every five years to prevent the miscarriage of justice and high-handed actions along with their usual administrative duties and that in accordance with the Emperor's instructions and under his command. Similar officials under the Viceroys of Uttarapatha and Avanti are required to do the same at least every third year. Pradesikas were the corresponding Rajavachanika Mahamatras in the provinces under the Viceroys, it may be conceded that the Rajjukas were the Rajavachanikas.

The usual administrative duties assigned to the Rajjukas in P.E. IV and in the prose version of the Kurudhamma Jataka cannot but remind us of the great officers of state (Agronomoi) who had the charge of the market. According to Strabo, they superintended the rivers, measured the land as was done in Egypt, and inspected the sluices by which water was let out from the main canals into their branches so as to ensure an equal supply of it to all. They had the charge of the huntsmen and were entrusted with the power of rewarding or punishing them according to their deserts. They collected the taxes and superintended the occupation connected with land, as those of woodcutters, the carpenters, the blacksmiths and the miners. They constructed roads and at every ten stadia set up a pillar to indicate the byroads and distances.

Raychaudhary aptly observes that as far as the measurement of the land goes, these magistrates may be connected with the Rajjukas as represented in the Kurudhamma Jataka, and that as regards the power of rewarding and punishing people, they have a point in common with the Rajjukas of Ashoka. If we look more closely into the matter, it cannot but appear that Strabo has simply sought to state the duties of various officers, the superintendents of various departments, as well as the Pradeshtris which are detailed in the Arthashastra. The activities mentioned are all referable ultimately to the office of Kautilya's Samahartri and *ex hypothesis,* to that of Ashoka's Rajjuka.

Thus indeed may be shown the executive side of all administrative affairs of a province for which either a Kumara Viceroy or a Rajjuka as a Governor or Imperial Commissioner was held responsible to the Emperor.

Department of Dharma

This came into existence with the first appointment of the Dharmamahamatras by Ashoka in his thirteenth regnal year. The scope of its activity may be determined by the various duties assigned to the Dharmamahamatras who functioned at one and the same time as Moral Sponsors, Imperial Almoners, protectors and promoters of religious interests throughout the Empire and outside, and may be also as religious advisers to the Emperor. The office of the Dharmamahamatras developed evidently out of that of the Dharmasthas or Jurists who functioned either as judges or as interpreters of the Sacred Law in a civil court of justice.

There is no evidence to warrant the surmise that the Dharmamahamatras interfered with the usual course of justice. "The question of treatment with mercy, sympathy or leniency of persons shut up behind the prison bars came indeed within their province. The only point of similarity between a Dharmastha and a Dharma-mahamatra is that the former, too, had the authority to treat with mercy a tirthakara (founder of a school of thought), an ascetic (tapasvin), a diseased person, one who is wearied due to hunger and thirst or invalid due to old age..., one who has come from another country, one who has already suffered much from punishment, and one who is penniless, but that again only in the capacity of a Judge. The Dharmamahamatras, on the contrary, figure prominently as royal almoners, dispensers of royal mercy, and, above all, as helpers of the cause of religion.

The Dharmamahamatras were appointed to discharge the following duties:

- In connection with all religious sects: (a) to establish the 'norm' effecting an increase in virtue and to work for the welfare and happiness of the virtuous amongst them, (b) to encourage the true spirit of tolerance enabling them to intelligently appreciate one another's faith and point of view and work together in harmony and concord for growth in the essence of the thing; and (c) to equitably distribute royal favour and do various other kinds of business as necessity arose.

- In connection with the royal family, including Ashoka's brothers, sisters and other kith and kin: (a) to distribute charity, (b) to found permanent institutions of piety; (c) to satisfy their hankering for knowledge of the truth and the law of duty; and (d) to persuade them to honour and hold all sects of religion.
- In connection with the inhabitants of Yavana, Kamboja, Gandhara, Rishtika, Petenika, and other western peoples, as well as the old and destitute, beggarly Brahmins and ascetics, and slaves and servants: (a) to work for their good and happiness and (b) to protect those who are devoted to religion against harassment and molestation; and
- In connection with the jail administration: (a) to provide one bound in chains with ransom, (b) to protect him against molestation, or (c) to grant him release in certain special and extraordinary circumstances."

In the matter of ensuring the growth of all sects in the essence of the thing (saravadhi), the Dharmamahamatras were variously assisted by the Stryadhyaksha Mahamatras, the Vrachabhamikas, and many other classes of officers. In the matter of welfare of the various sects including the Buddhists (Samghatas), they were variously assisted also by the Mahamatras attached specifically to this or that particular sect. In the matter of distribution of royal charities and of those of the Queens and the Princes of the blood, they were assisted by these Mahamatras and many other departmental heads. And in the matter of promulgation and propagation of the fundamental principles of piety, they were assisted within Ashoka's Empire by the Purushas and such touring officers as the Rajjukas and the Pradesikas, and outside by the Dutas or Emissaries.

Stryadhyaksha Mahamatras: They were undoubtedly the officers called Stryadhyakshas or Daradhyakshas in the Mahabharata. The Arthashastra speaks of the Antarvamsikas as well as the Ganikadhyakshas or Superintendents of Courtezans.

They were, according to the Vinaya Pitaka and Buddhaghosa's Commentary on the Ratthapala Sutra, the Mahamatras placed in charge of the family establishment of a King.

Mukherji Rightly Observes: "Regarding women, perhaps it was necessary to preach the dharma of toleration to them as a class. That there were Mahamatras attached to the royal harem is also indicated by Kautilya; because they had to deal with ladies, their special qualification emphasised is sexual purity, and they are to be placed in charge of the places of pleasure both in capital and outside. Again, in the Vinaya there is a reference to the appointment of religious preachers for the royal harem."

The Stryadhyakshas were, according to Raychaudhary, the 'Guards of the Wives' or 'Superintendents of Women of the King's household'. As the Great Epic attests, 'they were to see to the safety of the Queens and their female retinues whenever they were sent out under their care.' The Arthashastra insists on keeping away the Queens 'from the society of ascetics with shaved head or braided hair, of buffoons, and of outside prostitutes, and not allowing chances to 'women of high birth' other than appointed midwives, to see them'. Though the word ithi (itthi, stri) generally means a wife or married woman, it stands also for the womenfolk as distinguished from men.

If so, the duties of the Stryadhyakshas of Ashoka need not be confined to the Queens and other women of the royal or imperial household. In other words, it is conceivable that, as suggested by Hultzsch, they might as well function as the Ganikadhyakshas of the Arthashastra. It must have been their principal duty to guard the interests of women in general and of women in particular so as to keep them away from mischief.

The women in general included the courtezans, prostitutes, actresses, and the like. It must have been also their duty to guard them so as not to corrupt social morality, particularly the morality of the Brahminas and the Sramanas belonging to different religious orders. But it was no less their duty under Ashoka's regime to arrange for their sound moral and religious education, or to persuade them to honour and support all religious teachers irrespective of sect or creed.

Vrachabhumikas: The Vrachabhumikas whose business, like that of the Stryadhyakshas, it was to cooperate with the Dharmamahamatras, to ensure the growth of different religious sects in the essential matters are not expressly described as Mahamatras, though from the context of R. E. XII it might appear that they, too, formed a class of them. It is certain that their designation had something to do with vracha.

Various interpretations of vracha have so far been suggested on the strength of its equation with vraja. Accordingly the Vrachabhumikas may be taken to represent the officers, such as the elephant-riders, the chariot-trainers, and the like to whom was assigned the duty of proclaiming the imperial messages to the people at large.

Dutas: They were the imperial emissaries to the territories and courts of such independent 'frontagers' or 'borderers' as the five Greek potentates as the Cholas, the Pandyas, the Satiyaputras, the Keralaputras and the Tamraparnyas. The primary duty of the Dutas was the faithful delivery of the imperial messages. According to the Arthashastra, the duties of the envoys or emissaries consisted in 'transmission of messages, maintenance of treaties, issue of ultimatum (pratapa), gaining of friends, intrigue, sowing (seeds of) dissension among friends, fetching secret force, carrying away by stealth relatives and gems, gathering information about the movements of spies, bravery, breaking of treaties of peace, winning the favour of the envoy and government officers of the enemy". The King is advised to receive a foreign envoy in the presence of the Council of Ministers. The Dutas are distinguished into three classes according as they possess the lesser and lesser of ministerial qualifications to be employed as Plenipotentiaries (nisrishtarthah) or as *Charges d' affaires* (parimitarthah), or as mere conveyers of royal writs (sasanaharah). Ashoka's Dutas appear to have been at the most *Charges d' affaires* or 'agents entrusted with a definite mission', namely, that of good will. It was through them that Ashoka sought to achieve the conquest by piety in the territories outside his own. The Dutas might herald religious missions, though as emissaries they were all imperial officers. It is not inconceivable that some of the Dharmamahamatras were deputed as Dutas by Ashoka.

Judicial Administration

As for the administration of justice, a clear distinction is sought to be made in the Arthashastra between the cases to be tried by two kinds of tribunals: one for the trial of civil suits and certain quasi-criminal cases where fines only were to be imposed, and the other for the trial of criminal offences involving such severe punishments as arrest, imprisonment, mutilation of limbs, and death-sentence, and some quasi-civil cases. In the towns of the sangrahana, dronamukha and sthaniya types and the places where the districts met, the first kind of tribunals was to be constituted of three Dharmasthas (jurists capable of interpreting the Sacred Law) and three Amatyas (judges capable of administering the King's Law, i.e., the laws in force). The second kind of tribunals was to be constituted of either three Pradeshtris or three other Amatyas.

The Arthashastra does not, however, enlighten us clearly as to the appellate jurisdiction of the first kind of tribunals over the second, and the procedure to be followed in preferring and hearing appeals. It is simply by implication that the King represented the final court of appeal.

The criminal offences are those which involved arrest, imprisonment, and death-sentence as punishments, and those which are relegated by Kautilya to the tribunals formed by three Pradeshtris or three other competent Amatyas. It is, however, clearly stated in P.E. IV that in case of a death-sentence three days' respite was to be granted for having the judgement reviewed by the Rajjukas as well as allowing the persons to die to be prepared for death in case the appeal failed. The Rajjukas became the final court of appeal since the delegation of the royal or imperial authority in this matter to them.

Going by Ashoka's statement, taken in its literal sense, we are to understand that the kinsmen (natika) of the convicts were the persons expected to make the judges reconsider their case for the sparing of life. In Ashokan texts, the word natika may be taken not only to mean the relatives of a person, near or remote but also widely the kinsfolk, friends, associates, comrades and companions, even neighbours, in short, all persons who are interested in his welfare,—all active well-wishers. As a legal term, employed and interpreted in the Jatakas, the expression nijjhapana means "convincing the judge of the innocence of the accused," and according to the gloss, "openly claiming one's innocence by producing witnesses and persuading the judge to believe it.' But Mr. S. N. Mitra would cite three relevant texts from the Milinda to suggest that here, in Ashokan context, the term signifies not "revising the case, but interceding on behalf of the criminal not only with the King but also with the royal agents.' He would go even further and contend for the interpretation of Ashoka's expression 'for the sparing of life' as implying rather 'the barest sparing at life and reduction of punishment than release." The main text quoted reads thus in its translation: "Just as, a great King, a person powerful on the strength of his wealth, fame, prosperity and people, causes a heavy punishment to be commuted on account of his (great) influence by way of intimate contacts in the case of a relative or friend who has received a heavy punishment from the King (i.e., judge)." Whichever of the two be the more correct interpretation, the idea of interceding in its primary sense of 'pleading with a person for another' is there. In the Ashokan text, the natikas were the typical persons expected to intercede or plead with the judges for a convict or convicts on whom the death sentence had been passed. Whether or not Ashoka actually thought of the bare or full sparing of life is more or less a matter of construction. Anyhow Ashoka's statement, as it is, does not preclude the idea of full sparing or total release. It is interesting to note that the Divyavadana legend preserves the tradition of Ashoka as abolishing capital punishment altogether, although it lacks corroboration from the edicts.

As to the chance given to the unfortunate convicts to prepare for death and for better life in the next world, the interpretation of Ashoka's clause, niludhasi kalasi, signifying the time for observing the fast and giving gifts, has equally been open to dispute. "At the time of death," "when the time is over," "within the limited period," "when the time (of grace) has expired", "even in the time of their imprisonment," "in a closed dungeon,' "when the time (of respite) has expired," and "though their hour of death is irrevocably fixed' are the various suggestions hitherto offered. Although in Pali the word *niruddha* is also used in the sense of *mata* or dead, we may easily rule out the first of them, for here, as argued, the clause stands for the time which is *niruddha,* instead of the time of the *niruddha.* Fortunately, we now have two literary parallels to take us out of the wood. First we have the Pali idiom, *maggassa niruddha-vetilyam* meaning "at the time when the road was closed to traffic." Secondly, we have the Arthashastra idiom, niruddho desakalabhyam, to mean 'when the payment of the subsidy is limited by place and time," "when it is made payable at the specified place and within the specified period of time." In both the instances we have the idea of a limited or fixed period of time.

The edicts of Ashoka do not enlighten us as to the actual forms in which the death sentence was executed. The Arthashastra broadly distinguishes between putting to death with torture and putting to death without torture. Beheading and drowning may certainly and impaling doubtfully be mentioned as methods of execution without torture. The different forms of torture are listed in the Pali Nikayas and detailed in the Arthashastra. The offences that were punishable by death with or without torture have been carefully defined in the Arthashastra, and the reader may be referred to it for details. The Pali texts mention robbery with violence as a typical offence which was punishable with different forms of death. The atavis, meaning the predatory tribes or gangs of thieves with the forest as their hiding place,—warns with the words "Let them be judicious and not get killed", the extreme course of action taken in the Pali typical case.

Jail Administration

The Arthashastra not only speaks of the superintendent of jails as the officer placed in charge of prison but also prescribes certain specific rules for the guidance of jail administration. It distinguishes between the lockup (charaka) and the prison proper (bandhanagara). The rules prescribed provide that no obstruction should be caused to any prisoner in such of their daily avocations as sleeping, sitting, eating or easing nature. No person should be put in the lockup without the declaration of the grounds of provocation. The prisoners should not be subjected to torture (pariklesa) or deprived of food and drink. They must not be beaten to death, unnecessarily harassed or molested. In the case of women, particular care must be taken to see that no rape was committed either in the lockup or within the prison. The criminals condemned to death were put in the prison until execution.

Servitude, indebtedness and imprisonment were painted alike by Buddha as states of woe. A person would come out of them with a great sigh of relief. The philosophic opinion and the general law of the land were both in favour of granting relief to and releasing persons suffering from them. The authoritative verses cited in the Arthashastra enjoin: "Once in a day, or once in five nights, jails may be emptied of prisoners in consideration of the work they have done or of whipping inflicted upon them, or of an adequate ransom paid by them in gold. Whenever a new country is conquered, when an heir-apparent is installed on the throne, or when a Prince is born to the King, prisoners (should be) set free." The prose text of the Arthashastra enjoins: "On the days to which the birth-star of the King is assigned, as well as on full-moon days, such prisoners as are young, old, diseased or helpless (anatha), shall be let out from the jail (bandhanagara): or those who are of charitable disposition or who have made any agreement with the prisoners may liberate them by paying an adequate ransom."

The Ashokan word for prison is simply bandhana. Ashoka, too, shows much concern for making arrangements to provide the prisoners with money to pay the ransom, to protect them against coercion and oppression, and to see them released, especially in the case of such prisoners as were minors or mere tools, or burdened with the maintenance of family, or entitled to consideration by reason of their good conduct, or aged.

In S.R.E. I, Ashoka expresses his earnest desire that the city magistrates should always endeavour so that there may be no sudden restriction on man's liberty or sudden torture. "Well established is the rule", says he, "that if a single person suffers either arrest or torture, and there occurs on that account a sudden imprisonment (or death), others, the blood relations and many people distantly related feel grieved." Ashoka says that within the first twenty five years of his reign he had effected twenty five jail deliveries (bamdhana-mokhani katani), evidently once in one year. He does not tell us, however, on which particular occasion such jail deliveries were ordered. Obviously when he stated this fact, he kept a particular occasion in view, although we have no means of ascertaining what that occasion was. From the importance attached to the Tishya and Punarvasu days, the first, eighth, fourteenth and fifteenth days of the lunar half month, the first full-moon day in each of the three seasons, the first half month during the Indian Lent, as well as to other auspicious days in this edict, it may be inferred that the general rules which guided Ashoka's action were, more or less, the same as or similar to those met with in the Arthashastra. There is no reason to infer from either that ordinarily the whole prison or all prisons were emptied of all prisoners on any occasion.

Provincial Administration

Certain amount of anomaly is apt to arise regarding the relation between the imperial and provincial governments from the fact that Ashoka was at the same time the administrative head of the province of Magadha and that of the Empire of Jambudvipa. It is, however, certain that the domain proper was divided into a number of provinces, divisions, districts and smaller administrative areas for the purpose of administration, each with its official headquarters. The term ahara, as employed in Ashoka's inscriptions (Schism Pillar, Sarnath), denoted the jurisdiction of a certain body of administrative heads. The village was undoubtedly the smallest unit of administration. In the inscriptions we have mention of just one village, namely, that of Lumbini which was exempted from the payment of religious cess and granted the privilege of paying as revenue one-eighth of the total produce of land instead of one sixth.

City Administration

Ashoka distinguishes his capital Pataliputra from other towns that are described, according to their location, as outer (bahira). Among these outer cities or towns, we have an incidental mention of Tosali and Samapa situated in the province of Kalinga, Suvarnagiri and Isila situated in the Southern province, Ujjain situated in the province of Avanti, Takshashila situated in the province of Uttarapatha, and Kaushambi situated in the home province of Vatsa. Pataliputra served as the official headquarters of the imperial government, as also of the home province of Magadha. But nowhere in the inscriptions are the cities and towns classified according to their sizes and importance. The Arthashastra classifies them broadly into four types called sthaniya, dronamukha, kharvatika and sangrahana.

The account given by Strabo of the city administration under the early Maurya regime is remarkable for perspicuity and clearness. It is not quite correct to say with Vincent Smith and others that this account differs materially from the Indian model of city administration as supplied in the Arthashastra. Though the light shed on city administration by the Edicts of Ashoka is scanty, one cannot fail to observe that fundamentally it manifests the same traditional system to be in vogue.

According to Strabo, the officers, i.e., City Magistrates, who had the charge of the city (evidently meaning the Maurya capital) were divided into six bodies or boards of five each. The first body looked after all things relating to industrial arts. The second body attended to the entertainment of foreigners. The third body kept records of births and deaths with a view not only to levying a tax but also in order that births and deaths, of both high and low, might not escape cognizance of government. The fourth body superintended trade and commerce with an eye to weights and measures so as to ensure that the products in their season were sold by public notice. The fifth body supervised manufactured articles which were sold by public notice. The sixth body used to collect the tenths of the prices of the articles sold. Such are the functions which these bodies separately discharged, while in their collective capacity they had charge both of their special departments and also of matters affecting the general interest, such as the keeping of public buildings in proper repair, the regulation of prices, the care of markets, harbours and temples.

Though the Arthashastra does not in such clear terms speak of the city administration being vested in six separate bodies or boards of five each functioning in their individual as well as collective capacity, it will be a misconstruction of the model given in the Arthashastra of the city administration to take it to mean that it was entrusted to a single officer called Nagaraka. The Arthashastra envisages a system of city administration, which was modelled, upon the whole, on the administration of a distinct administrative unit (janapada) divided into four districts, each placed under a Sthanika with some Gopas under him. The Sthanikas with the Gopas as their subordinates were the four district officers under the Samahartri or Collector general of Kevenue. Thus in matters of revenue collection the Samahartri may be said to have formed a Panchayat together with four Sthanikas. There must have been other Panchayats similarly constituted for the discharge of other administrative functions.

In the case of a city, which, too, was divided into four wards, there appear to have been four Sthanikas, each placed in charge of a ward, with a number of Gopas as his assistants. In respect of the functions other than the collection of revenue, detailed in the Arthashastra as well as by Strabo, there were conceivably other officers to form different Panchayats with the Nagaraka. Here one is to imagine that the city administrators were responsible for the proper discharge of their duties either to the King or to a Kumara, or as the case might be, also to a Rajjuka. We have noticed that in the matter of judicial administration, the Arthashastra contemplates the existence of two kinds of tribunals, civil and criminal, one constituted of six judges, and the other of three magistrates. Let it not, however, be understood that I am holding brief for there being a complete agreement between the two accounts. Even as to there being a general agreement, the suggestion is merely a tentative one.

In S.R.E. I, Tosali and Samapa are spoken of as two cities, each of which was placed in charge of the City Magistrates called Nagara-vyavaharikas or Nagaraka Mahamatras. Thus the administration of neither was entrusted to a single officer. The city administrators were many, although from this edict it does not appear whether they had formed a single judiciary, a single body or board or more than one. In both the versions, the city administrators are addressed to in their collective capacity, no matter whether they had belonged to one body or to six.

The Arthashastra speaks of the Paura-vyavaharika and the Nagaraka without connecting them. The emolument allowed to the Paura-vyavaharika is equal to that meant for a Prince (kumara). Shama Sastri treats Paura and Vyavaharika as two separate designations, and take the first to signify 'the officer in charge of the town' and the second to mean 'the superintendent of law or commerce. This is not borne out by the text where Paura-vyavaharika is employed in a singular and not in a dual form. The Ashokan use of the designation Nagaraka as a variant of Nagara-vyavaharika sets at rest all doubts as to Paura-vyavaharika being the same designation as Nagaraka. To be more precise, the Vyavaharika is a general designation, while the designation of Paura vyavaharika is applicable only to a Nagaraka in charge of the capital city.

In S.R.E. I, Ashoka reprimands the Nagarakas for certain highhanded and rash actions on their part, sudden arrest, coercion and imprisonment, and takes steps to stop them. According to the Arthashastra, it was one of the main duties of a Nagaraka to try to detect internal thieves inside a fortified town, while the duty of a Pradeshtn consisted in detecting and bringing to book external thieves with the aid of the Sthanikas and Gopas. The designation of Vyavaharika does not necessarily imply that the duties of the Nagaraka Mahamatras were confined to those of Presidency and Police Magistrates; presumably the duties assigned to them embraced all administrative affairs of a city, including municipal. Thus they were not, except in their collective capacity, members of a single judiciary or magistracy.

Frontier Administration

The Arthashastra enjoins that forts should be constructed in the extremities of a territory and manned by the Antapalas or Wardens of the Marches whose main duty consisted in guarding the entrances into the kingdom, while the interior of the kingdom was to be watched by trap-keepers, archers, hunters, chandalas and wild tribes. The emolument allowed to an Antapala is equal to that of a Prince, or to a member of the Council of Ministers, or a Paura-vyavaharika.

Ashoka in his P.E. I, speaks of the Anta-mahamatras and insists on their following the general principles of administration as set out by him, namely, 'protection by piety, provision by piety, pleasing by piety, and guarding by piety'. The phrase 'so also the Anta-mahamatras' (hemeva amta mahamata) indicates that they had their special jurisdiction over the frontier districts, and were the Wardens of the Marches like the Antapalas of the Arthashastra or the Pratyanta Mahamatras of the Atthasalini. It is also not unlikely that they represented alike those Mahamatras who, like the Mahamatras of Tosali and Samapa, were competent to deal with the Antas or unconquered borderers.

Royal Domain

By his full title, Priyadasi Raja Magadha, Ashoka passed, as we saw, as the "King of Magadha and Emperor of Jambudvipa." The word by which he himself denoted the whole of his royal domain is vijita, vijaya, rajavishaya, or puthavi. The word vijita or vijaya implies that the royal realm which he field was held as though by the right of conquest. In R. E. XIV, his vijita is described as a vast or extensive one (mahalake, mahamte). The large extension of his Empire may be deduced from the very word puthavi which is etymologically defined as 'that which extends.'

In R. E. II, on the other hand, his own vijita is distinguished from the pratyantas or contiguously situated bordering territories of 'the Frontagers' (Antas). In S. R. E. II, the Antas are characterised as 'unconquered borderers' or 'independent frontagers'. The pratyantas represented, nevertheless, the territories of the Antas to which his Dutas ('envoys' or 'emissaries') had their access and where they were sent on certain definite missions. There were countries or territories even beyond them, which were not visited by his Dutas. It is, then, evident from Ashoka's own statements that his vijita was circumscribed by the bordering territories of the independent but friendly 'Frontagers'.

Even within his own Empire, we are to discriminate the portion which was at first entirely under his direct rule and subsequently under the direct rule of himself and his Viceroys, from that which was occupied by the semi-independent tribal territories or states. Thus his domain proper was further circumscribed by the surrounding semi-independent tribal territories.

Extent of Domain Proper: It cannot be strictly maintained that Ashoka's Book inscriptions indicate the broad outline of his Empire; these together with some of his Minor Book and Pillar inscriptions give us but a broad outline of his domain proper. In other words, his Empire was far wider than his vijita in the restricted sense of the term, and if we take into our consideration the independent but friendly territories of the Frontagers, the sphere of his moral and cultural influence was not only as wide as Jambudvipa but wider even than it to include in it certain parts of the three other Continents then known to the Indians, nay, gradually all of them in their entirety, as was expected by him when he viewed the world from the angle of a visionary. Ashoka's grandson and successor Samprati came to be claimed in the Jaina tradition to have been the 'Lord of Bharata with its three divisions.

Thinking, more or less, on the lines suggested by Professor D.B. Bhandarkar, one may take it that by the Book inscriptions was indicated the outline of his domain proper, by the Minor Book inscriptions was demarcated his domain proper from the semi-independent tribal States situate within it, and by the Pillar inscriptions the places personally visited by him in course of his pilgrimage.

The extent of Ashoka's domain proper, as outlined by his inscriptions, may be defined as follows:

In the south east it included the newly created province of Kalinga (i.e., Orissa), and extended as far as the western shore of the Bay of Bengal. In the south, it extended below the Krishna and the Tungabhadra to include the southernmost province with its headquarters at Suvarnagiri. In the west it included the countries of Sunaparanta and Surashtra as well as the Western province of Avanti, and extended as far as the eastern shore of the Arabian sea. In the northwest, it included the province of Uttarapatha or Gandhara, and extended at least as far north as Peshawar and Abbotabad, *on two sides* of the Indus, west and east, In the north, it extended as far as the Nepalese Tarai and the districts of Dehradun and Champaran.

As regards its extension in Bengal and Assam, the Pali Chronicles and Samantapasadika include in Ashoka's domain proper the port of Tamralipti. In the Pali Chronicles and Fa-hien's Fo-kwo-ki, Tamralipti is correctly described as the seaport (in Lower Bengal) which was reachable from Pataliputra by a boat 'following down the river Ganges in an easterly direction', and from which the seagoing vessels carried their passengers to Ceylon', and by implication, to other seaports. The Pali tradition speaks also of a land-route by which Ashoka arrived in one week's time at Tamralipti from Pataliputra across the Vindhya forest.

Raychaudhary bases his argument in favour of the inclusion of Bengal in and the exclusion of Assam from Ashoka's domain on the authority of certain Greek writers headed by Curtius, the Divyavadana and Hiuen Tsang's Si-yu-ki. "We learn from the Classical writers", says he, "that the country of Gangaridae, *i.e.*, Bengal, formed a part of the dominions of the King of the Prasii, *i.e.*, Magadha, as early as the time of Agrammes, *i.e.*, the last Nanda King. A passage of Pliny clearly suggests that the 'Palibothri', *i.e.*, the rulers of Pataliputra, dominated the whole tract along the Ganges. That the Magadhan Kings retained their hold on Bengal as late as the time of Ashoka is proved by the testimony of the Divyavadana, and of Hiuen Tsang who saw stupas of that monarch near Tamralipti and Karnasuvarna (in West Bengal), in Samatata (in East Bengal) as well as in Pundravardhana (in North Bengal). Kamarupa (Assam) seems to have lain outside the Empire. The Chinese pilgrim saw no monument of Ashoka in that country."

The extension of Ashoka's Empire in Bengal thus made out may be true to fact. But in the absence of any inscription of Ashoka throwing light on the point the evidences cited and relied upon must be treated all as presumptive in nature and inconclusive in effect. Hiuen Tsang was an eyewitness to the existence of four stupas built by Ashoka near the chief town of each of the four divisions of Bengal. Fa-hien, too, stayed for a long time at Tamralipti but he had to say nothing about any monument of Ashoka to be seen there. Thus the testimony of the later Chinese pilgrim lacks corroboration from the itinerary of the earlier visitor.

The Divyavadana mentions Pundravardhana in connection with an impossible episode of a ruthless persecution of the Nirgranthas by Ashoka's order, which was issued forthwith to avenge an insult meted out by them to an image of Buddha. The existence or worship of a Buddha image in Ashoka's time is yet to be proved. The cruel persecution of the Nirgranthas and Ajivikas attributed to Ashoka was against the spirit of the Maurya Emperor and the general trend of his edicts and inscriptions. The only relic of the Maurya time hitherto discovered at Pundranagara is the small Brahmi inscription from Mahasthan in the district of Bogra serving as it did to carry from the town of Pundra paddy and small coins to the settlement of the Shadvargikas. An additional support to the theory of inclusion of Pundravardhana might be sought from the Divyavadana definition of the Middle Country.

As defined in the Pali Vinaya Pitaka, "it extended in the east to the town of Kajangala, beyond which was Mahasala; on the southeast, to the river Salalavati." The Divyavadana on the other hand, "extends the eastern boundary to include Pundravardhana, roughly identical with North Bengal." Pundravardhana was indeed the first division of Bengal which lay contiguous to Kajangala as borne out by the itinerary of Hiuen Tsang and the Mahabharata description of Bhima's digvijaya in Eastern India.

Curtius and other Greek writers describe indeed Agrammes the Magadhan contemporary of Alexander as "King of the Gangaridae and the Prasii". What did the Greek writers themselves understand by the two terms, Prasii and Gangaridai?

According to Schawnbeck, the Greek word Prasii "bears a very close resemblance to the Indian word Prachyas (*i.e.*, 'dwellers in the East')." In the Indika of Megasthenes the Prasii are described as "an Indian people" the most distinguished people in all India in whose country is situated the city called Palibothra (i.e., Pataliputra). To the same effect it is stated in Fragment XXVII, "the greatest city in India is that which is called Palimbothra, in the dominions of the Prasians."

The Aitareya Brahmana distinguishes the Prachyas from the Dakshinatyas, Pratichyas, Udichyas, and Madhyamas, and defines them as the Eastern peoples who were 'anointed for overlordship'. It suggests that they were the ruling peoples who lived to the east of the territories of the Kurus, the Panchalas, the Vasas and the Usinaras. The Kurus and the rest were the typical Midlanders (Madhyamas).

If we take the name Prachyas in the Aitareya Brahmana and Great Epic sense, the Prasii of the Greek writers must be treated as the Eastern peoples of India identical with the Gangaridai or Gangaridae. But this equation is not maintainable in view of the fact that Megasthenes definitely represents the Prasians as the ruling people of Palibothra, i.e., the capital of Magadha, from which circumstance they were also known by the name of Palibothris, i.e., Pataliputrians. Megasthenes introduces the Gangaridai in connection with the Ganges system of rivers and the Ganges' course, both of which he correctly described. In one passage he says, "Now this river, which at its source is 30 stadia broad, flows from north to south, and empties its waters into the ocean forming the eastern boundary of the Gangaridai, a nation which possesses a vast force of the largest sized animals."

In another passage, he observes: "...it flows out with a gentle current, being at the narrowest eight miles and on the average a hundred stadia, in breadth, and never of less depth than twenty paces (one hundred feet) in the final part of its course, which is through the country of the Gangarides."

He clearly defines the Gangarides as a people who lived 'in the farthest off part' and whose King possessed '1000 horse, 700 elephants, and 60,000 foot in apparatus of war.' They are distinguished from a very powerful nation who occupied an extremely populous island in the Ganges, and whose King kept 'under arms 50,000 foot and 4000 horse.'

From Pliny's account of the Palibothri, it appears that the Gangaridai represented all peoples who lived along the whole extent of the Ganges' course, while, in one context at any rate, Megasthenes seems to make 'the Gangarides a branch of Kaligaa: *Gangaridum Calingarum Regia.* Pliny, too, 'mentions the Macco-Calingae and *Gangarides-Calingae* as separate peoples from the Calingae." "The tribes called Calingae", says Megasthenes, "'are nearest the sea, and higher up are the Nandei, and the Malli in whose country is Mount Mallus, the boundary of all that district being the Ganges." Prom this McCrindle concludes that 'the Gangaridae or Gangarides occupied the region corresponding roughly with that now called Lower Bengal and consisted of various indigenous tribes, which in course of time became more or less Aryanised."

The Allahabad stone-pillar inscription of Samudragupta leads us to think that probably the task of subduing such eastern frontier countries as Samatata (East Bengal), Davaka and Kamarupa

(Assam) was left to him to accomplish. The Great Epic account of Bhima's military expedition in the eastern region envisages the conquest of the whole of Bengal and Assam and agrees in all important respects with Hiuen Tsang's travels. The Mahabharata account may not, therefore, speak of an earlier state of things. But from this account and Hiuen Tsang's itinerary, it may be inferred that the Gangaridae as a people allied to the Calingae were no other than the dwellers of Tamralipta and Suhma, in short, of the modern district of Midnapore. The inclusion of this part of Bengal in Ashoka's domain proper is suggested, as we saw, by the Pali tradition. As for other parts of Bengal, including the district of Purnea on the river Kausiki, now included in the province of Bihar, it is not impossible that those adjoining the Middle Country came within Ashoka's domain proper, although we must wait for a more positive evidence to establish it.

Mauryan State

The historicocritical study of the Maurya State under Ashoka involves at every step the dispassionate consideration of these three points, each of importance: (i) the earlier Indian administration, particularly Mauryan, (ii) the innovations introduced by Ashoka, and (iii) the combined effect of both on the later systems, particularly one which is embodied in the Arthashastra as a prose treatise, ascribed to Kautilya Vishnugupta.

To put the matter in this fashion is to modify considerably the debatable assumption of Mukherji, Jayaswal, Jacobi, Sharma Sastri, N. N. Law, Bandyopadhyay and other writers that the Arthashastra in its extant prose form is a treatise written by Kautilya or Vishnugupta Chanakya, the uprooter of the Nanda dynasty, political adviser of Chandragupta Maurya and Chancellor of Magadha.

Such gifted writers, on the other hand, as Vincent Smith, Jolly, Hillebrandt, Winternitz and Otto Stein, who have doubted or challenged the above position, have erred on the wrong side by putting their implicit faith in the testimony of the Classical writers whose accredited authority was the Indika of Megasthenes. Even to the Classical writers like Arrian, much of what the Indika of the Greek ambassador to Chandragupta's court contained was fabulous and, therefore, incredible. It survives, moreover, only in a few fragments preserved or reproduced by some later historians and geographers. This fact alone goes to lessen the value of the work otherwise lost and render it into a work of questionable authority. Avoiding at all events these two extreme positions, the scientific historical method will be not so much to interpret and appraise the matters concerning Ashoka's state in the light of either the Indika or the Arthashastra as to see and show what actual light is shed on the subject by Ashoka's own records and the collective literary tradition of the age.

Whatever the actual date of its composition or compilation, the Arthashastra has certainly this advantage over both the fragmentary Indika of Megasthenes and the inscriptions of Ashoka that it presents a complete system of the Indian royal polity. The inscriptions of Ashoka keep us, on the other hand, entirely in the dark as to the military side of his administration. They give us but a *few glimpses, here and there, into the guiding principles of administration, its type* and basic character, its aims and methods, its machineries, the administrative divisions, the feudatory states, the foreign relations and policies, the personal epithets or titles of the King, the position and function of the King, the private life of the King, the position of the Queens, the King's near relations, his personal staff and agents, the Princes of the blood, the position, function and Constitution of the council of ministers, the King's power of legislation, the judicial system, the means of communication, the conveyances and means of transport, the King's prerogatives and proclamations, the nature of despatches, the method of supervision and inspection, the public works, the philanthropic deeds, the sources of revenue or state-income, the remission of taxes and duties, the decentralisation of power, the position and function of the Viceroys and Mahamatras, the rules of conduct for public servants, the war and peace, the suppression of revolts and internal troubles, and the like.

The oldest known stock-passages in the Pali and Ardhamagadhi canons bear ample testimony to the development of the science of royal polity in the country and in the interest evinced and active part played by certain Shramanas and Brahmanas in the matter. The Arthashastra itself quotes by name and criticises the views of different teachers and schools of political thought, and sets itself the task of defending and expounding the views of Kautilya.

- *Individual Teachers:* Dirghascharayana, ghotamukha, Vatavyadhi, Visalaksha, Pisuna, Pisunaputra. Kaunapadanta (all nicknames), Bharadvaja, Kaninka Bharadvaja, Kinjalka, Parashara and Katyayana.
- *Schools:* The Manavas, Parasharas, Ausanasas, Barhaspatyas and Ambhiyas.

The agreed opinion of the individuals and schools other than those who held dissentient views is obviously referred to the body of Acharyas (accredited teachers).

Among the individual teachers, Dirghascharayana (Pali Digha Karayana) was the Commander-in-Chief of Kosala and a younger contemporary of the Buddha. Ghotamukha (Pali Ghotakamukha) was a Brahmin contemporary of the Buddha. Parashara may be regarded as the putative author of the Mahabharata, and Katyayana as a Smriti-writer.

Among the schools, the Manavas and parasharas were exponents of the rules of polity embodied in the Smriti texts ascribed to them. The Barhaspatyas and Ausanasas represented the Smriti schools of law as well as the schools of politics. The Ambhiyas who are connected by Professor F. W. Thomas with Taxila, derived their name from Ambhi, King of Takshashila at the time of Alexander's invasion of India.

Vishnugupta's prose treatise preserves certain maxims of Kautilya in verse and reproduces many in prose, which must somehow or other be discriminated from their later elucidations in order to understand what was precisely in the immediate background of Ashoka's administration. The principles of royal polity and good government as well as the duties and responsibilities of Kings as inculcated by various sages in the Great Epic deserve careful consideration. The earlier Magadhan system of administration as may be envisaged from incidental references in the Pali and Ardhamagadhi texts is of an invaluable aid to the study of the same. Above all, the light must be constantly sought from the duties and ideals of the King overlord adumbrated and repeatedly emphasised in the Pali Nikayas including one of the Jatakas, and, to some extent, also from such Vedic texts as the Brahmanas, earlier Shastras and Upanishads.

Admittedly there is no ancient Indian term corresponding to the modern State, the nearest approximation being Rajya, nor is there any conception or definition exactly fitting in with the modern theory of State. But Ashoka certainly gives us a fairly clear idea of all the four elements of the Maurya State as it shaped in his hands, namely, the population, territory, sovereignty and government. He indicates and, in some respects, sets forth also the functions and aims, methods and contrivances, foreign relations and policies of the State, the Constitution and machineries of his government, and his achievements through it.

Extent of Empire

Ashoka's earthly Empire consisted of his domain proper and the semi-independent tribal territories. On the north, it was bounded by the Himalayan range. On the south, it abutted on the independent but friendly territories of the Cholas, the Pandyas, the Satiyaputras, the Keralaputras, and the Tamraparnyas. On the east, it extended as far as to the Bay of Bengal, at least after the annexation of Kalinga. On the west, it extended as far as to the Arabian sea. And on the northwest, it bordered on the independent but friendly Asiatic territory of Antiyoka.

"'Alexander indeed," says Arrian, "came and overthrew all in war, all whom he attacked, and would even have conquered the whole world had his army been willing to follow him. On the other hand, a sense of justice, they say, prevented any Indian King from attempting conquest beyond the limits of India." According to Megasthenes, the western side of India was bounded by the river Indus. But since the treaty following the Seleukidan war with Chandragupta the Maurya Empire extended not only beyond the Indus but also beyond the Sulaiman and Kirthar ranges to include in it the four former Greek satrapies of "the Paropanisadai, Aria, and Arachosia, the capitals of which were respectively Kabul, Herat, and Kandahar, and also Gedrosia, the modern Baluchistan," in short, the whole of Baluchistan and Eastern Afghanistan.

Pliny rightly observes: "Many writers, however, do not give the river Indus as the western boundary of India, but include within it four satrapiesmaking the river Cophes its furthest limit, though others prefer to consider all these belonging to the Arii. Many writers further include in India even the city of Nysa and Mount Merus. They include also the Astakani in whose country the vine grows abundantly."

As regards the geographical extension of Bharatavarsha or India proper, there is hardly any material difference to be noticed between the foreign and native accounts.

According to Eratosthenes and Megasthenes, for instance, "India is bounded on the eastern side, right towards the south, by the great ocean; -its northern frontier is formed by the Kaukasos (Himalayan) range as far as the junction of that range with Taurus; and the boundary towards the west and the northwest, as far as the great ocean, is formed by the river Indus.'

To the same effect is the description of Diodorus, according to whom "India, which is in shape quadrilateral, has its eastern as well as western side bounded by the great sea, but on the northern side it is divided by Mount Hemodos (Himadri) from that part of Skythia which is inhabited by those Skythians who are called the Sakai, while the fourth or western side is bounded by the river called the Indus."

As described by Hiuen Tsang, "The countries embraced under the term of India (In-tu, anciently called Shin-tu, Hien-tau) are generally spoken of as the five Indies. In circuit this country is about 90,000 li (15,000 miles); on three sides it is bordered by the great sea; on the north, it is backed by the Snowy Mountains. The north part is broad, the southern part is narrow."

The Markandeya Purana describes India as a typical peninsula with the great sea on the south, west and east, and the Himalaya on the north, and gives it a length of 1,000 yojanas from south to north.

The name Bharatavarsha is not employed by the Buddhists to denote India; their familiar term is Jambudvipa. This Jambudvipa may, for all practical purposes, be treated as India proper plus the inhabited tracts in the Himalayan region extending as far north as the Altyn range, if not still further up, as far west as the Hindu

Kush range, and as far east as the Namklu mountains. Jambudvipa, as defined in Buddhist literature, is the southern subcontinent of the mainland of Asia, situated to the south of Mount Sumeru and between the two subcontinents of Aparagoyana and Purvavideha, situated respectively to the west and east of the same mount. It excludes the eight upadvipas or adjoining islands of Bharatavarsha, Tamraparna (Ceylon) included.

Ashoka's Empire was not coextensive with either Bharatavarsha or Buddhist Jambudvipa in so far as it excluded from it the independent territories of the Antas in the south; it was wider than both in so far as it included within it the four Greek satrapies in Afghanistan and Baluchistan. As regards its extension towards the north beyond the Himalayas, it is still a disputed question, and it largely depends on the determination of the territories of the Nabha-lines of ruling tribes.

Jules Bloch is said so have once casually remarked that the inscriptions of Ashoka afford data for the first linguistic survey of India. But one may go even further and say that they afford data also for the first geographical survey of India. Accordingly, in connection with Ashoka's Empire, we may examine with profit the nature of the light these records throw on the traditional divisions of India.

Though the definition varies with different authorities, the geograpnical divisions of India are generally enumerated as five, *viz.*, the Eastern (Prachya, Purvanta, Purvadesa); the Southern (Dakshina, Dakshinapatha, Dakshinatya); the Western (Pratichya, Aparanta, Paschaddesa); the Northern, better the North-Western (Urddhva, Udichya, Uttarapatha); and the Middle (Madhyama, Madhyadesa, Antarvedi), The Markandeya Purana adds *two more divisions to the usual list of five, namely, the Vindhyan (Vindhyaprishtha)* and the Mountainous (Parvatasrayi). Pali literature, too, speaks of a sixth division but terms it the Himalayan (Hemavata, Himavanta-padesa).

The Eastern division was represented, according to the Aitareya Brahmana, VIII. 14, by the rulers who were anointed for overlordship (samrajyaya) and passed accordingly as Overlords (Samrat)); the southern division by those of the Satvat race who were anointed for military regime (bhaujyaya) and passed accordingly as Military Chiefs (Bhojas); the Western division by those of the southern and western peoples (nichyanam, apachyanam) who were anointed for self-rule (svarajyaya) and passed as Self-rulers (Svarat); the Northern division by the ruling peoples like the Trans-Himalayan Kurus and Madras who were anointed for sovereignty (vairajyaya) and passed accordingly as Sovereigns (Virat) and the Middle division by the ruling peoples like the Kurus, the Panchalas, the Vasas and the Usinaras who were anointed for kingship (rajyaya) and passed accordingly as Kings (Raja).

As to Middle division: The scope of the Middle division was gradually widened. Bodhayana placed it between the place of disappearance of the Sarasvati (*i.e.*, Vinasana) on the west and the Black Forest (Kalakavana) on the east, and between the Himalayas on the north and the Paripatra (Pariyatra) mountains on the south. Manu's Middle Country is placed between the Himalayas and the Vindhya range and taken to extend from Vinasana as far east as Prayaga (Allahabad). Rajasekhara extends it further east to include Banaras. The Gopatha Brahmana includes in it not only Kashi and Kosala but also Anga and Magadha. The Pali definition extends it still further east to include the country of Kajangala which is the modern district of Santal Parganas, while ultimately in the Divyavadana definition it includes even Pundravardhana or North Bengal.

As defined in Pali, the eastern *frontier of the Middle Country lay to the east of Mahasala beyond the township of Kajangala. It was* bounded on the southeast by the river called Salalavati, on the south by the town of Satakarnika which was probably the place of origin of the Satakarnis, on the west by the Brahmin village of Sthuna, and on the north by the Usiradhvaja mountain near Kankhal.

The countries of Kuru and Panchala, Anga and Magadha, Kashi Kosala, Salva and Matsya, Vasa and Usinara were contained in the Middle Country, according to the Gopatha Brahmana. The Pali list includes also the countries of Vriji and Malla, Chedi and Vatsa, and associates Surasena with Matsya instead of Salva.

It may, upon the whole, be premised that the Middle Country as known to the early Buddhists covered that middle part of Northern India which was watered by the entire Ganges system of rivers to the exclusion of those which now flow through Bengal.

This division is outlined on the north by Ashoka's Rock Edicts at Kalsi (Dehradun), Minor Pillar inscriptions at Lumbini and Nigliva (Nepalese Tarai) and pillars and Pillar Edicts at Lauriya Nandangarh and Rampurva (Champaran district), on the east by his Pillar inscription and palace at Kumrahar, Patna, on the south by his Minor Rock inscription at Sahasram (Shahbad district, Bihar), and on the southwest and west by his pillar at Samkasya, Schism pillar inscriptions at Sanchi and Kaushambi, Minor Rock inscription at Bairat, Pillar inscriptions at Mirath and Topra, and Rock Edicts at Kalsi. It was wholly included in his domain proper and Empire.

The Divisions

Vindhyan Division: The northern boundary of the Southern division was gradually pushed further and further south from the Ganges to the Pariyatra and Vindhya mountains, to the Narmada and the upper Godavari. Rajasekhara places it to the south of Mahishmati, once the capital of Avanti and now identified with Mandhata on the Narmada. While commenting on Hiuen Tsang's five Indies, Cunningham takes Southern India to denote 'the whole of the peninsula from Nasik on the west and Ganjam on the east, including the modern districts of Berar and Telingana.'

As I have sought to maintain, Dakshinapatha was at first the name of a trade-route, the Southern High Road, which extended from Rajagriha, the old capital of Magadha, to Pratishthana (modern Paithan) opposite Nasik on the right bank of the upper Godavari, not far from its source. Its extension may be divided into two stages, as pointed out by Rhys Davids, *viz,* (i) North to Southwest, from Shravasti to Pratishthana; and (ii) North to Southeast, from Shravasti to Rajagriha. The main stopping places between Shravasti and Pratishthana, beginning from the north, were Saketa, Kaushambi, Vanasa, Vidisha, Gonarda, Ujjaini (the later capital of Avanti), and Mahishmati (the earlier capital of Avanti). And the principal stopping places between Rajagriha and S'ravasti, beginning from southeast, were Nalanda, Pataliputra, Vaishali, Bhandagrama, Hastigrama, Pava, Kushinara, Kapilavastu, and Shvetavya. By the expressions, Pataliputrah Dakshinapathe and Avanti-Dakkhinapathe, one should understand either

'Pataliputra and Avanti on the Southern Road' or 'Pataliputra and Avanti in Dakshinapatha.' In the latter case, we may presume that Dakshinapatha as the Southern Road lent its name to the countries below the Ganges and above the Godavari across which it lay. When the name Dakshinapatha or Dakshinatya came to be applied to Southern India below the Pariyatra and Vindhya mountains or below the Narmada and Mahanadi, it simply meant the Deccan peninsula to which the Southern, better Southwestern, Road ultimately led.

The Markandeya Purana characteristically suggests a Vindhyaprishtha or Vindhyan division in between the Middle and Eastern divisions on the north and the Southern division on the south, and locates it to the east of the Western division. Its southern boundary is roughly the Narmada on the west, the Mahanadi on the east, and the Vindhya range in the middle. The Purana locates in it such typical peoples with their territories as the Uttamarnas, Dasarnas, Bhojas, Kishkindhyas, Anupas, Avantis, Virahotras, Karushas, Malajas (Malayas), Mekalas and Utkalas.

The northern boundary of this division which really formed the southern fringe of the Middle and Eastern divisions may easily be taken to be indicated by the Rupnath and Sahasram copies of M.R.E. Its western boundary may similarly be taken to be indicated by the Schism Pillar inscription at Sanchi.

Western Division: The Western division of India is outlined by Ashoka's Rock inscriptions at Sopara and Girnar in the west, and the Sanchi copy of the Schism Pillar Edict and the Bairat copy of M.R.E. in the east. This division contained his westernmost province of Avanti with its viceregal headquarters at Ujjaini. Kaushambi, Sanchi, *i.e.,* Vidisha, and Ujjaini were situated on the Southern Road. Bairat (Viratanagara) in the modern state of Jaipur was the capital of the Matsya country which, according to Bhandarkar, comprised parts of Alwar, Jaipur and Bharatpur. Eastern Matsya itself, like Vatsa with Kaushambi as its capital, was included in the Midland or Middle Country.

The Sopara set of Ashoka's Rock Edicts was incised at Shurparaka, which was known in the Buddha's time as a famous seaport in Sunaparanta, simply called Aparanta in the Pali Chronicles and the Samantapasadika. But it would seem that the Pali Sunaparanta is the same territorial name as Kukkuraparanta. The name Kukkuraparanta occurs in the Nasik Cave inscription of Vasishthiputra pulumayi along with Surashtra, Anupa, Vidarbha, and Akaravanti, and in the Junagarh Rock inscription of Rudradaman I along with Akaravanti, Anupa, Anarta, Surashtra, Shvabhra, Marukachchha, Sindhu-Sauvira, Nishada tracts, and the like, the dominions mentioned in Rudradaman's inscriptions being the typical countries of the Western division. The Kavyamimamsa list of such countries contains, among others, the name of Surashtra, Bhrigukachchha, Kachchha, Anarta and Arvuda. The Markandeya Purana, which contains a longer list, mentions, *inter alia,* the name of Nasika, Surashtra, Kachchha, Avanti, Arvuda, Tripura and Vidisha, while, according to Hiuen Tsang, the Western division appears to have comprised Sindh, Western Rajputana, Cutch, Gujarat, and a portion of the adjoining coast on the lower course of the Narmada.' The countries from the Mahabharata lists, which may be located in the same division, include Aparamatsya, Kantara, Avanti, Arvuda, Apara Kuntibhoja, Surashtra, Shurparaka, Nishada, Kalamukha (a cannibal tract), Kachchha Kukkura, Kundaparanta, and the like.

In the opinion of Bhagawanlal Indraji Aparanta denoted the whole western seaboard of Western India. But in the case of Sunaparanta or Kukuraparanta, as distinguished from Aparanta as the name of the Western division, Aparanta had presumably a limited territorial extension, which is represented now by Northern Konkan. Probably the whole of Konkan, north of Karnata, was sought to be denoted by the compound name Sunaparanta or Kukuraparanta, which was the southwestern destination of a caravan route extended from the Southern Road. The Mahabharata mentions two Kukura countries, one of which, namely, that which is not connected with Aparanta, might perhaps be located in North Kathiawar near Anarta.

I cannot agree with Dr. Sircar that Marukachchha, distinguished in the Markandeya Purana from Kachchha (Cutch), is a compound of two territorial names, namely, Maru denoting Western Rajputana and Kachchha denoting Cutch. It is evidently a variant of Bharukachchha or Bhrigukachchha (modern Broach, Barygaza of the Periplus). Marukachchha, as its name implies, was indeed a Desert Cutch, but the desert was not the Kantara or Marukantara of Western Rajputana; it was the desert adjoining Surashtra or Gujarat.

The Girnar version of Ashoka's Rock Edicts was incised at Girinagara, the capital of Surashtra, now identified with South Kathiawar. It is not improbable that in Ashoka's time the whole of Gujarat, including Anarta, was within the jurisdiction of Surashtra.

Southern Division: Ashoka's Empire excluded the independent but friendly territories of the Cholas, the Pandyas, the Satiyaputras, the Keralaputras and the Tamraparnyas but included those of the Andhras, the Parinda-Paradas and other Aparantas. It included also the entire territory of the Kalingas. We have two sets of Ashoka's Rock and Separate Rock Edicts within the newly created province of Kalinga, viz., one set in the Puri district and the other in the district of Ganjam. Both of these districts are included in the modern province of Orissa.

According to the Great Epic tradition, the territory of the Kalingas, which was reachable by a route along the seat-coast from the Ganges' mouth and lay beyond Tamralipti, Karvata and Suhma, included the river Vaitarani, if it was not exactly its northern boundary. Its southern limit along the seacoast may be guessed from the position of Ashoka's Rock inscriptions at Jaugada in the district of Ganjam as well as from the fact that Dantapura near Chicacole is mentioned in the Pali Mahagovinda Suttanta as the ancient capital of Kalinga. Raychaudhary may be right in suggesting that probably the name of Dantapura is still preserved in that of the fort of Dantavaktra in Ganjam. It is evident from the Hathigumpha inscription that the kingdom of Kalinga included Prithudaka or Pithunda on the seacoast, which was situated near the river Langala (Languliya). Hence it may be safely presumed that Kalinga comprised the whole of the seacoast from at least the river Vaitarani to the Languliya and abutted on the borders of the Andhra territory.

The river Salalavati, which formed the southeastern limit of the Buddhist Midland, may indeed be identified with the modern Svarnarekha which divides the state of Mayurbhanj and the district of Baleswar from that of Midnapore. Some of the hill-tribes and a branch of the Kalingas may be placed in the region between the Suvarnarekha and the Vaitarani.

The independent territories in the south lay, according to the specification suggested by Ashoka himself, below the province of Kalinga on the east, the southernmost province in the middle, and the province of Avanti on the west. It lay also below the Andhra and Parinda-Parada territories on the east, and the territories of the Rashtrikas and Bhojakas and their offshoots in the middle and on the west. And so far as Ashoka's inscriptions are concerned, the most eastern point of the dividing line is represented by the Rock inscriptions at Jaugada, the central part by those at Yerragudi, Brahmagiri and Gavimath, and the most western point by those at Sopara. On the east, the southern limit of Ashoka's Empire can indeed be pushed as far south as the upper Pennar, the region between this river on the south and the Krishna on the north being included in it. On the west the same may be pushed as far south as the tract about Karnataka. In the middle, Ashoka's Empire may be easily taken to have comprised the northern part of Mysore which is watered by the Tungabhadra and its southern tributaries. Whether or not the most southern limit of the same can be pushed further below depends largely on the location of Suvarnagiri, which was the viceregal headquarters of the Southern province.

As for Suvarnagiri, Mukherji inclines to think that "from its name, the 'gold mount', the place might be in the ancient gold-mining areas, and this edict has been found at Maski near Raichur, which shows numerous traces of ancient gold workings, a shaft of which is the deepest in the world known so far." This is identified by Hultzsch with Kanakagiri, south of Maski.

The proposed identification of Suvarnagiri with Kanakagiri, 'south of Maski and north of the ruins of Vijayanagara', is unconvincing for the simple reason that the Maski copy of M.R.E. differs materially from the Isila version in Northern Mysore. In the neighbourhood of Suvarnagiri one must expect not only a text of M.R.E. which is similar to that of the Isila version but also a set of Rock Edicts. The Yerragudi rock in the Karnool district, bearing as it does a complete set of Rock Edicts besides a version of M.R.E., which is substantially the same as that of Prahmagiri, Siddapura and Jatinga Rameshwara, satisfies, no doubt, this twofold test. But this rock, as appears from the M.R. E. incised on it, was situated rather within the jurisdiction of a Rajjuka than within that of a Viceroy-in-Council.

One must search for Suvarnagiri farther south in Mysore and in the upper valleys of the Kaveri. The Ramayana refers to a great mountain by the name of Ayomukha, which abounded in metallic ores and which lay in the centre of territories of the Andhras, the Pundras, the Cholas, the Pandyas and the Keralas and in a sandal district near the valleys of the Kaveri.

The territories around Ashoka's southernmost province below the Vindhya, below the Narmada and the Godavari, were, according to Ashoka's own showing, those of the Andhras and Parindapaladas and the countries of the Cholas, pandyas, Satiyaputras, Keralaputras and Tamraparnyas. These are obviously the territories mentioned in the Ramayana.

Northwestern Division: Uttarapatha and Dakshinapatha, as I am inclined to think, are two relative terms and both denoted at first two high roads or caravan routes, the former the Northern, better North-Western Road, and the latter the Southern, better South-Western Road, each with its various *branches and* extensions. Several roads having started from the main halting places on the South-Western Road, such as Shravasti Saketa, Kaushambi and Mathura on the right bank of the Yamuna, merged in the North-Western Road, and several roads having branched off from the North-Western, led to different destinations, such as Srughna, *i.e.*, Dehradun, Kekaya, and Sindhu-Sauvira. The well-known destination of the main road was Takshashila. The Ramayana speaks of two routes, longer and shorter, by which one might travel from Ayodhya (Oudh) to the Kekaya capital in Uttarapatha and back. The Kekaya territory itself "lay between the Vipasa or Beas and abutted on the Gandharva or Gandhara Vishaya."

Some of the roads that branched off from the South-Western Road passed through the Marukantara or great desert of Rajputana. The Mahaniddesa, the Serissaka story in the Peta and Vimana Vatthus, as well as some of the Jatakas mention the names of different parts of the North-Western Road which, like the main road, lent their names to the places in the Uttarapatha division across which they lay. Panini's aphorism, too, suggests that all these went together into the make-up of the Uttarapatha or North-Western Road.

Thus from the point of view of the Buddhist Midland the Uttarapatha was rather the Western North-Western than the Northern division of India. With Manu the river Drishadvati was the dividing line between the Midland and the North-Western region, while Rajasekhara takes the latter to have extended westward from Prithudaka (modern Pehoa) near modern Thaneshwar.

Broadly speaking, the North-Western division comprised that portion of India which was and is watered by the entire Indus system of rivers, and was and is placed between the river Drishadvati on the southeast and the Kubha or Kabul on the northwest. For Hiuen Tsang, as made out by Cunningham, this division 'comprises the Punjab proper including Kashmir and the adjoining Hill States with the whole of Eastern Afghanistan beyond the Indus and the present Cis-Sutlej States to the west of Sarasvati river.'

The North-Western division of Ashoka's time may be supposed to have comprised not only the whole of the Punjab, Sindh and North-Western Frontier provinces but also Baluchistan and Eastern Afghanistan. So far as the inscriptions of Ashoka along the banks of the Yamuna go, the Midland would seem to have included in it the region between this river and the Drishadvati.

In Pali literature Kashmira and Gandhara are excluded from the Haimavata division or the Himalayan region (Himavantappadesa), and Vajira is distinguished from Uttarapatha. The Dipavamsa uses the name Apararajagiri as a substitute for Vajira, which may be identified with the modern Bajauri in the North-West Frontier province.

The Uttarapatha division of India including the modern state of Kashmir and Jammu as well as the four Greek satrapies ceded by Seleucus Nikator to Chandragupta Maurya is represented by Ashoka's North-Western Province and the semi-independent tribal states of the Yaunas, Kambojas, Gandharas and other Aparantas. The southern boundary of these tribal states is indicated by the Shahbazgarhi and Mansehra sets of Ashoka's Rock inscriptions.

Himalayan Division: The Himalayan region (Himavantapadesa) of Jambudvipa extended northward, according to Pali legends, as far as the south side of Mount Sumeru. The Gandhamadana range with its two branches called Narada and Parvata is located in it. This range was penetrated by the ancient hermits. It contained seven great lakes, the two of which, *viz.*, the *Anotatta (Anavatapta) and the Chhaddanta, (Shaddanta) are frequently* mentioned in the Jatakas and several Buddhist legends including those of Ashoka. These lakes may even be seen today situated between the Great Himalayan range on the south and the Altyn range on the north. Anotatta Lake which is identified by Dr. Law with Manas Sarovar is said to have been surrounded by five mountain peaks.

A more or less clear idea of this part of Jambudvipa may be formed from the Great Epic description of Arjuna's northern military expedition, and Hiuen Tsang's travels.

The southern boundary of this division of India and Ashoka's Empire is indicated by the Kalsi set of Rock Edicts, the Ashokan monoliths at Nigliva, Lumbini and those in the district of Champaran. Ashoka evidently locates in it the semi-independent tribal states of the Nabhakas and Nabha-lines.

Eastern Division: The Prachya or Eastern division may be defined as consisting of the easternmost portion of Northern India extending as far northeast as the Patkai, Naga and Chin Hills. In Ashoka's time it must have comprised the province of Assam and the state of Manipur, as well as that portion of Bengal which lay beyond his domain proper and outside the Buddhist Midland as defined in the Divyavadana.

The western limit of this division is roughly indicated by the Pillars and Pillar inscriptions of Ashoka in the district of Champaran and the southern limit by the Dhauli set of Rock Edicts. The eastern extension of his Empire through Nepal and Assam depends on that of the semi-independent territories of the Nabha-lines of the ruling tribes.

Autonomous Regions

Aparantas and Atavis as Determinants: The position of Ashoka's Empire thus made out may be further tested by Ashoka's statements concerning certain semi-independent ruling peoples within his Empire, all of whom are broadly termed Aparantas. The Yaunas, *Kambojas and Gandharas are mentioned in R.E.V. as the most* typical *of* such Aparantas belonging to the Uttarapatha and Haimavata divisions, while the Ristika-Petenikas typify these Aparantas belonging to the Vindhya, Aparanta and Dakshinapatha divisions. The list supplied in R.E. XIII omits from it the name of the Gandharas but adds those of the Nabhakas and Nabhapamktis, and replaces the Ristika-Petenikas by the Bhoja-Pitinikas adding to them the name of the Andhra-Parindas or Andhra-Paradas. We are introduced in this very edict also to the Atavis (Atavikas or Atavyas) who lived within Ashoka's Empire. It is equally necessary to ascertain who they were and what tracts were inhabited by them in order to form a correct idea of the extent of Ashoka's Empire.

Ristika-Petenikas, Bhoja-Pitinikas: It may be reasonably presumed that Ashoka spoke of the Ristika-Petenikas and Bhoja-Pitinikas and other Aparantas with reference to Vindhya region in the broadest sense of the term. There exists a sharp difference of opinion on the signification of the two compound names. Jayaswal takes each of them to be a combination of two names, the Ristikas and the Bhojas representing the non-hereditary Ristikas and Bhojas, and the Petenikas the hereditary Ristikas and the hereditary Bhojas, while Bhandarkar treats petenika as an adjective to the Ristikas and the Bhojas, and takes the two names to mean the hereditary Ristikas and the hereditary Bhojas respectively. There are two Pali passages in the Anguttara Nikaya, in which Ratthika, Pettanika and Gamagamanika (*i.e.*, Bhojaka) are met with as official designations implying the enjoyment of varying degrees of sovereignty. In one passage Ratthika and Pettanika seem to go together, and in the other, they appear as two different designations.

Petenika as a territorial patronymic from Patitthana is improbable. Its Pali equivalent is Pettanika beyond doubt. Michelson rightly Sanskritises it as Paitrayanika, which is a patronymic from pitrayana. The Aitareya Brahmana broadly distinguishes between the Bhojapitaras and the Bhojas. In Jayaswal's opinion the intended distinction is between the hereditary and non-hereditary Bhojas. The distinction, as I am now inclined to think, is between the Bhojapitaras and the Bhojaputras, which is to say, between the parent or senior Bhojas and the offshoot or junior Bhojas. Jayaswal has obviously missed the force of the term Bhojapitarah which is a word like the Pali gopitaro, meaning the bulls who make seniors or elders among the cattle. Thus the distinction is between the Rishtika-Rashtrikas and Bhojas of the parent stock on the one hand, and their offshoots on the other, and not between the hereditary and non-hereditary Rishtika-Rashtrikas and Bhojas. The Rishtika-Rashtrikas and the Bhojas represented the parent tribal States and the Paitrayanikas their offshoots,—the branch States.

Let us now see how far this interpretation tallies with the epigraphic and literary representation of the Rishtika-Rashtrikas, the Bhojas and the Paitrayanikas. In R.E V, the Rishtika-Rashtrikas and the corresponding Paitrayanikas typify the Aparantas. In R.E. XIII, the Paitrayanikas are grouped together with the Bhojas instead of with the Rishtika-Rashtrikas. From a comparison of the two statements, it cannot but appear that the Rishtika-Rashtrikas and the Bhojas were two allied peoples, while the Paitrayanikas were just their offshoots or branches.

There must have been some definite reason for specifically mentioning the Rishtika-Rashtrikas and the Bhojas with their offshoots as the typical Aparantas and adding to the list the name of the Andhras and the Parinda-Paradas. According to the later traditional definition in the Puranas and the Kavyamimamsa, the Aparantas were the peoples within the Western division of India. Buddhaghosa records a tradition, according to which the Aparantas were the Indian, peoples that were originally immigrants from the Western subcontinent called Aparagoyana. "Some of the inhabitants came with Mandhata (*i.e.*, in pre-historic time) from Aparagoyana to Jambudvipa and settled down there. The country they colonised was called Aparanta.'

The Khoh Copperplate inscription of Samkshobha connects with the kingdom of Dabhala (Bundelkhand) the eighteen Forest kingdoms (ashtsdasatavi-rajya) 'the tiny kingdoms that must have extended (according to Bhandarkar) from Baghelkhand right up almost to the seacoast of Orissa'. In other words, going by this opinion, we are to locate these Forest kingdoms' in the Vindhya division of India which is said to have been inhabited and ruled, according to the Markandeya Purana, by such peoples as the

Uttamarnas, the Dasarnas, the Bhojas, the Kishkindhyas, the Anupas, the Tundikeras, the Vindhyan Avantis, the Virahotras, the Karushas, the Malajas (Malayas), the Mekalas and the Utkalas.

But to be more precise, the eighteen Forest kingdoms may be taken to correspond to the eighteen Vidyadhara settlements with their sixty towns, associated in the Jaina Jambudiva-pannatti with the Vaitadhya or Vindhya range. It was undoubtedly with reference to this very region that the Jataka tradition speaks of the sixteen Bhoja rulers (Bhojaputta) and the Hathigumpha inscription of Kharavela of the Vidyadhara settlements (Vijadharadhivasam) ruled by the Rathikas and the Bhojakas enjoying varying degrees of sovereignty. Many at least of the Forest kingdoms, mentioned in Sumudragupta's Allahabad Stone-pillar inscription, if not all of them, may be confidently referred to this very region.

If so, the total of eighteen Forest kingdoms or Vidyadhara settlements, ruled by the Rashtrikas and the Bhojakas, may easily be supposed to have been made up of the sixteen territories ruled by the sixteen Bhojaputras, *i.e.*, by the Paitrayanikas and the two parent states of the Rishtika Rashtrikas and the Bhojas, which is to say, of the Bhojapitaras. The parent state of the Rishtika-Rashtrikas was Rishtika (Pali Atthaka), and that of the Bhojas Vidarbha, both of these territories being placed in the Ramayana within the belt of the Vindhya the Narmada, the Godavari and the Krishna (Krishnavena), along with Avravanti, Avanti, Mahishika, Matsya and Kalinga.

Once King Bhimaratha of Vidarbha, King Arshtaka of Rishtaka (Atthaka) and King Kalinga of Kalinga acknowledged the suzerainty of King Dandakya of Dandaki, known as Dandakya Bhoja in the Arthasastra. The capital of Dandaka was Kumbhavati according to the Sarabhanga Jataka, Madhumanta according to the Ramayana, and Nasika according to the Mahavastu. The tradition in the Sarabhanga Jataka and the Arthasastra aver that King Dandakya perished with his kingdom for a heinous sin committed by him. It is also important to note that the Markandeya Purana, the Sarabhanga Jataka and both the Sanskrit Epics speak of two Avantis, the Purana of the Vindhyan Avanti and the Aparanta Avanti, the Ramayana of Avravanti and Avanti, the Jataka of the kingdom of Canda Pradyota and Avanti, and the

Great Epic of the Vinda Avanti and the Anuvinda (Upavinda) Avanti. The Purana distinction between the Vindhyan and Aparanta Avantis is evidently the same as that made in the Junagarh Rock inscription of Rudradaman I between the Purvakara and Aparakara Avantis. The Great Epic places the two kingdoms of Avanti in the Narmada region.

These facts go to locate the parent states of the Rishtika-Rashtrikas and the Bhojas to the south of the two kingdoms of Avanti, and, for the matter of that, to the south of the river Tapi or Tapti. Modern Berar preserves the reduced identity of the ancient territory of Vidarbha, the parent state of the Bhojas. The Hathigumpha inscription refers to the territory of a Shatakarni which lay on the west side of Kalinga. It alludes also to the Vidyadhara tracts, no doubt, in the Vindhya region, which were being ruled by the Rashtrikas and the Bhojakas. It is clearly suggested that Shatakarni's dominions included the town of Asika (Rishika) on the river Kanhapemna (Krishnavena, i.e., Krishna). This river appears to be no other than the Karavena mentioned in the Nasik cave inscription of the time of Nahapana and what is wrongly called Krishnavarna in the Markandeya Purana, having its origin in the Sahya mountains or Western Ghats. According to the Sankhapala Jataka, the river Kannapenna flowed through the Mahimsakarattha.

In the Mahabharata, VI. 9.69, the Mahishakas are associated with the Vanavasikas, the Karnatakas, the Vikalpas and the Mushakas. In both the Mahabharata and the Ramayana Rishika (Rishtika) is associated with Vidarbha (Berar) and distinguished from Mahishaka. In the Markandeya Purana, on the other hand, Rishika-Rishtika is replaced by Maharashtra, while in the Pali Chronicles Mahimsaka (Mahisaka) appears just as another name of Mahisamandala, which may be identified with the whole or northern portion of the state of Mysore.

The relative geographical positions of Rishika-Rishtika, Vidarbha and Avanti may be inferred from the list of places included in the dominions of Gautamiputra Shatakarni, as well as from the Pali list of halting places on the Southern Road. In the Nasik Cave inscription of Vasishthiputra Pulumayi, Rishika (Asika, Patanjali's Arshika), Ashvaka, Mulaka, Surashtra and

Kukkuraparanta (Pali Sunaparanta) are evidently mentioned as countries that lay to the southwest and west of Vidarbha, which is grouped with Anupa and Akaravanti. A similar territorial environment of Akaravanti is suggested also in the Junagarh Rock inscription of Rudradaman I, though to the exclusion of Rishika, Ashvaka, Mulaka and Vidarbha. Ashvaka and Mulaka were the two territories situated, according to Pali Canonical tradition, opposite each other, on two sides of the Godavari, while Pratishthana (modern Paithan), the capital of Mulaka, was the southwestern terminus of the Southern Road.

Mulaka on the left bank and Ashvaka on the right bank of the Godavari were evidently situated immediately to the east of Panchavati and Nasika, both of which were presumably included in the kingdom of Dandaka. This may enable us to locate Rishtika-Rashtrika or Maharashtra to the west of Ashvaka, to the south of Dandaka and to the east of Sunaparanta, and broadly in the region between the Godavari and the Krishna. Below Sunaparanta containing the Sopara set of Ashoka's Rock Edicts lay the coastal territory of Karnata to the east of which and to the south of Rishtika was the territory of the Mahishakas who are grouped together with the Vanavasikas and the Mushakas.

It may be supposed that Vanavasi lay in between Maharashtra in the north and Mahishaka in the south and extended from North Kanara as far east as to include in it the southwestern corner of Hyderabad containing two copies of Ashoka's M.R.E. at the town of Kopbal, while Mushaka, the territory of the Mushakas grouped in the Epics and the Puranas with the Vanavasikas, may be identified with Maski (Mosage) in the district of Raichur, Hyderabad, within the angle formed by the Krishna and its lower tributary called Tungabhadra.

From the location of the parent states of the Rishtikas and the Bhojas, it is clear that they were situated near about the southwestern end of the Southern Road. But the Rishtika-Rashtrikas and the Bhojas may be regarded as aparantas also in Buddhaghosa's sense, inasmuch as the Great Epic places them as peoples also in Uttarapatha or Punjab proper. The way in which Ashoka introduces them in his edicts leaves no room for doubt that they were not only neighbours as ruling peoples but also offshoots of one and the same people. According to the Aitareya Brahmana, the Bhojas as a people were all Satvats who anointed their rulers from amongst them. In the Puranas, they are described as offshoots of the Yadavas (i.e., Satvatas) of Mathura, and to the same scions of the Yadu family is attributed the foundation of Mahishmati, Avanti and Vidarbha. We learn from both literature and inscriptions that the scions of the ruling races like the Matsyas and the Chedis, too, founded kingdoms in the Vindhya region, even as far east as Odra, Utkala and Kalinga.

The Ristika-Rathikas and Bhojas of R. E. V and R. E. XIII were evidently the predecessors of the Rathikas and Bhojakas of the Hathigumpha inscription as well as of the Maharathis and Mahabhojas of the Satavahana period. The Satavahana inscriptions go to connect the Maharathis with Chitaldrug, Nanaghat, Karle and Kanheri (in North Konkan), the Mahabhojas with the Chutu rulers of Kanheri and Vanavasi, and the Mahasenapatis with Nasik and Bellary.

In the Yerragudi copy of M.R.E. we have mention of the Rathikas in addition to the Janapadas, to all of whom the Rajjuka in charge of the administrative area was to proclaim Ashoka's message of piety. These Rathikas were not probably to be mistaken for the semi-independent Ristika-Rathikas of R.E. V, their position being similar to, if not the same as, that of the Rashtriya Vaishya in Surashtra of Chandragupta Maurya's time.

Andhras and Parindas: In view of the fact that the Andhras are associated with the Parinda-Paradas and other Westerns in R. E. XIII, it must be presumed that-their territories lay near about the southwestern terminus of the Southern Road, i.e., Ujjaini, Mahishmati on the Narmada, or Pratishthana on the Upper Godavari. According to the Suttanipata, close to Pratishthana were the territories of the Assakas and the Mulakas, and according to its commentary, both Asmaka (Ashvaka) and Mulaka were Andhra territories. Mulaka lay to the north of Asmaka, which is to say, on the left bank of the Godavari. Hence it is easy to think with Bhandarkar that Mulaka abutted on the territory of Avanti. It is quite possible that the Asmakas or Asvakas had their settlement, as Raychaudhary suggests, also in the Uttarapatha or North-Western division and were no other people than those who were known to the Greek writers as the Assakenoi, and this may be taken to corroborate the truth in the tradition recorded by Buddhaghosa that the Aparantas were the peoples or races who had originally migrated into India from the Aparagoyana or Western subcontinent of Asia.

The Mahabharata, however, speaks of several Andhra peoples (Andhras cha bahavah). With Vincent Smith the Andhras were 'a Dravidian people now represented by the large population speaking the Telugu language, who occupied the deltas of the Godavari and the Krishna. But Srinivas Iyengar would seem to be more in the right in suggesting that 'the Andhras were originally a Vindhyan tribe and that the extension of Andhra power was from the west to the east down the Godavari and Krishna valleys.' 'The Serivanija Jataka locates Andhrapura, *i.e.*, the capital of the Andhras, on the river Telavaha which Bhandarkar identifies with the modern Tel or Telingiri and Raychaudhary inclines to treat as another name of the Tungabhadra-Krishna. Raychaudhary construes the evidence of the Mayidavolu plates of the early Pallava ruler Shivaskandavarman as implying that 'the Andhra country (Andhrapatha) embraced the Krishna district and had its centre at Dhannakada or Bezvada.'

In Ashoka's own record (R. E. XIII), the Parinda-Paladas are associated with the Andhras. The Kalsi Palada is phonetically the same name as Parada, as pointed out by Raychaudhary. The Markandeya Purana places the Paradas as a barbarous tribe in the Udichya-Uttarapatha or North-Western division along with the Aparantas, Gandharas, Yavanas, Kambojas and the rest. The Harivamsa and the Vayu Purana, too, mention them in a list of barbarous tribes (Mlechchhajatayah) along with the Shakas, Yavanas, Kambojas, Pahlavas, Khasas, Mahishikas, Cholas, Keralas, etc., some of whom belonged to Uttarapatha and some to the Deccan. On the other hand, the Pundras or Paundras and Pulindas are the two tribes who are associated in the Puranas with the Andhras and whose names approached those of Ashoka's Parinda-Paladas. The Markandeya Purana places the Pulindas in the Madhyadesa, the Aparanta as well as the Dakshinatya division. They are distinguished in the Matsya Purana from the Paundra (Pundras of the Ramayana). In this Purana the Paundras are associated with the Vaidisas, Mekalas and Gaunardas, and the Pulindas (Kulindas) with the Andhras, Shakas, Chulikas and Yavanas.

It need not worry us that the Paradas as a tribe who are placed in the North-Western division should be associated in Ashoka's R. E. XIII with the Andhras who were a Vindhyan as well as a Deccan people. Like the Chulikas, Mushikas and others, the Parinda-Paradas had their original settlement in Uttarapatha.

The Mahabharata speaks of the pulindas, Kulindas and Kaladas and places them all in South India, the Pulindas in association with the Vindhya Chulikas, and the Kulindas with the Kaladas. Here the Kulindas and the Kaladas are the same peoples as the Pulindas and the Paladas respectively, cf. Sindhu-Pulindakah and Sindhu-Kulindakah (Padma Purana, Bhugolavarnanam), Kakudha Katyayana, Pali Pakudha Kachchayana. One may be tempted to connect the Paradas with the river Parada mentioned in the Nasik cave inscription of the time of Nahapana.

From these facts, it may be inferred that Ashoka's Parinda-Paradas were no other ruling tribes than Paundra-Pulindas and Kulinda-Kaladas who were closely allied and had territories spread over a large area near about the territories of the Rishtika-Rashtrikas, the Bhojas and their offshoots.

Other Aparantas: The significant expression, 'other Aparantas', which occurs in E.E. V as an appendage to Ashoka's statement concerning the Ristika-Petenikas has, I think, been sufficiently explained in the foregoing account of the Ristika-Petenikas, the Bhoja Petenikas and the Amdhra Parimdas. The Rishtikas and the Bhojas with their offshoots, the Paitrayanikas, have been taken to represent the eighteen Forest-kingdoms in the Vindhyan region, and in Ashoka's time the semi-independent states near about the southwestern extension of the Southern Road between the Yamuna and the Godavari, and within the mountain belt of the Vindhya, the Riksha, the Pariyatra and the Sahya. The various peoples that are placed in this region in the Epics and the Puranas to the exclusion of those included in the dominions under Ashoka's direct rule came within the definition of other Aparantas.

Atavis: The position of the Atavis in relation to these Aparantas needs further orientation. In R E. XIII the Atavis are mentioned apart from the peoples that are introduced in R.E.V as Aparantas, while we have been inclined so far to identify the Rishtikas, the Bhojakas, and the Paitrayanikas with the ruling peoples of the eighteen forest territories or Vidyadhara settlements in the Vindhya region. Bhandarkar, too, inclines to identify the Atavis mentioned in E.E. XIII with the semi-independent Atavikas or Atavyas of the inscription of Samkshobha from Central India. How far is it correct to do so?

The Markandeya Purana mentions the territory of the Atavyas side by side with those of the Sabaras, the Pulindas, the Vindhyamuliyas, the Dandakas, the Vaidarbhas, the Paurikas, the Maulikas, the Asmakas (Asvakas), the Bhogavardhanas and the Andhras, and places all of them in Dakshinapatha. The Great Epic, II. N31. 2-15, seems to have counted the rulers of Matsya, Aparamatsya, Adhiraja, Nishada-land, Gosringa hill, Tarasa, Srenimanta, Nararashtra, Kuntibhoja, Charmanvatikula, Shaka, Paraseka, Vindavanti, Anuvind-avanti, Bhojakata, Venvatata, Kantaraka, Natakeya, Herambaka, Marudha, Ramyagrama, Nachina, Vata and Pulinda among the Atavikas of the Vindhya region, including, no doubt, the region covered by the Pariyatra branch of the Vindhya range of hills.

The Great Epic expression. Atavikan sarvan, is paralleled by sarvatavikarajyasya in Samudragupta's Allahabad Stone-pillar inscription. The Nasik Cave inscription of Vasishthiputra Pulumayi, too, speaks of the rulers of the hill tracts of the Vindhya, the Rikshavat, the Pariyatra, the Sahya (Western Ghats), the Krishnagiri (Kanheri), the Mahendra (Eastern Ghats), the Malaya and other ranges in the Western, Central and South India, But by the Atavis of R.E. XIII we may not, I think, understand, the rulers or ruling races of the hill tracts or forest kingdoms of the Vindhya region only. "The Atavis in the sense -Of jungle tracts, inhabited by semi-independent aboriginal tribes or used as hiding places by the gangs of thieves, were not confined to any particular place. The Jatakas clearly show that Atavis in this sense existed in each kingdom, and that the ruler of each kingdom had to reckon with the permanent or temporary dwellers of these areas. The Arthashastra speaks of a special class of officers called Atavipalas, and the Jatakas of the Atavirakkhikas.

Yaunas, Kambojas and Gandharas: As for the Yaunas, the Kambojas and the Gandharas, they are mentioned in R.E.V. as typical Aparantas, whose semi-independent tribal states were within Ashoka's Empire. E. E. XIII adds to this list the name of the Nabhakas (Sanskrit–Nabhagas) and the Nabhapamktis who were obviously the representative ruling races of the Haimavata region.

It must be also with reference to the western or northwestern end of the Uttarapatha or Northwestern Road that Ashoka represented the Yaunas, Kambojas, Gandharas, Nabhakas, Nabhapamktis and others as Aparantas or Westerns, inasmuch as their territories were situated near about it.

As regards the Yaunas, the Kambojas and the Gandharas, their semi-independent territories in Ashoka's time were situated in the Uttarapatha proper which is now covered by the North-Western Frontier Province.

The Pali texts mention Kashmira with Gandhara, otherwise called Gandharva-vishaya in the Ramayana. In one of the Jatakas, the Jataka No. 406, as pointed out by Raychaudhary, Kasmira is included in the kingdom of Gandhara. Some of the Jatakas represent Kasmira and Gandhara as two countries ruled by one King. Hekaitos of Miletos (549-486 BC) "refers to Kaspapyros (Kasyapapura, *i.e.*, Kashmir) as a Gandaric (Gandhara) city." We have got to see if the same was the state of things also in Ashoka's time.

The Gandharas or Gandharvas of Uttarapatha founded their territories on both sides of the Indus.The principal city of their trans-Indus territories was Pushkaravati or Utpalavati, which is now "represented by the modern Prang and Charsadda, 17 miles N. E. of Peshawar, on the Swat river." Takshashila (modern Taxila), which is now situated in the Rawalpindi district of the province of the Punjab, was the main city of the hinter-Indus territory of the Gandharas. Hiuen Tsang locates the kingdom of Gandhara, with Purushapura (Peshawar) as its capital, between the Sulaiman range and the Indus, the latter being mentioned as its eastern boundary.

In Ashoka's time, however, the major portion, if not the whole, of the trans-Indus territory of the Gandharas and the southern portion of their hinter-Indus territory were under his direct rule, and only the northern portion of both above Shahbazgarhi and Mansehra formed the semi-independent tribal state of the Gandharas.

In the Great Epic, the Yaunas, Kambojas and Gandharas are counted among the typical peoples of Uttarapatha, precisely as in Ashoka's R.E.V they figure as the typical Aparantas. In the Pali Assalayana Sutra, the Yavanas and Kambojas are represented as typical peoples of the North-West frontier countries. Yavana, Yauna or Yavana is the only name whereby all Greeks, whether Macedonian, pre-Macedonian or post Macedonian, were known to the Indians. But this name was obviously derived from Ionia, and the first Greeks known to the Persians and Indians were all, *ex hypothesi,* Ionians. It is, therefore, most probable, as opined by Jayaswal and others, that there was a pre-Alexandrian Ionian Greek settlement on the banks of the river Kabul, notably at Nysa.

As regards the Kambojas or Kambhojas, the Arthashastra classes them with the Saurashtras in so far as they lived by agriculture, trade and professional fighting. The Great Epic speaks of the Kambojas and Paramakambojas, just as the Mahaniddesa does of Yavana and Paramayona. The Kambojas are grouped together with the Daradas (Dards) and the Paramakambojas with the Lohas and Northern Rishikas. From these facts, it cannot but be inferred that there were two distinct settlements or territories of both the Yaunas and the Kambojas.

The country of the Daradas (Dards) was situated in a valley of the Dari on the right bank of the Upper Indus, watered by the river Darin or Daril and hence may be taken to have extended from Chitral to the Indus. Ptolemy "locates them east of the Lambatai (Lampaka, Langhan) and of Soustane (basin of the Swat river) and to the north of the uppermost course of the Indus." The modern Dardistan still preserves the name of the Dards. The Kamboja territory may thus be located somewhere in this very region between the Darada country on the north and the Yavana territory on the south, on the west side of the Indus.

In connection with the Pandavas' digvijaya, the Great Epic relates that after conquering the Daradas together with the Kambojas, Arjuna in his march towards the north proceeded northeast to conquer the robber tribes (dasyavah) and also the tribes who dwelt in the forest, and thereafter 'the allied forces (sahitan) of the Lohas, Paramakambojas and the Rishikas of the north' (i. e., Paramayishikas).

Professor Jayachandra Vidyalankara identifies the Paramakambojas 'with the Galcha speaking Yaghnobis in the valley of Yaghnob at the head water of the Larafshan river, a tract of country considerably to the north of the Pamirs and separated from them by the hill states subordinate to Bokhara.' He identifies the Rishikas of the north with the Yue-chis and the Kamboja country with Badakshan and the Pamirs. From the fact that the Kambojas and Vahlikas are often associated together in the Great Epic, he is led to think that their countries were conterminous.'

Arguing more forcibly the case made out by Vidyalamkara, Dr. Moti Chandra seeks to establish that the Lohas, Paramakambojas, Northern Rishikas and robber tribes must have been settled in the country which is now represented by the Tadzhik Soviet Social Republic which till recently was divided in the Russian Wakhan, Shignan, Roshan and Darwanz. It is clear even from Kalhana's description of Muktapida's northern campaign that the Kambojas, Tukharas, Bhauttas and Daradas were neighbours. If the Bhauttas be rightly relegated to Baltistan and Bolor and the Darads to Dardistan, the Kambojas can only be placed in Kafiristan, Balkh-Badakshan and the Pamirs. Dvaraka mentioned as the capital of the Kambojas in the Petavattu-Commentary need not create any prejudice against their being a people in the northwest of India, here Dvaraka being no other place than what is known in Persian as Darwaz in the north of Badakshan. The place which Ptolemy locates to the south of the Oxus under the name of Tambyzoi is identified by Sylvain Levi with Kamboja on the ground that Tambyzoi is only a Greek transliteration of the Austro-Asiatic spelling of Kamboja. In the time of the Muslim geographer Idrisi Badakshan bordered on Qanauj (i.e., Kamboja), then a dependency of India. Apollodorus mentions the Asii, Pasiani, Tochari and Sacarauli as the four nomad tribes who conquered Bactria. The Torogus source attributes the conquest to two peoples called Asiani and Saraucae. Here the Asii or Asiani correspond with Chang Kien's Yue-chi, and Asiani and Pasiani are but Iranian forms of the Indo-Aryan Asika-Rishika and Paramarshika.

There being nothing until now to show that there was any pre-Alexandrian Yavana territory on the east side of the Indus, it is conceivable that the distinction aimed at was one between the trans-Kabul Yavana territory and that between the Kabul river and the Upper Indus. It is quite possible that by the name Paramayona were meant the Yavana territories in Asia Minor which find mention in the Achaemenian inscriptions. Alexander's invasion of India was followed, however, by 'the establishment of a number of Yavana settlements in the Uttarapatha', *e.g.*, the city of Alexandria (modern Charikar or Opian) in Paropanisadae i.e., the Kabul region, Boukhepala on the spot where Alexander began to cross the Jhelam, Nikaia, where the battle with Poros took place, Alexandria at the confluence of the Chinab and the Indus, and the Sogdian Alexandria below the confluence of the Punjab rivers.

It is difficult, however, to say that by the Yavanas in Ashoka's edicts were meant the Yavanas other than the pre-Alexandrian Ionian colonists or 'Perso Greeks' who were associated with the Kambojas and Gandharas and other semi-independent peoples of the Uttarapatha within Ashoka's Empire.

The close association of the Yaunas or Yavanas with such other peoples of North-Western India as the Kambojas, Gandharas, Shakas, Madras, Kaikeyas, Sindhus and Sauviras is certain. The fact is well attested by the Epics and Puranas as well as the edicts of Ashoka, They passed as most esteemed of foreigners, though according to some authorities they were regarded as born of Sudra females by Kshatriya males. In Panini's time Yavanani was the only feminine form of Yavana, while Katyayana, Patanjali and other later grammarians found it necessary to recognise Yavani as another form, and to restrict the use of Panini's form to the writing of the Greeks. It will be unhistorical to father this difference between the two forms on Panini when evidently he was acquainted with only one form. The Mahavastu rightly represents the Yaunas as a ruling people with a republican form of government. The existence of a pre-Alexandrian Ionian colony somewhere on the bank of the river Kophen, Kubha or Kabul may be taken for granted. The pre-Macedonian Greek settlers in the borderland of Uttarapatha were known to Megasthenes and other Greek writers as Nysaioi (Nyseans) evidently for the reason that they planted their colony in the district of Nysaia named after

Mount Nysa with Nysa as its principal city. The location given of this city goes to show that it lay close to and was built on the lower slopes of the mountain which is called Meros (Meru, Pali Neru) and which, according to the legend in the Great Epic and the Puranas, was one of the four mountains that surrounded Mt. Sumeru, say Pamir Knot. Identifying Mt. Meros (the name meaning 'thigh' to the Greeks) with the Sulaiman range, and Mt. Nysa with a spur of the same, one may get very near to the site of the hill state formed by these earliest known Greek colonists on the northwestern confines of India. Holdich is inclined to locate the site of Nysa in the lower spurs and valleys of Kohi-i-Mor, while Bhandarkar would have us place it somewhere between the river *Kophen (Kabul) and the Indus. According to M. de St. Martin, the* existing village of Nysatta 'near the northern *bank of the river of* Kabul at less than two leagues below Hashtnagar preserves the traces of the name of Nysa, the place which 'ought to be of Median or Persian foundation, since the nomenclature is Iranian, the name of Nysa or Nisaya which figures in the cosmographic geography of the Zendavesta being one which is far-spread in the countries of Iran,' Ivy and the vine were known to have grown on Mt. Meros or Meron, whence Nysaia became known as a vine-growing country.

In support of his view that the Yavanas of E. E. XIII 'settled in large numbers in some outlying province of India long before Alexander' 'outside the kingdom of Antiochus Theos' and 'in Ashoka's Empire in a territory adjoining Gandhara but outside India,' Bhandarkar cites the evidence of the coins resembling those of the earliest type of Athens which are known to have been collected from the northwest frontiers of India.

The Nysians were known to have dressed themselves in muslin, worn the turban, and arrayed themselves in garments dyed of bright colours. They marched to battle with drums and cymbals. In them were found by the Macedonians certain customs and traits of their own. Three hundred of them joined the army of Alexander on their mountain horses and "followed him to battle in the plains of the Punjab.

There is no wonder that the territory of the takabhara (cap-wearer?) Yaunas is mentioned immediately after Skudra in the Achaemenian inscriptions or that, according to the legend recorded by Strabo, the Nysians recognised the Oxydrakai (Kshudrakas) who were evidently their neighbours as equally being the descendants of Dionysos. The admixture of blood through intermarriage between these two peoples may have been the fact behind the Brahmanical castigation of the Yavanas as born of the Shudra mothers by the warrior fathers.

The name of Kamboja or Kambhoja is older in Indian literature than that of Yauna or Yavana. The Vamsa Brahmana list includes *the name of a Vedic teacher called Kamboja Aupamanyava. According to Yaska's Nirukta, the Kambojas spoke a dialect in which* the original sense of an ancient verb, savati, was retained while it was lost among other sections of the Indian people. Yaska's remarks have led Grierson to think that 'they either spoke Sanskrit with an infusion of Iranian words to which they gave Indian inflexions, or else spoke a language partly Indo-Aryan and partly Iranian'. The verb savati is in Grierson's opinion an Iranian and not a Sanskrit word.

Yaska indulged only in a folk-etymology when he sought to account for the name of Kamboja or Kambhoja by taking Kam to be an abbreviation of *kambala,* meaning 'blanket', which is to say, of kamaniya, meaning 'a lovable thing'. Thus the Kambojas were Kambala Bhojas or Kamaniya Bhojas, the blanket being treated as a lovable thing. Their country was noted undoubtedly for 'many of the best kinds of skins, wollen blankets, blankets made of the fur of animals', but that does not mean that for this very reason the people became known as Kambojas or Kambhojas and their country as Kamboja or Kambhoja.

The Ganapatha on Panini's rule, speaks of persons who were shaven-headed like the Kambojas and Yavanas (Kamboja-mundah, Yavana-mundah). This was evidently based upon a legend like one in the Harivamsa purporting to say that King Sagara who was bent upon annihilating the Shakas, Yavanas, Kambojas, Paradas and Pahlavas relented and so he released the first after having half of their head shaved, the second and third after having the whole of their head shaved, the fourth after compelling them to keep their hair dishevelled, and the fifth after compelling them to keep their beards. The tradition gained ground in later Indian literature that these were the distinctive habits of these five peoples.

According to the Pali Assalayana Sutra, the Yavanas, Kambojas and other frontier peoples of the Uttarapatha region had altogether a different social organisation of their own, admitting only of two social grades of masters and slaves, with no impassable barrier placed between them. The Bhuridatta Jataka expressly states that the Kambojas followed a crude religion of their own, contrary to the accepted Ahimsa cult of the Indo-Aryans. Manu classes them as Kshatriyas who became degraded for the disregard of the purificatory rites.

In the Great Epic, the Andhrakas, Guhas, Pulindas, Shabaras, Chuchukas of South India, together with the Madrakas, are all described as inferior types of men, while the Yaunas, Kambojas, Gandharas and Kiratas of the Uttarapatha, together with the Barbaras, are castigated as peoples who lived as criminal tribes with predatory habits like those of hunters and vultures. And from Ashoka's R E. XIII, it is clear that the Yavanas were the last people to welcome the Indo-Aryan faiths propagated by the different sects of the Brahmanas and the Shrarnanas. In Buddhaghosa's opinion the Yavanas, Kambojas and other frontier peoples of the Uttarapatha region were Parasakavanna,, Persian or Persianised in their general habits, customs and usages. The Divyavadana speaks of a popular revolt in the Svasarashtra of Uttarapatha during the closing period of the reign of Bindusara. Raychaudhary inclines to think that probably the Svasas were the same people as the Khasas of Indian Literature.

As for the Achaomenian or Persian influence in this part of India, Raychaudhary rightly points out that Kurush or Cyrus (558-30 B. C), the founder of the Persian Empire, led in vain an expedition against India through Gedrosia (Baluchistan). According to Pliny, however, he was able to destroy the famous city of Kapisa. Arrian tells us that the Astacenians (Arshtakas) and the Assacenian (Asvakas), the two Indian tribes who inhabited the district west of the river Indus as far as the river Cophen (Kabul) and who may be identified with the Kambojas, 'were in ancient times subject to the Assyrians, afterwards to the Medes, and finally they submitted to the Persians, and paid tribute to Cyrus, the son of Cambyses, as ruler of their land.'

During the reign of Darius I (c. 522-486 B. C), the people of Gandhara (Gadara) appear among the subject peoples of the

Persian Empire. "Kshayarsha or Xerxes (486-65 BC), the son and successor of Darius I, maintained his hold on the Indian provinces. In the great army which he led against Hellas both Gandhara and 'India' were represented."

On one occasion, as Strabo tells us, the Hydraces (Kshudrakas) from 'India' (i. *e.*, the Punjab) were summoned by the Persians to serve them as mercenaries. None need be surprised, therefore, that the army of Darius III Codomannus (335 30 BC) included the Indians when he fought a battle with Alexander.

The Yavanas, Kambojas and Gandharas were Aparantas even in Buddhaghosa's sense, *i.e.*, they were peoples who immigrated into India from the trans-Sulaiman and trans-Kabul regions.

Nabhakas and Nabha Lines: Who were Ashoka's other Aparantas who held semi-independent territories in the Uttarapatha? In one context the Great Epic broadly divides the peoples of Uttarapatha into five ruling races, *viz.*, the Yaunas, Kambojas, Gandharas, Kiratas and Barbaras, and in another mentions and locates them in three different orders, *viz.*, those who dwelt in the northern portion of the Punjab proper including the North-Western Frontier Province and the whole of the State of Kashmir and Jammu, those who dwelt in the southern portion of the Punjab proper including the modern province of Sindh, and those who dwelt in the Central and Eastern Himalayan regions extending up to Assam and Manipur.

In the northern part of the Uttarapatha are placed the hill tribes and rulers of the Antargiri, Bahirgiri and Upagiri, the Brihantas of Uluka, the towns of Senabindu, Modapura and Vamadeva, Susaskula, the principal town of the Sudamas, the Ulukas of the north, the country of the Panchaganas, Devaprastha, the Parvatiyas, the capital of the Pauravas, the robber tribes, the Saptagānas, the Kasmirakas, the Lohitas, the Dasamandalas, the Trigartas, Darvas and Kokanadas, the Abhisaras, the people of Uraga (Urasa), Simhapura, the Suhmas and Cholas, the Vahlikas, the Daradas and Kambojas, the robber tribes who dwelt in the northeast, the Lohas, Paramakambojas and Rishikas of the north and the Rishikas proper. Beyond the Shvetaparvata (White range) are placed the Kimpurushas or Kinnaras, Guhyakas or Hatakas adjoining the Manas Sarovar, and war-like peoples of Harivarsha beyond which lay the land of Uttarakuru. And in the southern part of the Uttarapatha division, which lay to the west of the Midland, are located, among others, the Sudras and Abhiras who dwelt on the banks of the Sarasvati, Rohitakas, war-like and frenzied Mayarakas, Sairishikas, Mahehas, Sivis, Trigartas, Ambashthas, Malavas, Panchakarpatas, Madhyamakeyas, Vatadhanas, dwellers of Pushkararanya and other republican tribes who dwelt along the banks of the Lower Indus, Ramathas, Harahunas, Madras of Shakala, Pahlavas, Barbaras, Kiratas, Yavanas and Shakas.

Over and above the Gandharas, Yavanas and Kambojas, the Markandeya Purana refers the following peoples to the Udichya-Uttarapatha division: the vahlikas, Vatadhanas, Abhiras, Kalatoyakas, Aparantas, Sudras, Pahnavas (Pahlavas), Charmakhandikas, Sindhu-Sauviras, Madrakas, Satahradas, Lalitthas, Paradas, Mashikas, Ramathas, Rarkshahantakas, Kaikeyas, Dasamanikas, Barbaras, Angalaukikas, Nichas, Tusharas, pot-bellied Pahlavas, Atreyas, Bharadvajas, Prasthalas, Daserakas, such Kiratas as the Lampakas, Sunakaras, Chulikas, Jahnavas, Apadhas and Alimadras, Tamasas, Hamsamargas, Kasmiras, Tanganas, Chulikas, Hudukas, Urnas and Darvas. The Nirharas, Hamsamargas, Kupathas, Tanganas, Khasas, Kutsas, Pravaranas, Urnas, Darvas, Hudukas, Trigartas, Kiratas and Tamasas are specified as Parvatasrayis (Mountaineers).

The eastern Punjab States of Nabha and Patiala still preserve the name of Ashoka's Nabhakas and Nabhapamktis. The Nabha and Patiala were originally and are even now the Haimavata or Central Himalayan States above Kalsi and below Kasmira. In the Puranas, Nabhi figures as a mythical King of the Central Himalayan kingdom, the name Nabhi denoting the meeting place of the Greater or Eastern and the Lesser or Western extensions of the Himalayas. Raychaudhary inclines to think that the town of Na-pei-kia located by Fa-hien to the southeast of S'ravasti and to the west of Kapilavastu is perhaps reminiscent of the Nabhaka territory. The Central Himalayan States, too, pass as Northern in respect of the Midland.

The Great Epic locates in the eastern extension of the Himalayan range such peoples as the Anartas, Kalukutas, Kulindas and Sumandalas in the Kulinda territory, the dwellers of the island of Shakala, Pragjyotishapura, i.e., the kingdom of Kamarupa under the descendants of Naraka, the tribes who had their settlements in the valleys of the Lauhitya (Brahmaputra), *i. e.*, in the whole of Assam, and the Kiratas and Chinas who lived in the eastern and northeastern confines of Assam, say, in the Chin Hills, Manipur. Bhutan, Sikkim and Nepal as Himalayan territories to the west of Assam and to the north of the Buddhist Midland do not find mention in the Mahabharata. The present inhabitants of Bhutan and Sikkim are, in respect of their dialects and racial traits, Tibetans. The Tarai portion of Nepal, included in the Buddhist Midland and Ashoka's domain proper, was occupied by the Shakyas and Kauliya territories.

As attested by the Classical writers, the Uttarapatha was at the time of Alexander's invasion of India parcelled into innumerable small kingdoms and republics. "The Nandas of Magadha," says Raychaudhary, "do not appear to have made any attempt to subjugate these states of the Uttarapatha (North-West India). The task of reducing them was reserved for a foreign conqueror, viz., Alexander of Macedon he obtained assistance from many important chiefs like Ambhi of Taxila, Sangaeus (Sanjaya) of Pushkaravati, Kophaios or Cophaeus (of the Kabul region), Assagetes (Asvajit), and Sisikottos (Shasigupta) who got as his reward the satrapy of the Assakenians. The only Princes or peoples who thought of combining against the invader were Poros and Abisares, and the Malavas (Malloi), Kshudrakas (Oxydrakai) and the neighbouring autonomous tribes. Even in the latter case personal jealousies prevented any effective results.

Alexander met with stubborn resistance from individual chiefs and clans, notably from Astes (Hasti or Ashtaka), the Aspacians, the Assakenians, the elder Poros, the Kathians, the Malloi, the Oxydrakai, and the Brahmanas of the kingdom of Mousikanos. But all this was of no avail. A disunited people could not long resist the united forces of the Hellenic world led by the greatest captain of ancient Europe. Alexander succeeded in conquering the old Persian provinces of Gandhara and 'India, but was unable to try conclusions with Agrammes, King of the Gangaridao and the Prasii."

In connection with Seleucus Nikator and Chandragupta, Justinus observes: "He (Seleucus Nikator) carried on many wars in the East after the division of the Makedonian kingdom between himself and the other successors of Alexander, first seizing Babylonia, and then reducing Baktriane, his power being increased by his first success.

Thereafter he passed into India, which had, since Alexander's death, killed its governors, thinking thereby to shake off from its neck the yoke of slavery. Sandrokottos had made it free: but when victory was gained he changed the name of freedom to that of bondage for he himself oppressed with servitude the very people which he had rescued from foreign dominion. Sandrokottos, having thus gained the crown, held India at the time when Seleucus was laying the foundations of his future greatness."

Here we are not concerned, however, with all the tribes of the Uttarapatha and Haimavata divisions of Jambudvipa who were reduced to subjection by Chandragupta but with only those who held semi-independent territories within Ashoka's Empire. As far as Ashoka's Rock inscriptions at Shahbazgarhi, Mansehra and Kalsi, his Minor Pillar inscriptions at Nigliva and Lumbini and Pillar inscriptions in the Champaran district indicate, these tribal states were situated in the northern part of the North-West Frontier Province, the State of Kashmir and Jammu, the kingdom of Nepal, Bhutan and Sikkim, and the hilly portion of Assam. The ruling races who dwelt in these regions were typified by the Yavanas, Kambojas, Gandharas, Nabhakas and Nabha lines in the language of Ashoka, and the Yavanas, Kambojas, Gandharas, Kiratas and Barbaras in the language of the Great Epic.

Extent of Empire in the Light of Hiuen Tsang's Testimony: Hiuen Tsang was a personal witness to the stupas, sangharamas and stone-pillars, in short, monuments in several places in India of his time that were popularly known as pious and memorable erections of Ashoka. If his testimony can be relied upon, which I think is of a doubtful certainty, one may presume indeed that the places.

Where these monuments were found *in situ* were all included in Ashoka's Empire.

The Chinese pilgrim saw one stupa known to have been built by Ashoka on Mt. Pi-lo-sa-lo (Pilusara) near the capital of the country of Kapisa, and two stupas near the city of Nagarahara. The country of Kapisa abutted on the north on the Snowy mountains and on the remaining three sides it bordered on the Black ridge (Kalakuta) which is identified with the Hindu Kush. It lay at a distance of about 120 miles west from Lan-po (Lampaka, modern, Langhan, a small country lying along the northern bank of the Kabul river).

Kapisa was included in the Persian Empire, as we noted, during the reign of the first Achaemenian King Cyrus. The site of the town of Nagarahara, the old capital of the Jalalabad district, may be placed 'in the angle formed by the junction of the Sukhar and Kabul rivers, on their right banks,' The fact of inclusion of Kapisa and Nagarahara in Ashoka's Empire is rendered probable by the unambiguous testimony of the Classical writers regarding the inclusion of Paropanasidai, Aria and Arachosia in the Maurya Empire. The same remark holds equally true of the country of Saukuta (Taukuta, modern Sewistan) with Ho-si-na and Ho-sa-la as its two chief towns in which the pilgrim noticed 10 stupas attributed to Ashoka. If Pitasila and Avanda were places beyond the Sulaiman and Kirthar ranges and somewhere in Baluchistan, their inclusion in Ashoka's Empire is completely in accord with the testimony of the Classical writers vouchsafing for the inclusion of Gedrosia in the Maurya Empire.

The city of po-lu-sha (Purushapura, modern Peshawar), near which the pilgrim saw three stupas of Ashoka, and the city of Takshashila, near which stood four stupas, were evidently places in the trans-Indus and hinter-Indus Gandhara territories within Ashoka's domain proper. Similarly Udyana or Oddiyana, the city of Simhapura, the town of Sakala, Chinapati, Kuluta, Satadru and Parvata, which were honoured with the stupas of Ashoka, were all places in the Uttarapatha division within Ashoka's Empire.

As for the country of Kasmira where Ashoka was reputed as a builder of 500 sangharamas and a stupa, its inclusion in Ashoka's Empire is vouchsafed for by the testimony of Kalhana's Rajatarangini crediting Ashoka with the building of the town of Srinagara and speaking of Ashoka's son Jalauka as having been appointed the governor of Kasmira. So far as Ashoka's own records are concerned, the ruling races of Kasmira may come in either as some of the semi-independent Himalayan tribes representing the Nabha-lines *or as representing some of the unnamed Aparantas connected with the Yavanas, Kambojas and Gandharas, and there is no other* way.

Mathura, Thaneshwar, Srughna, Govishana, Ahikshetra (Ahich-chchhatra), Kanauj, Ayodhya, Hayamukha, Prayaga, S'ravasti, Kapilavastu, Ramagrama, Kushinagara, Banaras, Sarnath, Mahasala, Shvetapura, Vaishali, Vriji country, Pataliputra, Rajagriha, Nalanda, Gaya, Bodhgaya, Odra, Kalinga, South Kosala, Andhra, Ajanta, Vallabhi and Ujjaini, the places where the pilgrim came across monuments of Ashoka, need no comment as these were all included in Ashoka's Empire, and many of them even in his domain proper.

As regards Bengal, he saw a stupa of Ashoka near the town of Tamralipti, one near the town of Karnasuvarna, one near the town of Pundravardhana, and one near the capital of Samatata. The pilgrim's itinerary goes to exclude Assam and Nepal proper from Ashoka's Empire.

Chola and Dravida, where, too, the pilgrim saw the stupas of Ashoka, cannot be included in Ashoka's Empire. The pilgrim's Chola and Dravida constituted together the territory of the Cholas, better, the Cholas and Pandyas, which lay outside Ashoka's Empire.

Home Provinces

Precisely how many were the Home provinces we cannot say. The inscriptions of Ashoka, hitherto known, enable us to state that Banaras, Kaushambi, Viratanagara and Srughna were official headquarters of four divisions. One may include in the list of divisional headquarters such towns as Mathura, Gaya, Sahasram, and the town adjoining the rock at Rupnath. The Mahamatras of these divisions might also be regarded as Rajavachanikas, inasmuch as they were all entitled to receive directions from the capital and imperial agents in the provinces to carry out the imperial wishes.

The occurrence of three versions of Ashoka's Rock Edicts at Girnar, which was the ancient capital of Surashtra, at Sopara (Pali Supparaka), which was the capital and main port of Sunaparanta or Kukkuraparanta, and at Yerragudi in the modern district of Karnul gives rise to an administrative problem which is not easy to solve.

As regards Surashtra, we learn from the Junagarh Rock inscriptions of Rudradaman I that near Girinagara (Girnar) was excavated the Sudarshana Tank by Chandragupta Maurya's Vaishya Rashtriya named Pushyagupta. Subsequently, after the reign of Ashoka, the Yavanaraja Tushaspha built embankments and fitted the same with aqueducts. From the new reading amte in lieu of krite, it is evident that Tushaspha, probably a Perso Greek from the North-Western region of India, was a post-Ashokan chieftain or independent ruler of Surashtra as well as that the credit for the embankment of the tank and its aqueducts was due not to Ashoka but to Tushaspha.

If it be true, as supposed, that Rudradaman had a previous record to guide him regarding the origin of the tank and its embankment, etc., there is no escape from the conclusion that the Vaishya Pushyagupta, the excavator of the tank, was a Rashtriya of Chandragupta Maurya. Here the whole political and administrative mystery lies in the word Rashtriya which, according to the Amarakosha, signifies the brother-in-law (wife's brother) of a King. Amarasimha is here guided by the sense in which the word was employed in the Sanskrit dramas. So the commentator Kshirasvami is justified in pointing out that 'except in a play a Rashtriya is a Rashtradhikritra, i.e., an officer appointed to look after or supervise the affairs of a rashtra, state or province.'

With Kielhorn Pushyagupta, the Vaishya Rashtriya of Chandragupta Maurya, was the provincial governor of Surashtra, while with Raychaudhary he was probably 'a sort of Imperial High Commissioner whose position was comparable to that of Lord Cromer in Egypt.' Raychaudhary inclines to identify the Rashtriya with the Rashtrapala whose salary was, according to the Arthashastra, 'equal to that of a Kumara or Prince.'

Raychaudhary's suggestion is evidently based upon the assumption 'that Surashtra was probably an autonomous vassal state, or a confederation of vassal states, and not an imperial province.' The argument which leads him to this conclusion is worth quoting.

"The Kautilya Arthashastra refers to a number of Sanghas, *e.g.*, Kamboja, Surashtra, etc. The Kambojas find prominent mention as a separate unit even in the Thirteenth Rock Edict of Ashoka.

That Surashtra (Kathiawar) was antonomous in the time of Ashoka seems probable from the reference, in R.E.V, to various nations in the western border (aparata) in addition to those named specifically, and from Rudradaman's inscription at Junagadh which refers to the Raja, the Yavana Tushaspha, the contemporary and vassal of Ashoka. The Yavanaraja was probably a Greek chief of the North-West who was appointed one of the Mukhyas or chiefs of the Surashtra Sangha by Ashoka, just as Raja Man Singh of Ambar was appointed Subedar of Bengal by Akbar. His title of Raja probably indicates that he enjoyed a certain amount of autonomy."

This observation, which is otherwise very weighty, is shaky for these two reasons:

- That the verse in the Arthashastra speaking of the Kambhojas, the Surashtras, and the like as the guilds (corporations) of warriors who lived by agriculture, trade and wielding weapons, as distinguished from others who bore the title of Raja, may be taken to have referred to an earlier state of things, and
- That the new reading Ashokasya Mauryasyamte renders the contemporaneity of Ashoka and Tushaspha highly problematical.

As for the official designation of Rashtriya, Buddhaghosa tells us in one context, that during a processional state-drive of King Ajatashatru of Magadha the place assigned to the Rashtriyas (Ratthiyaputta) among his retinue 'was just between the Mahamatras who were nicely dressed and the fittingly dressed Brahmans shouting the joy of victory. The Rashtriyas themselves 'are said to have been gorgeously dressed holding swords and the like in their hands (vividhalankara-mandita nanappakara-avudhahattha).' In another context, he tells us that the King of the Kuru country came to see the Thera Ratthapala (Rashtrapala) with a retinue consisting of the Mahamatras, the Maharashtrikas, and such like persons *of higher* and higher ranks (Mahamatra-Maharatthikadinam vasena uggatuggatam eva parisam gahetva upasankami).

Squaring up the two, we may understand that Rashtriya and Rashtrika are one and the same designation. As for the connection of the Rashtriya or Rashtrika with Rashtrapala, some light may be thrown from the Pali Ratthapala Sutra and Buddhaghosa's comment thereon. From the Sutra itself, it is clear that Rashtrapala was the only son of a Sreshthi of Sthulakoshthita, a fertile and prosperous place in the Kuru country of the Buddha's time. The Sreshthi who was a Vaishya by caste lived in a right royal style. According to Buddhaghosa, the Sreshthin's was a Rashtrapala family (Ratthapala-kula). By definition, a Rashtrapala family was that of which the head was capable of maintaining and restoring the peace and order in a territory or any portion thereof in the event of party factions, capable of coping with or quelling any popular commotion or disturbance.

In the prose portion of the Chulla Sutasoma Jataka, the Commander-in-Chief (Senapati) is placed at the head of the Amatyas (Councillors and Officers), the Chaplain (Purohita) at the head of the Brahmans and the Rashtrika (Ratthika) is placed foremost among the Naigamas (Negama, i.e., the bankers, business magnates and rich landowners who functioned at the same time as Mayors, Sheriffs and Justices of the Peace).

If such were the office and worldly position of a Rashtriya or Rashtrika, there is no wonder that Pushyagupta, a Rashtriya under Chandragupta Maurya, should be described as a Vaishya in Rudradaman's inscription. But the question still is—Was he appointed by Chandragupta to function as the Governor or Imperial High Commissioner of Surashtra?

From Rudradaman's inscription, it is evident, no doubt, that the Yavanaraja Tushaspha became an independent chieftain or ruler of *Surasahtra,* the whole *of Kathiawar,* sometime after Ashoka. The ancient name of Junagarh itself indicates that the city with the hill-fort was built by a Yavana ruler. Rudradaman himself appointed a Pahlava (Parthian or Persian), named Suvisala, son of Kulaipa, as Amatya (Governor) for the whole of Surashtra and Anarta. Can we say that this was in keeping with the Maurya tradition, particularly Ashokan?

The Yerragudi copy of M.R.E. goes to show that the Imperial Agent or Commissioner at the place was a Rajjuka to whom the message to be proclaimed was despatched from the capital with the direction that he should, in his turn, commend it to the people (janapadam) as well as the Rashtrikas (Rathikani cha). If any inference is to be drawn from this, it is that in the janapada under this particular Rajjuka were the Rashtrikas besides the general populace. Whether there were any Mahamatras attached to this Rajjuka or not, this inscription has nothing to say. If the Rajjuka as Regent or Chief Commissioner virtually took the place of the Kumaras in the Home provinces, he, too, must have a body of Mahamatras to assist him in deliberation as well as administration. That which was at the Yerragudi area was *ex hypothesi* in Surashtra (Girnar), Sanaparanta (Sopara), Maharashtra (Kopbal), and Mushaka (Maski).

Broadly speaking, as Regent or Chief Commissioner for a particular janapada (large administrative area, a Home province or Division), the Rajjuka was responsible to the King as the supreme administrative head of a particular imperial territory. He was to carry on the administration of the janapada placed in his charge with the aid of the Mahamatras and the Rashtrikas. He was the official medium through which the King's orders, directions and instructions were to be communicated to the Mahamatras entrusted with the administration of towns or districts within his jurisdiction. The Purushas or Personal Secretaries of the King were the official agents to intimate to the Rajjukas the King's wishes, instructions and policy shaping the method of administration to be faithfully followed by them in order to please the King, to work to his satisfaction.

From this line of argument, it may be concluded that in the four outlying provinces the Rajjuka or his provincial substitute, namely, the Pradesika, was replaced later by a Kumara.

The janapada under a Rajjuka was divided into a certain number of aharas (smaller administrative areas, say, districts defining the jurisdiction of different classes of Mahamatras), with the kotavishayas (fort-areas or fortified districts) here and there (Schism Pillar Edict, Sarnath).

The capital of Ashoka was the seat of the Imperial Government. Here was his permanent residence, and within the palace area were located the Council Hall and the Secretariat. The subordinate officers in the Imperial Secretariat were known as Yuktas, and they were to work under instructions from the Purushas rather than from the Parishad or Council of Ministers which was a deliberative and advisory rather than an executive body. As clearly stated in P. E. IV, the Purushas or Personal Secretaries were intimately acquainted with the King's wishes.

The Purushas, as appears from R.E. VI, were probably also the Dapakas and Sravapakas to whom the King issued his oral orders concerning something to be communicated or publicly announced. They were the personal agents of the King to instruct the subordinate officers in the Imperial Secretariat as to how to codify the orders properly and effectively. The Yuktas in this Secretariat must have been attached also to the various departments of the Mahamatras, better Mantri Mahamatras, the Mantrins of the Arthashastra, to whom the King entrusted all urgent matters. It was the main duty of the Mantri Mahamatras as adepts in the science and art of royal polity to advise the ruler in all important and urgent matters and to take necessary diplomatic or administrative steps to save the state in times of emergency.

Sphere of Influence

Ashoka in his M. E. E., claims that the sphere of his moral and cultural influence was as wide as Jambudvipa. In Jambudvipa he was able to create that noble and unprecedented atmosphere of piety which enabled him to commingle the gods and men or men and the gods and entitled all to the attainment of the grand heaven (vipule svage aradhetave). This was indeed, according to the Pali Apadana and Buddhaghosa's Manorathapurani, the true signification of the honorific Devatanampiyo (Dear to the gods) applicable to a righteous King overlord:

> "In this Gentle Era", said Thera Pilindavachchha, "there was a lord *of men; of great personality was he, a mighty King overlord. In his* identity I became 'dear unto the gods' by establishing the multitude in the moral precepts of conduct and enabling them to get a happy destiny (in heaven, after death)".

Buddhist literature mentions Jambudvipa as one of the four Mahadvipas (Great Islands) of the earth as known to the Indians, the other three islands being Purvavideha, Aparagoyana, and Uttarakuru. Purvavideha is the Eastern subcontinent of Asia which is located to the east of Mount Sumeru, Jambudvipa is the Southern subcontinent which is located to the south, Aparagoyana is the Western sub continent located to the west, and Uttarakuru is the Northern subcontinent which is located to the north of the same mountain. The Mahabharata, too, speaks of the four Mahadvipas and locates them in the same way. It names, however, Purvavideha as Bhadrasva, and Aparagoyana as Ketumala.

In many respects the Great Epic account anticipates the description of Jambudvipa in the Markandeya Purana and other later works, according to which Jambudvipa is Just one of the seven islands or continents, the remaining six of them being situated to the south of Jambudvipa and one on the south side of the ocean forming its southern boundary.

Furthermore, Jambudvipa is said to have consisted of nine varshas or countries,—of seven, according to the Great Epic. Mount Sumeru is placed in the middle of the Ilavritavarsha and between the Gandhamadana range (towards the east), and the Malyavat (towards the west). It is also spoken of as the highest mountain of the earth which is surrounded by the four lesser mountains called Mandara, Merumandara, Suparsva, and Kumuda, and situated on four sides viewed from east to north.

From the east side of the Ilavritavarsha extends the mountain range of Gandhamadana to the east of which lies the country called Bhadrasvavarsha with the ocean as its eastern boundary.

From the west side of the same country extends north and south (east to west, according to the Great Epic) the Malyavat range to join with the Nila and Nishadha ranges. To the west of this range lies the Ketumalavarsha with the ocean as its western limit.

To the north of the Ilavritavarsha extends east and west the Nila or Blue range to the north of which is situated the country called Ramyakvarsha. On the north side of the Ramyak country extends east and west the Shveta or White range beyond which lies the Hiranmayavarsha. Farther north extends east and west the Sringavan range decked with peaks and beyond it is the country called Kuruvarsha (i. e., Uttarakuru) with the ocean as its northern boundary.

On the south side of the Ilavritavarsha extends east and west the Nishadha range to the south of which is Harivarsha. To the south of this country extends east and west the Hemakuta range bstween which and the Himalayan range lies the country called Kimpurusha-varsha. The last-mentioned range forms the northern boundary of Bharatavarsha or India proper with its eight upadvipas or minor islands, which include Tamraparna, i.e., the island of Ceylon.

Thus the Jambudvipa, as described in the Puranas, as also in the Great Epic, may be treated as coextensive at least with the mainland of Asia. The mountain system of Central Asia from the Himalayan range on the south to the Srinagavan (Tienshan) on the north may be rendered intelligible if we assume that the Ilavritavarsha is the highest plateau of the world which covered the whole of Pamir and western part of the tableland of Tibet, and that Mount Sumeru with the four surrounding mountains was situated in the midst of what is now called the Pamir Knot.

The Jaina work Jambudiva-pannatti divides the Himalayas into two ranges, namely the Greater (Mahahimavanta) and the Lesser (Chullahimavanta). The Greater range extends eastward down to sea (i. e., the Bay of Bengal) below the varshadhara mountain, say the Arrakanese Yoma. Similarly the Lesser range extends westward down to the sea (i. e., the Arabian sea) below the varshadhara mountain, say the Sulaiman and Kirthar ranges. Just at the junction of these two ranges it locates the Lotus Lake (Padmahrada) or Manas Sarovar consisting of two juxtaposed lakes, one on the side of the Eastern and the other on that of the Western range.

Eratosthenes and Megasthenes, too, speak of four parts, the largest of which was India. The parts were not, however, of the whole of Asia but those into which Southern Asia was divided. The smallest part was the region which was situated between the Euphrates and the Mediterranean sea. The two remaining parts were separated from the others by the Euphrates and the Indus, and lay, therefore, between these two rivers.

The main point of difference between the Puranic and Buddhist accounts of Jambudvipa lies in the fact that the former includes in Jambudvipa the Bhadrasvavarsha corresponding to the subcontinent of Purvavideha, the Ketumalavarsha corresponding to Aparagoyana, and the Kuruvarsha corresponding to Uttarakuru, while the latter excludes them.

Ashoka's sphere of influence coincided rather with the Jambudvipa as described in the Great Epic and the Puranas than with the Jambudvipa of Pali literature. It comprised the five Mediterranean countries in the west, the territories of the Cholas, Pandyas, Satiyaputras, Keralaputras and Tamraparnyas in the south, and Southern Asia around India.

In his R.E. XIII, Ashoka mentions 600 yojanas as the extent of the regions outside his Empire where he was able to achieve an effective conquest by piety. In this outermost zone of the sphere of piety he was able to create are located the territories of the five Greek rulers called Amtiyoka, Tulamaya, Amtekini, Maga and Alikasudara, and in the south, those of the Cholas, Pandyas, Satiyaputras, Keralaputras and Tamraparnyas.

Among his Greek contemporaries and allies, Amtiyoka is to be identified with Antiochus II Theos, King of Syria and Western Asia, and not with his father Antiochus I Soter, son and successor of Seleucus Nikator. Thus he was the nearest Greek 'frontager' of Ashoka. The nearest southern Greek 'frontager' of Antiochus I and Antiochus II was Tulamaya identified with Ptolemy II Philadelphus, King of Egypt. The nearest western Greek 'frontager' of Antiochus II was Amtikini, i. e., Antigonas Gonatas, King of Macedonia. The nearest western Greek 'frontager' of Ptolemy II Philadelphus was Magas, half-brother of Ptolemy and King of Cyrene in North Africa. The nearest western Greek 'frontager' of Antigonas Gonatas was Alikasudara better identified with Alexander of Epirus. 'Evidently the five Greek potentates were the direct descendants and successors of Alexander the Great's generals and successors and their territories were but once component parts of the Greek Empire left behind by the great Macedonian conqueror.' Upon the whole, all of them represented but the contemporary Mediterranean States and Powers. As regards the Asiatic dominion of Antiochus II Theos, it abutted on the northwest frontier of Ashoka's Empire.

The Chola territory lay between that of the Andhras on the north and that of the Pandyas on the south, and extended along the entire seacoast of Kolapattana or Coromondel, say roughly between the river northern Pennar and Kaveri. Buddhadatta's description leaves no room for doubt that in the south the Chola kingdom comprised the lower Kaveri valley, with Uragapura (modern Uraiur in Trichinopoly) as its capital and Kaveripattana (modern Pugar) as its inland river-port. Kanchipura (modern Conjeeveram) was once its capital as attested by the Skanda Purana and Hiuen Tsang. The journey of Buddhaghosa from Kanchipura to Anuradhapura lay obviously via Madhura (Madoura). The inhabitants of the Chola country are known in the Chronicles of Ceylon as Damilas (Dravidas). According to Raychaudhary, the Chola country "was drained by the river Kaveri and comprised the districts of Trichinopoly and Tanjore", which, however, leaves the question of its northern limit open.

The Pandya territory in South India corresponded, according to Raychaudhary, "to the Madura, Ramnad and Tinnevelly districts and perhaps the southern portion of the Travancore State, and had its capitals at Kalkai and Madura." But it would seem that there was a separate Tamraparnya territory in the southernmost part of the Deccan below those of the Pandyas on the east and the Keralaputras on the west,— a fact which is well attested by Hiuen Tsang. In the days of Ptolemy there were in the southern part of South India the kingdom of Karoura ruled by Kerobothros (Keralaputras), the kingdom of the Aioi (capital Kottiara) in South Travancore, the kingdom of Madoura (Madura) ruled by Pandion (Pandyas) and above that the kingdom of the Batoi (capital Nikama), that of Orthoura ruled by Sornagas (Chola-Nagas) and that of Sora (Chola) ruled by Arkatos.

Evidently the territories of the Satiyaputras and the Keralaputras, who are mentioned as peoples in the Mansehra version of R. E. II, lay to the west of those of the Cholas and the Pandyas and extended along the western seacoast of South India. The name of Satiyaputra or Satiyaputras is nowhere met with in Indian literature. The geographical name approaching Satiyaputra is Seriyaputa, which finds mention in one of the Barhut inscriptions. There still exists a difference of opinion as to the relative positions of the Satiyaputra and Keralaputra territories. From the manner in which Ashoka has mentioned them, it follows that the Satiyaputras had their territory above that of the Keralaputras. "Satiyaputra must have stood north of Keralaputra on the western side of the far south of South India, to the south of own vijita

From the location of Ashoka's Rock and Minor Rock Edicts, it may be inferred that the country of Satiyaputta or Satiyaputra lay along the western coast of South India to the south of Sopara (ancient Supparaka, Shurparaka) and the Chitaldrug district of Mysore, to the west of Mysore and to the north of Keralaputra." "Still the best suggestion on this point is one from R. G. Bhandarkar, drawing attention to the fact that along the westernmost portion of the Deccan tableland we have Maratha, Kayastha and Brahmin families, bearing the surname 'Satpute' which cannot but be treated as a modern transformation of Ashoka's Satiyaputa."

The Girnar variant Ketala for Kerala of other versions and absence of the variant Sacha for Satiya render dubious the equation of Satiya with Satya and all the identifications of Satiyaputra on that basis.

The Tambapamni of R. E. II may indeed be taken to stand both for the river Tamraparni and for the Tamraparnis as a people and their territory. But the Tambapamniya of R. E. XIII stand certainly for the Tamraparnyas as a people and their territory. And all that R. E. XIII contains is nothing but a restatement of what Ashoka has said in R. E. II. The question still is—where to place the Tamraparnyas and their territory?

There are apparently these three arguments that may be put forward in favour of the second view:

- That the Pali Chronicles and the Samantapasadika speak of the friendly relationship which existed between Ashoka and his contemporary, King Devanampriya Tissa of Ceylon, and give a graphic account of the conversion of Ceylon to Buddhism by the mission despatched during the reign of Ashoka.
- That Indian literature generally speaks neither of an Indian country called Tamraparni nor of a people known by the name of Tamraparnyas.
- That Ceylon was really known to Megasthenes and other Greek writers as Taprobane.

The fact which goes against it is that wherever by Tambapamni or Tamraparni is meant Ceylon, the word dipa (dvipa) or 'island' is associated with it. Megasthenes and other Classical writers speak of the sea-girt island of Taprobane.

Ceylon is called the island of Tamraparna or Tamravarna in the Great Epic and the Puranas. But as regards the Ramayana, Ceylon is known by the name of Parasamudra. The name Parasamudra (Greek, Palaesimundu) is met with also in the Arthashastra. In both the Ramayana and the Arthashastra, as we saw, Pandyakapata (kavata) is associated with Tamraparni. In both, Tamraparni denotes obviously a South Indian river and by implication only, a riverine region. This region is represented now- a-days by Tinnevelly.

In R. E. XIII the Tamraparnyas are placed below the territories of the Cholas and the Pandyas, and in R. E. II, below those of the Cholas, the Pandyas, the Satiyaputras and the Keralaputras.

The Markandeya Purana names four rivers, the Kritamala, the Tamraparni, the Pushyaja and Utpalavati that rise from the Malaya mountain. The Kritamala, which flows past Madoura, is identified with the Vaigai and the Tamraparni with "what is locally called Tambravari or with the combined stream of the latter and Chittar." The Tamraparni is described in the Ramayana as a great river, which goes to meet and dive into the sea (samudram avagahate), containing the row of islands covered with the beautiful sandal woods. It is connected, precisely as in the Arthashastra, with Pandyakapata noted for its gems and pearls. The Malaya mountain to which *the Markandeya* Purana traces *the source of the Kritamala, Tamraparni* and other rivers, is singled out in the Ramayana as the rocky landmark of the Tamraparni region, precisely as in the Mahabharata the mountain finds mention as the rocky landmark of Tamraparna. Malaya was the name of a mountainous district in South India, and also that of a mountainous part of Ceylon.

The Pali Chronicles apply the names Lanka, Sihala and Tambapanni to one and the same country and island of Ceylon. At the same time the Mahavamsa refers to Tambapanni as a district in Lanka, with a town of the same name as its capital, which is distinguished from Anuradhapura. The Sirisavatthu (Srisavastu), evidently a seaport, described as a Yaksha capital, is located in Ceylon. Vijaya, the eponymous Indian coloniser of this island, is said to have returned therefrom to Tambapanni and entered into a matrimonial alliance with the Pandu (Pandya) King of South India whose capital was South Madhura, i.e. Madoura. The Damila (Dravida) hordes under Elara who conquered Ceylon for the time being at least, are said to have come across from the Chola country.

As Megasthenes heard, Taprobane was a large island in the great sea, which was 'separated from the mainland by a river' and was 'more productive of gold and large pearls than India.' Its inhabitants were called Pelesimundu (Parasamudra).

In the Arthashastra, on the other hand, the Parasamudraka is distinguished from the Tamraparnika and Pandyakavataka regions, which are associated together in the Ramayana. It is also important to note that the Ramayana tradition speaks of dvipa (island or islands) in the river Tamraparni, covered by beautiful sandal woods (chanda-navanaschitraih prachchhanna-dvipa dharini). Thus there was at least one Tamraparni-dvipa in South India below the Pandya country, *as there was one in Lanka on the other side of the sea. And it is not unlikely that the* Pandyakapata is the modern Aruppakottai in the Ramnad district on the right bank of the river Vaigai. From these facts, one cannot but be led to think that Tamraparni (better Tamravarni from having copper coloured sand-beaches), which was originally a riverine region in the southernmost part of South India below the Pandya territory, came to denote afterwards, probably in about the Maurya time, also the northwestern seacoast region of Ceylon between the Nagadipa and the river Kalyani, and ultimately the island of Ceylon. This riverine region of South India must have the river valleys and deltas and entire sea coast areas below Pandya and included also the entire area occupied by the Tinnevelly district.

The location of Ashoka's Tamraparni as the land of the Tamraparnyas may now be placed on a solid foundation. In the Nagarjunikonda inscription, marked F by Dr. Vogel, Tambapamna (Tamraparna) is clearly distinguished from Tambapamni-dvipa. The Great Epic distinctly speaks of Tamraparni as a country south of Pandya, which in some contexts is included in Dravida, and locates in it the Gokarnatirtha and the hermitages of Agastya and his disciple. This Tamraparni with Mt. Vaidurya as its rocky landmark corresponds with Hiuen Tsang's country of Mo-lo kiu-ch'a (Malaya-kuta), with Mt. Po-ta-la-kia (Vaiduryaka) as its rocky landmark and placed south of Dravida.

The extension of Ashoka's sphere of influence, south of the Krishna-Tungabhadra, even south of Sopara and the river Pennar, thus made out, would seem to be substantially in agreement with the tradition recorded by Mamulanar, an ancient Tamil author, and other Tamil writers like Paranar and Kallil Attiraiyanar, regarding the 'Vimba Moriyar' ('Maurya upstarts') and their invasion of South India. "The invaders advanced from the Konkan, passing the hills Elilmalai, about sixteen miles north of Cannanore, and entered the Kongu (Coimbatore) district, ultimately going as far as the Podiyil Hill (in the Tinnevelly District)."

The only point needing further orientation is whether or no, the list of Antas or Pratyantas given by Ashoka in his R. E. II and R. E. XIII is exhaustive or typical only. From his mode of enumeration of the Antas or Pratyantas in R.E. II, it cannot but appear that the list produced was intended to be typical only, and not an exhaustive one.

In Pali literature the word pachchanta (pratyanta) is employed in a twofold sense: (1) to denote the outermost region of a principality, the frontier of a dominion forming nevertheless the hinterland, and (2) to denote the outlying districts or territories (pachchantima-janapadas), *i.e.*, the places outside the territorial limit of the Buddhist Midland. In the Allahabad Stone-pillar inscription of Samudragupta, on the other hand, the term pratyanta occurs in the sense of borderlands, bordering territories instanced by Samatata, Davaka, Kamarupa, Nepala and Karttripura. Strictly speaking, the term was applied to the erstwhile independent principalities outside the territorial limit of the Aryavarta or Aryandom.

So far as Ashoka is concerned, he has distinguished in R. E. XIII the Antas or Pratyantas listed in R. E. II from the semi-independent States and Atavis (Atavyas, Atavikas) within his Empire, the semi-independent States of which the ruling races are broadly termed Aparantas or Westerns in R.E. V. And in M.R.E., too, particularly in its Yerragudi copy, the Antas have been sharply distinguished from the populace under his direct rule, namely, the Janapadas and Rathikas. It should be noted that in Samudragupta's prasasti the Pratyanta principalities are distinguished not only from those included in the Aryavarta but from those forming the Atavika States.

As for the connotation of the term Antas or Pratyantas, Ashoka does not keep us at all in the dark. In his S. R. E. II, the Antas are expressly characterised as avijitas (Amtanam avijitanam), 'the unconquered ones', 'those who did not territorially belong to his domain or Empire, which amounted to saying, 'the independent borderers', 'the independent frontagers', 'the independent rulers or peoples around.' If so, it is difficult for me to agree with Bhandarkar in thinking that by the Antas in S.R.E. II Ashoka must have meant but the Atavis in R.E. XIII on the ground that to both of them he held out threats, both of them he wished to pacify precisely in same terms, or that both of them were mischief makers and creators of troubles from time to time.

In my opinion, Ashoka has placed the Antas, Aparantas and Atavis in three separate categories. The Aparantas and Atavis cannot be treated as Antas or Pratyantas unless we can show that Ashoka employed the term pratyanta also in the Buddhist sense to mean either the people of a frontier region or the territories outside the Buddhist Midland. By the expression pratyanta janapadas or frontier districts the author of the Divyavadana has evidently meant those located in Uttarapatha, such as the Svasarashtra and the city of Takshashila where popular revolts took place on account of misrule or high-handed tyranny on the part of the Maurya high officials. Ashoka's S.R.E.I bears evidence to such tyrannical action on the part of the City-judiciaries in the province of Kalinga, and by implication also in those of Gandhara and Avanti.

Kautilya's Arthashastra, too, contemplates a clear distinction between the Atavis and the Antas, the former being placed in charge of the Atavipalas and the latter in that of the Antapalas.

Here one might pertinently ask with Bhandarkar who were the independent borderers within the reach of the Viceroy-in-Council stationed at Tosali and the Lajavachanika mahamatras at Samapa, if they were not the Atavis? The nearest such borderers in the south were the Cholas and Pandyas. As for those towards the northeast, some light may be obtained from Pliny who speaks of a very large island in the Ganges which was inhabited by a single tribe called Modogalingae. Beyond them were the Modubae answering to the non-Aryan people called Mutibas in the Aitareya

Brahmana who occupied the country north of the Ganges, the Molindae identified *with the Maladas whom the Markandeya Purana places in the* Prachya division, the Uberae who are 'referred to the Bhars, a numerous race spread over the central districts of the region spoken of, and extending as far as to Assam', the Galmodroesi, Preti, Calissae, Sasuri, Passalae, Colubae, Oxexulae, Abali and Taluctae. The King of these is said to have kept under arms 50,000 foot-soldiers, 4,000 cavalry and 400 elephants.'

Pataliputra, the Capital

Whether of Ashoka's domain proper, or of his Empire, or of his sphere of influence, the centre was his capital called Pataliputra (R.E.V.)- It was known to Megasthenes and other Classical writers as Palibothra. It is known in Pali also by the name of Pupphapura (Pashpapura), a synonym of Kusumapura, by which the city is not infrequently designated in Indian literature. The evidence of the Pali Mahaparinibbana Suttanta and the Suttanipata is conclusive as to its earlier name Pataligama implying as it does that it was at first but a mere village, from which humble position it rose afterwards into the eminence of the greatest city in India under the Mauryas. The Pali evidence is important also for the reason that it supplies us with an authentic account of the circumstances that led to the fortification of Pataligama by King Ajatashatru of Magadha as a timely measure against the advance of his powerful rival, the Vrijis of Vaishali. From the same realistic account, it is clear that Pataligama situated on the southern bank of the Ganges, stood as an important halting place on a high road, known as the Southern Road in the Buddha's time. Just opposite to Pataligama and on the side of the rival territory of the Vrijis was the halting place called Kotigama.

The first step to the building of the city of Pataliputra lay in the fortification of Pataligama. The work was in full swing when the Buddha passed through this place in course of his last journey, and that under the personal supervision of the two able Brahmin ministers of Ajatashatru, Sunidha and Varshakara by name, who must have been well-versed in the science and art of town planning and fort-building, of which a comprehensive idea may be formed from the rules stated in detail in the Arthashastra, and no less from the Pali description of a well-fortified city in the

Mahaparinibbana Suttanta. The Buddha prophesied the future greatness of Pataligama Pataliputta and also mentioned the danger of its destruction by *fire or water, or internal discord." This prophecy* about Pataliputra, put into the Buddha's mouth, was prospective in its purpose but retrospective in fact.

The origin of the name of Pataligama had much to do with the Patali tree. The village was called Pataligama either because a Patali tree was its cognizance, or because it abounded in Patali trees, or because, as suggested by the Pali scholiasts, "on the day of its foundation several Patali shoots sprouted forth from the ground." Who changed the name of Pataligama after its fortification into Pataliputra is not known. But the traditions are unanimous that the capital of Magadha was for the first time transferred from Rajagriha to Pataliputra by Udayi, son and successor of Ajatashatru. The city as the capital of Magadha was definitely known by the name of Patatiputra in the time of the next King Munda, grandson of Ajatashatru. As Hiuen Tsang, the great Chinese pilgrim, came to know, the city which became afterwards known by the name of Pataliputra was at first called Kusumapura, because the palace of the King had many flowers," which, however, is doubtful. Whatever the origin and significance of the other name, Pushpapura or Kusumpura, the collective literary and epigraphic evidence goes to show that this poetic name was acquired later. This is not, however, to deny that the Maurya capital outgrew its humbler beginning. With these reservations we may readily accept the following comment of Vincent Smith on the position of Pataliputra:

> "Pataliputra, Chandragupta's Capital, was a great and noble city extending along the northern bank of the Son for about nine miles, with a depth of less than two miles. Much of the area is now covered by Patna, Bankipore, and sundry neighbouring villages. Kusumapura, the more ancient city, stood on the Ganges, and evidently became merged in Pataliputra, for the two names are often used as synonyms. The Maurya city was built in the tongue of land formed by the junction of the Son with the Ganges, a defensible position recommended by the writers of textbooks,

and frequently adopted by the ancient Indian in practice. The old river beds and even the ancient embankments of quay may still be traced. The city was defended by a massive timber palisade, of which the remains have been found at several places. The gates were sixty-four, and the towers five hundred and seventy in number. The palisade was protected by a deep moat."

The main advantageous position required in the Arthashastra of a city deserving to be used as a capital (sthaniya) is that it must be centrally located and possess all the easy communication facilities. Its position was in this respect really enviable. It was situated at the junction of the two great highways of commerce, namely, the Southern Road extending from Rajagriha to Pratishthana and the Ganges system of rivers connected with the coastal trade of India and the overseas trade of Eastern India.

The connection of the Southern Road with the Northern with its various branches afforded facilities also for land communication with such distant places in Uttarapatha as Takshashila and Pushkalavati. The internal arrangement and life of the city, with the imperial palace as the cynosure, may be easily inferred from the inscriptions, as also from the foreign accounts, the Arthashastra, and the typical description of the city of Sagala in the Pali work called Milindapanha.

The Population

The Indian technical terms denoting the population of a territory, *i.e.*, the ruled or subjects, are prakritayah (same as pakatiyo of the Hathigumpha inscription), Paurah, paura-janapadah, prajah, and sarva-prajah. As defined by Amarasimha, the prakritis denote the collective body of citizens.

Corresponding to Ashvaghosha's saravprajah we have the Ashokan expression savamunisa, "all men", janajanapada, or simply jana. In the wider sense of the term, the population consisted of pasumunisa, "men and animals", *i e.*, both citizens and denizens, further distinguished as bipeds and quadrupeds, birds and aquatic beings. In terms of religion, all men are represented by the term sava pasamda, "all sects", "all denominations", "all communities".

The population, in the political sense of the term, is spoken of as placed in three categories: (i) that within the territory under his direct government, and subsequently, within the territory under the direct rule of himself and his Viceroys, (ii) that within the semi-independent tribal or feudatory States, and (iii) that within the independent but allied territories, denoted respectively by the terms, janapada, aparanta-ataviyo-rathika, and amta. The population of the earth living outside the territorial limit of the unconquered antas or pratyantas is broadly distinguished as peoples whose countries were not frequented by Ashoka's Dutas (Envoys or Emissaries), *i.e.*, the territories to which they had no access.

The Antas were not Ashoka's subjects since they territorially belonged to principalities or dominions of which the sovereignty was vested in other rulers or ruling races; politically they were extra-territorial. They might, if at all, be regarded as intra-territorial only in a non-technical sense, on the strength of the good will cherished by Ashoka towards them as towards his own subjects, by virtue of the works of public utility and philanthropic nature Ashoka was able to accomplish in their lands, on the ground of acceptance of Ashoka's principles of piety or duty by them, in short, as Ashoka himself put it, by the right of cultural conquest (dhamma-vijaya) he was able to achieve. Thus they came indeed within the sphere of Ashoka's moral influence and became dwellers of the Greater India Ashoka aspired to found on the basis of good will and mutual understanding, particularly through appreciation by the outsiders of the goodness of human heart and the nobleness of human spirit and their tangible expressions in word and deed.

The Aparantas formed the population of certain tribal States within Ashoka's Empire that were internally free and externally only acknowledged the suzerainty of Ashoka, however real or nominal their allegiance to the imperial state might be.

The position of the Janapadas as the population proper, broadly divided into two classes, *viz.*, urban and rural, is self-evident. Even as representatives and supporters of different religious communities, their position is easily understandable.

The denizens consisting of beasts and birds and fishes, of the beasts of burden, live-stocks and games, formed in a sense the population under the name of pana, "life", "living beings", of a civilized state like the Ashokan.

The Territory

The Indian technical terms to denote territory are Janapada and Rashtra (Pali Rattha). The Kamandakiya term svarashtra stands for one's own territory as distinguished from Pararashtra, the territory of others. Ashoka's own words for territory, such as Vijita, Vijaya, Raja-visaya, Desa and Puthavi are met with in the contemporary, earlier as well as later Indian literature, particularly in Pali. The later Indian inscriptional term for territory is Vijaya-chakra or Vijaya-rajya instead of Ashoka's Vijaya. The literary as well as the inscriptional word Rajya (Pali Rajja) for territory is nowhere employed in Ashoka's inscriptions. Desa and Prithivi are treated as synonymous terms in the Arthashastra: desah prithivi.

An ideal territory including population is defined thus in the Arthashastra:

> "Has favourably situated cities and towns, with means to maintain its own population and others in times of calamity, well-guarded, with easy means of livelihood, averse to the enemy, can cope with neighbouring rulers, free from miry, rocky, marshy, uneven and thorny tracts, as well as from tigers, wild beasts and wild tracts, attractive, containing plenty of good cultivable lands, mines, timber, elephant forests and pasture grounds, excels in arts and crafts, has hidden passages, rich in cattle (livestock); not dependent on rainwater only, provided with land and waterways, has an extensive trade in various kinds of merchandise, can bear the burden of a vast army and heavy taxation, has a good and active peasantry, full of intelligent masters and servants, with a population noted for its loyalty and moral purity—these are the characteristics of a good territory."

Ashoka refers to his territory as a vast domain, with the city of Pataliputra as its capital. He alludes also to the outer towns containing his family establishments or residences, and to residences also of his brothers, sisters and other kith and kin. Among outer towns, we have mention of such important cities as Takshashila, Kaushambi, Ujjaini, Tosali and Samapa, Suvarngiri and Rishila. The existence of other towns may be inferred from the location of other inscriptions, *e.g.*, the city of Kapilavastu from the Lumbini Pillar inscription, that of Srughna from the Kalsi set of Rock Edicts, those of Rajapura and Abhisara from the Mansehra set, that of pushkaravati from the Shahbazgarhi, that of Girinagara (Jaina Girinara) from the Girnar, that of Surparaka from the Sopara, that of Viratanagara from the Bairat copy of M.R.E., that of Vidisha from the Sanchi Pillar inscription, and that of Gaya from the Barabar Hill-cave inscriptions.

It is only in respect of his conquest by piety, *i.e.*, the sphere of his moral influence, that Ashoka's domain was or might be claimed to have been as wide as Jambudvipa, which traditionally contained in Ashoka's time as many as 84,000 towns, large and small. His earthly Empire, as we saw, was less extended than Bharatavarsha.

As King of Magadha or Magadhan King (laja Magadha, Bhabru), his territory in the sense of his narrow royal domain, confined within the four corners of Magadha, or, at the most, of Anga-Magadha. To put it in the language of the Classical writers, he was just a King of the Prasii or Palibotris (Pataliputriyans). His imperial domain proper, *i.e.*, the major portion of his Empire which was under his direct government excluded the semi-independent territories of such oligarchical tribes as the Yaunas, Kambojas, Gandharas, Nabhagas and Nabha-lines on the north and northwest, and the senior Rashtrikas and Bhojas and their offshoots, as well as the Andhras and Parinda-Paradas in the south. His earthly Empire as a whole included in it also these territories as well as the wild forests occupied by the Atavyas of more or less nomadic habits and predatory propensities, but it certainly precluded from it the pratyantas or unconquered territories of the Antas who might otherwise be called Samantas.

Even these territories were sought to be distinguished from those beyond them by the fact of their having entered into some sort of an alliance, having some common bonds of friendship. Ashoka gives us to understand that these territories were favoured than against favouring by way of remaining quiet and pacified. The territories without lay beyond the range of his Dutas.

According to the general terminology of the Indian science of polity, the Samanta or 'Frontager' whose territory stood immediately contiguous (on any one side) to the territory of a King in the role of a conqueror was to be termed satru (the enemy); the Samanta whose territory lay just beyond that of the satru was to be termed mitra (the conqueror's friend); the Samanta who stood next to the mitra was to pass as udasina (the neutral); and the Samanta who stood just in the rear of the conqueror to help the latter's enemy was to go by the name of parshnigraha (the rearward enemy.)

In the frontal order the Arthashastra places the Samantas, each in front of the man behind, and carries their relative positions beyond the fourth degree. The nearest Frontager is termed ari (the conqueror's enemy), the next man, mitra (the conqueror's friend), the third man, arimitra (the enemy's friend), the fourth man mitra-mitra (the friend's friend), and the fifth man, arimitra-mitra (the enemy's friend's friend).

"In the rear of the conqueror, there happen to be situated a rearward enemy (parshnigraha), a rearward friend (akranda), an ally of the rearward enemy (parshnigrahasara) and an ally of the rearward friend (akrandasara).

A rival whose territory lies contiguous to that of the conqueror is a natural enemy. He who is antagonistic or creates enemies to the conqueror is a factitious (kritrima) enemy. An ally whose friendship is based upon family relationship and whose territory is next to that of the enemy is a natural friend. He whose friendship is courted for self-maintenance is an acquired friend. The Samanta whose territory lies close to those of both the conqueror and his enemy and who is capable of helping both is a mediatory ruler (madhyama). He whose territory lies beyond those of all of the above and who is capable of helping or resisting any of them individually is a 'superior' ruler.

The conqueror, his friend and his friend's friend constitute together a circle of states on one side. Thus one is to think in respect of all the four sides of the conqueror's territory of altogether four interstate circles.

The inter state relations which are carried to the highest degree of nicety in the prose treatise of the Arthashastra are far beyond the scope of the Maurya State under Ashoka.

On the western side of Ashoka's territory, the nearest frontager was Antiochus II Theos. The next man whose territory lay contiguous on the south to that of Antiochus was Ptolemy II Philadelphos. The frontager whose territory lay contiguous on the west to that of Antiochus was Antigonas Gonatas. The third frontager whose territory lay contiguous on the west to that of Ptolemy was Magas, and the third Frontager whose territory lay contiguous on the west to that of Antigonas was Alexander of Epirus. The territories beyond those of Magas and Alexander lay outside the range of Ashoka's foreign relations', diplomatic or otherwise.

On the southern side of his territory, the nearest frontagers were the Cholas and below them the Pandyas along the eastern sea coast. The nearest frontagers along the western coast were the Satiyaputras and below them the Keralaputras. Below all of them were the Tamraparijyas. The peoples whose countries lay on two sides of the Indian Ocean were all situated beyond the range of Ashoka's foreign relations.

The existence of some Antas or Samantas on the eastern and northeastern sides of his territory in Northern India may be inferred from Ashoka's S.R.E. II. The Pali tradition speaks of a Buddhist mission sent to Suvarnabhumi during Ashoka's reign, but it lacks as yet corroboration from Ashoka's inscriptions and reliable foreign accounts.

The independent peoples whose territories lay immediately beyond those of the Yaunas, Kambojas and Gandharas in Uttarapatha proper, and on the north beyond those of the Nabhakas and Nabha-lines are not expressly mentioned. It is vaguely stated that all the peoples in Jambudvipa, which in its northernmost reach extended up to the southern side of Mt. Sumeru, came under his moral influence, if not precisely under his rule.

The semi-independent peoples who were hinter-landers may be shown to have formed territorial gradations of buffers: the Yaunas and Kambojas above the Gandharas, and probably the Barbaras and Kiratas not only above the Yaunas and Kambojas of Uttarapatha but also above the Nabhakas and Nabha-lines of Central Himalayan region. Similarly in the south were the Andhras and Parindas below the Rashtrikas, Bhojakas and their offshoots in the Vindhyan and Narmada regions.

The poet Bhasa, two of whose verses may be shown to have been cited in the prose treatise of the Arthashastra, restricted the territory of a paramount sovereign of Rajasimha's type to Northern India situated between the Himalayas and the Vindhya hills and extending (east to west) from sea to sea.

Though the words chaturanta and chaturanta, mahi occur in the Arthashastra, from Shama Sastri's rendering of the actual definition of the domain of a King overlord in the same considered as a developed prose treatise, it appears that it was similarly limited to Northern India.

This might be made to tally with the Puranic definition of Bharatavarsha only by the following rendering of the passage from the Arthashastra:

> "Country is the earth, thereof the portion between the Himalayas and the ocean in extent one thousand Udichi yojanas *(i.e.,* judged by the Udichi or North Indian standard), measured lengthwise *(lit.,* not crosswise), forms the domain of an overlord."

"In it", precisely as according to the description of Jambudvipa in the Jaina Jambudivapannatti, "there are such varieties of land as forests, villages, waterfalls, level plains, and uneven grounds.... Time consists of cold, hot and rainy periods. The divisions of time are the night, the day, the fortnight, the month, the season, solstices, the year, and the yuga cycle of five years."

As appears from his inscriptions, Ashoka's domain, which in a sense was coextensive with Jambudvipa, contained mountains and hills (pavata), hill-caves (kubha), forests (ataviyo), and watery regions suitable for the purpose of fishery (kevatabhoga). The year, too, was divided into three seasons (tisu chatumasisu), the lunar months into fortnights (better, half months as in the Arthashastra), and days and the populace was familiar with the cycle of five years yielding an additional month (adhimasa) at the end of every half cycle within the third year.

Ashoka evidently placed the five Samanta territories in the west, as well as the five in the south, within an extension of six hundred yojanas from his Empire.

The Sovereignty

The Maurya State under Ashoka, precisely as under his father and grandfather, was apparently an absolute monarchy in its form, 'in the legal and political sense of the term' (in the words of Mukherji), and as such, its sovereignty or supreme power might be taken to have belonged to him, vested in his person. In his inscriptions, Ashoka has been variously represented, e.g., as Devanampriya Ashoka. He has referred to former Kings either as rajano or as Devanampriya. He himself has been referred to in the same set of edicts under the two titles of Raja and Devanampriya. One can say indeed on the authority of the commentary on the Harshacharita that Devanampriya was no more than a pujavachana or honorific, which, according to Patanjali, was on a par with such other honorifics as Bhavan, Dirghayus and Ayushman. But this, as applied to Ashoka, had, as will be shown anon, had a deeper signification of its own.

No ruler passed as a Raja until he went through the ceremony of coronation, anointment or consecration (abhisheka), in other words, of formal installation on the throne. To be a King a warrior had to be crowned and consecrated. Ashoka was duly anointed as King, his regnal years are all stated in terms of his abhisheka.

According to the tradition in the Dipavamsa, as we saw, he was anointed twice, the first time as Ashoka, and subsequently as Priyadarshin, which was in accordance with the prescription in the Brahmanas. As Raja, he passed as the King of Magadha or Magadhan King, and as Priyadarshin, he was to be considered the Emperor of Jambudvipa (India).

Two lunar constellations, *viz.*, Tishya or Tishya and Punarvasu, find repeated mention in Ashoka's inscriptions. The two constellations to which the Arthashastra attaches importance are called raja-nakshatra (i.e., the birth-star of the King in the role of a conqueror, the jata-nakshatra as it is otherwise termed, and desa-nakshatra (the national star, i.e., the coronation star). The scholars are divided in their opinion on the question of which is which. With Buhler Punarvasu was the birth-star of Ashoka, while with Bhandarkar it was Tishya or Tishya. The Tishya constellation which enjoys precedence over the Punarvasu was probably the birth-star, and the latter the coronation.

In connection with the Ashokan state the question may pertinently be asked—who was the legal sovereign and who the political? Under the British Constitution in which the King is only a figurehead of the state and which, therefore, entertains the idea of a limited monarchy, the legal sovereign is the King-in-the-Parliament. Under the Maurya Constitution as it shaped in Ashoka's hands the legal sovereign was the King and the Council of Ministers. The two points of difference between the two Constitutions are these: (i) in the former, the ministers who are appointed in name by the King, are chosen out of the people's representatives and as such, are subject ultimately to the control of the electorate, while in the latter, the ministers were all chosen and appointed by the King independently of any reference to the popular will; and (ii) in the former, the initiative in all matters of national well-being and policy lies with Cabinet as the executive body of the Parliament, and the power of legislation belongs entirely to its two houses and the Crown, while in the latter, the real initiative in all matters of national well-being and policy as well as the power of enforcing the laws, even if not exactly of enacting them, rested with the King himself. Minus the elective factor, the King-in-Council might be taken to be the legal sovereign of the Ashokan State. The relative positions of the King and the Council of Ministers changed with times and became, for all practical purposes, reversed. The general opinion is that the Ashokan Constitution is neither a limited monarchy of the English type nor an undiluted despotism of the Czarist type; it is something between the two.

R. E. VI goes to show that whenever King Ashoka gave verbal orders concerning any donation, announcement or proclamation to be made, or entrusted any urgent matters of state-business to the Mahamatras, these were, as a matter of course, referred to the Council of Ministers which met to consider them independently of the King. It was only the reporters (Prativedakas) who were present to watch its proceedings that were to be immediately reported to the King. There is nothing to indicate that the Council's decision was binding on Ashoka. According to some versions of R. E. III, it was the duty of the Council of Ministers to instruct the Yuktas (subordinate officers in the Imperial Secretariat) in the matter of codifying the King's orders. One cannot be sure on this point inasmuch as other versions appear to have assigned this duty to the Purushas instead of to the Parishad. In Bhandarkar's opinion "the Parishad was like a modern Executive Council which was an intermediate body between the King and the Mahamatras, and it appears that whereas, on the one hand, it saw that the written orders of the King were carried out by the different officials, it had, on the other, the power to scrutinise his oral orders before they were executed and to suggest what course of action would meet what pressing contingencies of the Mahamatras for the information and approval of the King, who was, of course, the final arbiter."

It is emphatically asserted by Mukherji that the King in India "was not the source of Law but rather its support." By way of an argument in support of this, he adds, "Sacred Law, according to Manu and other legal authorities, is derived from four sources, viz., (i) the Vedas, (ii) the Smritis, (iii) the practices of the pious (sishtachara), and (iv) the opinions of the pious on doubtful points, while the sources of secular law were the manifold groups and communities which legislated for themselves, so that 'whatever may have been practised by the virtuous, and by such twice-born men as are devoted to the law, that only he shall establish as law if it be not opposed to the laws of castes, communities (janapada), guilds and families' (Manu, viii. 41, 46)...' it is the quasi-instinctive postulates and conventions of group-life which came to be formulated as law, and not the mandate, command, or decree of a single, central authority in the state.' 'Law, under these conditions is not an artefact, but a natural growth of consensus and communal life.'

Mukherji's opinion, which is admittedly based upon Manu and other post-Ashokan Smriti writers, cannot decide the point at issue. It is besides too categorical in its assertion to bear scrutiny. We have a more thoroughgoing discussion of the question in the informative notes appended to Professor Rangaswami Aiyangar's Dewan Bahadur K. Krishnaswami Row Lectures on Rajadharma,

University of Madras. But, even Rangaswami Aiyangar, whose conclusion ultimately tallies with Mukherji's opinion, would seem to have proceeded on a doubtful interpretation of the data relied on.

In the Kautilya-vachana in verse (Arthashastra), it is opined that the adjudication of cases should be guided by these four things: dharma, vyavahara, charitra, and rajasasana, which find mention alike in the Law-books of Yajnavalkya and Narada. Kautilya allows to each that follows to have precedence over each that precedes (paschimah purvabadhakah) while, according to Aiyangar, Narada, reverses this order in maintaining that what precedes is to be given precedence over what follows (uttarah purvabadhakah). In Aiyangar's words, with Kautilya "each following overrides the preceding" and with Narada "what precedes overrides what follow." Here he has sadly missed, I regret to observe, the meaning of the word uttarah which is just a synonym of paschimah. So, in point of fact, Narada simply reiterated the opinion of Kautilya.

Immediately after this, Professor Aiyangar argues his case in the following manner to establish that it was beyond the province of the Indian King to make a new law:

"Shukra, who is also an Arthashastra authority, gives the King power to declare the law, but it must be in accordance with dharma and usage. He cannot make a new law. The royal edict is merely declaratory, and not innovative. This is specially indicated by Katyayana.

The edict has to conform to dharma, nyaya and desachara if it is to be operative. Yajnavalkya refers to the edict as 'dbarma as declared by the king'.

Without going into the question of the relative authority of the Dharmashastra and the Arthashastra as such, I find that Aiyangar's interpretation of the four terms, dharma, vyavahara, charitra, and rajasasana, as "smriti law, secular law, custom and edicts of the King" respectively is arbitrary, and he appears to have owed it to Jaiaswal. Kautilya himself defines, though enigmatically, the four things of which one stands superior to the other previously named, or the four terms employed by him in the following verse:

> "Here dharma (the fundamental principles of human action, the basic rules for the righteous and judicious discharge of man's duties in a socio-moral, politico economic and religiocultural order) is established on truth (the order or nature of reality as revealed, ascertained and affirmed), vyavahara (the procedure or operational feature of law) is concerned with the reliable evidence from witnesses called charitra, (the tradition or approved usage) is to be gathered from the people concerned, (and) sasana (the edict or the law as proclaimed or promulgated, the law in force) is in its essence the King's command (mandate or decree)".

The same is differently expressed thus:

> "If a ruler administers justice in accordance with the general law of piety or duty, the accepted moral principles of the cultured society (in short, righteously and judiciously), in accordance with the prescribed or definite law of procedure, the approved usage of a social group or locality, and the principle of equity as the fourth, he can conquer the earth extending as far as to the four seas."

And *in the* very first verse, Kautilya says:

> "By virtue of guarding the observance of respective duties of the four castes (lit., colours, social grades), and the four stages of life, maintaining the approved manners and customs of the populace and guarding against the deterioration of all good things and noble qualities, the King passes as the founder of a socio-moral, politico economic and religiocultural order".

The dharma-pravartakah is "the fountain of justice", according to Shama Sastri's rendering, which, to my mind, is too narrow to cover the meaning of the expression.

Even conceding to Professor Aiyangar that, so far as Brahmanism was concerned, the nature of the sacerdotal or sacred law (dharma) formed the fit subject of discussion in the Dharmashastra and the nature of the profane rajadharma or secular law was the fit subject of discussion in the Arthashastra as such, I do not see any reason for his inference from the evidence before us that the King in India was debarred from the power of legislating for the people, from being the supreme authority for making secular laws. According to modern jurists' finding, there is nothing of law as we now understand it in the Vedas or Sruti proper, and there is hardly anything of law in the older Dharmasutras, and, for the matter of that, in the earlier Sutra literature of the Brahmans. And on his own showing even such later Smriti texts as those of Manu, Yajnavalkya, Vishnu, and Parashara, devote but small spaces to the enunciation of the principles of rajadharma and secular law.

Neither Ashoka nor any other sane man of India claimed that he was the maker of the dharma, whether in the sense of the law of piety or duty which underlay the socio-moral, politico-economic and religiocultural order of men, or in the metaphysical sense of dharmata or the cosmic law, the order of reality.

The Buddha, for instance, stated his own position thus: "in so far as dharma in the sense of ancient or eternally abiding reality (paurana dharmasthitita) is concerned, it is a self-regulating order of cosmic life (dharma-niyamata), the suchness, realness and actuality of things (tathata, bhutata, satyata) which exists by its own right, independently of all truth-finders and pathfinders, which is to say, of all thinkers and teachers, divines and philosophers; only in so far as it signifies the pratyatmadharmasthitita, its nature is accessible to an individual contemplative through intuition at a supreme moment of experience or realisation. As thinker and teacher, he simply declared the truth with regard to the nature of reality as intuited by him per *se*, affirmed it, and pointed out the way of reaching or apprehending it, each individually by his or her own efforts, On the basis of that intuition or enlightenment was formed the basic concept of his thought which, in the sphere of religion and ethics, was interpreted, propounded and promulgated as a moral law. The path or the road which he discovered was not claimed to be new; it was the one trodden by the Enlightened Ones of the past millenniums. The *summum bonum* of human life and the ideal of human conduct and character which he set forth was shown to be in complete accord with the noble experience and life of all great contemplatives and saintly personages of the past.

Thus, like other great men of history, the Buddha said, "My work is to indicate rather than to originate." He, too, came not to destroy the Law but to fulfil it.

In reality, nevertheless, he came to set the wheel of the Law in motion, to occupy the proud position of the founder of a new kingdom of righteousness, of a great religion as we now say, inculcating, on the one hand, the fundamental principles of dharma in the sense of a psycho-ethical religion, and framing and enforcing the laws and disciplinary rules for his followers in the light of circumstances, amending, repealing or modifying them, on the other, as the circumstances changed. Thus *pari passu* developed two classes of Buddhist canonical texts, viz. the Dhamma or Sutra and the Vinaya or Anatti, the latter together with a system of judicial administration. The inner circle of his great disciples served the purpose of a Council of Ministers. The felt necessity for the framing of laws and rules, not to say, legislation, arose from varying circumstances. Great care was taken by the framer of the laws and rules of civic, criminal and ecclesiastical import that they were consistent with the psycho-ethical principles of Dharma and conducive to the growth of the kingdom of righteousness from within.

It should also be noted that the Buddha while he spoke of and laid down the fundamentals of human conduct, put himself in the double role of a King overlord (raja-chakravartin), which he would have assumed had he remained in the world, and of a Dharmaraja, which he had to play well as a Perfect type of Buddha.

Here the question arises—Whatever his mental attitude towards the Dharma as the eternal order of reality existing by its own right and the path which he discovered, was he not historically the founder of Buddhism and the framer of the laws and rules in the Vinaya Pitaka?

Ashoka's position, *mutatis mutandis,* was the same. Just as, on the one hand, the Buddha said, "Because of birth comes decay and death: whether Tathagatas arise or not, this element stands as the establishing of things as effects" and described the path which he discovered was an 'ancient path (puranam maggam) trodden by the Buddhas of the past ages', so, on the other, said Ashoka the Beloved of the gods: "Respectful attention must be paid to mother and father, likewise to seniors; tender regard for living beings be strengthened, truth must be spoken, these very attributes of piety must be propounded: likewise the teachers must be honoured by pupils with submissiveness and it must be fittingly propounded to the teacher's relatives.

This is the ancient tradition, and a thing of long standing is this, thus should it be practised". He, too, expressly stated that all that he did or wanted to do was directed to this single end, namely, the promotion of the cause of piety (dhamma-vadhi) throughout the length and breadth of his Empire. He, too, nowhere claimed that he was the originator of the Dhamma in the sense of the principles of piety or duty. With regard to the sufficient promotion of the cause of piety among his subjects, which was the real business of his as a ruler precisely as it was of the former Kings, he said that he tried to effect it by this twofold means, viz., the regulations of piety and the inculcation of the principles of piety, of which the second in his opinion was more effective than the first.

Now, what were the many and sundry 'regulations of piety' that had been promulgated by him and out of which just one was placed on record, namely, the game-laws embodied in P. E. V? From the general tenor of Aiyangar's argument, one may deduce that these regulations were not pieces of legislation or enactments, they having been merely declaratory of existing laws, rather customary laws, codified in the Brahmanist Law-books. The vulnerable point in his argument is that the authorities cited, such as Manu, Yajnavalkya, Vishnu, and Medhatithi, are all post-Ashokan, the majority post-Christian in date.

With regard to the regulation of piety in P. E. V, it may be observed that, though Ashoka was a strong advocate of the principle of non-injury to life, having taken human nature as it then was, having taken into his consideration the social habits of his subjects in general, as a wise ruler he could not reasonably expect to enact any such law as meaning total prohibition for all men and for all times, if he would like it to be really operative and effective. So minimisation of the slaughter of life was the express aim of this particular regulation carrying legal force, to avoid calling it technically a piece of legislation for want of a legislature elected by the people having voting rights. There is nothing of the kind to be seen in the older Dharmasutras, such as those of Gautama, Apastamba, Bodhayana and Vasishtha. In this regulation a few species of birds, fishes and quadrupeds were declared inviolable on this twofold ground: (i) that they were neither eaten by men, nor (ii) did they come into man's use.

From the first of the two grounds stated by Ashoka, it is evident that the creatures included in the list of inviolables passed as uneatables. Behind it were the authoritative views of the Buddha and the older Smriti writers as to what animals should be eaten as food and what animals should not be eaten. Upon the whole, Ashoka's list of inviolables may be shown to be specially in agreement with those of uneatables in the Law-books of Bodhayana and Vasishtha with whom the achara (custom) of the Midland was the standard. But the question which interested the earlier Brahmin Lawgivers was of eating and not eating certain creatures as food, and in this respect their interest was the same as that of the Israel Law giver Moses.

The standpoint of the Mosaic law as well as the socio-domestic law of the earlier Smriti writers was hygienic and aesthetic, while that of Ashoka's regulation was humanitarian. The remark which applies to Moses and earlier Smriti writers, applies equally to the Buddha's prohibitive injunction. Further, Moses meant his domestic rules of eating for the Israels, the Buddha for his followers, and the Smriti writers for those of the twice-born classes, while Ashoka's regulation was meant for all his subjects as it should be in order to pass as a law of the land. Equity, custom, progressive moral idea of the society and expediency guide modern legislation as they must have guided Ashoka's regulations, and, for the matter of that, all rajasasanas. If the later Smriti writers insisted on this point, as I find they did, they were very sensible and prudent. But that was not to say that Ashoka or any Indian King of the past was debarred from the right to legislate for the people, specially that Ashoka's regulations were not pieces of legislation.

The question of political sovereignty is not so easy to answer as that of legal in the case of the Ashokan State. In a Constitution such as the British, political sovereignty may be said to belong to the electorate in the sense that 'the legal sovereign is bound in the end to carry out its wishes'. It must have been in view of the absence of any elective system in the Maurya State that Professor Mukherji characterised it as an absolute monarchy in the legal as well as political sense of the term. The upshot of his remark is that under the Maurya Constitution the King was responsible to none but himself, his God or conscience. But to understand and appreciate the real situation we need not attach undue importance to the elective system which exists in the limited monarchy of England or the modern democracy of any other country of Europe or America. To speak of the British Constitution in particular, it cannot be said that its political sovereignty belongs to the British people as a whole for the obvious reason that it has not extended the franchise to all as, for instance, was done by the Greek City States. Instead of looking at the narrow technical aspect of the matter, let us better look to the essential point in the definition of political sovereignty. The political sovereign, according to its accepted definition, is 'that power in the State whose will prevails.' As distinguished from the legal sovereign, the political sovereign is unable to enact and enforce the laws directly.

In all the monarchical States of Ancient India but those in which the reigning monarch happened to be a reckless, ruthless and incorrigible tyrant, political sovereignty theoretically inhered in the impersonal authority of Dharma and actually belonged to the ruled, the subjects, or the people at large, who were the real beneficiaries of the State.

When only the Police type of State prevailed in India, occupied with the business of maintaining law and order within the territory, the Upanishad teacher proclaimed: "Dharma is the King of Kings (kshatrasya kshatrah), there being nothing mightier than it. It is by (the power of) Dharma that the weaker person controls the stronger as it were by (the might of) a ruler. Dharma is satya, therefore, when one affirms the satya, he affirms the dharma, or when one affirms the dharma, he affirms the satya. Thus verily it becomes an affirmation of both."

The Buddha expanded this Upanishad idea of Dharma when he, too, came to declare: "Dharma is the King of King overlords (dhammo ranno chakkavattissa raja). Here a King overlord who is virtuous and a righteous monarch, depending on the dharma, honouring the dharma, respecting it, submitting thereto, acting as the standard-bearer of the dharma, having the dharma for the banner of his imperium, and acknowledging the sovereignty of the dharma, provides the lawful protection and safeguard among his own people, and alike among the subordinate rulers, the army, the Brahmans and rich householders the townfolks and country people, the Sramanas and Brahmanas as religious teachers, (nay, even) among the beasts and birds. Thus verily by dharma he sets the wheel in motion (i.e. founds paramount sovereignty) of which the course cannot be resisted by any inimical human being whosoever."

Ashoka himself, who sought to fulfil the chakravarti or imperial ideal of the Buddha, insisted on rearing up by the dharma, providing by the dharma, pleasing by the dharma, and guarding by the dharma, He, too, desired that the rulers should administer the dharma, standing firm in dharma and virtue.

In the early Upanishad phraseology, dharma was just another word for rita. Dharma in the sense of Law was but the regulative principle of human conduct and compelling instrument in a socio-moral order, which was an actuality or truly existent fact (satya) and in consonance with the order of reality considered in its five contexts, viz., the physical order (adhilokam), the astronomical order (adhijyautisham), the procreational or biological order (adhiprajam), the cultural order (adhividyam), and the individuality of persons (adhyatmam). The dharma to be practised is the law of piety or duty in accordance with the past tradition or established usage.

As explained by Buddhaghosa, the dharma to be respected by a King overlord who was virtuous and a righteous monarch stood for the ten psycho-ethical principles of human conduct and character as also for the traditional path of virtue, the precedent.

The dhamma spoken of by Ashoka was essentially the law of piety or duty. With him the tradition was the tradition of piety established by the former Kings of India.

The Buddha, to be true to the ideal he had set forth, left behind him a Constitution for the Brotherhood founded by him, which was to be worked out and maintained by the impersonal authority of the Dhamma in the sense of the collective body of the Doctrine and the Discipline promulgated by him. He declined to nominate his successor on the ground that he never thought that he was the leader of the Sangha or that the Fraternity waited for his lead. The Doctrine embodying the principles and rules of conduct and character was to take his place in his absence.

As for the power of the collective body of subjects or citizens of the Ashokan State, and, for the matter of that, of other monarchical states of Ancient India, it is not enough to say with the writer in the Cambridge History of India that the Indian King was no Sultan with the sole obligation of satisfying his personal caprice, or with Mukherji that even apart from the living sense of his moral responsibility to his people, there was an important limitation upon his autocracy from the fact that he was not the source of Law.

The agreed opinion in the matter is that there was no unchecked monarchical despotism in India. Raychaudhary has convincingly sought to show that the power of the monarch was checked, in the first place, by the Brahmans, or, as we might also say, the Brahmanas and Sramanas who were the repositories, interpreters and disseminators of national culture. The second check came from the ministers and village headmen who aided in the consecration of the King and whom the King consulted regularly on important occasions. The third check (and we may say, the main check) was exercised by the general body of the people 'who were distinct from the ministers and Gramanis, or Gramikas, and who used to meet in an assembly styled Samiti or Parishad in the Upanishads'.

The late lamented Dr. Jaiaswal was at pains to show that the Council of Ministers as a body politic evolved out of the Vedic popular assembly called Samiti or Parishad (Pali Parisa), and that as such, it retained its representative character. The Purohita (Royal Chaplain) who administered the oath to the monarch at the time of his installation and the Ministers or Councillors with whose consent and whole-hearted support he was to be installed on the throne were generally viewed as the trustees of popular interests. The presence and assent of the army, the important officers, the leading people of the community, and the collective body of the town and countryfolks was indispensable.

The Pali Mahagovinda Suttanta, while narrating a story of the past stage of Indian monarchy, describes the Purohitas as 'kingmakers' (rajakattaro, Sk. rajakrits or rajakartris). The Satapatha Brahmana, too, speaks of an earlier state of things when it represents the Suta (Charioteer) and Gramani (Leader of the Host) as kingmakers, and makes them as well as other Ratnins (the chief members of the royal household and of the civil and military staffs) as recipients of the sacrificial honours at the time of the King's coronation. Other Ratnins comprised the Chief Queen (Mahishi), the Royal Chaplain (Purohita), the Chamberlain (Kshattri), the Treasurer (Samgrahitri), the Tax-Collector (Bhagadugha), the Keeper of the Dice (Akshavapa), the Companion in the Chase (Govikartana), the Courier (Palagala), and, above all, the Commander-in-Chief (Senani).

The Pali Nikayas including the Jatakas in verse amply testify to the importance of the Councillors and Officers (Amachchas, Parisajjas) and Village Headmen (Gamikas) in the body politic of a royal state. But the power behind them all was the will of the collective body of the people, the town and the countryfolks (pora-janapada, ratthika-negama). When this went against the King, he had to go. When it went against the King and his Purohita and Ministers, they all had to go. The whole position may be realised from the following conversation between the King of Sivi and the people of Sivi in the Pali Vessantara Jataka:

"The King was told:

> The bidding of the Sivi folk if you refuse to do The people then will act, may thinks, against
>
> your son and you.
>
> The King replied:
>
> Behold the people's will, and I that will do not gainsay."

The career of the King and his ministers was not interfered with so long as they were not found guilty of misrule and their conduct not reprehensible. When the citizens of Magadha became sick of the unworthy conduct of the successors of King Bimbisara, all of whom happened, according to the Pali Chronicles, to be parricides, they rose up together against the last monarch of the line and replaced him by his minister. According to the Padakusalamanavaka Jataka, when a King and his Purohita were found guilty of theft, the investigating officer brought the matter to the notice of the councillors and the citizens, and the latter got rid of both and elected a good man as King. In the case of Vesantara, the people of Sivi were enraged when the Prince gave away the state-elephant whose presence in the kingdom was necessary for guarding against drought and food scarcity.

Thus it may be shown that the popular will ultimately prevailed in Ancient India and that it was expressed in extraordinary circumstances, no matter how. Rebellion or resort to physical force is everywhere the last weapon at the hands of the populace of a country. But we shall be far from the truth to think that in India of the Maurya age the people had not various civic institutions of their own,— societies, corporations, and trade guilds and their respective leaders, to express their will in a constitutional or semi-constitutional form. The idea of natural leadership was generally prevalent. From the various 'set forms of speech' (kammavachas) met with in the Grihya Sutras, the Vinaya Texts and the Arthashastra, it is easy to infer that the parliamentary proceedings were not unknown.

Government: The government of a territory is, according to modern definition, the machinery through which the will of the State is expressed. It involves the consideration of two things, *viz.*, the Constitution and its actual working, both of which are comprehended by the system of administration.

The familiar Indian word for administration is rajyasasana or rajadanda-parichalana. In the Buddha's phraseology, administration means anachakka-pavattana, *i.e.*, setting the wheel of the sovereign command in motion. The same is implied in Kharavela's inscription by the expression, supavatavijayachaka (supravartta-vijaya-chakra). The poetic imagery behind it goes to compare the running of a government to the driving of a royal chariot (raja-ratha). The Indian conception of government centred indeed round the imagery of a chariot, just as the modern conception does round that of a machinery.

In the Upanishad poetry, the chariot stands for the living body or organism, soul for the lord of the chariot, intelligence for the charioteer, mind for the rein-holder, the organs of sense and action for the horses yoked to the chariot, and the objects of sense and action for the field to be traversed by them:

In the case of a government, the King (raja) is the lord of the chariot, the chief minister (amachcha) is the charioteer (sarathi, suta), the commissioner (rajjuka) is the rein-holder, the officers (yuktas) are the horses yoked to the chariot, the commander-in-chief (senapati mahamatra) is the doorkeeper or guard.

In connection with the chariot procession came in the King's mother, chief Queen, the crown Prince, the chaplain, the banker, the master archer (or measurer of capacity), and the courtesan.

The Constitution

Ashoka's was a unitary form of government, inasmuch as all the powers of the State were centralised in the King and the Council of Ministers, and all the state-policy emanated from the capital, *i.e.*, from Pataliputra.

In the earlier part of Ashoka's reign, precisely as in that of the reign of his father, the central government was responsible for the administration of the Empire, especially that of his domain proper. With the appointment of his Viceroys in the four of the outlying provinces, there took place the delegation of certain powers to them, although the policy, official directions and changes in the method of administration continued to be dictated from the centre. The four outlying provinces were the North-Western (Uttarapatha), the Western (Avanti), the Eastern (Kalinga), and the Southern (Mahishamandala). Clearly in the case of the Eastern Province, we find that it had two administrative divisions, the major and the minor, each with its official headquarters, namely, Tosali and Samapa. The Southern Province is also shown to have comprised two such administrative divisions, the major with Suvarnagiri and the minor with Rishila as their respective headquarters. Though such a clear case cannot be made out for the other two provinces, from the setting of the edicts, it may not be difficult to guess that the North-Western Province, too, consisted of two such divisions, the major with Takshashila and the minor most probably with Pushkaravati as their respective headquarters, and that the Western Province was constituted of two divisions, the major with Ujjaini and the minor probably with Vidisha as their respective headquarters. The Mahamatras placed in charge of the minor division of the province of Kalinga are represented as Imperial Commissioners. It may be inferred from this, that prior to the appointment of the Kumara Viceroys, the Mahamatras in charge of the administration of the major division of the province also passed as Rajavachanikas. The same remark applies to the Mahamatras entrusted with the administration of different divisions in other outlying provinces as well. As distinguished from the Mahamatras in charge of the divisions in Home provinces, those placed in frontier provinces appear to have been designated Antamahamatras, competent to deal with matters relating to frontiers (pachamta) and frontagers, in accordance, of course, with instructions from the capital.

The Legislature

The lawmaking organ of the Ashokan State was composed of the King and the Council of Ministers, the initiative and the right of final approval lying with the former. The enactments went by the name of Regulations carrying legal force.

The King of India was the highest judiciary of a monarchical state. He represented the final court of appeal. P.E. IV goes to show that in the latter part of his reign, Ashoka delegated his own judicial authority to the Rajjukas and to corresponding state officials as regards provincial governments. In cities like Tosali and Samapa, the administration, judicial or otherwise, was entrusted, as will be shown further on, to a body of City-judiciaries corresponding, more or less, with the Paura-vyavaharika or Nagaraka of the Arthashastra.

The supreme head of the Executive organ, too, was the King. All the orders, verbal or written, directions, instructions and policy shaping the method of administration and supervision, as well as the mode of carrying out the King's wishes emanated from the King and passed through the Council of Ministers before they took their final shape. These orders, directions, etc. were codified in the Secretariat by the Yuktas under instructions from the Purushas or the Parishad and officially despatched for execution to the Rajjukas, and in the case of the outlying provinces, to the Kumara Viceroys since their appointment, who in their turn communicated them to the divisional or district heads. All despatches from the major division to a minor one in a province had to be sent on the joint authority of the Kumara Viceroy and the Mahamatras attached to him and with proper official courtesy observed. The same courtesy was equally observed even when the King himself addressed anything to a religious fraternity like the Buddhist Sangha (Bhabru).

It may be shown that this was in accordance with the convention established long before. It may further be shown that the forms and style of Ashoka's inscriptions conformed to the prevalent rules that became systematised later in the prose treatise of the Arthashastra. As for the promulgation of an ordinance or the proclamation of an imperial message, certain written copies were supplied from the capital to select centres from which other copies were to be made, circulated and suitably placed as far as went the jurisdiction of the officers concerned. These were to be also permanently incised on rocks and pillars (Schism Pillar Edict, Sarnath, M.R.E., Rupnath, Sahasram). In communicating with the people of wild tracts (ataviyo), the officers commissioned to do the work were to verbally inform them. The communication with the Antas or Samantas was maintained through the Dutas.

Law and Order

The maintenance of law and order which is one of the essential duties of every state of stable character did not suffer in the least under the Ashokan regime. That the criminal laws were most rigorous in the country is reflected by Ashoka's inscriptions as well as borne out by the collective literary evidence. The prisons existed, sudden arrest (akasma bandhana) and coercion (parikilesa) ending in imprisonment (bandhanamtika) was not altogether out of the mischief of the law. The life behind the prison bars was a state of woe and it needed safeguards and humane consideration. The wild tribes and gangs of thieves (ataviyo) were a source of trouble to the State. But whenever they caused or tried to cause mischiefs within the territory, the miscreants were severely dealt with and warned. Frontiers were zealously guarded and drastic measures, if necessary, were taken, to prevent the frontagers from planning encroachments on the home territory or creating any disturbance from outside. It was considered a bounden duty of the State to see that the people were not harassed or oppressed by any officer and were not driven into a state of rebellion by highhandedness on the part of government servants.

The Ashokan was not, however, a police type of government. It represented, on the other hand, a far advanced culture type performing all the ministrant functions, e.g., keeping itself fully informed of the actual condition of the people, whether it is prosperity and happiness or the opposite; identifying itself by an enlightened sympathy with them, taking care of the poor, the needy, the aged, the children, the oppressed, the virtuous, and the persons engaged in disseminating culture, ensuring the reasonable and human treatment of slaves and servants, promoting the cause of piety (dhamma-vadhi), doing works of public utility and humanitarian kind, and, above all, educating the subjects to an excellence of moral and national character.

Military Strength and War Policy

We have no means other than Greek accounts of ascertaining the exact military strength of the last Nanda or that of the first Maurya King. Among the Classical writers, Curtius assesses the military strength of Agrammes, the last Nanda King, as consisting of 20,000 cavalry, 200,000 infantry, and 2,000 four-horsed chariots besides a most formidable force of 3,000 elephants, while Diodorus and Plutarch increase the number of elephants to 4,000 and 6,000 respectively. "The Maurya (i.e., Chandragupta) raised the number of the infantry to 600,000, and of the elephants to 9,000. But his cavalry is said to have mustered only 30,000."

We regard to Ashoka, the Pali Chronicles make it certain that his army, like that of other Indian monarchs, comprised all the four divisions called *haya gajanararadha* in Kharavela's inscription. In the inscriptions of Ashoka, we have mention in R.E. VI and M.R.E. (Ye), of the elephant-riders (hathiyaroha), the chariot-masters (yugyachariya), and the trained horses (vinita). His military strength may only be guessed from the account he has given of his war with the Kalingas. Ashoka while speaking of the casualties suffered by the Kalingas, mentions 1,50,000 men made captives, 1,00,000 wounded, and as many as that (*i.e.*, 1,00,000) who died (mata). From his painful reminiscences, it would seem that he found the Kalinga army to be a formidable force. To overpower such a strong adversary, the Maurya army under him must have been by far the larger and stronger.

Certain it is that the territorial ambition impelled him to wage the aggressive war on the Kalingas. Profound reflections on aftereffects of a war such as this, by which the cause of culture is bound to suffer most, brought about a great change in his life and career. Thenceforward he came to set the highest prize on dharma-vijaya or conquest by piety.

Here I am just to add that in so far as Professor Rangaswami Aiyangar observes that "this is a clear declaration by Ashoka of his preference of the method of extending his suzerainty or sphere of influence without recourse to arms as against the policy of force, and violence which succeeded in Kalinga," I have nothing to gainsay. But I do not see much reason why he should consider Hultzsch's translation of Ashoka's dhammavijaya by 'conquest by piety', as distinguished from "conquest by arms", 'a forced interpretation', when in the edict itself it has been contradistinguished from sarasaka (sarashakya) or sayaka vijaya.

Aiyangar's argument is vitiated in this as well as a few other instances by the wrong assumption on which it is based. We are not to say with Mr. Ramchandra Dikshitar that Ashoka made use of the 'well-known expressions popularised by Chandragupta's great Minister, Kautilya.'

The prose treatise of the Arthashastra distinguishes between three kinds of conquerors, *viz.*, the righteous (dharma-vijayi), the avaricious (lobha-vijayi), and the demoniac (asura-vijayi), while the earlier distinction, as met with in the several Jatakas and Ashoka's R.E. XIII, and as implied in the words of Buddha, is between two kinds of conquest, *viz.*, dharma and asura, dhamma and adhamma, dhamma and sarasaka, dhammena *(i.e.*, adandena asatthena) abhivijaya and adhammena *(i.e.*, dandena satthena).

From this, it is clear as Professor Raychaudhary, too, has sought to maintain, that behind Ashoka's nomenclature was the chakkavatti ideal of the Buddha. The conception of three kinds of conquest, which must have developed out of the earlier two, takes us rather beyond the time of Ashoka.

Now, following up Aiyangar's trend of thought, we can say that the standpoints of Ashoka and the Arthashastra are diametrically opposite, the concern of the former being the noble way of a conqueror who is fully conscious of his superior strength and that of the latter the diplomatic way of a weaker ruler having to deal with powerful neighbours intent on invasion and conquest.

From the foregoing discussion of the general state policy of Ashoka, we may concede so far that however noble, lofty and idealistic Ashoka's Dhammavijaya might be, in actual practice and as circumstances needed, the Epic Dharma-vijaya as a diplomatic art from the point of view of a superior power could not altogether be dispensed with. It is this Epic idea of Dharma-vijaya that has been advocated under Rajadharma in the later Smriti works inculcating that "as far as possible recourse to arms should be avoided, and after victory in battle, if a battle becomes inevitable, no harassment of the conquered royal family or people should be permitted." Ashoka kept in view this kind of Dharma-vijaya, which was really a conquest by arms, when he opined: "In a conquest possible indeed by the force of arms, let them (*i.e.,* his descendants) like to practise forbearance and light punishment, and think of that conquest only which is the conquest by piety", he certainly made a distinction between the Dharma-vijaya as it was (with recourse to arms) and the Dharma vijaya as ought to be (without recourse to arms).

5

Ashoka, the Conquerer of Hearts

Ashoka's Religious Faith

Ashoka's personal religion may be taken to be Buddhism although there is also a view that it was Jainism, That he was a Buddhist is apparent from several of his Edicts and other proofs. In the Minor R.E. I, he tells us of the stages in his progress towards Buddhism; and, according to the reading of M.R.E. I, Maski and Rupnath, by Hultzsch, he also openly declares himself in that Edict to be a "Shakya," and a "Buddha-Shakya," i.e., a Buddhist; in the Bhabru Edict he speaks with an air of authority over the church, pointing out several passages from the scriptures to be recited and meditated by the monks and nuns, and also by the laity, male and female, and declaring his faith in the Buddhist Trinity; in the Minor Pillar Edicts at Sarnath, Kaushambi and Sanchi, he stands out as the Defender of his Faith, and proclaims the penalties for schism; while, according to tradition, he himself held a Council which defined the canon under the presidency of Moggaliputra-Tissa, who produced the *Kathavatthu* treatise for the purpose. There are also other facts pointing to the same conclusion: his pilgrimage to the holy places of Buddhism, his various measures for protecting animal life, his abolition of meat diet for the royal household, and abjuration of all amusements connected with the pain, or slaughter, of animals; his abolition of bloody sacrifices, his observance of the Uposatha Buddhist holidays, and his appointment of the Dharma-mahamatras to look after "the interests of the Sangha" *(Samghathasi),* as distinctly specified, and not for their supervision, as is implied by the expression used for the other sects. Lastly, we may note Ashoka's attachment to a definite Buddhist symbol in the Edicts, the symbol of the White Elephant, indicated by an inscription at Girnar at the end of R.E. XIII, and represented by a figure cut on the rock at Dhauli and incised at Kalsi with the label *gajatame,* "the most perfect elephant." The elephant recalls the Buddha descending in that form into the womb of his mother, so that there is here an attempt on the part of Ashoka to dedicate his Edicts, as it were, to the Buddha. Along with this association of the inscriptions with the Elephant, we should also note the association of the Ashokan Pillars with the four animals of the Elephant, the Bull, the Horse, and the Lion, figuring as their capitals, and chosen for the purpose as symbols of different stages in the life of the Buddha. Thus the Elephant typifies the Conception, the Bull (as presiding over) the Nativity, the Horse the Great Departure (Renunciation), and the Lion, "the lion among the Shakyas" (*Shakyasimha),* the appellation by which the Buddha was known.

Ashoka, however, did not inherit, but was a convert to, Buddhism. Like his predecessors, he freely allowed the slaughter of animals in the royal kitchen every day, prior to his conversion. It may be noted that he did not become an absolute vegetarian even after his conversion. His meat diet was limited to the flesh of antelopes and peacocks even in 258 BC, some six years after his conversion, and, though the antelope was discarded later, it is not definitely known if the peacock was given up finally as an article of his food. The exhaustive list of animals and birds specified for protection in the Pillar Edict V, issued as late as 243 BC, does not include the peacock. Similarly, he indulged in all the customary merry-makings of Kings before his conversion. And he has been described in all tradition as being up to usurping the throne by violence against his eldest brother, hardly a less legitimate claimant. Lastly, even as a Buddhist lay disciple, he did not desist from a bloody battle fought to the bitter end. Thus no stories such as those anxiously invented by the Buddhist theologians are needed to prove the miraculous power of Buddhism in converting an ordinary King into the saintliest of men. The facts speak for themselves.

Tradition gives different versions of the story of Ashoka's conversion. The Ceylonese legends ascribe it to the young son of his eldest brother Sumana, the boy's name being Nigrodha. Next Tissa, son of Moggali, is mentioned as his preceptor. This divine is reckoned as the fifth Vinaya teacher from the time of the Buddha, his predecessors being Upali, Dasaka, Sonaka, Siggava and Chandavajji. Tissa was sixty years old at the time of Ashoka's coronation, and he died at eighty, succeeded by Mahendra. Yuan Chwang names Upagupta as Ashoka's preceptor in Buddhism, but Upagupta has been identified with Moggaliputra Tissa. The preceptor's first educative measure was to take his royal pupil out on a long pilgrimage already described.

The Emperor also lived under the influence of other Buddhist saints of the times. Among these are mentioned Sumitra and Tissa whose death is said to have been followed by much confusion in the church, due to the heretics outnumbering believers. At last the confusion had to be settled by convoking the Third Council under the King's spiritual director, Tissa, as already related. The Council sat for nine months. It is not easy to define the degree of his devotion to his new faith. It is partly proved by his own statement in the M.R.E. I that he had intimately associated himself with the Sangha, and also by his dedication of his son and daughter to the direct service of the Sangha.

The legends go much farther to prove his devotion by relating the story that on completion of one of his religious edifices he made a gift of the Empire to the monks and bought it back from them three times. This tradition is repeated by Fa-hien who refers to a great tope built by Ashoka at Pataliputra and to a stone pillar near it, fifteen cubits in circumference, and more than thirty in height, "on which there is an inscription, saying, 'Ashoka gave the Jambudvipa to the general body of all the monks, and then redeemed *it* from them with money.' This he did three times". But the few references in the Edicts to the Sangha breathe rather a spirit of authority than of submission, while his civil officers, the Dharma-Mahamatras, were asked to control the Sangha as much as the *parishads* of other sects. Buddhaghosa records a tradition that Ashoka so far controlled the church as to personally expel schismatics, "giving them white garments." His stern attitude towards schism in the church, as expressed *in* his Sarnath, Sanchi, and Kaushambi Edicts, of course, demonstrates his zeal for its welfare.

This brings us to the question of Ashoka's toleration as permitted by his zeal for Buddhism. In the first place, he did not choose to impose his personal faith on his people, although he was so zealous in its service. In the second place, he held the scales evenly between the competing claims of different religious sects to the royal patronage, as shown by his grant of cave-dwellings to the Ajivikas, or promoting the interests to Brahmans, Ajivikas and Nirgranthas equally with the Buddhists through the instrumentality of his officers, the Dharma-Mahamatras, superintending their affairs at state expense. He also favoured the sect of worshippers of the previous Buddhas by doubly enlarging the stupa of Buddha Konakamana and paying a personal visit to the shrine. In the third place, his own Edicts breathe consistently a lofty spirit of toleration. Liberality to Brahmans and Sramanas is always emphasised as a public duty and unseemly behaviour to them equally condemned.

In his own "pious tours," he made it a point of "visiting ascetics and Brahmans, with liberality to them". He passed a, special decree removing the previous distinction obtaining between sects in respect of their rights of residence. In another Edict it is stated that "the King does reverence to men of all sects, whether ascetics or householders, by gifts and various forms of reverence." While encouraging discussion among different religious schools—a time-honoured feature of Indian intellectual life—he deprecated criticism "without reason," "because the sects of other people all deserve reverence for one reason or another," and "he who does reverence to his own sect, while disparaging the sects of others, wholly from attachment to his own, with intent to enhance the splendour of his own sect, in reality by such conduct inflicts the severest injury on his own sect." Thus the King's only care was "that there should be growth in the essence of the matter in, and respect for, all sects". In a later Edict he asserts. " I devote my attention to all communities, for the followers of all denominations are honoured by me and the honour is paid in various forms. Nevertheless, showing personal regard for them is the chief thing in my opinion." It is, however, to be remembered that Ashoka's toleration what appealed most to the essentially spiritual mind of Ashoka were not its external elements, its rituals and regulations, so much as its aids to inner development or self realisation As a Buddhist, Ashoka takes more interest in the regulations for the life spiritual than in those for the collective life of the Sangha, though as Emperor he was keenly interested in its prosperity and preventing and punishing disunion in the Sangḥa.

The particular cast of his mind is, indeed, envisaged in the different canonical texts selected by Ashoka for the religious instruction of his co-religionists of all classes in the Bhabru Edict. He shows a preference for the ideal of the *Muni,* as set forth in two of the texts cited by him, viz., the *Munigatha* and *Moneyasute,* the recluse who is free from all desire, has renounced the world, and lives to himself in solitude and meditation leading up to *nirvana.* In the *Aliyavasani* is emphasised the need of simplicity and asceticism as regards food, dress, dwelling, and the need of meditation. The necessity for strenuous self-exertion in spiritual life is emphasised against the unforeseen hindrances to it from the *Anagatabhayani,* such as disease, decay, famine, war, or schism.

No less are the internal hindrances to it, which are to be guarded against by constant self-examination, scrutiny of every act of the body, mind, and speech, as laid down in the *Laghulovada.* Thus it is apparent from these citations of the texts that what appealed most to Ashoka in Buddhism was its ideal of purity and asceticism, and the aids it prescribes for the life spiritual, rather than its external rituals and regulations or those special and sectarian elements which distinguished Buddhism from other systems.

This also leads us to infer that by the word *Sangha* as used in the Edicts. Ashoka meant the entire Buddhist Order, which in all probability remained undivided up to his time, so that Ashoka's Buddhism was not the particular Buddhism of any of its special sects or schools. This view, though borne out by the Edicts, is not *in* consonance with tradition, according to which, by the time of the third Buddhist Council held at Pataliputra in the tenth year of Ashoka's reign, there were already in the Sangha not only its two divisions, called *Theravada* and *Mahasanghika,* but also two subdivisions of the former and four of the latter. But the tradition may be brought into conformity with what we find in the Edicts, if we suppose with some scholars that the second Buddhist Council at Vaishali really came off at the time of Ashoka (called Kalashoka in tradition) when the Sangha was for the first time threatened with a schism, due to the Ten Points about Discipline raised by the Vrijian monks who were, however, defeated in the controversy, and the split in the Sangha was averted. This explains Ashoka's fear of schism, and his measures to prevent it, and his references in the Edicts to the Sangha as an undivided unity which must be preserved at all costs. His intolerance towards dissent or schism was only due to his desire to nip it in the bud before it was too late: the intolerance could be commended if it had anticipated, and had not followed, the schism.

We shall now treat of his public religion which he sought to present before his people. Negatively, we may say that it was not to be identified with any of the then prevailing faiths of the country. It was certainly not Buddhism, his own religion. "We hear from him nothing concerning the deeper ideas or fundamental tenets of that faith; there is no mention of the Four Grand Truths, the Eightfold Path, the Chain of Causasion, the supernatural quality of Buddha: the word and the idea of *Nirvana* fail to occur; and the innumerable points of difference which occupied the several sects are likewise ignored". As also pointed out by Vincent Smith: "the zeal of Ashoka for Buddhism is proved not by his presentation of Dharma, but by his references to the canon, by the cast of his language, by his pilgrimages to Buddhist holy places, and by his active control of the church", i.e. by what does not appear in the principal Edicts.

The *dharma* of the Edicts is not any particular dharma, religious system, but the Moral Law *independent* of any caste or creed, the *sara* or essence of all religions. It has a twofold aspect (i) practical and (ii) doctrinal. In its practical aspect, it prescribes a comprehensive code of conduct embracing the Various relations of life.

Dharma: If to appreciate a great man of history is to appreciate the doctrine or ideal with which he identified himself, it is meet that, after considering the position of Ashoka the man and King, we should take up his Dharma for discussion.

The inscriptions of Ashoka contain two sets of records: one relating to the Saddharma or Good Faith which he professed as his religion, and the other to the Dharma which he propounded and promulgated. If so, the question arises—how far is the Dharma which he propounded and promulgated consistent with the Saddharma professed by him? Thus the consistency between the Saddharma or religion of Buddha Shakyamuni and the Dharma of Ashoka is the main problem which engages our attention here.

There are divergences of opinion on the real nature and character of Ashoka's Dharma. Three main views on the subject are that of Fleet, that of Vincent Smith, and that of D. R. Bhandarkar.

In Fleet's opinion Ashoka's Dharma is but a form of Rajadharma consisting in the politico-moral principles such as those embodied in the Great Epic. Fleet's opinion may be shown to have been based on the evidence supplied by Buhler.

Vincent Smith opines that the principles promulgated by Ashoka are common to all religions without being identical with those of any one of them. It is in agreement, more or less, with this view that Mukherji is inclined to appraise Ashoka's Dharma as something like a universal religion.

Both Senart and Hultzsch are inclined to interpret Ashoka's Dharma in the light of Buddha's Words. The most powerful advocate of this opinion is Bhandarkar with whom Ashoka's Dharma is nothing short of that aspect of primitive Buddhism which is meant for the upasakas or lay worshippers of Buddha. Both Bhandarkar and Raychaudhary rightly draw our attention to the ideal of the righteous chakravartin upheld by Buddha.

The position taken up by me is that Ashoka's Dharma *is* wholly consistent with the principles of secular Buddhism and not altogether inconsistent with those of other systems of faith and thought, and there is no reason as yet to give it up. Treat it as a form of Rajadharma or as a form of Buddhist Upasakadharma, or even as a form of Universal religion, this position remains unaltered. The acute observation of Rhys Davids that there is not a word about God or the soul in Ashoka's Dharma, not a word about Buddha or Buddhism, makes no difference to it.

As Rajadharma: The Rajadharma in the narrowest sense of the term is based on the Science of Government of which the main problem is what is expedient or inexpedient, conducive or not conducive to the strength of the state. Closely allied to this is the Science of Wealth of which the main problem is what increases and does not increase material resources. Accordingly the Rajadharma was sought to be founded on both." To be broadbased, the Rajadharma has to take cognizance of and uphold the approved social customs and usages and the general principles of law and equity— subjects that come within the scope of the Trayi or Vedic system of which the main problem is what is lawful and equitable and what is not. To be full-fledged and unerring, the Rajadharma has always to seek guidance from speculative philosophy, which came to be recognised as "light to all kinds of knowledge, easy means to accomplish all kinds of action and receptacle of all kinds of virtue."

The extant prose treatise of the Arthashastra represents the final and most methodical form of the Rajadharma which developed in different Brahmanical schools of political or quasi-political thought. The Rajadharma section of the Mahabharata and the Karika of 6,000 verses presupposed by the Arthashastra may be treated as two typical earlier Brahmanical treatises on Rajadharma. Though the Pali Jatakas have many maxims in common with the Great Epic and the Ramayana, particularly the former, through them as well as the Rajavagga of the Anguttara Nikaya and the Agganna, Chakkavatti-sihanada, Lakkhana and Singalovada Suttantas of the Digha Collection was advocated an ideal form of Rajadharma, which in its general tone and spirit and even in phraseology the same as that followed and upheld by Ashoka.

The first question is—What is Dharma from the point of view of Rajadharma? To this, the Upanishad teacher returns the answer— Dharma is the King of Kings. To the question—What is the King of a King Emperor? Buddha returns the selfsame answer: Dharma is the King of a King Emperor. The former declares that there is nothing higher than Dharma, wherefore by Dharma the weaker person rivals the stronger, precisely as by the might of a King. The latter, too, declares the paramountcy of Dharma among men, in the present life as well as the life to follow. So far as the social order is concerned, both maintain the superiority of the warriors as rulers over other social grades, even over the worldly Brahmans.

According to the Upanishad teacher, to affirm Dharma is to affirm Satya or Rita, and *vice versa.* Thus to affirm any one of them is to affirm both. This may be interpreted in two different ways: (i) that Dharma in the sense of the socio-moral order which is an existing fact or actuality is a derivative out of the cosmic life, which has either evolved by the Divine will out of or is founded on the world order; (ii) that Dharma in the sense of the moral or Divine law with its foundation in righteousness or piety is the guiding principle of the socio-moral order in which we find ourselves. Prom the point of view of Rajadharma, Dharma may be interpreted as law in the narrow legal sense of the term with its foundation in rajasasana or rajanusasana, i.e., the will of the sovereign authority of the state. Whether we treat it as the moral, sacred or Divine law or as the King-made or state-enforced law, it is a body of rules which carries with it the sanction from some unchallengeable sovereign authority, whether it be the prevailing collective will and good sense of the society or community, or the express will of the King or state. The essence of both is justice, or, as one might say, both are only means to an end, which is justice. It is desired that to be used as a means of human good and happiness as well as of progress, the King-made or state enforced law must always be subservient to the moral Sacred or Divine law.

Buddha's view concurs with that of the Upanishad teacher in so far as he, too, maintains that the socio moral order of men is the result of an evolutionary process of cosmic life. The difference between the two lies in the fact that in Buddha's account of the process the notion of the operation of any arbitrary will, whether it be in the name of Brahmin or God, is eliminated. With Buddha Dharma or moral law as the guiding principle of the socio-moral order is divine only in so far as its end or underlying purpose is concerned. It is rather the collective experience, good sense and idea of expedience that guide and have guided the course of evolution of the socio moral order. Buddha traces the origin of kingship or state in popular consent which is behind all forms of social contract.

The common upshot of both the views, however, is that the Law is above the King, and not that the King is above the Law.

The ideal of life or the ideal behaviour, conduct or action is, according to the Brahmanist view, one which is set forth by the best among the Brahmans who are the leaders of thought and the accredited teachers of men. According to the Buddhist view, the leaders of thought and the accredited teachers of men are the Sramanas and the Brahmanas or the Brahmanas and the Sramanas, while the best or foremost of all,—the agra—is the Buddha.

The perennial source of Dharma is either Brahmaveda as with the Brahmanist, or Dhammaveda or Atthaveda as with the Buddhist. Dharma is characterised in the Jatakas as 'the good old rule', which is to say, the tradition of piety or duty, the traditional path of virtue. Thus Buddha speaks of the porana-Vajjidharama constituting the national tradition of the Vrijis of Vaishali, the rules of life backed by noble precedents, customs and usages. The Dharma enforced by rajasasana or the sovereign authority of the state is to promote the growth of men in such Dharma and not to hamper it. We can say that this is the common Indo-Aryan conception of Dharma from the point of view of Rajadharma with this difference, however, that in the Brahmanist line the tradition is to be adhered to more in the letter, the departure being allowed to take place only through legal fiction or ingenious interpretation of the texts, and in the Buddhist line the tradition is to be followed more in the spirit, it meaning that the path of virtue or that body of rules which accords with both the supposed original state of the purity of man's nature, the instinctive prompting of unsophisticated human mind and the ideal born of the supreme religious experience and profound meditation of the Enlightened Ones.

With Ashoka, too, the Dharma from the point of view of Rajadharma is 'the good old rule', 'that which is of long standing'. There exists even a verbal correspondence between the two ideas, Ashokan and Buddhist:

- esa porana pakiti.
- esa te poraniya pakati.

Though in R.E. III Ashoka lays equal stress on letter and spirit, in S.R.E. I he takes his officers to task that they failed to catch the import of his instruction as far as it went.

According to the Brahmanist and traditional definition, the raja is one who pleases his subjects. Buddha qualifies it by adding to it the saving clause— dhammena, meaning 'righteously', 'judiciously', 'in accordance with the law of piety or duty': Dhammena pare ranjetiti raja, the verb ranjeti being paraphrased by sukheti pineti, 'makes happy, pleases.' The force of dhammena is sought to be augmented and emphasised by the explanatory clause: dhammeneva, no adhammena, 'righteously indeed, not unrighteously', which is to say, discriminately, and not indiscriminately. Thus the exercise of discretion on the part of the King is explicit in Buddha's definition. Consistently with this, the righteous King Emperor is expected to provide the lawful safety, cover and protection, depending on dharma, showing due respect to Dharma, venerating, reverencing and worshipping Dharma, honouring it in all humility, holding the banner of Dharma, raising the flag of Dharma, and acknowledging the authority of Dharma. Here safety means the safety, of oneself and that of others, and four are the means of safety, viz, moral fortitude, non-harming mental attitude, friendly heart, and compassion; cover means the means of preventing discomforts and guarding means guarding against the action of thieves and other enemies of men and the country.

Ashoka, lays down the same as the general principle of administration when he says: "This is the rule, namely, that which is called rearing by Dharma, providing by Dharma, making happy by Dharma, guarding by Dharma". He desired that his descendants and successors would administer the law of piety by taking each his stand on Dharma and virtue:

Dhammamhi silamhi tistamto dhammam anusasisamti. This reminds us of Buddha's admonition in the Sutranipata, verse 250: Dhamme thito ajjave maddave sato.

> "Standing on Dharma, being in moral rectitude and gentleness of spirit."

Anything approaching the above principle is the following maxim quoted in the Arthasastra:

> "(The King in a newly-acquired territory) should allow those customs in vogue among others to prevail, though these are not observed (in his own country). He should not allow any unrighteous custom to prevail, and should stop it, though it is observed by others."

The meaning of the saving clause 'by Dharma' is not far to seek. The performances of animal sacrifices followed by sumptuous feasts and convivial gatherings, the chariot-processions held in honour of the gods, the royal chase, and the like were the traditional means of entertaining the people. According to Aelian, "Ashoka's grandfather, Chandragupta, used to hold annually a great festival for animal fights. There were butting contests between rams, wild bulls, elephants, and even rhinoceroses, and also races between chariots drawn by two oxen with a horse between them." "It was by the twofold means, namely, the display of darpa, nritya, gita (songs) and vadita (instrumental music), and the organisation of utsava (festive occasions) and samaja (popular gatherings) that Kharavela sought to exhilarate the citizens of the Kalinga capital as the joy celebration of success in his first military campaign. Thus it is opined in the Ramayana: utsavan cha samajas cha vardhane rashtravardhanam. The festivity and popular gathering increase the popularity of the state. The Arthashastra, too, recommends the organisation of yatra, samaja, utsava and pravahana. Kautilya in one passage refers to utsava, samaja and yatra, where the drinking of wine was unrestricted for four days, and in another passage points out the conqueror's duty of conciliating the conquered people by respecting their national devotion to their country, their religion, and their institutions, viz., their utsava, samaja and vihara.

The Great Epic praises in no uncertain terms the pious deed and unrivalled fame of King Rantideva and his Queen in daily killing in the royal kitchen two thousand cattle to feed the people with meat and that invariably during the period of chaturmasya. It extols the viharayatra as sarvakamaprada, "fulfilling all desires for enjoyment", and expressly declares going a hunting to be proper, fitting.

These traditional means of pleasing the people are deprecated by Buddha. The most unfortunate feature of the contemporary social life regretted by Buddha is that even certain classes of the Sramanas and the Brahmanas took delight in them. The animal sacrifices are undervalued, and the release of helpless creatures brought to the sacrificial ground for slaughter by the monarchs in obedience to the dictates of good conscience awakened in them by the Buddhists among the recluses is extolled. The hunting expeditions of the monarchs are shown in several Jatakas to have ended in granting the boon of 'No fear' (abhaya) to all antelopes, to all quadrupeds, to all bipeds (birds), to all aquatic beings (fishes).

Ashoka in his very first edict, holds that no sacrifices should be performed by immolating living beings and no convivial gatherings held as he found many faults in them. He did not, however, condemn the popular gatherings wholesale, without discrimination. He did not omit to mention that there were certain gatherings calculated as good by him. Even with regard to such gatherings as were approved by him, e.g., popular religious demonstrations by the display of celestial mansions, celestial elephants, and the fiery and other divine forms, he was of opinion that these were by far the less effective as means of promoting the growth of the people in piety than the two novel methods introduced and tried by him, viz, imparting instructions in the law of piety or duty and issuing the proclamations of piety. The pleasure excursions typified by hunting expedition were replaced by the pilgrimage of piety. The rites of piety came to be preferred to the divers popular rites that found sanction in secular Brahmanism.

As regards the general method of administration, Ashoka advocates one fulfilling the ideal of the mean between two extreme courses of action, namely, one in which is manifest the character of men determined by such immoral dispositions as malignity, irascibility, cruelty and oppressiveness, and the other in which is manifest the character with non-application, indolence and weariness for exertion as its traits. This middle method grew out of a changed ideology. Extremism in thought as well as the mode of life was the order of the day when Buddha started his career as a teacher of gods and men. As against such extremisms, he propounded his doctrine of the Middle Path, which was not without its salutary effect on the course of the political thought of the country. In the case of a righteous ruler, the Jatakas recommend the middle method as the best method of government: anumajjhani samachare, "he should practise the *felt mean*" The argument advanced in its support is that if too mild a method is followed, the ruler becomes disregarded, and if too rigorous a method is followed, he is apt to provoke hostility.'

Though the term *niadhya* is missed, Kautilya apparently advocates the same method and virtually in the same language in prose:

> "Whoever imposes severe punishment becomes repulsive to the people, while he who awards mild punishment becomes contemptible. But whoever imposes punishment as deserved becomes respectable."

The Arthashastra rightly refers to the earlier agreed opinion that "whoever is desirous of the progress of the world shall ever hold the sceptre raised" This is the opinion which is advocated in the Great Epic by Kanika Bharadvaja and Manu's Law-book, Though the acclaimed advanced political thinker of the eminence of Kautilya prefers a method which is verbally the same as that in the Jatakas and the edicts of Ashoka, its underlying spirit is different, it being that of 'paying in the same coin by way of awarding rewards or punishments'. Referring to the atavis, Ashoka, on the contrary, expresses himself thus: "Even he who today does mischief is considered pardonable by the Beloved of the gods, whom he can pardon". In other words, Kautilya's method leans to the policy of 'Tit for Tat' words, Kautilya's method leans to the policy of Tit for Tat, while Ashoka's middle method inclines more towards tolerating or forgiving the miscreants as long as their actions do not exceed the limits of patience.

The difference in the underlying spirit between the two middle (methods is more manifest in the two forms of conquest by Dharma, one advocated in the Great Epic and the Arthashastra, and the other by Buddha and Ashoka.

The Great Epic distinguishes between Dharmavijaya and Asuravijaya, while the Arthashastra distinguishes between the three types of conquerors, viz, Dharmavijayi, Lobhavijayi, and Asuravijayi. "The first is satisfied with mere obeisance on the part of the weaker King who seeks his protection; the second is satisfied with what he can safely gain in land or money; and the third satisfies himself not merely by seizing the land, treasure, sons and wives of the conquered but by taking the life of the latter as well.' This is the very idea of Dharmavijaya which is behind Kalidasa's account of Baghu's digvijaya. The Dharmavijaya on the part of

Raghu consisted 'in depriving a defeated or weaker King of his glory but not of his territory'. "This is well exemplified by Raghu's traditional treatment of his rival, the lord of the Mahendra Mountain, made captive and then released, the capture and liberation of the Deccan rulers by Samudragupta, and the subduing of the Rathikas and Bhojakas and the Magadhan King Bahasatimita by Kharavela. When some of the Shaka rulers and generals posed sometimes as Dharmavijayi, presumably they acted on this very principle of Dharmavijaya.

I cannot but maintain, as against the opinion of Mr. T. N. Kamachandran, that this is different in its fundamental character from the Dharmavijaya of Buddha and Ashoka. The Epic or Kautilian Dharmavijaya is just the best form of what Ashoka calls Sarasaka or Sayaka Vijaya, i.e., armed conquest, the necessity or possibility of which is not denied by him. The essential feature of the Epic Dharmavijaya is brought out by Ashoka himself when he says that even where it is a necessity, forbearance and light reprisal should be preferred.

With Buddha the Dharmavijaya is a fuller form of conquest by Dharma achieved over an extensive Empire by a King overlord without the infliction of any punishment, without the use of any weapon. According to Buddhaghosa, here 'the infliction of punishment' may mean the imposition of fines, the issuing of orders for massacre, as well as the use of the armed forces, and 'weapon' means all weapons for torturing others. The Pali scholiast explains the phrase, dhammena abhivijiya, as meaning achieving a fuller form of conquest by making it a point not to take the life of a King who comes as desired by the rival King, and following such other principles of action.

It is evident from Buddha's account of the position of the Chakkavatti-monarch that he seeks to achieve such a fuller measure of the conquest by Dharma not out of the consciousness of his weakness but out of that of his irresistible strength in army, wealth and territorial solidarity. Buddhaghosa has not fully brought out the significance of this form of conquest as described in the Chakkavatti-sihanada Suttanta. This may be realised from the Ashokan definition of Dharmavijaya according to which it consists negatively in not thinking of a new territorial conquest through a war of aggression entailing untold miseries and endangering the cause of culture, and positively in assuring the neighbouring states of the King Emperor's good will and desire to respect the laws of territorial integrity besides winning their affection and earning their gratitude through philanthropic and cultural missions.

The ideal feeling relation between the ruler and the ruled is desired by Ashoka to be one that subsists between the loving parent the loving children. The ruler is to inspire this confidence in the ruled that he is to them like a solicitous parent keenly interested in their welfare and eager to connect them with good and happiness. The ruled are to assure the ruler that they are to him like his children. Thus the parental feeling or attitude on one side is expected to be reciprocated by the filial feeling or attitude on the other. This is the best conceivable feeling relation which is expressible in terms of domestic relationship. The analogy is not, however, to be pressed too far, nor is it to be inferred from this that the Ashokan, and, for the matter of that, the ideal Indian government is a parental form of government, founded and run entirely on a domestic model.

In the Great Epic, the Arthashastra, the Buddhacharita, and other Indian works just the ruler's side is emphasised when it is enjoined that the King should look at, be solicitous about the welfare of, or do favour to his subjects precisely as he would do in the case of his own progeny. Ashoka too, lays stress on this side only when he states his own position in the words: "All men are like unto my progeny". But he goes a step further when he claims that he cherished the same parental feeling also towards the people of the neighbouring states.

The scriptural authority for the idea of the mutual feeling relation between the ruler and the ruled is the Mahasutasoma Jataka. The verbal agreement between the two statements will at once indicate the fountainhead of Ashoka's ideal:

- Yatha pita athava pi mata anukampaka atthakama pajanam, evam eva no hotu ayan cha raja, mayam pi hessama tath'eva putta.
- Atha pita hevam ne laja ti. Ath(a) atanam anukampati hevam apheni anukampati. Atha paja hevam maye lajine.

The supreme importance of the position of a King or King overlord in worldly life is recognised by all alike in India. In the authoritative verses cited in the Arthashastra, the King is represented as the founder and upholder of a socio-moral order. According to Buddha, just as a Buddha is the founder of a religious order and propounder of a system of faith and thought, so a righteous universal monarch is the founder of a socio-moral order and propounder of a system of piety and duty. In the Jaina Agama, too, the Chakravartins are regarded as worldly counterparts of the Tirthankaras. The Nijjhatti and the Dhammaniyama may be shown to have occupied the same place in Ashoka's rajadharma as the Dhamma and the Vinaya in Buddha's sasana or system of faith and thought.

In the opinion of the Brahmanical thinkers, however, the King is expected to be the founder and upholdei of only that kind of socio-moral order which is based upon the gradational system of varnasrama-dharma,—of four hereditary social grades and four stages of effort, while in Buddha's ideal scheme the hereditary basis of the four social grades and the graduated system of self-training except on the ground of expedience are denied.

Though the population is broadly divided into Brahmans and Ibhyas in Ashoka's rajadharma as well as in Buddha's social scheme, there is nothing in the edicts to indicate that Ashoka intended to be the upholder of the Brahmanical system as such. In accordance with the ideal set up by Buddha the righteous King overlord is responsible not only for giving the people a good rule making for their welfare and happiness, both here and hereafter, but also for their sound moral and religious education. Thus his part as an anusasaka implies the double function of an efficient ruler and a sound educator of mankind, which Ashoka tried to discharge to the best of his capacity.

According to the Brahmanical thinkers, the tried policies of government consist in conciliating, bribing, creating dissension, and employing force: In Buddha's terminology, these go by the name of four sangahas or sangahavatthus and consist in offering presents and timely help, exchanging the greetings of courtesy, doing good,and fellow-feeling. The wily art of creating dissension and division, and all forms of diplomacy and duplicity are condemned. In the former, there is the utter lack of sincerity; in the latter, the tone is of sincerity. In the former, the four policies are vitiated by the diplomatic motive of self-aggrandisement; in the latter, the four sangrahas are intended to win the heart and to earn the gratitude of all. It is more the idea of four sangrahas which guided Ashoka whose ambition was to win the affection of all men, not to care for any other glory or fame than that the people should be inclined to learn the ideal of piety or duty and to be trained therein, and to depute those officers to deal with the people who are not harsh in their language, not fierce in their nature but are of winsome cordiality.

With Ashoka pasamda is not a term of contempt; it denotes a religious order, sect or denomination. Its phonetic development out of the S.K. Parshada is traceable through its Shahbazgarhi variant prashamda. By the expression, save pasamda, he referred to all religious orders, sects, denominations or schools of thought in India of his time. He broadly divided them into persons following the two modes of life, the pravrajitas and the grihasthas, the former renouncing the household life and the latter keeping to it. The pravrajitas are broadly distinguished as the Brahmanas and the Sramanas, or as the Sramanas and the Brahmanas.

The grihasthas figure in his edicts as the lay adherents and supporters of the different sects and schools of the pravrajitas. Though *ipso facto* the grihasthas themselves were divided into different groups of devotees or worshippers of popular deities, the fact cannot be directly inferred from the edicts. Among the pravrajitas, the typical names mentioned are the Brahmans, the Ajivikas, the Nirgranthas and the Samghasthas. The Buddhists are distinguished as monks and nuns, and upasakas and upasikas. The same kind of distinction holds good also in the case of other orders of the pravrajitas. It is evident from this that women were till then allowed to renounce worldly life and to join the orders of the pravrajitas. The Brahmans represented numerous orders of the pravrajitas as well as Brahmin householders in the service of the state and of the society at large.

Ashoka desired that all the sects should dwell everywhere in his dominions. He insisted on putting up seemly behaviour and giving alms and making gifts to the Brahmanas and the Sramanas, particularly on personally waiting upon them. He knew them to be the persons in whom were well established the principles of piety or duty, such principles as respectful attention to high personages, respectful attention to parents, respectful attention to preceptors and teachers, and seemly behaviour to friends, associates, comrades and relations as well as to slaves and servants, besides strong devotion. He knew them to be the custodians of higher forms of culture and civilization as well as the disseminators of learning and culture in all parts of the country and outside.

If they were affected and distressed, the cause of man's progress in culture and civilization would greatly suffer. Accordingly he completely changed his mind and launched upon a new career of cultural conquest throughout his Empire and throughout the world with the Brahmanas and Sramanas as the brave soldiers of the Aryan faith, and appointed a special class of imperial officers, the Dharma-mahamatras, to look after them while they were carrying on their noble missions. He liberally helped them with alms and gifts and honoured them in various ways. He tried to persuade them to cooperate with one another for their healthy growth in knowledge and matters essential so that they might be better equipped for the great work before them. He dedicated four beautiful cave-dwellings to the Ajivikas in the Khalatika hills. As regards the Buddhist Sangha, he sought to prevent division among its members, even by promulgating a penal ordinance. For the guidance of the Buddhists who were his co-religionists he selected several texts out of the growing corpus of Buddha's Words and commended them for their constant study and meditation.

The information furnished by Megasthenes and other Classical writers about the philosophers or wise men of India of the 4th century B. C. is, in both detail and substance, the same as that which may be gathered from the inscriptions of Ashoka and the Pali Nikayas and Jatakas. The philosophers are broadly distinguished as the Brachmanes and the Sarmanes, or as the Sarmanes and the Brachmanes. The Brachmanes are described as the wise men whose lives were regulated by the rules prescribed in the Grihya Sutras, and as those persons who spent the first period of their lives as brahmacharis or resident pupils in the schools of different teachers and the second period as grihasthas or married householders. Their graduated system of training, ideal of simple living and high thinking, marrying many wives, reluctance to communicate their knowledge of philosophy even to their wives, and wrapping up their doctrines about immortality and future judgement, and kindred topics, in allegories, after the manner of Plato and the like are noticed. It is rightly observed by Megasthenes that their ideas about physical phenomena were very crude, for they were better in their actions than in their reasonings, inasmuch as their belief was in great measure based upon fables.

The Sarmanes are distinguished as the Hylobioi who live in the woods, the Hylobioi who are the physicians, those who practise hard penances, and those who are diviners and sorcerers, adepts in funeral rites, and who go about begging both in villages and towns. Megasthenes mentions that there were religious women who pursued philosophy with some of the Hylobioi. Clemens likens the Hylobioi to the Enkratetai among the Greeks, and distinguishes, as held by Colebrooke, the followers of Boutta (Buddha) from the general body of the Hylobioi.

Pseudo Origen speaks of a sect of philosophers among the Brachmanes par excellence who abstained from animal food and all victuals cooked by fire, went about naked, and lived on the banks of the river Tagabena. With them God was light, the Word, and the body the outermost covering of the soul. The leader of one such sect in Alexander's time was Mandanis, a Dandamis, one of whose unworthy disciples was Sphines whom the Greeks called Kalanos probably for the reason that he greeted a person by uttering the auspicious word kalyanam. This sect of the Gymnosophists, if not precisely a sect of the Ajivikas, was at least a sect of the Achelakas or Avadhutas closely allied to the Ajivikas.

Though the Nirgranthas or Jainas are not expressly mentioned,' their inclusion among the Indian Hylobioi is evident from the reference to the ascetic practice of remaining 'for a whole day motionless in one fixed attitude, say in the posture of one called ubbhatthika in Pali.

Regarding the collective body of the philosophers in India Diodorus accurately observes that they were in point of number a minority, but in point of dignity predominant over all. They, being exempted from all public duties, were neither the masters nor the servants of others. They were, however, engaged by private persons to offer the sacrifices due in lifetime, and to celebrate the obsequies of the dead, for they were believed to be the most dear to the gods, and to be the most conversant with matters relating to Hades. In requital of such services they received valuable gifts and privileges, while to the people at large they rendered great service. When the people gathered together at the beginning of the year, they forewarned them about droughts and wet weather, propitious winds, health and disease, and other useful topics, so that they and their ruler might make adequate provision against a coming deficiency.

Nowhere in a Brahmanical work, whether it be the Great Epic or the Ramayana, the Arthashastra or any of the Law-books, is recognised a religious other than one who is a Brahmin by birth and qualities and a Brahmanist by religious conviction and ideal of life, who, in spite of his being an anchorite or ascetic renouncing everything of the world sannyasin, parivrajaka, yati or bhikshu, is expected to be the upholder of the Vedic system sanctifying the socio-moral order based upon the scheme of four castes and four stages of effort.

The attitude of the Arthashastra towards the Shakyas (Buddhists), the Ajivakas, and such like 'runways' is naively hostile, and the language in which it introduces them, opprobrious. They are indiscriminately stigmatised as Vrishala pravrajitas. The rule it prescribes is to the effect that "when, without making provision for the maintenance of his wife and sons, any person embracing asceticism, he shall be punished with the first amercement; likewise any person who converts a woman to asceticism" may be taken also to go against their interests. In the Ramayana, may be in an interpolated verse, Buddha is bluntly maligned as having been a thief and an atheist. The Brahmin Parivrajakas like Markandeya took Buddha to be a bhunaha, bhunaha obviously for the reason that his opinion went against household life. If at the time of a sacrifice any Sramana was sighted, the Brahmin performer of the sacrifice felt sore offended and tauntingly remarked, saying, "Here comes the shiveling, the Sramana, the Vrishala!" In some of the Grihya Sutras, the prejudice against the Sramanas is sought to be made deep-rooted by giving a religious sanction to the superstitious belief that the sight of a Sramana in a dream portended evil.

John Caird is rudely shocked by the utter inconsistency between 'All is Brahman' doctrine of the Early Vedanta pantheism pantheism and the grossest monstrocities of the Brahmin-sanctioned polytheism. Here he was anticipated by Buddha, in one point at least, namely, that the boasting nature and fury of a Brahmin was wholly inconsistent with his acclaimed proficiency in Vedanta and advance in religious life. The only redeeming feature of the Arthashastra polity is that in B.K. III, Ch. 16, it ordains that the orthodox ascetics (asraminah) and the heretics (pashandas) 'shall, without disturbing each other, reside in a large area' (mahatyavakase-vaseyuh), the newcomer being 'provided with the space occupied by an old resident, and that whether hermits of the Vanaprastha order, or the Yatis and Brahmacharins of the orthodox orders, or the heretics, may when found to be delinquents, in the name of the ruler, perform penances, offer oblations to gods, observe fasts, and the like in lieu of the payment of fines imposed, while in cases of defamation, theft, assault and abduction of women they shall be compelled to undergo the usual punishment, the guiding principle for the ruler being that he shall forbid under penalty imposed by law the wilful or improper conduct among the runaways': pravrajyasu yathacharan raja dandena varayet.

The authoritative maxim in the Arthashastra also desires that the King should honour the Siddhatapasas, making them to dwell in his kingdom. But this is not to be mistaken for Ashoka's desire to see all sects dwell everywhere in his domain, in spite of their verbal agreement. The former keeps in view only those hermits or ascetics who are experts in magical arts and endowed with supernatural powers and may be employed to ward off providential visitations.

Totally different is the attitude of Buddha towards the Sramanas and the Brahmanas. In his terminology, the religious who is a Brahmana is at the same time a Sramana, and *vice versa*. As Sramana the bhikshu stills his nature by getting rid of sins, and as Brahmana he washes away his sins. The religious status of a person is sought to be determined by the state of purity and all-round spiritual advancement, and not by birth or family or any outward sign. The persons of all social grades are entitled alike to this status provided that they stand the test of saintship. The Sangha or Gana (the latter as in the case of the Jainas) is a common brotherhood or sisterhood of all persons who have come away from the world to live and work together in the pursuit of a common ideal of life irrespective of caste or family. Thus the value is set upon man as man, and not upon man in relation to any accidents of birth or social life.

A difference existed nevertheless between the Sramanas and the Brahmanas as such, and it is freely recognised in the early literature of the Jainas and Buddhists. Mahavira generally passed as Samana Mahavira, and Buddha as Samana Gautama. The Wandering ascetics who were born in Brahmin families and belonged to the religious orders to which admission was restricted to persons of the Brahmin caste are bodily distinguished as Brahmana Parivrajakas from the rest who are called Sramana pravrajitas. According to the Sutranipata Commentary, the Brahmans stigmatised the Sramanas as Vrishalas, not because they were all Vrishalas by caste but because they freely admitted even the Vrishalas or Kudras into their orders and interdined with them. Among the pravrajitas or 'runaways', the Tapasas or hermits formed a class by themselves.

All of them belonged to the Vanaprastha order, and were mostly twice-born or persons of the three upper social grades, there having been rarely any Tapasa from among the Shudras, touchable or untouchable. In the early literature of the Jainas and Buddhists, precisely as in the inscriptions of Ashoka, the pravrajitas are broadly represented by the Sramanas and the Brahmanas. They were the objects of love as well as veneration to the people. They were the accredited teachers of religion and ethics to them. In a territory from which they were driven out, the people are shown to have become morally degraded and impious. It is, therefore, repeatedly insisted that a righteous ruler aspiring to be a universal monarch owes a primary duty to them, which consists not only in entertaining them with food and drink, clothing and shelter, but also in paying due homage to them, properly observing the rules of continence on the sabbath days, and waiting upon them for the cultivation of wisdom through instructions and discussions.

The legal authority of the King or state to inflict punishments on the priests and 'runaways' if they were found guilty of criminal offences of any kind or to take drastic measures against the recurrences of mischievous and irreligious actions on their part has nowhere been questioned either in the Arthashastra or in Buddhist literature. On the other hand, there are clear prescriptions and positive evidences to establish the existence of such an authority. The promulgation of a penal ordinance by Ashoka for the suppression of schisms in the Buddhist Order or even in a particular community of Buddhist monks and nuns may be shown to have its precedents in the past action of the Kings of Northern India. The measure adopted by Ashoka is preserved in the Theravada tradition with a note of approval and without any adverse comment. It Was, moreover, in accordance with both the Vinaya rule and the early Buddhist religious sentiment. As the Pali legend suggests, the King exercised this authority with the consent of the leading men of the Sangha. "The Buddhist law," as Mukherji observes, "has its counterpart in the Brahmanical law, according to which mischief-makers who tried to create or foment dissensions in the village communities and assemblies were punished by banishment."

Buddha enjoins it as a noble duty on the part of a righteous King-Emperor and he should ask the virtuous Sramanas and Brahmanas, approaching them from time to time— what is wholesome, what is unwholesome, what is blameworthy, what is blameless, what is cultivable, what is not cultivable, what is that which being done, makes for harm and suffering for a long time, and what is that which being done, makes for good and happiness for a long time.

Ashoka describes the Sramanas and the Brahmanas as suvihita or 'well-established ones', by which he meant the accredited religious teachers in whom the desired principles of piety or duty were established (yesu vihita). The Hathigumpha inscription speaks of 'the honoured recluses who are well-established', while the Theragatha praises visiting the well-established saints as a meritorious deed.

"With Ashoka the supreme deity was doing good to the whole world, and there was greater duty than it.

To the same effect and virtually in the same language the Bajadharma Section of the Great Epic enjoins:

- hitartham sarvalokasya;
- sarvalokahite ratab;
- sarvalokahitam dharmam kshatriyeshu pratishthitam.

The authoritative dictum quoted in the Arthashastra represents the ideal ruler as one who is devoted to the good of all beings: sarvabhtttahite ratab.

The Mahamora Jataka speaks of the righteous King-Emperor as a ruler who grants the boon of 'No fear' to all beings: abbayam cha yo sabbabhutesu deti.

It is said of Buddha, the religious counterpart of the righteous King-Emperor, that he was brought forth by Maya for the good of the many: bahunam vata atthaya. Gautama the Recluse might be praised by the outsiders as the well-wisher of all living beings: sabbp-panabhuta-hitanukampi.

'The whole world' is rather a vague term. By this the Mahamangala Jataka understands the world of the devas, the pitris, the reptiles, and the rest of beings. The beings may be conveniently distinguished as suprahuman, human and infrahuman. The supra-human world is svarga—heaven, the human world is prithivi—earth, and the infrahuman world is apaya—hell. The heaven is the grand world in the sense that there one can obtain and enjoy grand results, or to use Buddha's phraseology, unbounded joy and happiness. The infernal world is a terrible state of woe—of apaya-duggati vinipata in Buddha's words. In Buddha's terminology, the devas were either the gods by birth, such as Indra, Varuna, Agni, the Lokapalas, the sun, the moon, and the stars, or the gods by purity, such as the Sramanas and the Brahmanas held in high esteem as the accredited religious teachers, or the gods by courtesy and popular consent, such as the Kings and Princes. The infrahuman world included also the whole of the animal kingdom—the world of bipeds, quadrupeds, birds, fishes, and the rest. This is comprehended by Buddha's expression migapakkhi. The earth consists narrowly of the domain proper of a ruler, the vassal states, and the bordering territories of allies, enemies or strangers. The Rajadharma of Ashoka, precisely like the Rajadharma of the Great Epic and the Arthashastra and the Raja-chakravarti-Dharma of the Nikayas and the Jatakas, is intended to secure and promote man's interests here in the present world and hereafter in the other world.

The expression 'doing good to the whole world' had a positive meaning for Ashoka. By this he meant that he should make all energetic efforts to see that 'all were free from the innate proneness to sins, that 'all men were actively joined with all good and happiness, both of this world and of the next', that 'the people might sufficiently grow with the growth in piety and sense of duty', that, 'they might elevate themselves'. With Ashoka parisrava is just another word for apuna, meaning 'demerit. In Mahavira's phraseology the two concepts of parissava and asava and their opposites go together, while in Buddha's terminology parissaya stands for lurking danger, the internal spring of impiety and the unwholesome. Ashoka employs the word vadhi as the opposite of hini the word dharmahani occurring in the Bhagavad Gita. Buddha employs antithetically two verbal forms, abbhunna-meyyam and na apanameyyam.

The secret of success in this matter lies, according to Ashoka, in readiness to action and prompt dispatch of state business. Ashoka says that he had no satiety in respect of readiness to action and prompt dispatch of state business. Here the great Maurya Emperor had just followed the wise adage of the age which is traceable almost in the same language in the Great Epic and the Arthashastra quotation of verses:

Mahabharata:

> "Readiness to action on the part of the Kings, which is the secret of success in royal administration."

Arthasastra:

> "Of a King, the vow indeed is exertion, the performance of sacrifice the discharge of duties, the offer of fees the equal attention to all, and the baptizm the consecration.

> In the happiness of the subjects lies the happiness of the King, and in their happiness his welfare. The (personal) welfare is not dear to the King, but the welfare of the subjects is dear.
>
> Hence the King should always be active and administer state-business. The root of advantage is readiness to action, of disadvantage it is the counteractive.
>
> In the case of unreadiness to action surely perish that which is gained and that which is to be gained. He obtains the fruit (desired end) from the promptness in action, and gains in the wealth of advantage."

Though no Pali dictum showing verbal agreement with that of Ashoka is traced so far, it is incontestable that the whole emphasis of Buddha's teachings is on utthana, which is but a synonym of appamada (earnestness), dalhaparakkama (strong power of action), attakara purisakara (self-willed action), bala (strength of the will), viriya (mental energy), and the like. The Dhammapada inculcates that the glory of a person goes on increasing if he is ready for action, mindful, pure in deed, discreet in action, self-restrained, virtuous and earnest.

Just as in Ashoka's edicts the different aspects of the concept of utthana are sought to be expressed by such terms as parakrama (power of action), pakama (strenuous exertion), usaha (zeal), and uyama (effort), dhiti (fortitude), and patimna achala (resolve unshaken), so in the Dhammasangani, we have for the concept of samma-vayama (right exercise of the will) such contributory terms as viriyarambha (energetic initiative), nikkama (strenuous exertion), parakkama (power of action), uyyama (effort), ussaha (zeal), ussolhi (ardour), thama (stamina), dhiti (fortitude), asithila-parakkamata (unabated powerful activity), anikkhittachhandata (unabandoned will to act), anikkhitta-dhurata (steadily keeping on to the path of action), and anikkhitta-sampaggaha (steadfast adherence to the path of action).

With Buddha appamada is the single term by which the whole of his teaching might be summed up. In the Kosala Samyutta, II. 7-8, Buddha mentions appamada to King Pasenadi of Kosala as the single principle of action which stands embracing both the interests, viz., that which appertains to the present existence and that which appertains to the future existence. Here he advises the King to base on this very principle all his duties, private and public, as thereby he might keep him active, wakeful and guarded together with his family members and vassals, his subjects and officers, and his treasury and storehouse.

"Figuratively only utthana means the active state of mind and body. The opposite state of ustana, according to S.R.E. I, is represented by anavuti (non-application), alasiya (indolence), and kilamatha (fatigue).

As observed elsewhere, "Ashoka's principle of utthana or parakrama seeks its fulfilment through atthasantirana, 'prompt dispatch of state business', and is directed to doing good to the whole world, to making all beings happy here and enabling all men to attain to heaven hereafter, particularly to promote other worldly interests. It required all including him and his officers to apply themselves ceaselessly and eternally to the noble cause espoused by way of faithfully and effectively discharging the duties assigned. In short, action, and action alone, was the underlying principle of Ashoka's Dhamma and system of administration."

The two means by which Ashoka sought to promote the cause of piety and human duty in the world are appositely called nijhati and dhammaniyama, the first corresponding to the Pall nijjhatti, and the second to saddhammaniyama. In Pali the term nijjhatti implies the sound method of reasoning, the appeal to reason and understanding, the way of convincing each other by fact and reason, as distinguished from ujjhatti or the obstinate way of suppressing reason by resorting to a kind of *argumentum ad verucundum*. The niyama is the order regulating the path of action which is inviolable. Ashoka sought to give effect to the means of nijjhatti or moral persuasion by the inculcation of the fundamental principles of piety or duty (dhammanusathini), the proclamations of their usefulness, and the tangible works of public utility. The second of these is the duty assigned in Pali literature to the Dhammaghosakas. The way of dhamma-niyama was sought to be given effect to by Ashoka through regulation or legislation,

Ministration to the whole world is possible through the discharge of certain essential duties that are traditionally known in Pali as dasa-raja-dhamma or dasarajavatta. The number ten may be raised to twelve by following a slightly different mode of enumeration. The categorisation of the duties is evidently based upon a certain statement of Buddha, which is just illustrative and not exhaustive. The essential duties of a ruler lie, according to the Arthashastra and other Brahmanical works on royal polity, to the seven elements of sovereignty, *viz.*, himself, the ministers and other officers, the territory and population, the defences, the financial resources, the army, and the allies. These may be taken to consist, according to Buddha, of the obligations to the ruler himself (attani), to his own people, to his own territory, to vassals, to the friends and allies, to the fighting units, to the Brahmans and other needy householders, to the slaves and servants, to the people of towns and districts, to the Sramanas and the Brahmanas, and to the beasts and birds and other animals.

As for the duty to himself, Ashoka's expression is 'just as he feels concern for himself'. The Pali idiom is precisely the same: "just as I feel concern for myself." The earlier Buddhalogy as developed in the Buddhavamsa, the Chariyapitaka and Jataka Nidanakatha speaks of a long course of preparation undergone by the Bodhisattva for serving these three great interests: doing good to oneself, doing good to one's people, and doing good to the world. The first is individual, not to say egotistic; the second is national, not to say parochial; the third is universal, not to say altruistic. These are reduced to two in the Jatakas, viz., in the interest of oneself and in the interest of others. The right application of oneself is considered the best course of wisdom. Before taking the responsibility of instructing others one should first establish oneself in what is proper. To do so one must stand firm in piety and be endowed with moral rectitude and gentleness of nature, be well established in virtue. In words of Ashoka, standing firm in piety and virtue, they will be administering the form of conduct. The philosophic argument behind it is that the enlightened self-interest is *ne plus ultra.* If one holds oneself dear to him, one should guard oneself well. The Arthashastra, cites the word of wisdom according to which the King himself being well-disciplined in sciences, should devote himself to the task of regulating the conduct of his subjects. The object is that he should be the pioneer in noble deeds,—the leader of the multitude, himself being firmly devoted to the practice of piety. He is to be the adikara or first-doer, an epithet applied in the Jaina Agama to the founder of Jainism: aigare titthagare. Ashoka says, "Doing a good deed is difficult. He who does it first, does a difficult thing. But many a good deed has been done by me".

All the authorities agree in saying that the first duty of the King fit to rule is self-preparation through education, learning and training, and that the means thereof is constant contact with men of experience. They also agree in insisting on his protecting himself as well as others against all possible harm. But Kautilya's King, like Machiavelli's Prince, is advised to live always in a world of suspicion and dread, which is full of enemies, internal and external. He is to trust none, neither his wives nor his sons, neither his ministers nor his officers; neither the food which is cooked nor the bed which is prepared for him, not even his friends, far less his enemies, not even himself.

Buddha's righteous King Emperor is expected to live, on the other hand, in a world of trust and security where all are imbued with the same spirit of Dharma and all are devoted to the pursuit of the common ideal of life. Ashoka's world is such a world of trust and security where all should be working for piety.

By the expression 'own people' are narrowly meant one's family members consisting of wives and sons (children). Mother and father are to figure most prominently among them. One's own people may be taken also to include brothers and sisters and other kinsfolk. Ashoka speaks of parents, teachers, wives and sons, brothers and sisters, other kinsmen, other Princes of the blood. Along with kinsmen he mentions friends, associates, comrades and companions, all comprehended by Buddha's expression mittamachcha or natisuhajja. He does not omit to refer also to the neighbours. He distinguishes one's people as those who are closely and those who are distantly related, as those who stand near and those who stand afar. With sons go grandsons, great-grandsons and the descendants after them. He speaks in the same breath of father, son, brother, master, friend, associate, even down to neighbour. Though the individual words are met with in all literature of India, there is little doubt that Ashoka's language or manner of speaking is almost verbally the same as that in the Buddhavachana. Ashoka's word vijita for one's territory is typically a Pali word.

The Nikayas mention the Shakyas as vassals under the King of Kosala. Such vassals within Ashoka's Empire were the Yavanas, the Kambojas, and the rest. The idea of vassals is rather obscure in the Great Epic and the Arthashastra. Samanta in the sense of independent neighbours is as much a Pali or Sanskrit word as Ashokan, while the word Anta or Pratyanta in the same sense is peculiarly Ashokan. Ashoka's Barnbhanibha is the very same expression as the Pali Brahmanibbha or Brahmana-gahapatika by which the needy people of the-world are meant. Even the Brahmanas and the Sramanas in one aspect of their earthly existence, namely, mendicancy, may be taken to have been meant by the expression Brahmanibbha. In the Pali Nikayas and Jatakas, precisely as in Ashoka's Edicts, the Brahmanas and the Ibbhas, or the Brahmanas and the Sramanas are often associated with the four classes of beggars, viz. kapana meaning 'those in a pitiful condition, the poor people suffering from bodily infirmity', addhika or street-beggars, vanibbaka or 'those beggars who induce the public to offer alms and make gifts by proclaiming the merit that accrues from alms-giving and gifts, and yachaka or 'the beggars imploring the public to spare anything, however little or insignificant. Ashoka's anathas, vudhas (age-worn persons), kapana-valaka, and dasa-bhataka are rightly grouped with persons deserving of compassion. One may take along with them also other persons in distress, such as those who are shut up in prison (bamdhanabadha) and those sentenced to death. The sick implied in R.E. II are to be counted also among the distressed.

The expression negama-janapada which is the same as pora-janapada applies to the people of towns and districts who are variously engaged in the transactions of life, particularly commercial.

The expression samana brahmanaas distinguished from brahmana-gahapatika applies to the 'runaways' who are the accredited religious teachers of men.

And the expression migapakkhi (lit., beasts and birds) applies to all animals, whether bipeds or quadrupeds, terrestrial or aquatic.

The territory gained by a King is rightly said to be of three kinds: that which is newly acquired, that which is recovered, and that which is ancestral. In Ashoka's case the territory of the second kind is out of the question as he is not known to have lost any portion of his territory. The major portion of his territory is ancestral, Kalinga being the only territory newly acquired. It is the agreed opinion of all Indian political thinkers that the primary duty of a King or King Emperor is to see his territory consolidated, or to guard it carefully if it is a newly conquered one.

In the ancestral territory the reigning King is advised in the Arthashastra to cover the faults of his father and to manifest his own virtues. The instance of King Siri Meghavanna who tried to make ample amends for certain tyrannical and revengeful acts of his father Mahasena might here be cited from the history of Ceylon.

Ashoka in his edicts, does not think of his father or immediate predecessor but only of the former Kings who had through several ages built up a noble tradition of piety. The works of public utility done by them was also being done by him just to keep up the tradition, though these in his opinion had but slight effect. As for himself, he tried to fulfil their noble intention to see the people grow sufficiently with the growth in piety by adopting two novel methods.

With regard to the newly acquired territory the King is advised in the Arthashastra to adopt, among others, the following means of pacification:

Trying to cover the faults of the fallen enemy with his virtues and excelling his virtues by doubling his own. Devotion to his own duties and works. The showing of favours, the offering of presents, the giving of gifts, the bestowing of honours, and the doing of what is agreeable and good to the subjects. The adoption of the same mode of life, the same dress, language and etiquette so as to avoid appearing as "a stranger in the habits of life. The evincing of personal interest in their national, religious and social festivals and functions. The honouring everywhere of religious orders. The offering of land, articles of use, and other gifts and presents to persons noted for their learning, eloquence and piety. The release of all prisoners and the doing of favour to miserable, helpless and diseased persons. The prohibiting of the slaughter of animals for half a lunar month during the period of chaturmasya, for four nights during the full moons, and for a night on the day of the birth-star of the conqueror King and on that of the national star; the prohibiting as well of the slaughter of females and young ones and the castration of males.

One may observe that in this particular context the Arthashastra prescribes all the noble principles of rajadharma advocated by Ashoka through his edicts and that the prohibitions are precisely those embodied in his Regulation of Piety. But we lose all zest in the Arthashastra prescriptions and prohibitions as soon as we learn that these are all meant to give the conqueror a good appearance before the people of a conquered territory. One is likely to wonder where-from the Arthashastra got the idea of these advantageous prohibitions when these are bodily against the rules of secular Brahmanism. Consider for instance, Ashoka's prohibition of the branding of horses and cattle with marks on the Tishya, Punarvasu and chaturmasi full-moon days, as well as for half a month during the period of Chaturmasya. The Arthashastra has no prohibitory rules regarding the time of marking the cattle. The most auspicious time for marking is the Kartika full-moon or the star Bevati in the month of Asvayuja, according to the Law-book of Vishnu. The Asvalayana Grihya Satra adds the full moon day of Vaisakha, while the Sankhayana Grihya Sutra prefers the new moon after the month Phalguna and the star Revati after the full moon.

"Ashoka's Regulation was meant to restrain the people of India against the killing of she goats, ewes, and sows, if they were found to be with young or in milk, as also against the killing of their offspring, if they were within six months of age. Among the Smritikaras, Gautama alone, as pointed out by Buhler, forbids the meat of animals whose teeth have not fallen away. In the Nigrodhamiga Jataka, a doe desiring to put off her turn of going into the execution-block, pleads her case, saying, 'Sire, I am now with young. There is not a word about the cow and her calf in the edict in this particular connection. The oxen (gone) certainly find mention alongside of goats, rams and pigs in the context of the rule for branding. Following the custom of the Middle Country, Bodhayana and Vasishtha prohibited the meat of milch-cows and oxen, Kautilya penalises the killing of the calf, the bull, and the milch-cow. The Buddha raised his strong voice against the killing of cows, and succeeded in persuading some of the contemporary rulers and leading Brahmin teachers of the Middle Country to put a stop to the practice. The killing of milch-cows, oxen, and calves must have been out of the question in the Middle Country of Ashoka's time."

The identity of Ashoka's samdaka figuring in his list of inviolables (avadhyas) is still open to dispute, Buhler takes it to mean the bulls set at liberty that serve in India as stud bulls. If it really stands for such bulls, the reader might be referred to the Arthasaastra prescribing rules to punish with the first amencement a person who causes the leading bull of a herd to fight with another bull, and with the highest amencement when such a bull is injured thereby.

Though both the grounds and purposes of the game laws in P.E. V and the Arthaststra are different, the birds, fishes, and quadrupeds declared as inviolables are for all practical purposes the same. "From the qualifying clause, 'that neither come into (men's) use nor are eaten', Ashoka's purpose seems to have been to stop for good the unnecessary killing or torture of inoffensive creatures, not because they were *mangalyas* or sacrosancts (as in the Arthashastra). The abandonment of the practice of going on hunting expedition on his part must have been in accordance with the dictates of his new religious conscience, His intention of minimising the slaughter of and inflictions of cruelty on living beings which is clearly expressed in R.E. I is perceptible also behind all the restrictive measures contemplated in his Regulation."

On the question of the King's or King Emperor's obligations to the needy, the destitute, the minor, the aged, the diseased, the distressed and the fallen the Indian systems of rajadharma are hardly at variance.

To take, first of all, the case of the diseased among men and animals. With regard to them Ashoka tells us that he made throughout his dominions as well as in the territories of his friendly neighbours arrangements for two kinds of treatment, one suitable for men and the other for animals. To implement it he caused medicinal herbs and roots and fruits to be supplied and planted wherever these were not available. The arrangements made by him may not strictly be taken to mean that he founded hospitals for men and cattle. Almost to the same effect and in the same language the Rajadharma section of the Great Epic enjoins:

> "Medicinal herbs and roots and fruits and four classes of physicians should particularly be collected."

According to the Arthashastra, when pestilences and epidemics occur as a national calamity, the King should try to cope with them by such remedies as secret arts, medicines, and pacificatory and purificatory ceremonies. The medicines are to be applied by the physicians and the pacificatory and purificatory ceremonies are to be performed by the siddhatapasas. In the case of cattle diseases, the King should perform the ceremony of nirajana as well as the worship of the family deity. But elsewhere the Arthashastra speaks of the treatment of the diseases of cattle, horses and elephants by expert physicians.

With regard to the helpless, the aged, the miserable and the distressed, Ashoka ordained seemly behaviour and appointed the Dharma-mahamatras to work for their good and happiness. The religious mendicants are taken along with them. Among the prisoners, those burdened with the maintenance of family and those advanced in years were made entitled to special consideration in the matter of ransom, leniency and release.

The Nikayas and Jatakas abound in admonitions to the Kings persuading them to feed the mendicants of all description, to give them alms, and to liberally help them with gifts out of faith and without worried mind.

Regarding men and animals in old age, the general principle laid down in the Jatakas is:

> "The officers in their old age as well as the cows and horses should not be engaged in work as before, and they should be given due consideration on account of the good service rendered when they were in strength."

In keeping with the general spirit of the age the Arthashastra lays down the following rules to safeguard the interest of religion and the religieux, the infants and invalids, women and children, the poor and the helpless:

> "The King shall personally attend to the business of the gods, of the Brahmanical ascetics, of the heretics, of the Srotriyas, of cattle and sacred places, of minors, the aged, the afflicted and the helpless, and of women, either in the order of enumeration or according to the gravity or urgency of the duties."

> "The King shall provide the orphans, the aged, the diseased, the afflicted, and the helpless with maintenance. He shall also maintain (helpless) women when they are carrying and the children they give birth to."

According to the Arthashastra, on the days connected with the birth-star of the King and the full-moon days 'such prisoners as are young, old, diseased or helpless shall be let out from the jail, or those who are of charitable disposition or those who have made any agreement with the prisoners may liberate them by paying an adequate ransom'.

The authoritative maxims quoted in the Arthashastra mention the conquest of a new country, the installation of the heir-apparent, and the birth of a Prince as the special occasions for jail delivery. "Once in a day," they say, "or once in five nights, jails may be emptied of prisoners in consideration of the work they have done, or of whipping inflicted upon them, or of an adequate ransom paid in gold."

As regards the prisoners on whom death sentence has been passed by the court, Ashoka says that he granted them three days' respite either to give a chance to their kinsmen to have their cases reviewed for the sparing of life, or at least to observe religious fast and offer gifts within the specified time of death, to prepare, in other words, for death. Nothing corresponding to this is to be found in the Arthsastra or elsewhere in Indian literature.

Servitude, indebtedness, disease, imprisonment and long journey, particularly one across a wildnerness are mentioned by Buddha as typical states of woe from which men seek release. Servitude is described as the hard lot of slaves and hirelings, of slaves and servants in the words of Ashoka. Though indebtedness is not expressly mentioned in the edicts, it is included in the general problem of poverty and destitution dealt with by Ashoka and others. As a contributory-cause of servitude and imprisonment, indebtedness may be regarded as a subhead of both.

Long journey, especially one across a wilderness, means the suffering of the travellers including caravan merchants from fatigue as well as risks of life and fortune from the action of thieves and robbers. The construction and maintenance of roads, guarding them against inroads of thieves, highway robbers, wild tribes and animals, providing guides and escorts, shade-trees, inns and caravansaries, and the like are all meant for ensuring the safety and comfort of the travellers. The planting of shade-trees at every half *kos*, the sinking of wells and excavation of tanks, the construction of resting sheds and water-stations, the laying out of fruit gardens and retreats, the founding of almshouses, and similar other institutions of comfort were admittedly the time-honoured tradition of piety established by the former Kings of India which was just kept up by Ashoka.

All of them come within the scope of ishtapurtam praised in the Brahmanical Law-books as works of merit. Similarly the Buddha praises the laying out of flower gardens and fruit gardens, the making of forest retreats, the construction of bridges, etc., the building of water-stations, and the digging of wells and tanks as meritorious works of public utility by which persons become entitled to go to heaven.

According to the Arthashastra, it was the duty of the superintendent of passports and the Antapalas and Atavipalas to guard the frontiers, forest tracts and uninhabited tracts with a view to the safety of travellers and the control of travels and traffic, while the Pradeshtris were specially charged with the duty of removing all thorns or internal troubles arising from the action of thieves, robbers, and the like. It recommends certain amount of leniency on the part of the judges in dealing with the cases of persons suffering from the fatigue of long journey. In Buddha's opinion it is one of the seven main conditions of national welfare that legal protection should be vouchsafed for worthy visitors so that they may be induced to visit the land and when they come they may find the place quite comfortable. The Arthashastra refers to rest-houses among the charitable institutions in a town or city that were open to wandering ascetics and travellers. The wayfarers going along a highroad are required to catch hold of any person whom they find to be suffering from a wound or ulcer, or possessed of destructive instruments, or tied of carrying a heavy load, or timidly avoiding the presence of others, or indulging in too much sleep, or fatigued from a long journey, or who appears to be a stranger to the place in the localities such as inside or outside the capital, temples of gods, places of pilgrimage, or burial grounds. Among the Classical writers, Strabo refers to a board of town officers who attended to the entertainment of foreigners, assigning to them lodgings, keeping watch over their modes of life, escorting them on the way when they leave the country, taking care of them when they are sick, burying them if they die and forwarding their property to the relatives of the deceased.

Slavery existed in different forms and degrees of servitude in India even when Megasthenes came as an ambassador to the court of Chandragupta Maurya, nay, it existed even in earlier times. The treatment of slaves was, nevertheless, so liberal and humane that slavery, even if it existed in the country, was nothing as compared with its Greek or Roman form. One of the remarkable facts, noted by Megasthenes about India was that all the Indians were free, and not one of them was a slave.

Though the Lakedaemonians and the Indians agreed so far in this matter, the former held the Helots as slaves, but the latter did not even use aliens as slaves and much less a countryman of their own. The statement of the Greek ambassador about the non-existence of slavery in India has rather been misconstrued by his modern critics. Diodorus truly represents the account of Megasthenes when he says, "Of several remarkable customs existing among the Indians, there is one described by their ancient philosophers which one may regard as truly admirable; for the law ordains that no one among them shall, under any circumstances, be a slave, but that enjoying freedom, they shall respect the equal right to it which all possess." Thus Megasthenes was concerned with the ideal advocated by the philosophers and religious teachers and the underlying spirit of the law of the land,

and not with the actual state of things. If we say that in England and Burma there is no harlot in the eye of law, we do not certainly mean that there is no harlot in fact; all that we intend here is a distinction between *de jure* and *de facto*. Speaking of the philosophic and religious standpoint, he was careful to observe: "Those, they thought, who have learned neither to domineer over nor to cringe to others will attain the life best adapted for all vicissitudes of lot: for it is but fair and reasonable to institute laws which find all equally, but allow property to be unevenly distributed."

The Arthashastra emphatically declares that servitude is not verily consistent with the condition of an Aryan, though it may not be improper among the unclean to sell or buy children for servitude. The general tenour of the laws prescribed in this great work is to afford all possible chances to the slaves to regain their free state.

Buddha not only abstained himself from receiving slaves, male and female, as gifts but also restrained his disciples from it. He prohibited 'traffic in human beings' on the part of the laity. In accordance with the Jataka maxim, no person should offer himself to slavery.

Taking servitude to be an existing social institution, Ashoka pleaded for seemly behaviour. Buddha defined in a concrete form the nature of such a behaviour, and the Arthashastra prescribed the laws for its regulation by the state.

Going by Ashoka's statement that he had enacted many regulations of piety, we cannot but understand that all of them were intended to give a practical effect to the principles of piety or duty enunciated in the edicts and promulgated through them. These regulations having not all been placed on record, to make an idea of what they might be we have no other alternative but taking our guidance from the theoretical scheme of the whole duty of a noble householder as advocated by Buddha and to a great extent to infer from the state-enforceable laws of conduct as prescribed in the Arthashastra.

Upasakadharma: The term upasaka is employed in the edicts to denote, precisely as in the Buddhist and Jaina works, the householders included in a religious community as lay adherents and supporters of a distinct body or sect of the Sramanas or the Brahmanas. The feeling of veneration and the cherishing of serene faith determined the devotional attitude of the upasakas and upasikas. Each sect or school of thought had its own doctrinal tradition, not to call it a scripture in the absence of writing being used for the purpose of recording and transmitting that tradition.

The upasakas attached to a particular sect were supposed to believe that all that was embodied in such a tradition was well said. Apart from their adherence to this or that sect or school of accredited religious teachers, the upasakas were mere householders belonging to different social grades and orders. As householders their lives were regulated by certain social customs and usages, certain rules of decorum and conduct, and certain laws of the land enforced by the state, while as upasakas they were temperamentally disposed to cultivate certain special virtues and to shun certain vices emphasised by the ministers of the faith in which they were believers.

Rajadharma being primarily concerned with secular affairs of men, it is ultimately reducible to Upasaka or Grihastha Dharma. The difference between the two lies in the fact that there is state sanction behind the former, while the latter has nothing behind it but the force of customs and social approval or disapproval, not to call it social and religious sanction. The common aims of both are the attainment of good and happiness here and the attainment of heaven hereafter; the attainment of Nirvana or Moksha is far beyond their scopes.

The chief interests of both centre round the three topics of dana, sila, and sagga (heaven), here dana and sila being just the two means to the attainment of heaven. The heaven in popular belief is a paradise of unbounded joy and happiness—a higher world or state of existence where a pious man reaps the great fruit of his meritorious deeds on earth, the celestial mansions, celestial elephants, fiery and other celestial forms symbolise the paradise of popular fancy which in the eye of the divines and philosophers is but a fools' paradise. This paradise is either the heaven of Indra, or that of the four Lokapalas, otherwise called Maharajas, or at the best the divine world of Brahma who is endowed with eternal youth and unsurpassed glory. The commingling of the gods and men in Jambudvipa is claimed by Ashoka as his most remarkable achievement through strenuous exertion. Ashoka's expression, misibhuta, is explained in the Jataka Commentary in a physical sense, meaning 'brought into close bodily contact so that they might appear as clasping each other's hand.

Thus here by commingling we are not to think of comradeship in heaven which is possible only after death but of coming together on earth in human form, e.g., in a mixed congregation of gods and men listening to an important religious discourse. To be a god, even one of an inferior rank, was the popular aspiration of a person practising a certain kind of virtue, conforming to a certain rule of conduct, keeping a certain religious vow.

According to the Classical writers, the Brachmanes of India were regarded as 'dear to the gods.' This enviable position was contested by the Sramanas, and no less by a righteous King Emperor like Ashoka bearing the title of Devanampriya. The persons who became gods after death came down to the earth to express their gratefulness to the righteous universal monarch. To erect a ladder between heaven and earth was the ambition of the Devanampriya as of other powerful monarchs and saints. The practice of virtue came to be popularly extolled as the ladder for climbing up to heaven. The sculptural representation of the ladder by which Buddha descended at Samkasya in one of the Bharhut panels, with Shankara and Brahma as umbrella-bearers, is too naively physical to retain the charm of the poetic metaphor behind the popular legend.

With regard to the position of Ashoka's Dharma as a form of Upasaka "Dharma, we may do no better than quoting below the significant observation of Rhys Davids according to which "It was the Dhamma for layman, as generally held in India, but in the form, and with the modification, adopted by the Buddhists. The curious thing about this Dhamma, as a description of the whole duty of man, the good layman, is, especially when we consider its date—its extraordinary simplicity."

Bhandarkar has ably discussed in this connection the importance of the Singalovada Suttanta to which attention was drawn for the first time by me. This discourse of Buddha on the whole duty of a good householder was not unreasonably esteemed as Gihivinaya or 'Institute for the householders' The Mangala Sutra, with the Mahamangala Jataka in its background, is but a poetical summary of the Singalovada Suttanta.

The interest of the longer prose discourse lies in the fact that it sets out a scheme of the whole duty of a good householder, which is conceived on a reciprocal or relational basis and may as such serve as the doctrinal basis of a Law of Persons. The six typical relations of reciprocity are those between parents and son, teachers and pupil, husband and wife, kinsman and kinsman, friend and friend, master and slaves and hirelings, the Sramanas and Brahmanas and the lay supporter.

There is nothing to prevent one from adding to these such other relations as those between King and subject, brother and brother, brother and sister, neighbour and neighbour, senior and junior, the rich and the poor, men and lower animals. The edicts of Ashoka presuppose all these relations, the systematic way of thinking in India in terms of such relations being peculiarly Buddhistic. The stress is laid in the edicts on the most elementary duties probably under the thought that when these are fulfilled, the rest are bound to follow. Consistently with its limited scope a state can regulate the minimum of human good, leaving the maximum to be achieved by the collective effort of the nation or community. The elementary, principles of piety or duty inculcated by Ashoka, consist in the following:

- respectful attention to parents;
- respectful attention to teachers and preceptors and honouring them in all humility;
- respectful attention to high personages;
- respectful attention to seniors or men of experience, following their advice and waiting upon them;
- seemly behaviour and liberality to the Sramanas and the Brahmanas, as well as waiting on them;
- seemly behaviour and liberality to friends, associates, comrades and kinsmen;
- seemly behaviour to slaves and servants;

- cherishing parental feeling towards the subjects and cherishing filial feeling towards the King;
- the non-slaughter of life and the non-harming attitude of mind towards living beings.

The idea of mutual obligations in the discharge of duties by householders is clearly suggested in Ashoka's instruction—This should be propounded by a father or a son or a brother or a, husband or a friend, associate or relative, or even by neighbours: This is good, this should be done".

The definitive modes of performing the duties stressed by Ashoka are catechetically enumerated as follows in the Singalovada Suttanta: Five are the typical modes of discharging one's duty to one's mother and father, viz., maintaining them out of a feeling of gratitude that he was reared up by them, doing their duties, keeping up the family tradition, deservedly inheriting their property, and performing funeral duties.

Five are the typical modes of discharging one's duty to one's teachers and preceptors, viz., rising up from seat at their approach, waiting upon them for instructions, attentively listening to their words, rendering personal services and preparing the lessons given.

(e) Five are the typical modes of discharging one's duty to the Sramanas and the Brahmanas, viz., friendly bodily action, friendly vocal action, friendly mental action, keeping the door of hospitality open to them, and supplying them with their temporal needs.

Five are the typical modes of discharging one's duty to one's friends, associates, comrades and relations, viz., offering help and presents, pleasing with sweet words, doing good to them, expressing fellow-feeling, and keeping up amity among them.

Five are the typical modes of discharging one's duty to one's slaves and hirelings, viz., employing them according to their capacity, giving them proper meals and wages, attending them in times of illness, sharing with them delicacies and special dishes, and occasionally granting-them leave.

The Arthashastra prescribes the state enforceable laws relating to the slaves and hirelings, It prescribes similar laws to regulate man's duty to his parents, wife, children, brothers and sisters:

> "When a capable person other than an apostate (patita) neglects to maintain his children and wife, mother and father, minor brothers and sisters, or widowed girls, he shall be punished with a fine of twelve panas.
>
> When, without making provision for the maintenance of his wife and sons, any person embraces asceticism, he shall be punished with the first amencement."

Universal Religion: The term Universal religion' as applied to Ashoka's Dharma is sweetly vague in its connotation; it is Just an empty word of praise until the meaning in which it is used is precisely defined. One can say that it is non-credal in its stress and non-sectarian in its spirit,—non-credal in the sense that it eschews all matters of theology and speculative philosophy, and nn-*i* sectarian in the sense that it nowhere intends thrusting any man's views and beliefs upon another. As Rhys Davids puts it, "There is not a word about God or the soul, and not a word about Buddha or Buddhism." The Four Noble Truths, the Causal Genesis, Nirvana, and other distinctive tenets of Buddhism find no place in it. The word Dharma which, according to Rhys Davids, corresponds with the Latin *forma,* means 'good form', and the two main points discussed in Ashoka's Dharma are what is proper for good men to do and what is improper for them not to do, or, as one might say, what are the things that lead to sin, to demerit and vice or innate proneness to sin, in short, to the state of woe and the utter degradation of human nature, and what are, on the other hand, the things that lead to much good, to unbounded merit, in short, to grand heaven which is a state of unbounded joy and happiness and to the elevation of human nature. These are indeed the two main points with which religion is concerned, whether it be Buddhism or Jainism, Brahmanism or popular Hinduism, Christianity or Islam.

Ashoka's Dharma is broadbased upon the principle of tolerance. The Ashokan idea of toleration differs, however, from the general Indian idea in that it offers a scheme of active co operation among all sects for their growth in essential matters, and does not leave any sect to itself under the comfortable belief that all faiths lead ultimately to one and the same goal. It wants all sects and exponents to come together for frank and free interchanges of their thoughts and ideas in a mutually helping spirit. It urges that men of all sects should listen to and study each other's doctrines so that all may be well-informed and possessed of noble traditions. If there be any criticism in the course of discussions, it should be as light as possible and always to the point, but there must also be due appreciation of other sects in this or that point. One must not unduly extol one's own sect and condemn another sect because it is not one's own. He who does that, does so because of his devotion to his own sect and with the desire of glorifying it. In doing so, he not only does a great disservice to other sects but also digs the grave of his own sect. Concord, therefore, is good, and at the root of it is self-restraint, particularly the guarding of the tongue.

Ashoka's samavaya is not precisely the modern Hindu idea of Dharma-samanvaya or harmony of all religious faiths. The basic idea of this harmony as advocated by "Ramakrishna Paramahamsa is traced in the Rigveda dictum—"They designated one and the same Deity by many a name". The Advaita axiom is upheld by Rishi Uddalaka when he declares the ultimate reality as one without a second, and by Buddha when he maintains that truth or reality is one. In the immediate background of Ashoka's tolerance is the exclusive, mental attitude which finds its characteristic expression— "What I affirm is the only thing true and everything else is false". In a tone of disapprobation Buddha observed: eke samana-brahmana sakam yeva vadam dipenti jotenti, paravadam pana khumsanti. "Certain Sramanas and Brahmanas edify and glorify verily their own doctrine, but deprecate the doctrine of others." Here one may notice even a verbal correspondence with Ashoka's words; atpapasamda-puja parapasamda-garaha, atpapasam Jain dipayema iti. The Great Epic goes a step further when it cites the time honoured opinion of the exponents of piety according to which neither the condemning and honouring of oneself nor the condemning and extolling of others is the practice of the Aryans.

Now, to consider some of the behests of Ashoka's Upasaka Dharma. The first of them is respectful attention to mother and father. This corresponds to Buddha's expression mata-pitu-upatthanam. The valedictory address in the Taittiriya Upanishad enjoins: matridevo bhava, pitridevo bhava. "Honour thy father and thy mother" is one of the ten commandments in the Old Testament. The second is respectful attention to teachers and preceptors. Respectful attention (susrusa) is one of the five typical modes of fulfilling one's duty to teachers and preceptors.

These are covered also by the following stanza from the Dhammapada:

Sukha matteyata loke, atho petteyyata sukha, sukha samannata loke, atho brahmannata sukha. The third is non-slaughter of life and non-harming mental attitude towards living beings (anarambho prananam, avihimsa bhutanam). That this is a common behest of Jainism and Buddhism goes without saying despite the fact that the expressions are more Buddhistic than Jaina.

The universality of Ashoka's Dharma may be particularly appreciated with regard to its psycho-ethical concepts. In answer to the self-put question—Wherein does the Dharma consist? Ashoka mentions the six principles of which the first two are apasinave and bahukayane. Here apasinave corresponds in a sense to apaparisrava meaning 'little demerit', 'little sin', better 'little proneness to sin.' In the Jaina Acharanga Sutra, parissava and asava are treated as synonyms. Evidently the two terms represent two sides of piety, namely, negative and positive: 'little evil' and 'much good.' The second term, bahukayane or 'much good' as an abstract moral quality, finds its fulfilment in many good deeds, In E.E. IV, however, the expression bahukalanam is employed in a concrete collective sense.

The two directly antithetical terms are kayane (kalyanam) and pape (papam) in which case asinava must be treated as a resultant moral factor following from a sinful deed,—from an act of demerit. Corresponding to kayana and papa in P.E. II, we have in R.E.V the use of the two antithetical terms sukatam and dukatam. It may be noted that in the religious literature of India, whether Buddhist, Jaina or Brahmanical, punya and papa, sukrita and dushkrita, sadhu and asadhu, and the like are frequently met with as antithetical pairs of terms. In the opinion of Bhandarkar asinava corresponds more to the Jaina anbaya than to the Pali adinava, none of the Buddhist enumerations of the passions and acts with reference to adinava being suited to the Ashokan context. The Pali adinava is explained by Buddhaghosa in the sense of amadhurabhava, upaddava and dosa. In the Nikayas, adinava in the sense of 'fault' occurs as a synonym of okara and samkilesa due to which all passions become very painful and disappointing. In the phrase, adinavo ettha bhiyyo, the term stands for trouble. The Itivuttaka Commentary connects adinava also with such malevolent passions as kodha and mana. In the Amarakosha, adinava, asrava and klesa signify three allied afflictions due to a disease, the first for the general weakening of the system, the second for the infuriating of the organs, and the third for the ailments. Referring to the Acharanga Sutra, Bhandarkar observes: "Jainism specifies eighteen kinds of papa or sin and forty-two kinds of asravas. These two lists have four malevolent affections in common, called kashayas. Two of these are krodha and mana, exactly two of the passions named by Ashoka. The isya of Ashoka, again, is to be found in the Jaina list of the papas, as Irshya or dvesha; chamdiye and nithuliye are alone not traceable, though they are covered by the malaffection himsa mentioned under asrava. Thus the use of the term asinava (anhaya), distinction between it and papa, and the inclusion of at least three passions of the Jaina lists are enough to convince anybody that in all likelihood, Ashoka has here adopted and assimilated same psychological concepts of Jainism."

Here the evidence of the Aupapatika Sutra would seem more conclusive. In this Sutra, the adjective anhayakare, meaning 'causing affliction, anhaya having to all intents and purposes the connotation of the term asinava, is applied to a malevolent mind needing control. The other predicates of such a mind are chhedakare (swayed by the passion of cutting), bheyakare (swayed by the passion of piercing), paritavanakare (causing distress), uddavanakare (afflicting) and bhaopaghaie. This mind is characterised as savajje (impure), sakirie (offending), sakakkase (rough), kadue (paining), nitthure (cruel), and pharuse (rude).

From the logical setting of the Buddhist psycho-ethical concepts it is easy to understand that the terms kodha and upanaha, issa and machchhera, mana and mada, chandikka and assuropa often go together as complements. The same may equally hold true of the two terms nitthuriya and tudana, Ashoka's nithuliya and tulana.

The term kodha, here translated by the English 'anger', presupposes an agitated state of mind, implies an infuriated condition of the self, burning with wrath, and produces the disposition to strike, to hurt, to kill. The complementary term upanaha implies harbouring resentment, a brooding state of mind which follows as a sequel to anger. Anger has fury for its distinctive feature, its functional tendency is to strike, and its resultant is an inimical action.

The term isya, here translated by 'malignity' in preference to 'envy' or 'jealousy', has either envy for other's prosperity or non-forgiveness for its distinctive feature, its functional tendency is to produce disgust, and its resultant is disappointing. The opposite of issa in the sense of 'envy' or 'jealousy' is machchhera or meanness, niggardliness. It is in the other sense of non-forgiveness that isya as a mental disposition is allied to kodha.

The term mana stands in Pali for both conceit and conceitedness, an unwholesome mental state which may arise both from a wilful overestimate and a wilful understimate of oneself. It has vanity for its distinctive feature, its functional tendency is to produce pride and boasting, and its resultant is conceitedness. The complementary term mada signifies the pride of birth, the pride of wealth, position, learning, etc. The extolling of oneself and the condemning of others are due to mada. For the association of mana with the passion of kodha in Pali the reader may consider the following admonition of Buddha:

"Give up anger, conceit should be completely given up."

The Pali equivalents of Ashoka's chamdiye and asulope are chandikkam and assuropa. The Pali scholiasts explain chandikka as meaning rigidity, which is the state of a rigid person, while, as defined in the Amarakosha, the chanda is a person whose nature is fierce. Thus Ashoka's chamdiye may preferably be translated by fierceness. The Mahaniddesa Commentary defines assuropa as the distemper of mind, while others take it to mean that violent passion in man which causes tears in others. The Pali word assuropa stops us from equating asulope with asulopa, just as Ashoka's asulope prevents us accepting asurupo as a variant ingeniously suggested in the Pali Commentary, Nithuliye, here translated by cruelty, has nitthuriyam for its Pali equivalent. The adjective nishthura as applying to speech or words is paraphrased in the Amarakosha by kakkhata, paurusha, krura, and the like, the first two having their equivalents in Ashoka's a-khakhase a-phalusam.

The remaining term tulana, here translated by oppressiveness, has been equated by some with turna which is not justifiable for the reason that turna is not used as a substantive. Its Pali equivalent is tudana, meaning pidanam.

The concepts belonging to the category of bahukayane or 'much good' are daya, dane, sache, sochave, madave and sadhave. The four concepts of sayame, bhavasudhita, katamnata and dadhabhatita are connected with dana. These are reduced in the same edict to two, viz., sayame and bhavasudhi. The concepts of savrabhutana(m) akshati, samyama and samachariya are grouped together with madava in R.E. XIII. The two terms, anarambha and avihimsa, are mutually complementary.

The guiding principle of Ashoka's Dharma, precisely as that of Buddhism and other early Indian systems of faith and thought, is the principle of action which is presented by such terms as ustana (readiness to action), parakrama (power of action), pakama (strenuous exertion), uyama (effort), and usaha (zeal, ardour). The opposite states of mind and body are represented by anavuti (non-application), alasiya (indolence) and kila-matha (weariness for exertion). The whole activity is to proceed on the twofold basis of dhamma (piety) and sila (virtue) which is the same as to say, through the practice of piety (dhamma-charana) and that of seemly behaviour, and it is to be directed towards feeling concern for oneself, feeling concern for one's own people, and doing good to the whole world.

The first pair of terms consists of daya and dana. Here daya, translated by pity, has anuddaya for its Pali equivalent According to Buddha, anuddaya presupposes fellow-feeling, sympathy and a friendly heart. From the set of synonyms given in the Amarakosha, it is evident that daya presupposes compassion which is felt in the heart, and that it has two expressional forms, viz., anukampa (feeling concern) on the part of seniors and anukrosa by juniors. In Buddha's terminology avihimsa has the positive connotation of karuna, karunna or sakarunabhava, i.e., the compassionate state of mind which finds its expression in feeling concern for the good of all beings. According to the Bhagavad Gita, daya means feeling pity for all beings. Pity as a noble feeling stands opposed to cruelty. Dana, which may be translated by liberality, charity or charitable disposition is a tangible expression of daya. Dana implies tyaga, which is both the spirit and the act of self-sacrifice. Ashoka speaks of various forms and acts of dana. In P.E. II, he expressly refers to 'giving the eye' and 'granting the boon of life to the lower creatures' (pana-dakhinaye). The monumental acts of piety mentioned in P. E. VII are all concrete instances of dana. By the eye is meant, of course, the eye of wisdom, and not the fleshy eye. It is with reference to the eye of wisdom that Ashoka declared the gift of the doctrine to be the best of all gifts. Dana implies, according to Buddha and others, the visagga, e.g., dhamma-samvibhaga, dana-samvibhaga, dana-visaga. Dana in itself is not a great thing in spite of the generally accepted maxim of the age that it is good. Ashoka speaks of the four moral qualities that go to enhance the value of dana, viz. sayaine, bhavasudhi or bhavasudhita, katamnata and dadhabhatita of which the equivalents are met with in the Great Epic and the Jataka. The very word bhavasuddhih is met with in the Great Epic, in the following ethical precept of Vidura:

Here sayama stands for restraint in body, speech and mind, bhavasudhita for the purity of motive, for what is called akshudrata in the Great Epic; katamnata for gratitude or gratefulness which consists not only in acknowledging the service rendered by the benefactor, not only in not harming the benefactor, but also in rendering the service in return and dadhabhatita for firm devotion, strong faith. The valedictory address in the Taittiriya Upanishad insists on giving out of faith and not giving without faith (asraddhaya adeyam), Buddha's word saddhadeyyam conveying the same idea. Ashoka speaks of the restraint practised with regard to the whole of life, and the restraint in the form of guarding one's tongue. In the Pali list of terms, samyama is sought to be distinguished from dama, the former meaning, according to Buddhaghosa, the restraint in accordance with the prescribed rules of conduct and the latter the control of the senses.

The next two categories of Ashoka's Dharma are sacha and sochaya, both of which are included in Buddha's list. In Pali, however, the first is combined with dhamma, and the second with uposatha, which is conceived as the abode of virtue. The combination of satya and dharma is as old as the older Upanishads. In Ashokan context, precisely as in that of the Pali Lakkharia Suttanta, the two terms, satya and dharma, are devoid of all metaphysical connotation. As Buddhaghosa rightly points out, here the first term stands for truthfulness in utterances, and the second for the system of piety relating to the ways of performing the ten wholesome acts. That in Ashoka's terminology, too, the first term stands for truthfulness in utterances is evident from the insistence on speaking the truth. According to the general Indian notion, the truthful speech carries with it also the idea of a speech, which is pleasant, sweet, and appealing. So the adage goes to teach:

> "satyam bruyat priyam bruyat, ma bruyat satyam apriyam".

As Buddha puts it, "Abandoning lying speech, Gautama the Recluse who has completely abstained from it, is the speaker of truth, given up to truth, truthful, utters words that are worthy of trust and not to be slightly doubted by the world. Abandoning harsh speech, Gautama the Recluse who has completely abstained from it, utters speech which is faultless, sweet to the ears, lovable, goes into the heart, agreeable to many, pleasing to many." By the expression 'that which is sweet to the ears" Buddhaghosa understands that which is sweetly worded, and by 'that which is lovable' he understands that which is sweet in meaning. Ashoka, too, insists on uttering words that are not harsh, impetuous, rude and that are full of winsome cordiality.

The sweetness in meaning gets its due emphasis. The word sachcha conveys also the idea of sachchapatinna implying as it does the resolve to keep the fealty to the oath taken, to keep the agreement entered into or word given, to keep the promise made under all circumstances, however trying. The notion of such a resolve is comprehended by the term dhiti which is met with in S.R.E. II. To be worth the name, both the dhiti and the patimna must be of an unshaken character. The four principles of sachcha in the above sense, dhamma, dhiti and chaga (self-sacrifice) are grouped together in the moral of the Vanarinda Jataka. The term sochaye, here translated by purity, really implies the sense of purity or the consciousness of being oneself pure in body, speech and thought. This may be treated as the prerequisite of a pious deed or an act of virtue, e.g., the observance of the sabbath.

The next pair of terms is composed of madave and sad have. In the Pali lists maddava is invariably combined with the concept of ajjava. Corresponding to the grouping of tapas, danam, arjavam, ahimsa and satyavachanam in the Chhandogya Upanishad we have in the Jataka the categorisation of the following concepts:

> Danam silam parichchagam ajjavam maddavam tapam akkodham avihimsam cha khantin cha avirodhanam.

The word ajjava signifies moral rectitude or uprightness, which lies behind Ashoka's principles of uniformity in procedure and uniformity in justice. By maddava is meant gentleness, mildness, which is the opposite of intrepidity accounting for all rash acts of violence, detention and coercion.

In sadhava we have the concept of nobleness which underlies all noble deeds. The noble deeds are all good deeds. The kalyanas or good deeds emphasised in the Jataka are precisely those repeatedly mentioned in the edicts.

The concept of khamti (kshanti) is combined with that of lahudamdata. In the Mahahamsa Jataka, we have the succession of the four concepts of akkodha, avihimsa, khanti and avirodhana. According to the scholiast, friendliness is at the back of the first, compassion is at the back of the second, the third implies the notion of toleration or forbearance, and the fourth means non-hostility. Though khanti and titikkha are often used as synonyms, the former is taken to mean the toleration of a person who is physically stronger by one who is physically weaker and the second to mean the toleration of a weaker person by a stronger man. The Buddhist khanti is far more than the Christian idea of forbearance in that in the practice of this moral quality the oppressed are expected not only to patiently bear the pain of oppression caused but also to think well of the oppressor. In the Bhagavad Gita, kshama (i.e., kshanti) is succeeded by dhriti or moral fortitude.

Cultural Conquest

Dharma-vijaya: With Ashoka, precisely as with Buddha and other Indian thinkers, Dharma was not only a way of life or means of elevation of human nature but also a weapon for the conquest of men's hearts, a royal means of bringing about a permanent cultural understanding between the countries and peoples and building a new nation or imperialism on that very foundation. It remains yet to be seen how the Dharma-vijaya of Ashoka served to place India between the cultures, to create, in other words, a Greater India with universalism as its ideal for the furtherance of the common cause of humanity.

Ashoka's Dharma-vijaya was just one of the four great cultural conquests made by the Indo-Aryans in pre-Muslim India, the other three being the Digvijaya of Agni, the Dharma-vijaya of the Great Epic, and the Trailokya vijaya of the Karandavyuha.

Definition of Dharma-vijaya: Conquest is the dominant thought of a heroic age, a warrior King, a war-like people, a virile race, a militant faith. It presupposes in all cases consciousness of strength, a sense of certainty about the Tightness of the cause espoused, a strong conviction about the success to be attained, a vision of the future to follow, an intrepid will to act, an unabated zeal to proceed, a great power of endurance to withstand the obstacles on the way, a sense of preparedness, a capacity to adjust means to ends, an uncommon energy for incessant action, and a well-disciplined army to carry out the orders. Its motive factors or springs of action maybe either greed, malevolence and folly or magnanimity, amity and wisdom. It is possible by some kind of weapon. If it is possible by the sword, it goes by the name of Sarashakya or Sayaka-vijaya, and if by piety, it deserves the name of Dharma-vijaya. The weapons other than those implied by Dharma are taken to be comprehended by the antithetical term Adharma. The sword symbolises the violent method with all its strategic skills and accessories resorted to on the failure of the diplomatic means of conciliating, bribing and causing dissension. Dharma stands for the peaceful method with all its friendly acts of give and take. Where greed is found to be the motive factor, the conquest is to be classed as Lobha-vijaya, and where malevolence is the motive factor, it is to be called Asura-vijaya.

With these two forms of conquest is to be contrasted what is called Dharma-vijaya or conquest by Dharma. As a moral concept, the Dharma vijaya implies some amount of human consideration and mental discipline to conform to the laws of approved human conduct.

As defined in the Arthashastra, the Lobhavijaya aims at what may be safely gained in land or money and the Asura-vijaya aims not merely at seizing the land, treasure, sons and wives and all of the conquered but also at taking his life, while the aim of Dharma-vijaya is fulfilled with mere obeisance or surrender on the part of the conquered. In the words of Kalidasa, the Dharma-vijaya consists in robbing the conquered King of his glory but not of his territory. Ashoka's Dharma-vijaya consists, on the other hand, in the expression of good will and the assurance of territorial integrity, the friendly acts of public utility, and the advancement of the cause of humanity through piety.

Professor Nilkanta Shastri Poignantly observes: "Whatever the relative ages of our texts, the classification of conquests and conquerors in Hindu political theory is logically complete, and has the ring of antiquity, and we may take it that the expression Dharmavijaya was first carried in contrast to lobha-or artha and asuravijaya": The Jataka distinction between Dhamma and Adhammavijaya and Ashoka's distinction between the Dhamma and the Sarasaka presupposes the idea of just two kinds of vijaya, one the Dharma and the other Artha or Asura.

The idea of Dharmavijaya developed in the Brahmanical as well as the Buddhistic line of thinking. The common point between the two conceptions is that both are free from the thought about territorial aggrandisements. The mere acknowledgement of supremacy by the weaker powers was sufficient, according to the Arthashastra, to satisfy the demand of Dharmavijaya. It appears from the Great Epic account of the Digvijaya of the Pandavas that the offering of presents, or of revenues, or of both was to be the tangible expression of obeisance or submission on the part of the conquered.

Though mere ultimatum or negotiation through the envoys sometimes sufficed to effect it, the Brahmanical Dharmavijaya was undeniably a conquest by the sword. Ashoka rightly characterised it as a milder method of conquest where forbearance and light punishment were to be practised and preferred. The Buddhistic Dharmavijaya was to be achieved, on the other hand, without the employment of the sword or armed force but certainly by means of the doctrine meaning the superior ideal of humanity.

In neither case, the Dharmavijaya implied the idea of disbanding the army or lessening the military equipment; it presupposed, on the other hand, the sufficient strength and preparedness of the army and the full military equipment backed by adequate state resources and other elements of sovereignty. As Buddha emphatically puts it, invincible shall be the position of the righteous King overlord, not shaken by any human rival or enemy, internal or external, and the territory under his benign sway and protection shall be undisturbed, free from all signs of aggression and oppression, throneless, populous, prosperous, secure, tranquil and unulcerated.

There is not the slightest hint in the edicts and legends of Ashoka that he either disbanded the army or was not fully prepared to cope with the menace to the security of life and property of the citizens arising from the mischievous action of the Atavis or to his territory arising from the inimical action of the independent neighbours.

Arrian's remark that 'a sense of justice prevented any Indian King from attempting conquest beyond the limits of India must not be taken to mean that any Indian King was lacking in the ambition of gaining the coveted position of a chaturanta or conqueror of the earth extending as far as the four seas, i.e., of a supreme lord of Jambudvipa. Brahmanism went to encourage the predatory instinct in man by according a popular religious sanction to the periodical hunting and military expeditions on the part of a warrior-King and a war-like people. It tended to foster the idea of conquest, no matter whether it was actuated by an avaricious, demoniac or righteous motive. The worldly motive was thereby kept in the forefront and the cultural motive in the background. In the Brahmanical tradition the Digvijaya of Agni was shown to have proceeded side by side with the Digvijaya of the warriors, the latter reaching its consummation in the performance of either the horse-sacrifice or the still grander sacrifice called Rajasuya, each containing in its programme the holding of a Sabha or Coronation Durbar.

With Buddha the Dharmavijaya achieved without the employment of the sword or armed force implied the welcoming by the rival monarchs or powers of the cause of piety espoused by the righteous King Emperor or superior power, and this was precisely the underlying thought of the Dharmavijaya of Ashoka. As the great Maurya Emperor himself puts it, "This, of course, is considered the chief conquest by the Beloved of the gods, namely, the conquest by piety. This has been achieved by the Beloved of the gods here as well as among ail the borderers, even over a distance of six hundred leagues, the Greek King named Antiochus and four other Kings beyond the said Antiochus, namely, Ptolemy, Antigonas, Magas Alexander, and constantly the Cholas, and Pandyas, even the Tamraparnyas. So also here, in the King's territory, among the Yaunas and Kambojas, the Nabhakas and Nabhapamktis, the (parent) Bhojas and their offshoots, the Andhras and Parinda-Paradas—everywhere follow the moral instruction of the Beloved of the gods. Even where the envoys of the Beloved of the gods do not go, even they hearing of the system of piety and moral instruction of the Beloved of the gods, abide by and will abide by the Law of Piety". The essence of Ashoka's Dharmavijaya may be shown to have been recorded in the Gupta coin legends: sucharitair svargam jayati. "He conquers even the heavens by virtues."

Dharmavijaya of the Great Epic: We have in the Sabhaparva of the Great Epic a graphic account of the digvijaya or military campaigns undertaken by the four Pandava brothers and of its sequel—the Rajasuya sacrifice performed by King Yudhishthira, all under the guidance of Krishna Vasudeva. Its main narrative is concerned, however, with the great battle of Kurukshetra valiantly fought and won by the Pandavas under the same guidance of the Superman and God incarnate and with the laudable object of founding a dharmantjya. The victory at the battle of Kurukshetra, too, was consummated by the performance of a horse-sacrifice by the Pandavas and the convening of a Coronation Durbar. The Bhagavad Gita contains a philosophic explanation of the battle of Kurukshetra, while the Sanatsujatiya Gita presents an elaborate explanation of the doctrine of apramada or principle of action which characterised Ashoka's Dharma and guided all his noble undertakings and efforts, and which, as a matter of fact, was the distinctive tenet of all the heroic Indo-Aryan faiths of the past rooted in sraddha.

The digvijaya of the-Jaina King Kharavela as described in the Hathigumpha inscription, the digvijaya of the great Hindu King Samudragupta as described in his Allahabad Stone-pillar inscription and the digvijaya of Raghu as described by Kalidasa in his Raghuvamsa partake all of the nature of the digvijaya of the Pandavas as described in the Great Epic and fall, therefore, within its scope.

The idea of this digvijaya occurred to Arjuna after the killing of Jarasandha, the most powerful monarch of the Brihadratha dynasty of Magadha and a renowned scion of the Chedi race of warriors who were hostile to the aspirations of the Andhaka-Vjrishnis or Yadavas of Western India. Krishna Vasudeva himself belonged to the Satvata or Andhaka Vrishni family of Dwaraka which was matrimonially connected with the Pandavas as well as the Chedis of the Chedi country. The express motive behind this digvijaya is stated to be the increase of the liquid reserve and financial strength of the rising state by the collection of booties consisting in revenues and valuable presents, This motive is praised as warrior-like in spite of its being predatory and earthly.

Four brothers started in four directions, each in one direction on an auspicious day, at an auspicious moment and under an auspicious asterism. Arjuna who proceeded to the north conquered the whole ' northern division of Jambudvipa comprising the upper half of the Punjab proper, the whole of the state of Kashmir and Jammu, the Himalayan region extending as far east as the Upper Assam Valley, Manipur and Chin Hills, and the trans-Himalayan hill-tracts and countries extending as far north as the southern boundary of Uttarakuru. The list of the conquered included monarchs, ruling classes, hill tribes and savages. All of them were reduced to the position of karadas. Bhima who proceeded to the east conquered the countries east of Kuru including Bengal and the Lower Assam Valley. Sahadeva who proceeded to the south conquered the countries that lay *tot* the south of Kuru and whole of the southern division of Jambudvipa extending as far down as Pandya and Dravida, Chondra-Kerala and Simhala. The western countries that lay to the west of Kuru extended as far west as the

Lower Indus Valley and even included the territories of the Pahlavas, the Barbaras, the Yavanas and the Shakas. The Rajasaya sacrifice was performed thereafter at Hastinapura. A grand feast was given. A sabha was held to establish the paramount sovereignty of Yudhishthira and the divinity or supreme personality of Krishna. The military campaigns involved all the three forms of conquest.

Such a wide geographical vision of Jambudvipa together with an intimate knowledge of the individual countries and peoples as we obtain from the Great Epic account of the digvijaya is inconceivable previous to the reign of the Nandas and Mauryas of Magadha. The inclusion of the name of the Shakas, Yavanas and Pahlavas in the list of conquered peoples and territories means that the account in the Sauti Pauraniki version of the Great Epic is Gupta or pre-Gupta but definitely post-Ashokan, post-Shunga and post-Kushana. Whether such an account of the digvijaya appeared or not in the earlier Vaisampayana or pre-Paninian version of the Great Epic is still a disputed question.

The geographical references of Panini may be shown to be on a par with those in the pre-Ashokan Pali Canonical texts which confine our vision to Jambudvipa. These allusions lead us to think of the countries and peoples in the Uttarapatha or Punjab proper, comprising the Upper and Lower Indus Valleys, the Himalayan region, the Middle Country to the west of modern Bengal, the Western India and the Central India. These hardly take us further south than the river Godavari.

In such post-Ashokan Pali Canonical works as the Mahaniddesa, Buddhavamsa and Apadana we have mention of India's trade-relations, internal and external. Even such a distant country as China finds mention in the Buddhavamsa and Apadana. The Mahaniddesa list includes the name of Suvarnabhami, Tamraparni and Yava. The Baveru Jataka refers to India's seaborne trade with Baveru. The geographical vision of India's trade-routes and trade-relations which these works give us agrees in many respects with that in the prose-treatise of the Arthashastra which in its extant form can hardly be treated as a pre-Christian work. Sylvain Levi has successfully tried with the help of the Brihatkatha to locate many of the places mentioned in the Mahaniddesa along the eastern seacoast extending from India to China and Java. But these places, e.g., Ajapatha Mendapatha, Masikapatha, Takkola, Angaloka, Tangana, Yavana, Paramayona, Alasanda, may all again be connected with the North-Western trade-route and located in the Punjab proper or near about.

Referring to the Ramayana, too, one may observe that the Pali story of Dasharatha locates the place of Rama's exile in the Himalayan region, and that the earlier version of the Rama story did not push Rama's wanderings with Sita and Lakshmana beyond the banks of the Godavari. The realistic account of the land-route by which Rama reached Pandyakapata and the region of the Tamraparni river to have a view of the Parasamudra or Ceylon from the Indian shore and other incidental geographical references that appear in Valmiki's epic are post-Ashokan but not, perhaps, post-Christian.

The account of Kharavela's military campaigns goes to show that he had by-passed the main territory of his contemporary Shatakarni in carrying his conquest up to the town of Asika (Rishika) on the Krishhvenva (Krishna), humbled the Rashtrikas and Bhojakas of the Vidyadhara countries (along the Vindhya range of hills), compelled the King of Pandya in the extreme south to send him presents, subdued Brihaspatimitra, the contemporary ruler of Anga-Magadha, drove back a contemporary Yavana King to Mathura, and defeated the rulers of Uttarapatha.

It is easily understandable even to common sense that the Rajasuya sacrifice was availed of as a socio-political and semi-religious device for proclaiming and establishing the paramount sovereignty of Yudhishthira. What is bewildering to common sense is the question —was it the proper occasion for proclaiming Krishna Vasudeva as the Superman and Supreme Being and establishing his divinity. The bewildering and overwhelming of common sense instead of organising and enlightening it is the main trend of the Great Epic thought which is vitiated throughout by its diplomatic undercurrent. Let us for the present examine the arguments put forward in the Great Epic in favour of the proposal for the unanimous acceptance of Krishna as the divinity, the supreme human personality, the highest object of popular adoration and the worthiest recipient of the homage of the sacrifice.

When among the invited, Shishupala of the Chedi royal house raised a dissentient voice, expressed resentment and openly challenged the propriety of the proposal, Yudhishthira gently besought him to agree to the proposal and tried to pacify him by advancing an *argumentum ad hominem* as well as an *argumentum ad verucundum.*

Of the three arguments advanced by Bhishma, the first is worldly, the second rational, and the third theological i.e., questionable. The first argument is based on the maxim:

> "A warrior becomes a victor in war by conquering another warrior. He who releases the conquered King after bringing him into subjection becomes a guru (superior) to the latter."

At the Rajasuya Durbar there was not a single monarch present who was not conquered by the Pandavas through the power of Krishna. Many powerful Kings were conquered by Krishna in battles. So he became a guru to all of them. The whole world became established in him in the sense, no doubt, that he came to hold then the balance of power in India.

The second argument proceeds on the axiom that he who excels the wise in moral and personal qualities is to be deemed most worthy of the homage:

> "Gunair vriddhan atikramya Harih archyatamo matah".

Krishna excelled even the wisest among the Brahmans in his knowledge of the Vedas and Vedangas and the mightiest among the Kshatriyas in his fighting strength (baladhikya). The moral and personal qualities with which Krishna was endowed consisted of liberality, skill, learning, heroism, judiciousness, fame, superior intelligence, lineage, luck, endurance, contentment and prosperity: Danam dakshyam srutam sauryam hrih.

> "kirtir buddhiruttama, santatih Srir dhritis tushtih pushtis cha niyatachyute".

On this ground alone Krishna might be claimed to have been the teacher, the father and the guru, entitled to the homage by the consensus of opinion:

> "Tam enam lokasampannam acharyam pitaram gurum arghyam architam archarham sarve samkshantum arhatha".

The third argument which is extraordinary rests on the popular veneration of Krishna as Divinity or God incarnate, the highest personality in all the worlds of life and existence:

> "Urddhvam tiryag adhas chaiva yavati jagato gatih,
> sadevakeshu lokeshu Bhagavan Kesavo mukham".

It passes common human comprehension how a human being, however mighty and perfect and great in soul-power, might be eulogised as the inexhaustible first cause and the final cause of the world:

> "Krishna eva hi lokanam utpattir api chavyayah,
> Krishnasya hi krite visvam idam bhataip characharam".

The Great Epic has not, however, concealed from view the other side of the picture. It has put into the mouth of Shishupala what might be the bold criticism of the whole affair of this Rajasuya sacrifice. Krishna's motive is construed to be self-establishment by taking full advantage of an earthly situation:

> "Ayuktam atmanah pujam tvam punar bahu manyashe, havishah prapya nishyandarn praasita Sveva nirjane".

The things came ultimately to such a pass that there was no other alternative left but to stop the arrogance of Shishupala by a furious method, to silence the critic and to crush the rising party by killing its leader and spokesman. Krishna took Upon himself the opprobrium of beheading Shishupala with his chakrayudha. Before this drastic step had been taken Shishupala's mother interceded on his behalf and Krishna promised in the presence of all to forgive him. But to common sense the act of beheading is irreconcilable with the solemn promise of forgiving. The argument of the strong prevailed. Such is the rule of the majority which is guided by a mob psychology and is not infrequently arbitrary and tyrannical. This is not again the only instance recorded in the Great Epic where the critic having the moral courage of expressing his honest opinion was hooted out of the court. When at the victorious conclusion of the battle of Kurukshetra all the Brahmans led by the greed of gifts and favours came in to pronounce their blessings on Yudhishthira, one of them had the audacity to condemn his action saying that he had gained this earthly sovereignty at the cost of many of his own people. The rest of the interested Brahmans uttered *hum* and decried the fellow, saying in one voice that he was not a Brahmin but a charvaka or goblin in disguise. Such has been the way of the madding crowd, the thoughtless world. When a person succeeds by hook or crook in establishing Bob Roy's simple rule of might is right, the priests with their blessings, the Pandits with their learned interpretations, the sycophants with their flatteries and the followers with their devotional sentiments change it into a divine rule of right is might.

Now let us see if the position at all improves by the philosophic explanation of the battle of Kurukshetra offered in the Bhagavad Gita which is the most authoritative Book of the Hindus. According as we take this battle to be a historical event or an internal affair of oneself, a battle against one's internal enemies, the Bhagavad Gita teaches either a war philosophy or a religious method of self-realisation through self-conquest. Whether the one or the other, the foundation of a dharmarajya is its avowed aim. In one respect, this dharmarajya means a Holy Empire of India without, and in another, a kingdom of righteousness within.

The Holy Empire of India is sought to be founded by an internecine and global war in the sub continent which resulted in the destruction of all great warriors, the destruction of the Kurus, the descendants of the Pandavas, the annihilation of the Yadavas and the Brihadrathas; and the general emasculation of humanity. The Great Epic goes to show that the New World sought to be created through the battle of Kurukshetra was a world of desolation and despair, the inhabitants whereof began to utter in their helplessness the pitiful cry of Ha Krishna, Ha Krishna! The thrilling narrative of Bama's exploits in Valmiki's epic ends similarly in the most catastrophic tragedy of the destruction of the most prosperous city of Ayodhya in the north and that of the equally prosperous city of Svarnalanka in the south. Both the religion of the strong justifying all diplomatic artifices, violent methods, valiant feats, nefarious acts and self-aggrandisements in the name of God, Divine purpose, Holy Empire and New World, and the religion of the infirm seeking consolation in the Lord's name and through the thoughtless fatalism of some kind are equally reprehensible. The war philosophy, developed in the Great Epic in general and the Bhagavad Gita in particular, seeks to establish the following beliefs: (a) that all beings are the creatures of time of which the decree is unavoidable; (b) that the Divine Will works through and ultimately prevails in all the dramas of life in heaven and on earth; (c) that the world-order and the astronomical universe are far far greater than a man, however powerful and mighty he may be; (d) that the race-instinct is the real goading factor in man's life than the momentary prick of conscience or reflective mood; and (e) that there is a mightier power than all earthly lords, led by the demoniac spirit of arrogance, self-conceit, atheism and defiance of all divine laws, to act as the arbiter of their fate.

So far as the war philosophy of the Bhagavad Gita is concerned, its arguments are irrelevant, incongruous and unconvincing as answers to the points raised by Arjuna from the common sense point of view. When brought into the battlefield, Arjuna felt sad to think that to commence the battle was to fight against his own kith and kin, teachers and elders and other persons for whose good and happiness be would desire victory, sovereignty and fame; if they were all killed, for whose sake he would attain it, what was the use of attaining it? An internecine war is likely to result in the destruction of one's own people which in its turn results in the loss of the chastity of women. The promiscuity of sex-relations leads to the loss of the purity of the blood and fusion of races which in its turn leads to the loss of the family tradition and race heritage. When the high tradition is lost, the whole human race is overtaken by corruption, impiety and sin.

When Ashoka reflected upon the scene of carnage and bloodshed and aftereffects of the aggressive war waged on Kalinga, it occurred to him: "In conquering indeed an unconquered country, the slaying or dying or deporting which occurs there is considered an extremely painful and serious matter by the Beloved of the gods. Even more serious than that is this, that those who dwell there, whether the Brahmanas or the Shramanas or other sects of householders in whom are established this respectful attention to high personages, to them occurs hurt or death or deportation of beloved ones, or that even (as regards) those well-controlled ones whose affection has not diminished, if those who are their friends, associates, comrades and relatives encounter disaster, on that account that, too, becomes a cause of hurt to them. This is a common reaction to all men and a serious matter in the opinion of the Beloved of the gods.".

Instead of considering the points raised by Arjuna, Vasudeva simply accuses him of cowardice, insinuating that inwardly he was afraid of risking the fame of a great warrior earned by him, and proceeds with his grandiloquent discourses that are incoherent, and ultimately reveals his omniform to overawe the earthly hero, wanting Arjuna to do his behest.

The Dharmarajya in the sense of a kingdom of righteousness within is sought to be founded in the Bhagavad Gita also on a set of beliefs indispensable to its syncretic philosophy of life and action. Looked at from the point of view of the literary history of India, the Gita literature started by way of a deflection from the Upanishad. But for the synthetic religious setting of jnanayoga, karmayoga and bhaktiyoga, the docetic Satvata cult of Purushottama, and the shifting of emphasis from jnana and karma to bhakti the Bhagavad Gita has hardly any originality of its own as regards its ideas, principles and practices that are mostly drawn from different sources.

The catalogue of ethical concepts which gets prominence through the perorations of the poetical discourse was the fullest development, as we sought to show, from its humbler beginning in the instruction of the Upanishad teacher Ghora Angirasa who is represented as the guru of Krishna. The interested reader of the Upanishads is likely to be amazed at Krishna's being in the role of a Teacher himself of all the wisdom of the past and the future,—the pupil of whom it is said that at the time of his death, he took refuge in the Deity applying to Him the three attributes of being the under saying, immutable and living one: akshitam asi, achyutam asi, pranasamsitam asi. It is further said that he ceased to thirst for things worldly on hearing Angirasa's instruction. No part of a teacher is assigned to him even by mistake. It is nevertheless important to watch how the idea of a grand edifice of religious thought came to be developed out of such crude materials. In the Gita, Krishna Vasudeva, the friend, philosopher and guide, is represented as saying to Arjuna, a typical warrior of fame and worldly man with strong common sense and goodness of nature:

- Believe that thy real self is the soul in a bodily garb, which is cast away when it is worn out and replaced by a new one in the process of metempsychosis;
- Believe that the soul which is thy true self is the entity that outlasts all apparent changes, it being by its essential nature unborn, undying, unchanging, immutable, imperishable and untouchable by all thy actions;
- Believe that the soul within thee and the soul within the universe are identical in their nature;
- Believe that thy first duty is to look into thyself and find out thy true self and the true self of the rest of things and beings by lifting the veil which hides the true nature and identity of the two;
- Believe that thy folly lies in coming away from God and coming into thyself, being deluded by the thought that thou art different from Him;
- Believe that with the true vision of reality thou wilt see thee in the all and the all in thee, and ultimately nothing and none but God;
- Believe that placed that thou art in life, the utmost thou canst do is to purify thy motive;
- Believe that the right way to work in life is to surrender thy will to the Divine and to feel always that thou art not the agent but only an instrument to His will fulfilling itself;
- Believe that the possession of the godly estate far outweighs in value that of the demoniac;
- Believe that God is the alpha and the omega of the universe, the almighty and the infinite, the incomparable, the

imperishable, the inexhaustible, the immanent, the transcendent, the greatest of the great and the smallest of the small;

- Believe that all the modes of knowing, all the methods of action, and all the forms of worship are the manifold mode of approach towards Godhead, and hence meant ultimately for Him; and
- Believe that all the social grades and all the human institutions are to be respected and utilised and not to be interfered with, these being created by the Divine will.

Thus indeed was laid the stable and spacious philosophic foundation of the Hindu faith (sraddha) enlivened with devotional sentiment (bhakti), the faith consisting of a set of beliefs, laying down certain principles of human conduct, commending certain rules of life, and emphasising certain religious practices. A grand order of harmony, full of life, meaning, truth, good and beauty, is conceived to enable us to realise and appreciate the unity as truth behind the puzzling diversity or multiplicity of existences, forme, motives, expressions, thoughts, tendencies and actions. This order had behind it the Vedic and Upanishadic conception of the organic unity of the visible universe of the world, of life, of the society, as well as of the state, with a division of labour among the component elements or constituents of each. Herbert Spencer is the modern advocate of such an organic theory carrying too far the analogies between a living organism on the one hand and the material universe, the world of life, the society and the state on the other.

Unfortunately for India the fanciful organic idea was sanctified in Hinduism into a captivating religious faith. The popular poetical imagery seeking to represent the alternate appearances and disappearances of the cosmic system in a fixed rotatory order in the analogy of a wheel turning round and round on its eternally fixed axle stood against the idea of a forward movement. In the cumbersome scheme of harmony where the diverse races of men with their distinctive traits, the different social grades and trade-guilds with their special caste privileges and handicaps and exclusive occupations on a hereditary basis, etc., were sought to be accommodated and the scope of their existence, competition, education and environment had to be narrowed down and curtailed. The rigidity of the restrictive rules as to *connubium* and *commensality* compelled them to live, move and have their being within hidebound compartments of an insular and unalterable socio-political and religio-economic organisation.

In bringing the social organisation of men into harmony with the world order of life, it began to work no better than the social organisation of the ants or wasps or honeybees, on the commodious principle of a division of labour, each class or section of men functioning as a cog fitted only for a special work of life. The social scheme thus sanctified in the name of the Divine order and dispensation went to present an aggregate of human beings permanently placed in divers groups, functioning as different limbs and organs of a living body, each being intended for a specific duty and all contributing to the well-being of the whole which is a unity with the diversity of functions.

But the irremovable artificial barriers placed between one group or class and another served to make them all 'dependent on a common care taker, divine or human'. The scheme of religious toleration proposed with non-intervention as the best policy went similarly to present congeries of faiths, all kinds of belief, all modes of approach, all forms of worship under the convenient axiom 'whatever is, is right in its own place'. Thus the multitudinous popular cults, even those rooted in the grossest kind of superstition, were justified and allowed chances to exist and thrive side by side with higher philosophic thoughts and religious ideals.

The Hindu needed, as a modern saint points out, their supreme Deity, whether He be Shiva, Vishnu, Shakti, Rama, Krishna or Kalki, to be one who can hold the balance of power or maintain the harmony of the turbulent world by his unsurpassed "might, illumine the minds of all by his unsurpassed knowledge, who can create, preserve as well as destroy,—who is omniform, omnipresent, omnipotent and omniscient, overwhelming, overpowering and all-conquering. The India-wide digvijaya and pilgrimage (tirthayatra) on the part of the Pandavas and Karna, as described in the extant Sauti version of the Great Epic, and finally the great battle of Kurukshetra fought and won by the former resulted in the founding of such a grand Holy Hindu Empire of a feudal type. On this very model was built the powerful Gupta Empire under the aegis of which we reach the Augustan age of Sanskrit language and literature, Indian arts and crafts, religions and philosophies, dramas and kavyas, opulence and enjoyment. All the earlier currents and cross-currents of linguistic development met at last to make Sanskrit the *lingua franca* of the cultured laity. The prasastis or royal panegyrics composed either by the court poets or Pandits in terms of hyperboles, mythological fancies and allegorical equivoques came to extol the later digvijayas as unprecedented achievements of far-reaching consequence in the annals of human history and culture. These are conspicuously lacking in the homely Prakrit diction and simplicity, the direct appeal and sincerity of the edicts of Ashoka.

The analytical method of the earlier systems of science and thought, the formulation of ideas, the epitomising of thoughts in aphorisms, etc. were followed by elaborations, scholastic niceties and logical discussions. The heroic spirit of the earlier age which was sought to be enlivened in the Bhagavad Gita with the devotional sentiment of popular religions yielded place to the erotic and tended to find its satisfaction in the grandeur and aesthetic grace of arts and crafts. The clever art of diplomacy was degenerating into a degraded form of sychopancy in the sphere of religion and of life. Slavery not only continued to exist but tended also to become more numerous in its form and to assume a feudal character. As the Sukraniti indicates, the Council of Ministers was gaining more and more in power to deprive ultimately the King of his right of vetoing, which meant gaining in more power by the Brahmin Peshwas for creating feuds and divisions.

Trailokya-vijaya of the Karandvyuha: The Satvata cult of Purushottama as advocated in the Bhagavad Gita, was not without its lasting effect on other faiths in India, Buddhism included. In this cult Krishna was claimed to be the soul in the heart of all, the creator, preserver and destroyer of all living beings. He is the Vishnu among the Adityas, the sun among the luminaries, the Marlchi among the winds, the moon among the stars, the Sama among the Vedas, the Vasava among the gods, the mind among the organs of sense, so on and so forth.

These were evidently the current Hindu ideas in the immediate background of the Trailokya-vijaya of later Buddhism. This vijaya is defined in the Karandavyuha and other later Mahayana works as a form of religious and cultural conquest to be achieved by offering Brahmatva *par excellence* to the worshippers of Brahma, Vishnutva *par excellence* to the worshippers of Vishnu, Shivatva *par excellence* to the worshippers of Shiva, Yakshatva *par excellence* to the worshippers of the Yakshas, Rakshatva *par excellence* to the worshippers of the Rakshas, Pisachatva *par excellence* to the worshippers of the Pisachas, and the like.

Trailokya-vijaya as a distinctive epithet of Buddha is met with as early as the 7th century AD in the inscriptions of the Chandra Kings of East Bengal. But the Trailokya-vijaya career of Buddhism must be associated with the Palas of Eastern India headed by Dharmapala Vikramashila during whose peaceful and prosperous reign several new Buddhist Universities were founded in Bengal and Bihar, notably the Somapura Mahavihara at Bihar Sarif and the Vikramashila Mahavihara probably at Sakri Gali, South Bihar and the earlier world-famous University of Nalanda was quickened into a most vigorous life. These Buddhist seats of learning of various sizes and degrees of importance and the newer ones that were subsequently ushered into existence were all in a flourishing state under the liberal patronage of the Pala rulers.

The Mahabodhi Sangharama which was caused to be erected at Bodhgaya by King Kitti-Siri-Meghavanna during the reign of Samudragupta for the accommodation of the monks from Ceylon was in a thriving condition when Hiuen Tsang visited the place during the reign of King Harshavardhana of Kanauj in the middle of the 7th century AD. The same continued to flourish even thereafter under the Pala rule.

The new stream of the Chinese pilgrims headed by I-tsing began to flow into India to bear a glowing testimony to the greatness of India, the sacred land which had produced the world religion of Shakyamuni and was the cradle of a mighty Aryan civilization. One among the late medieval pilgrims from China, namely, Chiang Hsia-pias (AD 1021), did not omit in his hymn composed in honour of the Bodhgaya Temple to pay his best compliment to Ashoka as the righteous Emperor who lived in the right perception of the truth of the religion of Buddha and as the great builder of Buddhist shrines in India whose noble fame travelled far and wide.

The trade-relations of India with Suvarnabhumi (Burma and Further India), Suvarnadvipa (Java), Sumatra and Borneo not only facilitated intercommunication between India and those countries and islands and led to the foundation of Indian colonies in the Pacific islands but resulted also in the spread of Buddhism and Hinduism. So far as Suvarnabhumi is concerned, the substitution of the name of Suvarnabhumi for Suvarniagiri in the tradition of the Buddhist mission under Sona and Uttara went to associate the name of Ashoka also with the history of introduction of Buddhism into Burma.

Though the successive waves of Buddhist mission had reached the shores of Burma, first probably from South India and finally from Ceylon, from the time of the Chandras of Bengal and during the reign of the Palas, the districts of Tippera and Chittagong served as the connecting link between the Buddhist art tradition of Bengal and Bihar, while the Hindu art tradition which has left its impress on the Buddhist religious monuments of Pagan in Upper Burma was evidently carried by the architects and craftsmen brought over from Orissa. The legacies of the Buddhist art-tradition from the Deccan and the island of Ceylon came to be prominent in the frescoes in several Pagodas of Pagan. The Shailendras of Suvarria-dvipa (Java) under whose patronage and with whose munificence the shrine of Borobudur was built were contemporaries of the Palas.

The earlier Buddhist mission to Bhota or Tibet is known to have been led by Padmasambhava during the reign of Srong-tsan Gampo, 'the most renowned of Tibetan kings', who introduced Buddhism into his kingdom under the influence of his Buddhist consorts from China. Nepal was then subject to Tibet and Tirhut too became subject to it. From the latter half of the 7th Century onwards the Lochavas or Pandits from the Land of Snow came in larger and larger numbers to different Buddhist seats of learning for the study of Buddhist and Indian works during the reign of the Palas. It was during this very reign that the later and more successful Buddhist mission to Tibet was led by Atisa (Dipankara-srijnana) in the first half of the eleventh century.

Between the Guptas and the Palas was the powerful and prosperous reign of Harshavardhana of the Pushpabhuti family who succeeded in founding a fairly large Empire in Northern India extending from Valabhi in the extreme west to Assam in the extreme east. His reign is noted for the visit of the great Chinese pilgrim Hiuen Tsang who left behind him a detailed account of India of his time as well as of the countries in Central Asia through which he passed on his way to and back from India. Harsha's system of administration, though less rigorous, was structurally the same as that of the Guptas. 'The provinces were governed in detail by tributary Rajas.' The only redeeming feature of it, and one connecting it with the tradition of the Maurya administration under Ashoka was the 'incessant personal supervision which he (Harsha) effected by constantly moving about'. The large-hearted practice of religious toleration is another notable point of historical connection of Harsha with the tradition of Ashoka. Nalanda was up till then the only great centre of Buddhist learning which had attained to the eminence of a University.

Be that as may, the secular side of Indian life was being regulated, as we shall see enough of it under the Digvijaya of Agni, by the law-books of the Brahmin jurists and the rituals of the Brahmin priests and dominated by Hinduism in matters of religious belief and forms of worship.

Digvijaya of Agni: The Digvijaya of Agni which is presupposed by the Dharmavijaya of Buddha and Ashoka signified the spread of Vedic religion and culture and the establishment of supremacy of the Brahmans as a social grade and a privileged class of priests, teachers, law-givers, mystics and philosophers. Agni was regarded as the first and most important god of the Vedic Indians both as the purifier of all impurities, external and internal, and as the carrier of oblations to different gods. Agni whose essence is heat is fire on the earth, lightning in the firmament and sun in the sky, Agni manifests itself in various forms, terrestrial and celestial, As fire, Agni is the lord of every home, whether worldly or religious, whether in the common habitat of men or in the forest home. One can say indeed that it was by the genial warmth of fire that all the seeds of culture sprouted in India and Iran, nay, in all the ancient cradles of civilization. So far as India is concerned, Agni as sacrificial fire symbolised the Vedic cult of yajna in the widest possible sense of the term, which is to say, the whole of Vedic religion and culture as handed down, interpreted, elaborated, disseminated and utilised by the different schools of Brahmans and Brahmin teachers.

To understand the real historical significance of the Digvijaya of Agni, it is necessary to differentiate broadly the two successive stages in the development and expansion of the Indo-Aryan culture and civilization, the earlier stage represented by Vedism and the later stage by Brahmanism. By the former we are to understand the one phase of the Indo-Aryan culture and civilization into which we can have glimpses through the windows of the collection of inspired hymns in the Rigveda and the Atharva-Angiras collection of charms, spells, incantations, imprecations and vratya hymns in the Atharvaveda. The corridors to the first were formed by the Sama collection of the Vedic psalms and the Yajur collection of the Vedic rituals, while that to the latter was formed by the Grihya hymns from the Rigveda adapted to the needs of domestic and social rites. It is through these corridors that one can pass from Vedism into Brahmanism.

The Vedic civilization which is characterised by race virility and indomitable spirit of man to resist and overcome the dreaded and inhospitable natural forces, the pestilences due to drought and the prevalence of epidemics, the rivalry of the hostile powers and the mischiefs caused by the savages was primarily the civilization of the Saptasindhu, *i.e.*, of the Uttarapatha or Punjab proper watered by the Indus system of rivers. As may be easily inferred from the list of fourteen rivers mentioned by name in the Nadi-stuti hymn, the Aryandom became widened during the closing period of the Rigveda so as to include in it even the region between the Ganges and the Yamuna. Two easternmost rivers of the older Aryandom were the Srasvati and the Asmanvati. The remaining ten rivers, including the Kubha (i.e., Kabul) belonged all to the Indus group. The Digvijaya of Agni implied in secular life the victorious career of the five confederate sects or clans of a war-like people representing the Vedic Aryans. The same implied in religious life the establishment of the cultural tradition of the seven Rishis. The traditional number of the leading Rishi families increased with time, it being known in Buddha's time as ten. The Vedic civilization presupposes the powerful and materially advanced civilization of the Indus Valley of which the highly interesting but imperfectly understood remains have been unearthed at Mohenjo-daro and Harappa. The historical tradition in the Rigveda speaks eloquently of the victory of King Sudas over ten Kings and of his extensive power and munificence. The Digha Nikaya preserves the tradition of a magnificent old buried city, which was once the prosperous capital of a righteous King overlord called Sudarshana the Great. The site of this city is misplaced. The name Sudarshana which is also an epithet of the sun may be suggestive of the fact that its bearer was a warrior of the solar race. Nothing would be more astonishing to think than that Vedic Aryandom had extended further east than the river Shatadru, or that in the Vedas there is mention of any people or country outside the Uttarapatha. The Gandharis who are incidentally mentioned in the Rigveda and the Atharva 'apparently as a despised people', in the latter, along with the Mujavats, Angas and Magadhas, were a people of Uttarapatha. We may be certain about the Angas having been a people of Uttarapatha, inasmuch as even in historical times there was a distinct tribal tract by the name of Angaloka or Angana, which existed side by side with Tangana.

The pre-historic sites hitherto discovered in South India and Ceylon abound in dolmens, cists, stone implements and other remains of a rude state of civilization attained by man in the palaeolithic and neolithic ages. None of them has so far yielded any evidence of man's progress reaching up to the chalcolithic stage. The latter stage was abundantly reached in Sumer or Shinar in Mesopotamia and in the two ancient buried cities of Harappa and Mahenjo-daro, *i.e.*, in the pre historic civilization of the Indus Valley. The Pali tradition of the old forgotten buried city preserves the name of Kusavat reminding us of the earlier Sumerian city of Kush (Kish), the glory of which was eclipsed by the rise of Baveru (Babylon) to importance, while the name of Sumer with its Biblical variant Shinar cannot but remind us of Mt. Sumeru with Sineru as the Pali variant of its name. The marked advance in civilization was made by human races in Egypt in the valley of the river Nile (Aigyptos), in Sumeria and Asia Minor in the valleys of the Euphrates and the Tigris, and in the Punjab proper in the valley of the Indus. A similar advance was made in China in the valley of the Yangtse. In the history of Babylonia, Assyria and Chaldea we get nothing but an account of the subsequent development of the Sumerian civilization. In the rise of the Hittites in Asia Minor as a powerful rival of both the Egyptians and the Mesopotamians one can trace not only the historical process of amalgamation of the two earlier forms of civilization but also a new type of civilization, which is more European than Indo-European in its essential features. From the Egyptian, the Babylonian and the Hittite stages, it is easy to watch the rise of the Phoenicians, the Israels, the Achcemenians, the Greeks and the Romans as civilizers of mankind on the Mediterranean shores.

The traditions of India refer all to the region of Mt. Sumeru or Sineru, say the tableland of Pamir, as the centre of the then known earth extending as far as to the four seas and dividing the four subcontinents. This very region was remembered to have been the scene of contests between the Devas and the Asuras for supremacy with varying results. There is also a tradition, though a late one, that the higher and more powerful races of men came to India from the Western, Northern and Eastern subcontinents. The Uttarapatha or Punjab proper within the belt of the Western Himalayan range was indeed the portion of Northern India which became the most ancient of higher civilization and culture. It is here that one must trace the early settlements of divers races and scenes of conflict amongst them in pre-historic and historic times. It lay exposed to powerful invasions from outside and had to bear the brunt of first attacks and onslaughts of hostile and invading forces.

The worship of idols or concrete representations of various divinities was widely prevalent in all the ancient cradles of civilization and centres of culture. The first move in the direction of progress was aniconic, meaning as it did a struggle of the higher mind to get away from the concrete to find heart's delight in the realm of the abstract. With the open condemnation of idolatry and the monotheistic conception of Jehovah as the wrathful and Almighty God of the Hebrews commenced the history of Judaism as a higher religion in the eastern Mediterranean countries and later on that of Islam with its conception of Allah as the All merciful and Almighty God. With the conception of the gods and goddesses as finalities of beauty commenced the history of Greek religion. With the birth of a higher religious poetry in the Riks tending to transform the concrete into the abstract and to endow the gods and goddesses with divine attributes of an ethical and aesthetic kind commenced the history of Vedism in the Saptasindhu.

Superseding the Egyptian Book of the Dead, Sumerian Psalms and Hittite state-treaties and religious texts by their dignified utterances, elevated moral tone, broadness of outlook, religious fervour, self-consciousness, imaginativeness and philosophic insight, the Rigvedic hymns came to represent a great upheaval of human mind and to raise the level of culture and standard of civilization. The Rigveda supplied to Brahmanism the sacred texts to be chanted as psalms, the mantras or charming ritual formulas of mystic potency, the notion of purifying agency in Agni, that of the source of light and heat in Surya, that of sovereignty in Indra, that of an orderly universe in Varuna, that of organic individuality of the universe and of human society in Purusha or Narayana, that of a divine architect in Vishvakarman, that of vitality in Anila, that of a scientific attitude towards the problem of creation in the Nasadiya hymn, that of Brahma or Brahmin in Hiranyagarbha, and that of the Four Indian Graces in asa, Sraddha, hri and sri. The commercial spirit of the earlier civilization was at the back, nevertheless, of the business like relationship between the deity 'invoked and the invoking priest promising the offer of oblations in return of the services to be rendered.

The historical tradition in the Manu-samhita places the beginning of the history of Brahmanism in a narrow strip of land between the Shrasvati and the Drishadvati, honouring the region as Brahmavarta or Brahmaland. The customs and usages of all the castes and mixed castes in that land, as handed: down from generation to generation, were acknowledged as good (sadachara). The subsequent development of Brahmanism through interpretation and instruction as a system of religious thought is located in the countries of Kurukshetra, Matsya, Panchnla and Surasena, all together constituting the land of pride hallowed by the advent of the renowned Brahmans. Whatever its southern limit, the Pariyatra mountain', the Vindhya range, the river

Narmada or the Godavari, the name of Aryavarta was restricted to the northern half of India proper, while the peninsular south was given the distinctive name of Dakshinapatha or Dakshinatya.

Referring evidently to his Empire, Ashoka says that there was no locality other than the solitary Yavana territory where the distinct bodies of the Brahmanas and the Shramanas were not, and where the people had not sincere faith in one or another of them, which means that already before the promulgation of R. E. XIII in his 13th or 14th regnal year the whole of his Empire with the single exception of the Yavana country was Aryanised. In the face of this clear statement the question is apt to arise—when and by whom was the Indo-Aryan civilization and culture spread over the whole of South India and Ceylon, and ultimately over the whole of Jambudvipa in the Buddhistic as well as the Great Epic sense of the term?

We have so far sought to maintain that South India proper and the island of Tamraparni had not loomed large in the geographical vision of Jambudvipa or Bharatavarsha before the Mauryas and Nandas. In support of this one may confidently cite the testimony of Megasthenes and later Classical writers from Arrian to Pliny, all of whom broadly divide Northern India into two portions, the northwestern portion, i.e., the Punjab proper, watered by the Indus system of rivers, and the eastern portion covering the whole of the Buddhist Midland and the Lower Bengal watered by the Ganges system. They give us but a rough topographical outline of India proper in the manner of the Pali Mahagovinda Suttanta. The account given of the trans-Himalayan countries and races is similar to those embodied in the Great Epic, the Puranas, the Jatakas and the Jaina Jambudvipa-prajnapti. They offer us a fair account of Kalinga and a bare indication of India's seacoast trade from the mouth of the Ganges to that of the Indus; even the traditional distances from the mouth of the Ganges to Cape Calingaon and the town of Dantagula (Dantapura) to Tropina (Tripontari or Tirupantara opposite Cochin), to the cape of Perimula (a projecting point of the modern island of Salsette near Bombay), and to Patala (Prasthala at the Lower Indus Valley) are mentioned. The geographical account of Taprobane (Tamraparni, Ceylon) and its trade-relations with South India and the kingdom of Kalinga is fairly accurate. A true picture of the political conditions of Northern India is held before us when the Punjab proper situated to the west of the Yamuna is stated to have been held by the Macedonian army under Alexander and the eastern portion called Gangaridae by such a powerful rival as Agrammes, the last Nanda King. It is also a correct statement of the fact that Sandrokottos (Chandragupta Maurya) grew powerful by the unification of the fighting peoples and states of the Punjab proper under his leadership and widened the growing Magadha Empire by the annexation of the Punjab proper, as well as the four trans-Sulaiman territories ceded by Seleucus Nikator. Though the Puranas refer to Mahapadma, the founder of the Nanda dynasty, as an exterminator of all Kshatriyas, as a monarch who brought all under his sole sway, the inclusion of Kalinga in the Magadha Empire and a considerable portion of the Deccan below the Godavari remains still to be proved, though its probability cannot altogether be ruled out.

Among the Classical writers, Plutarch and Justin definitely speak of Chandragupta Maurya as a monarch in possession of India by overrunning and subduing the whole of the country 'with an army of 600,000 men.' In the Mudrarakshasa, too, the supremacy of the first Maurya is said to have extended from the Himalayas to the shores of the southern ocean. This, as Raychaudhary suggests, may have been just a conventional description of the position of a chakravartin.

The Tamil traditions make 'frequent allusions to the Mauryas in the past having penetrated with a great army as far as the Podiyil Hill in the Tinnevelly district." The opinion differs as to who the Maurya leader was, Chandragupta or his son Bindusara. Seeing that they are stigmatised as Vamba Moriyar or 'Maurya upstarts', Raychaudhary inclines to identify him with the first Maurya. On the strength, on the other hand, of Taranatha's specific statement that sixteen kingdoms were overthrown by Bindusara Mr. Sathianathaier of the Jaiaswal school of historians thinks that overwhelming is the evidence in favour of the second Maurya being the conqueror of Tondamandalam if it was within Ashoka's Empire. In the edicts, however, Ashoka gives the credit to none but himself for the Dharmavijaya achieved in the independent territories of the Cholas, the Pandyas, the Satiyaputras, the Keralaputras and the Tamraparnyas, as well as in the semi-independent states of the parent Rashtrikas and Bhojas and their offshoots and the Andhras and Parinda-Paradas.

Manu's first Brahmaland (Brahmavarta), which is located between the Shrasvati and the Drishadvati, excludes the earlier Vedic Aryandom between the river Kabul and the Sutlej. The Markandeya Purana speaks of two Brahmin settlements in Uttarapatha, viz., those of the Atreyas and the Bharadvajas—the Brahmans whom Arrian connects with the country of the Mushikas in the region of Sindh. Pliny takes the Brachmanes of this region "to be, not what they actually were, the leading caste of the population, bat a powerful race composed of many tribes."

The compilation of the Vedic hymns in the form of four different Samhitas, which took place, according to tradition, in the land of the Kurus, the acceptance of them as the greatest book of wisdom of unquestionable authority, the preparation of different reactions of them, adherence to any one of them in preference to the rest in respect of their ritual values, the necessity felt for committing them to memory by methodical chanting instead of to writing, etc. gave rise to various schools of Brahmin hymn-chanters, priests and teachers. In the historical process of Brahmanism one may trace the course of origin and development of an enormous literature, sacred and profane, technical and popular, philosophic and scientific. There was no sphere of man's existence and activity, individual or domestic, socio-moral or politico-economic, religious or philosophic, where the usefulness and indispensability of the Brahmans as a class was not acutely felt.

As shown by Dr. B. C. Law, the early Jaina and Buddhist books place the Brahmans either in the usual social environment or in the hermitages. "In the first connection, they are introduced either as those who were in the service of the King or as those who had followed different professions of their own. In the second connection, they are introduced as those who went out of the social environments and lived the life of tapasas or isis in forest homes called assamas with or without families and resident pupils. Of those in service of the King, the most important were the amachchas and mahamatras. The yachakas and others were no better than assistants in the office of the Purohita. Partly in connection with the King, they held the position of mahasalas or heads of Vedic institutions. They came to represent the sotthiya class of Brahmans who were occasionally employed as dutas. The Brahmans also filled the office of senapatis and issatthas or yodhajivas, chariot-drivers, trainers of elephants, legal experts and judges. To the people in general they rendered services as Purohitas and priests, as physicians and druggists, as astronomers and architects, as ballad-singers and matchmakers."

In dealing with the Digvijaya of Agni we are primarily concerned with the Shrotriyas, Purohitas and Ministers, all of whom were Brahmans, and the Tapasas, called Hylobioi by the Greek writers, who lived in the woods, where they subsisted on leaves of trees and wild fruits, and wore garments from the bark of trees. They represented the various orders of Indian hermits practising hard penances, developing supernormal faculties and holding communion with God or gods and the different schools of Rishis or hermit teachers. Among the Tapasas were men of all the three twice-born classes, and hardly any from among the Shudras and untouchables. The householder Brahmans and the Tapasas were equally the performers of sacrifices, believers in the practice of penances and upholders of the doctrine of purity, bodily or otherwise.

Going by Ashoka's statement, we have to say that the main agents for the Aryanisation of India or Greater India uptil the 13th year of his reign were the various orders of 'runaways' and schools of thought represented by the Brahmanas and the Shramanas. Among them, the Brahmanas alone were popularly venerated in largest number as teachers of religion and philosophy, morality and piety in the three later stages of effort. As 'runaways', they mostly figured as Tapasas and Parivrajakas. Even among the Shramanas who had not either strictly adhered to the Vedic rules of life or openly challenged them, the majority were Brahmans. The only powerful rivals of the Brahmans in the matter of higher knowledge and social importance were the Kshatriyas. Leaving out of account the case of Vishvamitra among the leading Vedic Rishis, we find in Pravahana Jaivali, the Kshatriya leader of the oligarchy of the Panchalas, Pratardana, the son of Divodasa, and

Ajatashatru, the King of Kashi the three distinguished Upanishad teachers who were approached even by the Brahmin seekers of truth for the sake of higher knowledge. The Jatakas glorify the Kuru tradition of righteous rule established by King Arjuna, and the tradition of righteousness and renunciation established by the Janakas of Videha, the Brahmadattas of Kashi and the Shivis of Uttarapatha. In the Hathigumpha inscription, the Jaina King Kharavela is described as a worthy descendant of a long line of Rajarshis among the Chedi Princes.

Parsva who was the founder of an order of Shramanas in Eastern India with ahimsa as its main principle was a Prince from the royal House of Kashi. Though Mahavira and Buddha who were respectively the founders of the two most powerful orders of Shramanas and Kshatriya schools of thought, the most eminent and distinguished among their disciples and later followers were all persons from Brahmin families. Thus the Brahmans made all the noble heritages in Indo-Aryan religion and culture ultimately their own. But to appreciate the Digvijaya of Agni we must leave the Shramanite Brahmans out of consideration, particularly the Shakyaputriyas or Buddhists, Ashoka's Samghasthas.

The history of the Brahmans as priests and their usefulness and influence shows parallel to that of the Babylonian priests and their wide influence in Western Asia among the Assyrians, the Chaldeans, the Hittites, the Mittanies and others with this difference, however, that they have an unbroken history up till now. The tradition of the Brahmans as law-givers and framers of the rules of life and conduct shows a parallel to that of the Jewish Prophets and Patriarchs.

The Brahmans, too, cherished the tradition of the successive advent of the Manus or Patriarchs. The legend of a great Flood during the dispensation of Manu Vaivasvata, as narrated in the Satapatha Brahmana, cannot but remind one of the Biblical legend of the Flood at Babylon in the time of the Patriarch and Prophet Noah. Although the maximum span of man's life as one hundred years was recognised in the Vedic hymns, it is represented as-120 years in the Aitareya Aranyaka, which, too, is a point of agreement with the Jewish tradition of the time of Noah.

The Brahmans of India, like the Jewish Patriarchs in Syria, were guided by the idea of purity and impurity, the clean and the unclean, in the matter of framing rules regarding eatables and non-eatables, and the rules prescribed by both were in many respects similar. The earlier Brahmanical rules that held ground, particularly in the Midland, are clearly presupposed by Ashoka's argument, "that are not eaten", behind his list of birds, fishes and quadrupeds made inviolables under the law. The Mosaic code of prescriptions and prohibitions having many points in common with Manu's, had behind it the belief in the Divine sanction as communicated to Noah, enjoining that "every moving thing that liveth" was meant by the Creator to serve as "meat" for even as the green herb had he given him all things. The Divine sanction as stated in the Chhandogya Upanishad and Manu's Code is even verbally the same:

> "The Creator had meant all these as food for life; all that is stationery and all that moveth were to serve as food to life."

> "What will be my food? Whatsoever is the living thing, even the horses and vultures (birds?)."

The earlier sanction allowing to man "every herb bearing seed, which is upon the face of all the earth, and every tree, in which is the fruit of a tree yielding seed" to be for meat had to be modified under the exigency of terrible circumstances, such as the cataclysmic Flood. This is missed in the Brahmanical tradition.

The Patriarch Noah is credited in the Biblical tradition with the building of an altar for making burnt offerings unto the Lord of every clean beast and of every clean fowl, the sweet savour whereof was appreciated by Him. This is another remarkable point of agreement between Brahmanism and Judaism in that both insist on not eating the meat of any beast or fowl that has not been sacrificed on the altar built unto God.

In the opinion of Megasthenes, all that had been said regarding nature by the ancients was asserted also by philosophers out of Greece, on the one part in India by the Brachmanes, and on the other in Syria by the people called Jews. Clemens boldly maintained that the Jewish philosophy had preceded the philosophy of the

Greeks. As regards the story of creation, the main point of agreement between Brahmanism and Judaism is that, according to both, in the beginning was God, and God alone, and it was by His will that the heaven and the earth, the beings and the things, the man and the woman were created, the usual language in both for the expression of the creative will of God and its product being "Let there be and there was."

It is rather sad that the Gentile and Brahmanical traditions are full of curses, the pronouncement of which is a proof of one's moral weakness and morbid state of mind. Viewing in the light of both, we are to witness the dramas of life of which the plots are laid in effective curses and counter-curses, the prospect of blessedness being far off from the view.

In both, the position of woman is lowered and made subordinate to that of man. In the eye of the Brahmanical law the woman needs protection in all the three stages of her life and does not deserve to be free. As known to Megasthenes, the Brahmans did not communicate a knowledge of philosophy to their wives, "lest they should divulge any of the forbidden mysteries to the profane if they became depraved, or lest they should desert them if they became good philosophers."

With the householder Brahmin teachers and ministers suspicion or distrust was as much the guiding factor in conjugal life as in the system of royal polity, particularly that which was embodied in the Arthashastra ascribed to Kautilya. Panini spoke indeed of devotion to one's country or nation, and the Arthashastra of the importance to be attached to the national star, but the Brahmanical rajadharma having been concerned about one man's show, was far from arousing national sentiment or making the people conscious of their nationhood.

The Brahmans as priests made the age-old popular superstitions deep-rooted in man's mind instead of eradicating them by having used them as the basis of mangalas or auspicious domestic rituals and ceremonies, arranged stage by stage. They allied themselves with the masses who were worshippers of various tribal gods and goddesses, of divers benevolent and malevolent spirits, and were mostly animists. They utterly failed to develop a congregational life in their religion. Even in such common matters as eating, there were no fixed hours when meals were to be taken in common, but each one ate when he felt inclined, the contrary of which would be, in the opinion of Megasthenes, 'better for the ends of social and civil life."

The great stumbling block in the way of the development of a healthy and strong national life in India was the caste system creating irremovable barriers between men and men, class and class, occupation and occupation. The most unfortunate feature of it was that it was founded on an apparently captivating organic idea of the universe, the society and the state, the scientific and philosophic drawback of which has not as yet been fully considered and understood. Though the Purusha Sukta presenting this fond idea found its place in the Rigveda, the idea itself may be shown to have been more Brahmanical than Vedic. The subsequent history of Brahmanism shows nothing but a process of gradual hardening of the castes, creation of differences even in the heights of sepulchres after death, and that of social divisions within divisions, all causing social and civic injustice. As known to Megasthenes, the body-politic was so divided in India in the 4th century B. C. that no one was allowed to marry out of his own caste, or to exercise any calling or art except his own, for instance, a soldier could not become a husbandman, or an artizan a philosopher.

The Shrotriyas as founders and heads of residential Vedic schools and colleges were' recipients of brahmadanas or royal fiefs enabling them to maintain those institutions independently of state control. Through the Digvijaya of Agni and with the wider and wider extension of Aryandom there came to be a network of those institutions seeking to convert India into a free gift for the spread and establishment of Vedic culture and Brahmanical socio-religious order, the varnasrama dharma. It was among these great Brahmin teachers that there arose men with lofty vision and keen insight and true seekers of philosophic truth and propounders of higher religious ideals. The early Upanishad teachers were mostly Brahmans of this class.

The Shrotriyas as Shrotriyas were not, however, the persons to be credited with the expedition in the annals of the Digvijaya of Agni. They were rather the consolidators of new territorial gains. The daring explorers of uninhabited and at first inaccessible forest tracts or woodlands in the mountain ranges or along the different rivers, the builders of peaceful and sombre religious homes with sylvan surroundings having a divine aroma about them, gay with the life of fauna and flora, lively with the movement of spirits, and endowed with idyllic beauty and charm were the Tapasas or Hermits of various orders among whom flourished the great rishis endowed with psychic powers, spiritual visions and personality. They were attracted by the natural beauty of the woodlands and through them developed the aranyaka or vanaprastha life, the science of medicine and astronomy, and the schools of Samkhyayoga or adhyatinavidya.

In the solitude of woodlands they practised hard penances, cultivated friendly feelings towards all, lived on the bounties of nature, and bravely went to meet death instead of allowing death to come to them. It is in their line that one must trace the continuity of the tradition of Vedic poets, sages and seers. With the spread of hermitages over the whole of India extended the range of krishnasara, and of sacrificial fire, which is to say, of the Digvijaya of Agni. Their mission was to sanctify the earth with sacrificial fire, to convert it, in other words, into a holy land.

The rivers, lakes and springs where they performed ablutions for the purpose of self-purification, the places where they built their hermitages, performed sacrifices and laid to rest their bones became tirthas or places of pilgrimage to the Hindus. The gradual advance of the sacrificial fire in all the four directions and increase in the number of tirthas are traceable through literary references and inscriptions, the list of tirthas given in the Sauti version of the Great Epic having been unthinkable in pre-Ashokan and pre-Christian times.

The typical list of seven tirthas we have from the Buddha confines our geographical vision to the Midland between the Shrasvati and the Phalgu. Even as known to Megasthenes, the course of advance had not gone in the south beyond the river Tagabena. Tradition associates the first expedition to the extreme south with Agastya. That which was at first a mere foot-track to walk from one hermitage to another became afterwards a high road, notably the Southern Road connecting Rajagriha with Paithan on the Godavari. 'The neighbourhood of the hermitages became sites afterwards of many important cities.' The hermitages that were surrounded by non-Aryan and aboriginal settlements needed from time to time the help of warrior Kings and Kshatriya Princes to secure them from the inimical action of the rude natives, the savages including cannibals. Thus the building of hermitages and that of the new Kshatriya states proceeded almost *pari passu.*

If the Hermits were, as Bhandarkar rightly thinks, the passive evangelists of Vedic religion and Indo-Aryan culture, there arose in Northern India and not long before the rise of Buddhism powerful bodies of active propagators of the same. They were the Wanderers and Recluses, the Brahmana Parivrajakas and the Shramanas of various orders and schools of thought. The new order emerged at first out of and as a further step from the order of Hermits, and resulted later also from direct renunciation of worldly life. They indeed became known to Megasthenes and other Classical writers as two classes of Indian philosophers, viz., the Brachmanes and the Sarmanes.

Theoretically they were all homeless in the sense that they themselves did not build abodes for them but sought for temporary shelters in abodes built for them by others, the royal pleasances, called aramas or viharas having been originally the places where they used to halt for a night in course of their wanderings. Even when the permanent abodes were built for them, they came to be known by those names.

The Brahmarnas and the Shramanas differed from each other not only in their outward signs, but also in their thoughts and ideals and general attitude towards the social and political institutions based on Vedic tradition and caste distinction. The general effect of the new movement was the undervaluation of the civic life and social rites under the control of secular Brahmanism. The Ajivikas among the Brahmanite Shramanas and the Nirgranthas (Jainas) among the Shramanite Brahmans appeared as heterodox in the eye of the orthodox Brahmanist. Though some were Shaivite, some Vaishiavite, and others Jaina, all of them were believers in the practice of hard penances and profound meditations, and all were in different ways confirmed believers in the existence of souls as abiding entities in individuals that are not subject to the laws of change. None but the Nirgranthas amongst them openly challenged the Brahmanist position and developed a religious and cultural tradition, which is in some important respects similar to that of the Shakyaputriyas or Buddhists. When Ashoka spoke of the Aryanisation of almost the whole of India by the different denominations of the Brahmanas and the Shramanas other than the Samghasthas or Buddhists, he had precisely kept in view the evangelical activities of the Hermits, the Brahmin Wanderers and such typical Shramanas as the Ajivikas and Nirgranthas.

Dharmavijaya of Ashoka: As propounders and propagators of Indo-Aryanism tending steadily and invariably to set higher value on the religious and cultural side of man's life and civilization, the Hermits, Brahmin Wanderers, Ajivikas and Nirgranthas were the precursors of the Shakyaputriyas. This fact is stated in no uncertain terms by Ashoka in his E. E. XIII. The same is borne out by the evidence of the Pali Nikayas and corroborated by the testimony of Megasthenes and other Classical writers. The Chronicles of Ceylon not only lead us to infer that the worship of the Nagas and Yakshas, of Vishnu Utpalavarna and the ascetic god Shiva was prevalent among the primitive dwellers of the island but also clearly state that King Pandukabhaya, the brother and immediate successor of Vijaya, caused hermitages to be built for the Hermits, retreats for the Brahmin Parivrajakas, and suitable abodes for the Ajivikas and Nirgranthas. They had held the ground before the arrival of the Buddhist mission under Mahendra in the 3rd century B. C. Even referring to the time of King Vattagamani (1st century B. C), the Chronicles tell us that they had had their rights and privileges left intact through twenty-one reigns since Pandukabhaya.

According to Jaina tradition, the Nirgranthas under their accredited leader Bhadrabahu went to South India during the reign of Chandragupta Maurya. That the Jinakalpika or Digambara Jainas got a strong foothold in South India as far back as the 4th century B. C. may be taken for granted, and the Deccan proper, particularly the Canarese country, is still one of the strongholds of Jainism. That the Ajivikas, too, got an early foothold there and maintained their identity as a distinct religious sect up till the 13th or 14th century A. D. may be seen from the ancient Tamil works as well as a number of South Indian inscriptions.

The pronounced cumulative effect of the pre-Buddhistic Brahmans-Shramana movement was felt and acknowledged by Alexander, the great Macedonian conqueror, in going to deal with Dandamis (Dandin), the leader of a Brahmanical sect of Gymnosophists, evidently of Shaivite persuasion and closely allied to the Ajivikas, who established themselves somewhere in the Punjab. The Ionians were the first among the Greeks noted for their commercial enterprise and came to the near east to be Persianised and to found a colony round the city of Nysa on the river Kophen or Kabul during the reign of the Achaemenian Kings of Persia, better Iran. They became in the matter of their social organisation and religious beliefs allied with the Kambojas, the Gandharas and other autonomous tribes of the Upper Indus Valley as early as Buddha's time and remained so even till the reign of Ashoka and to a still later period. There is nothing to be disbelieved or thought improbable when Megasthenes says that the Macedonians under Alexander came across at the threshold of India beyond the river Kabul a people whose manners and customs were akin to those of the Greeks. The Bharidatta Jataka contemptuously refers to the Kambojas as a people with the barbarous habit of killing the insects, moths, snakes and frogs (obviously for the purpose of eating) and believing in killing them as a meritorious act.

According to Arrian, the regions beyond the Indus on the west were inhabited up to the river Kophen (Kabul) by two Indian tribes, the Astakenai (Arshtakas, Rishtikas) and the Assakenos (Asvakas) who were in old times subject to the Assyrians and submitted subsequently to the Persians, paying the tribute to the Achaemenian King Kyros, son of Kambyses.

Schwanbeck Rightly Observed: "The Aryan Indians were from the remotest period surrounded on all sides by indigenous tribes in a state of barbarism, from whom they differed both in mind and disposition. They were most acutely sensible of this difference, and gave it a very pointed expression. Other races, and these even Indian, since they had originated in an intermixture of tribes, or since they did not sufficiently follow Indian manners, and especially the system of caste, so roused the common hatred of the Indians that they were reckoned with the barbarians, and represented as equally hideous of aspect".

The Greek knowledge of India was imperfect prior to Alexander's invasion. The stories then current in Greece went nevertheless to depict her 'as a land of righteous folks, of strange beasts and plants, of surpassing wealth in gold and gems.' Although the Greeks came to India forming foreign elements in her population, ruling or otherwise, first as Ionians, next as Macedonians, and afterwards as Bactrians, they continued to be known by the name of Yavana or Yavana, the Indian and Achaemenian equivalent of Ionian. "Although", as poignantly observed by Vincent Smith, "the direct effects of Alexander's expedition on India appear to have been small, his proceedings had an appreciable influence on the history of the country. They broke down the wall of separation between west and east, and opened up four distinct lines of communication, three by land and one by sea. The immediate formation of Greek kingdom in Western Asia ensured from the first a certain amount of exchange of ideas between India and Europe. The establishment of the Greco-Bactrian monarchy in the middle of the third century B. C. brought about the actual subjugation of certain Indian districts by Greek Kings."

Alexander's military expedition directed to Asia and Africa was designed undeniably also to spread the Greek civilization among the Barbarians, and accordingly his troops were accompanied by many men of letters, including the Sceptic philosopher Pyrrho of Elis and a follower of Democritus named Anaxarchns. But his pride as the son of the mighty god Zeus and the conqueror of many nations was humbled by two persons he met, one a robber who tried to convince him of the fact that he by his actions and intention was only a greater robber, and the other a famous leader of the Indian Gymnosophists who tried to convince him of the fact that there was even a far greater conqueror than he by having nothing to call his own.

Onesikrates was deputed to fetch Dandamis the great Indian ascetic leader in Uttarapatha. "The Emperor Alexander, the son of the great Jupiter, who is lord of the human race, has ordered that you should hasten to him, for if you come, he will give you many gifts, but if you refuse, he will behead you as a punishment for your contempt." When this message was thus delivered to him, "he rose not from his leaves whereon he lay, but reclining and smiling he replied in this way: The greatest God can do injury to no one, but restores again the light of life to those who have departed. Accordingly he forbids murder and excites no wars. But Alexander is no God, for he himself will have to die. How, then, can he be the lord of all, who has not yet crossed the river Tyberoboas, nor has *made the whole world his abode, nor crossed the Zone of Gades, not* has beheld the course *of the* sun in the centre of the world? Therefore many nations do not even know his name. Let Alexander threaten with this them that desire riches or fear death, both of which I despise. For Brahmanes neither love gold nor death. Go, therefore, and tell Alexander this—Dandamis seeks nothing of yours, but if you think you need something of his, disdain not to go to him."

> "When Alexander heard these words through the interpreter, he wished the more to see such a man, since he, who had subdued many nations, was overcome by an old naked man."

Whilst the earlier evangelists of Indo-Aryanism were spread upon the face of India and Ceylon, Buddhism, the religion of Shakyamuni, remained confined till the earlier part of Ashoka's reign to the territorial limits of the Middle Country. The two countries in Western India outside the Buddhist Midland were Surasena and Avanti where two important centres of Buddhism were founded in Buddha's lifetime, and just a sporadic attempt was made by a disciple of Buddha to preach the new Gospel of righteousness and piety to the rude and fierce people of Sunaparanta. There were several semi-independent tribal states within Ashoka's Empire but outside his domain proper where the Indo-Aryan culture and social organisation resting on caste basis were not well established.

Since Ashoka had declared the Dharmavijaya or Conquest by Piety to be a state policy, the religious and cultural movements within the definition of Indo-Aryanism assumed a new aspect of self-consciousness on the part of the Brahmanas and the Shramanas of various orders and schools of thought. The appointment of the Dharma-mahamatras as a class of imperial officers was purposed *inter alia* to ensure the personal safety of these active preachers and passive evangelists of Indo-Aryanism in those tribal areas as well as of those of the local people who became their adherents. Ashoka did not, however, mean to restrict the range of his noble cultural conquest to his domain proper or to his Empire. He was out for a world conquest through it, and for this India needed a religion like Buddhism.

In Buddhism was found a religion with vigorous missionary zeal. It had behind it the stupendous dynamic personality of the Buddha and the highest ethical perfection of man. Although on its philosophic and spiritual side it showed in many respects the continuity of the philosophy of the Upanishads, and on its secular and popular side it showed in many respects the continuity of the socio-religious and politico-moral system of the pre-Paninian Mahabharata, it differed fundamentally from both. The Brahmaveda of the Upanishads came to be replaced, supplemented and superseded by the Dharmaveda of Buddhism. The basic concepts of both had behind them two different kinds of intuition or mystical experience as to the nature of reality, one in which the static nature and the other in which the dynamic nature presented itself. While atman remained the underlying notion of the Upanishad doctrine, anatman became the prevailing idea of Buddhism. The difference between the fundamenal axioms of both was analogous to that between the Parmanidean and Heraclitean axioms in Greek philosophy.

The main points of difference between secular Brahmanism on the one hand and Buddhism on the other were that one was sacerdotal, the other rational in form; one clannish, the other universal in spirit; the commitment of one was to forms and procedures, that of the other to the inner essence of the thing; that one sought to base domestic and social relations on caste basis, the other on that of morality and piety. Thus no other form of government than monarchical found favour in Brahmanical rajadharma, while in Buddha's view the form, whether monarchical, oligarchical or democratic, was immaterial, if the state in any form had fulfilled all its main obligations. The same as to the forms of marriage, the forms of manifold duties. However lofty the purpose set before the state or earthly sovereignty, the Brahmanical rajadharma could never abandon, in no stage of its development, the Tit for Tat policy.

Jainism, which has acted throughout its history as a halfway house between Brahmanism and Buddhism, nay between all isms that were come across its path, was, at least so far as its doctrine of ahimsa, non-harming mental attitude towards all beings and things, moral rectitude, idea of moral responsibility, denial of God, rejection of caste barriers, and the like are concerned, a definite move towards Buddhism. And yet its ascetic predilections, religious vows, penitent heart, such categories of its thought as bandha, samvara, nirjara and moksha go to indicate that its main mental obsession was one of the bondage of sin, and its struggle was to release the soul therefrom.

The task was left to Buddhism to shift the emphasis from thraldom to freedom, abstinence from killing to the cultivation of friendliness and compassion, from the prevention and cure of diseases to the generation and development of healthy states, from the arrest of the course and possibility of degradation and deterioration of human nature to the progressive paths (paripuri) of the life. Buddhism was the only religion of India which vigorously espoused the educational and cultural cause of humanity and did not go to form a new society among its lay followers by the enforcement of a social code of its own in spite of its giving a clear direction to the path of progress, and rational and refined human behaviour. There was no other religion before Christianity which had boldly proclaimed that hatred does not cease by hatred, and that it ceases only by amity and love. Its doctrine of the 'mean' (madhya) between any two extreme courses of thought and of action did not fail to exercise its potent influence on the later political thought of India.

Ashoka's scheme of the toleration of faiths based upon Buddha's (and partly also upon Mahavira's) doctrine of samyak (all-round consideration, comprehensiveness) stood for frequent cultural contacts, healthy discussions, helpful criticisms and hearty interchanges of thoughts and ideas, and had not cherished the non-intervention policy of the Bhagavad Gita.

How long could an administration be efficiently run if it were based on suspicion and mutual distrust? How long could a state be at peace with the neighbouring peoples and powers if its foreign relations were always guided by the fourfold diplomatic means of conciliating, bribing, causing dissension and waging wars, as contemplated in Brahmanical rajadharma? The sordid art of diplomacy was sought to be superseded by the nobler policy of Dharmavijaya, both within and without, without the least thought about impairing the strength of the state and its military efficiency. The imperial envoys were despatched to convey the good wishes from this side to foreign courts and peoples, to carry on works of public utility and to promulgate the most elementary but fundamental principles of piety or duty in which lay the real happiness of men and the elevation of humanity.

Buddha was at pains to indicate the baneful reactions of drastic and vindictive measures adopted by a state on the life of the people. Going by his trend of thought, the supreme duty of a state that stands for the ideal of righteousness should be to educate the people to live better life and to help them by all means in their struggles for existence and in leading a decent and happy and comfortable life. Ashoka's scheme of Dharmavijaya fully recognises the wisdom in this line of thinking.

Buddhism was not made a state religion by Ashoka. It was Ashoka's personal religion, and he publicly stated that it was so. But the principles of the Dharma that he had advocated were neither propounded nor promulgated in the name of the Good Faith or any other religion. Buddhist missions were despatched to different places in India by the then head of the Buddhist Church, the most Venerable Moggaliputra Tissa, who was held in high esteem by him.

The places to which they are said to have been sent in the Chronicles of Ceylon are all now found to be indicated by the find-spots of the Kalsi, Mansehra, Shahbazgarhi, Girnar and Sopara versions of his Book Edicts, the Hyderabad and Northern Mysore copies of his Minor Book Edict. Suvarnabhumi and Tamraparni are the two places that are not explicable by the find-spots of the hitherto discovered inscriptions. Once we assume that Suvarnagiri was the earlier name on the list replaced later on by Suvarnabhumi, the case of both the places can be met by the inscriptions in which they find mention, one as the official headquarters of the most southern province, and the other as the most southern of the independent countries in South India.

The historical foundation of the tradition regarding Moggaliputra Tissa and the personnel of the mission to the Himalayan region is evident from the Sanchi relic-casket inscriptions. The development of such later Buddhist sects and schools as the Haimavatas (Central Himalayan), the Uttarapathakas (Northwest Indian), the Vajriyas (Extreme northwest Indian), the Purvasailas, Aparasailas, Rajagriyas and Siddharthakas (all Andhrakas) presupposes earlier missionary activities in these places. According to the tradition recorded by Hiuen Tsang, the Buddhist mission under Mahendra was directed first to the country of Malayakata, situated below Dravida,—the Tamraparni of the Great Epic—from which country he must have gone across to Simhala, i. e., the island of Tamraparni. The contemporaneity of Devanampriya Ashoka of India and Devanampriya Tissa of Ceylon and the political and cultural relationship between the two countries in their time may now be established beyond all doubt by the evidence of the most ancient of the Brahmi inscriptions of the island so far found carrying us back to the time of Uttiya, the brother and immediate successor of Tissa. There seems to be much force in the argument seeking to locate the site of Ashoka's Suvarnagiri in the proximity of the Yerragudi rock.

The Dutas or Emissaries were the imperial agents of Ashoka through whom the mission of his Dharmavijaya was sought to be fulfilled in the territories of five Greek contemporaries forming then the five Mediterranean States, as well as in the five independent territories of the Cholas, the pandyas, the Satiyaputras, the Keralaputras and the Tamraparnyas representing then the five most powerful Dravidian nations of South India. The semi-independent tribal states of such Northern Northwestern ruling peoples as the Yavanas, the Kambojas, the Gandharas, the Nabhakas and the Nabhalines, and of such Southern and Southwestern ruling peoples as the parent Rishtikas and Bhojas and their offshoots, the Andhras and Parinda-Paradas are also expressly included within the range of his embassies. So far as the latter were concerned, the Dharmamahamatras appointed in his 13th regnal year were charged with the duty of looking after the safety of the Indo-Aryan preachers and their local supporters. Were they officials who were employed also as Ashoka's Dutas? That they were not Buddhist missionaries is evident from the

Chronicles of Ceylon that expressly state that the Dutas forming the embassy despatched by Ashoka with coronation presents and happy wishes to his Ceylon contemporary Tissa consisted of Ashoka's nephew Mahaarittha, his Brahmin Chaplain or Councillor, and a Vaishya Treasurer and they were the precursors of the Buddhist mission led by Mahendra. The only means by which Ashoka paved the way for the Buddhist mission which followed was to disclose the fact of his embracing the Buddhist faith in the personal message conveyed to his distant friend and ally, thereby persuading him to do the same. Even if Ashoka had done so, it is difficult to say what actual effect it had produced as an earlier step. The account of Mahendra's mission goes, however, to show that its success in the island of Ceylon rested at first entirely on his personality and powerful preaching.

The veracity of Ashoka's statement concerning the despatch of embassies to the five Greek territories and the claim to the great success attained there through his new plan of Dharmavijaya has been challenged—a bit rudely by Rhys Davids. The cogent arguments by which this may be set at rest are as follows:

- The restricting of the list to five names, faithfully Indianised, cannot but speak of sincerity and accuracy on the part of Ashoka.
- The orderly manner of introducing them, keeping evidently in view the contiguity of the five Greek territories was rendered possible only by a correct information about the relative geographical positions of the territories concerned.
- The reality of the Dutas (envoys) despatched by Ashoka to the Antas, including the five Greek 'frontagers', cannot be disbelieved. Ashoka needed the employment of these agents not only to initiate or encourage various works of piety and public utility, not only to inculcate the principles of piety, not only to proclaim Ashoka's happy messages of piety, year after year, but also to assure the 'frontagers' of his sincere desire to respect their territorial integrity and of his solicitude and good wish.
- The treaty with Seleucus of about 302 BC was followed by the despatch to the court of Ashoka's grandfather of

> the famous envoy, Megasthenes, an officer of Arachosia, while Ashoka's father Bindusara received at his court the homage of the next envoy, Deimachos, from Antiochus Soter. A third envoy named Dionysios was sent to the court of Pataliputra by Ashoka's contemporary, Ptolemy Philadelphos of Egypt, either in his time, or in that of his father.' These facts are recorded by the Greek writers and ignored in Indian literature. Similarly Ashoka records the fact of despatch of envoys by him to the courts and territories of his five Greek 'frontagers', and the Greek writers ignore it. The exchange of envoys by way of reciprocation of courtesy on either side was only too natural under the circumstances to be dısbelieved. The Besnagar Garuda Pillar inscription records the name of Heliodoros as a Bactrian Greek ambassador from Maharaja Antialkidas to the court of King Kashiputra Bhagabhadra."

To these might be added also the argument: "Evidently the five Greek potentates were the direct descendants and successors of Alexander the Great's generals and supporters and their territories were but once component parts of the Greek Empire left behind by the great Macedonian conqueror. It was indeed between the two Empires, namely, the Mauryan and the Macedonian, that friendly intercourse and exchange of embassies remained possible until the reign of Ashoka."

Although, as seems probable, Ashoka got the idea of promulgating the edicts from the Achaemenid Kings of Iran, his epithet, Devanampriya or Beloved of the gods, was Indian in origin, and the toleration of other faiths was a marked feature of his Dharma. These two features characterise the famous Rosetta stone inscription of the 2nd century B. G. caused to be written by Ptolemaios, King of Egypt.

Two immediate and lasting effects of Ashoka's Dharmavijaya were: (i) that it gave impetus and offered chances to Buddhism to become a great force in Asiatic and world civilization, and (ii) that it placed India between the cultures.

In the opinion of Dr. Otto Stein "that position of India between the cultures cannot be better circumscribed than by a word of one of the noblest rulers in the history of mankind: dhammavijaya.

India's relation towards West and East was never defiled by waging wars for material gain and only self-defence forced the weapons in her hands. Thus she won her victory in accordance with the command of Dharma, be it religion, be it morality, call it culture or humanity. That is the importance of India's role in the history in which a place hardly shared by any other country belongs to her, from the remote past upto this day, that is her unique and noble position between the cultures."

Change of Heart

During Ashoka's grandfather's time the Kalinga army had only 60,000 infantry, 1,000 cavalry and 700 elephants. During Bindusara's reign and at the beginning of Ashoka's reign Kalinga must have improved its armed forces considerably.

The mighty Magadha army marched towards Kalinga. Ashoka himself went at the head of his vast army.

The Kalinga army resisted the Magadha army and fought bravely. They were not afraid even of death. But their valour and sacrifices were in vain. Every thinner and finally it accepted defeat.

Ashoka won a glorious victory.

'What Have I done!

True, Ashoka was victorious and Kalinga was his.

What was the price of this victory?

One of Ashoka's own inscriptions describes it:

One and a half people were taken prisoners. A lake was killed during the battle. Many more died as a result of the war.'

Ashoka who led the army saw the battlefield with his own eyes.

As far as his eye could see he saw only the corpses of elephants and horses, and the limbs of soldiers killed in the battle. There were streams of blood. Soldiers were rolling on the ground in unbearable pain. There were orphaned children. And eagles flew about to feast on the dead bodies.

Not one or two but hundreds of terrible sights greeted Ashoka's eyes. His heart was broken with grief and shame.

He felt unhappy over the victory, which he had won at the cost of so much suffering. 'What a dreadful deed have I done! I was the head of a vast Empire, but I longed to subjugate a small kingdom and caused the death of thousands of soldiers; I widowed thousands of women and orphaned thousands of children. With these oppressive thoughts in his minds he could not stay there any longer. He led his army back towards Pataliputra with a heavy heart.

The Noblest Victory

'The victory of Dharma brings with it love and affection. Devanampriya believes that, however small may be the love gained by its victory, it brings ample reward in the other world."

This is what Ashoka has said in one of his inscriptions.

The teaching of Buddha brought peace to Ashoka who was haunted by memories of the agony he had seen in Kalinga.

Buddha's message of non-violence, kindness and love of mankind appealed to the unhappy Ashoka. A disciple of Buddha. Upagupta initiated him into Buddhism. From that day Ashoka's heart became the home of compassion, right living, love and non-violence. He gave up hunting and eating meat. He put an end to the killing of animals for the royal kitchen. Realising that it was not enough if he lived a righteous life, he proclaimed that all his subjects also should live a life of righteousness.

'Of all victories, the victory of Dharma is the noblest. One may win a piece of land by fighting a war. But by kindness, love and pity one can win the hearts of people. The sharp point of the sword spills blood; but from Dharma springs the fountain of love. The victory won by arms brings fleeting joy but the victory of Dharma brings lasting joy Ashoka realised this truth. So he taught his subjects this lesson:

> 'All people should live a life of truthfulness, justice and love. Respect your parents. Treat your teachers and relatives with affection. Be modest in their presence. Give charity. Do not be unkind to animals. No one should think that he end his religion are the greatest. All religions preach the same virtues. Just as

it is bad to indulge in self-praise and slandering others, it is bad to condemn other religions. Respect for other religions brings glory to one's own religion.'

Ashoka did not think of the good of only his subjects; he thought of the good of all mankinds'. He wished to win the hearts of people and to serve the world through religion and through good will and good action. He decided to dedicate his energy and all his powers and wealth to this goal.

The first thing that Ashoka did to spread righteousness among his people was to undertake a pilgrimage. It took place two years the Kalinga war. His pilgrimage started with his visit so Sambodhi, the holy place where Gautama, the Buddha breathed his last. He visited other holy places during the pilgrimage. Ashoka has explained in his own words the purpose of his pilgrimage. 'To meet Brahmins and Shramanas and to give gifts to them. To meet the elders and to honour them with gifts of gold. To meet people and to preach the law of Dharma and to discuss Dharma.' These were the important objects.

Spreading the Message of Dharma

Ashoka was not content with visiting holy places. He believed that the message of Dharma should not become stagnant like standing water. He wanted it to spread within India and outside, too. He wanted the people of the world to bathe in its pure steam and purify themselves. Therefore he undertook a great task which could would be enduring. He got the laws of Dharma engraved on rocks and stone pillars both inside and outside the country. These inscriptions related to Dharma, social ethics and moral living. Ashoka himself has proclaimed that his desire was that his message should reach the people of all lands and enable them to follow and propagate the Dharma for the welfare of the world. Such inscriptions can be seen even today both in India and outside. In India they have been discovered in Madhya Pradesh, Gujarat, Uttar Pradesh, Maharashtra, Orissa, Andhra Pradesh and at Siddapura of Chitradurga District, Koppala and Maski in Raichur District of Karnataka. Outside India they have been found in Peshawar District in Pakistan as well as near Kandahar in Afghanistan and on the borders of Nepal.

Seeds of Dharma

We read in history about many Kings who put up inscriptions about their invasions, charities, donations and the extension of their territories. But it is only Ashoka who got inscriptions carved on rocks and pillars, which lead people from untruth to truth, from death to immortality and from darkness to light. To this day they are like lights of wisdom. The laws of Dharma are like the seeds of virtue sown in the hearts of the people. They are steps leading to salvation.

In order to foster greater understanding regarding Dharma, Ashoka took a bold and firm step. He wished to show that all religions teach the same path of virtue. In one of his inscriptions Ashoka says, 'We must respect the followers of other religions in every way. By doing so we can help the growth of our religion and we can help other religions also. If we act in a different way it will harm our religion and also other religions. The man who wants his religion to spread rapidly and honours only his religion and speaks ill of other religions will harm the interests of his own religion. The power of all religions should grow. Devanampriya does not consider charity and worship more important than this.' He appointed officers called 'Dharma - Mahamatras' in order to spread these ideas among the people. These officers met people of different religions and lived among them; they helped to remove the mistaken ideas they had about other religions and to know what was good in them. Often the money set apart for religious purposes in spent otherwise. Sometimes though it seems to have been spent for religious purpose, selfish people pocket it. It was the duty of the Dharma - Mahamatras to see that the money meant for religious purposes was spent properly. They toured the Empire and visited the courts of justice also. They set right the errors in the conduct of affairs and in the awards of punishments. Such officers do not seem to have been appointed anywhere else in the history of the world. Besides these, other officers also toured the Empire once in five years according to the orders of the Emperor and spread the Dharma among the people.

Religious Conference

After seventeen years of Ashoka's rule, unfortunately difference of opinion arose among the Buddhist monks and there was a split. There were many lazy and bad monks given to evil ways. These wilful sannyasins were a curse to Buddhism. Buddhism was, therefore, losing its power. Ashoka felt unhappy over this. In order to save Buddhism for total eclipse and to increase its influence, Ashoka threw out many lazy monks from the Buddhist fold. He invited the worthy and the serious - minded monks to Ashokarama in Pataliputra for a conference. Moggaliputra Tishya presided over the conference attended by the Buddhist monks from the Four Corners of the country. Ashoka sat with the great teaches and sent for each Bhikshu and asked him, "What did Lord Buddha teach?" He discussed many things with them. After long discussions what Lord Buddha had taught came out clearly and unambiguously.

Buddhism gained a new strength from this conference. Ashoka did not like other Kings send his armies to foreign lands to conquer them. He who declared that the victory of Dharma was the real victory sent Buddhist monks to other lands the light he had received from Buddhism. He sent Buddhist preachers to Syria, Egypt, Macedonia, Burma and Kashmir. To Ceylon (Sri Lanka) he sent his own children Mahendra and Sanghamitra. As a result off this, Buddhism spread to all countries in East Asia.

Pillar at Sarnath

In the twentieth year of his reign, Ashoka undertook his second pilgrimage with his daughter and Upagupta. This we learn from his inscriptions. During this pilgrimage he visited the ruins of Vaishali and the places where Buddha used to rest. From Vaishali Ashoka travelled east and came to Ramagrama. He visited the stupa at Ramagrama built by a King who had collected and preserved the sacred bones of Buddha after his death. Later he also visited Lumbini, Kapilavastu, Shravasti, Gaya and other holy places. Wherever he went he caused pillars and stupas to be erected in memory of his visit. They remind us even today of the visit of Ashoka to those holy places.

There is one such memorial pillar at Sarnath. On the top of a stone pillar about fifty feet high there are beautifully carved figures of four standing lions. The figures of four standing lions. The figures of four standing lions. The figures of the lions are now to be seen in the official emblem of the government of free India, and the Ashoka Chakra adorns the national flag of India. In this way the government of India has paid a deserving tribute to the ideal King, Ashoka. But unfortunately the pillar at Sarnath is broken and mutilated. So we can see only fragments of the pillar. Of the eighty-four thousand stupas said to have been built by Ashoka, the stupa at Sanchi is both famous and splendid. To this day this fifty-four feet stupa stands on a high pedestal and forms a semicircle. Besides these stupas and pillars, Ashoka built cave dwellings, rest houses and Buddha Viharas in large numbers. They not only proclaim Ashoka's teachings but also are examples of the splendid architecture of those days.

Ashoka, the Builder of Monuments

We shall now discuss the greatness of Ashoka as a builder. The greatness has been somewhat exaggerated, if we are to consider only the tangible evidence proving it. Tradition, however, makes Ashoka a mighty builder, the builder of cities, of innumerable stupas, viharas or monasteries, and pillars and rails of stone, bearing inscriptions or artistic sculptures The *Divyavadana* [ch. xxvii] ascribes Ashoka's building activity to the desire which he expressed to his preceptor, Upagupta, in the following words: "Those places which were inhabited by the Lord Buddha—those I shall visit, worship, and mark with memorials for the benefit of remote posterity." The testimony of tradition is confirmed to some extent by that of Ashoka's own words in his Edicts.

Tradition ascribes to Ashoka the foundation of two cities. The first is Srinagara, the capital of Kashmir, where Ashoka is said to have built 500 Buddhist monasteries together with other edifices, some of which were consecrated to Brahmanical worship. The tradition is recorded by Kalhana in his *Rajatarangini*, but, earlier than Kalhana, by Yuan Chwang who makes the additional statement that "Ashoka gave up all Kashmir for the benefit of the Buddhist church". The Chinese pilgrim saw about 100 Buddhist monasteries then still existing in the country, and also saw "four Ashoka topes." The second city built by Ashoka was in Nepal which he is said to have visited with his daughter, Charumati, and her Kshatriya husband, Devapala, who chose to settle there, building respectively a nunnery and a monastery. In commemoration of the royal visit were built the city of Deo-Patan (Devapattana), and four stupas still standing in their archaic style.

More than the builder of cities is Ashoka the builder of monasteries or stupas, according to the legend which describes them to be as high as hilltops. The *Mahavamsa* relates that the Emperor once asked his preceptor, Moggaliputra Tissa, the question, "How great is the content of the Dharma taught by the Master?" to which the divine replied: "There are 84,000 sections of the Dhamma." Then Ashoka said: "Each one of them will I honour with a *vihara.*" Thus he proceeded to have 84,000 viharas built by all his subordinate Kings in 84,000 towns selected all over India, including the Ashoka monastery built by himself at Pataliputra. This tradition is, however, differently told by Fa-hien. According to him, Ashoka "wished to destroy the eight topes (i.e., those built over the relics of the Buddha's body distributed at his death among eight different peoples), and to build instead of them 84,000 topes" on the theory that the bones of the human body comprised 84,000 atoms.

But archaeological evidence makes us sure about only a few of the stupas or viharas ascribed to Ashoka. From his own words in the Edicts, we only learn that he enlarged to twice its size the stupa of Konagamana, the previous Buddha, at Nigliva and built for the sect of Ajivikas three sets of cave-dwellings in the Barabar hills of Bihar, while archaeological inference ascribes to Ashoka the great stupa at Sanchi (forming the nucleus of the structure built round it a century later and to be seen now), as also a stupa at Bharhut with elaborately carved railing bearing inscriptions in Ashokan scripts. The latter stupa has now disappeared, and parts of its richly sculptured railing on view at the Indian Museum in Calcutta are all that now remain of that ancient structure.

We may note that Yuan Chwang in the seventh century AD made definite mention of more than 80 stupas and viharas associated by tradition with Ashoka, besides the 500 viharas of Kashmir and other large groups of same in different localities vaguely indicated. One of the stupas found by Yuan Chwang to the northwest of Vaishali, which was erected to mark the place where the Buddha in one of his previous births ruled as a Chakravarti, may be identified as the stupa now found at Kesariya, the stupa of the Raja-kesari, if it may be so taken.

Ashoka was also a great builder of monolithic pillars, of which but few are now extant and can fee definitely ascribed to him. Fa-hien noticed only *six* pillars, of which two were on each side of the door of the Jetavana Vihara at Shravasti with a *wheel* and *ox* on their tops; one at Sankasya, "about 50 cubits high, with a *lion* on the top of it," and niches containing shining images of the Buddha on its four sides; the fourth, an inscribed one, on the way to Vaishali from Kushinagara; the fifth, also an inscribed one, at Pataliputra, already described, and the sixth in the same locality, "more than 30 ft. high with a *lion* on the top of it".

The Mauryan structures in brick are sought to be distinguished by the size of their bricks, but the size, it must be noted, is not at all a very reliable indication of architectural chronology. There is revealed as much variety of dimension among bricks of the early strata and periods as of the obviously later ones.

The success of Mauryan engineering was also manifest *in* the domain of irrigation. The inscription of Rudradaman (AD 150) relates how the beautiful Sudarshana lake was constructed on the mountains Raivataka and Urjayat (near Girnar or Junagadh) by artificially damming up the course of their streams, Palasini, and others. It is also stated further in the inscription that the reservoir was "ordered, to be made by the Vaishya Pusyagupta, the provincial governor *(Rastriya)* of the Maurya King, Chandragupta, and adorned with conduits *(pranali)* for Ashoka the Maurya by the Yavana King, Tusaspha, while governing *(adhisthaya)."* Thus the lake was equipped "with well-provided conduits, drains and means to guard against foul matters." We are in this connection reminded of the remark of Megasthenes that there were officers in Mauryan administration whose duty was "to measure the land and inspect the sluices by which water is distributed into the branch canals, so that every one may enjoy his fair share of the benefit."

The Mauryan engineers were good at town-planning, too. Pataliputra, the capital of the Magadhan Empire since the days of Udaya, the grandson of Ajatashatru (as stated in the *Vayu Purana)*, who first laid its foundation at which the Buddha made a prophecy of its future greatness, had become developed by the time of Chandragupta Maurya into a mighty city fulfilling that prophecy. As seen and described by Megasthenes, "it stretched in the inhabited quarters to an extreme length on each side of 80 stadia, with breadth of 15 stadia, in the shape of a parallelogram, encompassed all around by a ditch for defence and receiving the sewage of the city, which was 600 ft. in breadth and 30 cubits in depth." Its inner line of defence was formed by a massive timber palisade, "pierced with loopholes for the discharge of arrows, crowned with 570 towers, and provided with 64 gates." Megasthenes further notes that of the cities of India, of which "the number is so great that it cannot be stated with precision," those on the banks of rivers or on the seacoast are built of wood instead of brick to escape from floods, while those "on commanding situations and lofty eminences are built of brick and mud." This wooden city was dominated by the royal palace which excelled in splendour the palaces of Susa and Ekbatana, with its gilded pillars adorned with golden vines and silver birds, and its extensive grounds studded with fishponds, and beautified by many ornamental trees and shrubs. Thus with his Empire, Ashoka inherited all that won it, and made it great—a large army, an efficient administrative organisation, and, last, but not least, its wealth of artistic and architectural achievements and traditions. Thus some of the polished pillars are rightly ascribed by Ashoka to his predecessors who could build a great city, and the most gorgeous palace of the East.

Ashoka also made important contributions to the expansion of the city and palace, the magnitude of which made Fa-hien attribute them to supernatural agency. Seriously and sincerely does Fa-hien observe: "The royal palace and halls in the midst of the city, which exist now (i.e., about 650 years later) as of old, were all made by spirits which he employed, and which piled up the stones, reared the walls and gates, and executed the elegant carving and inlaid sculpture-work—in a way which no human hand of this world could accomplish". This passage hints that Ashoka replaced much of the old wooden materia of the palace by stone which was so successfully utilised ii other monuments of Ashoka in the different parts of hi Empire.

Archaeological exploration has been able partially to unearth a few remnants of the Mauryan palace. The work was begun by P. C. Mukherji who dug up several fragment: of polished stone that could not be mistaken as parts of are Ashokan column. It was resumed many years later by Dr. D. B. Spooner whose excavations have brought to high polished Chunar sandstone pillars in parallel rows, 15 ft apart, indicative of a hall of 100 pillars in the Mauryan palace showing a similarity of design to the Achaemenin palaces of Persia. There was also discovered, 17 ft. below the surface, a wooden floor, on which there is a deposit of eight.

An Ashokan Pillar at Pataliputra was seen, it may be remembered by both Fa-Men and Yuan Chwang. Besides examples of architectural achievements, we may also consider some of the minor arts of the period. At Parkham near Mathura was found a colossal statue of a man, 7 ft. high, in grey and highly polished sandstone, and bearing an inscription in Ashokan script. A complementary female statue was also found at Besnagar, and quite lately two statues were discovered at Patna and Didarganj. These statues in their unifacial images betray the primitiveness of the art. Dr. A. K. Coomaraswamy considers these as examples of the "folk art" of the times, as distinguished from the *court* or official art. Similarly, the art of coining was not very advanced, considering the crude punch-marked coins of the period with their unsymmetrical forms and symbols stamped indiscriminately upon their surface.

Likewise some of the contemporary terra-cottas discovered show only "coarse primitive reliefs." "Indeed, so far as is known at present, it was only in the jewellers' and lapidaries' arts that the Maurya craftsman attained any real proficiency, and in this domain his aptitude lay, not in the plastic treatment of form, but in the high technical skill with which he cut and polished refractory stones or applied delicate filigree and granular designs to metal objects. The refined quality of his gold and silver work is well illustrated in two pieces of jewellery which were discovered on the site of Taxila in company with a gold coin of Diodotus, a large number of local punch-marked coins, and a quantity of other jewellery and precious stones. Of the stonecutter's art, also, some beautiful examples are furnished by the relic caskets of beryl and rock crystal from the stupas of Bhattiprolu and Piprahwa, the latter of which is probably to be assigned to this epoch". We may add to these examples the very inscriptions of Ashoka which are executed with perfect accuracy in very well-cut letters.

From the archaeological we may now proceed to consider the artistic aspect of these monuments of Ashoka. That in their best examples they exhibit a high level of technical and artistic accomplishment is admitted on all hands. But there is a doubt as to how far this art is Indian in its origin and character, and especially in some of its finished forms which we see among the Ashokan monuments. As its excellence is seen mainly in the treatment of animals, of their muscles, veins, and claws, and also of plants, and birds, the art has been taken as naturalistic, and, to that extent, as foreign to Indian artistic traditions and ideals. It is taken to be inspired by Greek Art which alone in that epoch of world's history distinguished itself in the modelling of living forms. A negative evidence for the foreign inspiration in Ashokan Art is sought to be found in the fact that its best examples belong to the same epoch which witnessed crude and primitive examples already mentioned, such as the statues in the round found at Mathura, Besnagar, and Patna, of which the indigenous origin cannot be disputed, so that we are forced to account for the evolution of an art that could produce at the same time such an extreme difference in the quality of its examples. Thus the best examples, the Ashokan Pillars, are traced to foreign influence. While some of their elements are traced to Greece, others are traced to Persia. Their so-called bell-shaped capitals, their smooth unfluted shafts, their polish, and even their inscriptions are traced to Persia.

This, however, does not seem, on a closer examination, to be a completely correct view of the subject. Even V. A. Smith was not prepared to go so far in ascribing foreign origins to Ashokan art. He considers, for instance, the treatment of the bull and the elephant in the Saraath abacus as being entirely Indian in both subject and inspiration, and not as in any way the outcome of a half-caste art. According to Havell, the supposed Persepolitan bell-capital is a misreading of the Indian lotus. Further, Codrington points out that the Persian capital is not quite closely related to these early Indian bell-capitals, and does not show itself to be a necessary part of the structure of the Ashokan pillar. "The Persian bell is conceived as part of a compound capital, and is always crowned by a further member, the lines of which curve upwards and outwards, the whole suggesting the flourishing head of a palm tree with a ring of drooping half-dead leaves clustering below round the stem. Above this comes a quadruple bracket-like member with upper and lower incurving volutes, between which and the final member is nothing but a bead-and-reel fillet. Above this, the head and bent-back forelegs of the surmounting beast jut out, without any sort of abacus or intermediary platform. The typical Achaemenid pillar-shaft was also fluted, not smooth, whatever its rudimentary form may have been". As regards the pillars themselves, it is to be noted that while those at Persepolis and elsewhere are structural, the Ashokan ones are purely monumental. Nor is the idea of raising the pillars completely foreign to India. The raising of religious symbols for common reverence is a time-honoured Indian practice. Hindu temples have always before them their banner-torch or light-pillar, which are often adorned with the special symbol of the god, a wheel, or a trident. Vedic literature, itself, by its descriptions of the banner of Indra, and of sacrificial posts, points to far-distant origins of these pillars. The Ashokan pillar is the descendant of those royal or tribal ensigns or standards which were set up to mark off the sacrificial areas for ancient Vedic ceremonies. The Indian purpose of these pillars is, again, declared in their very locations. Rummindei and Sarnath called for pillars commemorative respectively of the Buddha's Nativity and first teaching. The pillar at Nigliva associates itself with the fifth of the previous Buddhas. A group of pillars guides the pilgrim's progress towards the Buddhist holy places.

It is not, however, to be claimed that Ashokan art does not reveal any trace of foreign influence. It is only difficult to trace it to a particular source or country in that age of frequent and fruitful intercourse between India and the outside world. The influx of foreigners to India for purposes of trade and business called for the institution of a Foreign Office in the chief cities of India under Ashoka's grandfather, Chandragupta Maurya, as stated by Megasthenes, the Greek ambassador to his court. And we have already seen from Ashoka's own words in his edicts how largely and religiously did he seek to cherish and cultivate these foreign relations with the then most prominent Western countries and seats of Hellenic culture and civilization. The fact of the matter was that in that age of intercourse and interchange of ideals, the arts of different countries were bound to reveal some common elements and features which in the case of India and Persia might be traced to a common source from which the entire culture of the East or Asia has sprung.

6

Ashoka's Religious Role

Ashoka, as a Buddhist

It is scarcely necessary to state that Ashoka was a follower of Buddhism. All Buddhist records tell us that he had espoused that religion. On the other hand, there is no work, literary or scriptural, which says that he had embraced any other faith. But what do his inscriptions teach us? This is the only and real question we have to answer. When the inscriptions of Ashoka began to be studied and only a few were known, H. H. Wilson ventured to dispute his Buddhist faith, and Edward Thomas held that Ashoka was a Jaina at first but became a Buddhist afterwards. But it is no longer permissible to call in question the Buddhist faith of Ashoka. That is now established beyond all doubt by the Bhabru Edict, otherwise-called the Second Bairat Edict. It opens with Ashoka expressing his reverence for Buddha, Dhamma, and Sangha, exactly in the well-known trinitary formula of Buddhism. There are other records too, which point to the same conclusion. The views of Wilson and Thomas were based upon unreliable readings and inaccurate interpretations, and are no longer countenanced by scholars. The question regarding which difference of opinion is now possible is: when did Ashoka become a follower of Buddhism? The scholar who considered this question last was the late Dr. J. F. Fleet. He held that the Dhamma inculcated in the rock and pillar edicts was in no way the Buddhist Dhamma, because in them Buddha is not mentioned at all and the Sangha only once and in such a way as to place it on a par with other creeds. The object of these edicts, says Dr. Fleet, was thus "not to propagate Buddhism or any other particular religion, but to proclaim the determination of Ashoka to govern his kingdom righteously and kindly in accordance with the duty of pious Kings." In other words, the term dhamma, used in the rock and pillar edicts, Fleet takes as the ' ordinary *dharma* of Kings, which is laid down in the Manava-dharmasastra, 1, 114, as one of the topics of that work.' According to him, Ashoka was converted to Buddhism in the thirtieth year from his coronation, that is, two years after the pillar edicts were engraved.

Evidently, Fleet ignores the fact that the Dhamma Ashoka refers to in his rock and pillar edicts is intended for being put into practice, not by himself or his officers, but by all men. Obedience to parents, respect for teachers, seemly behaviour towards relatives and so forth, as we shall see later on, are some of the practices of Dhamma taught by Ashoka. This Dhamma cannot possibly be *raja-dhamma,* which represents a code of duties for a King and his officers to perform and not for his people.

The Rummindei inscription, again, informs us that in the twentieth year of his reign Ashoka visited in person the place where Buddha was born and did worship there. It is evident from this that already in his twentieth regnal year he was a Buddhist. The words of the inscription clearly mean that Ashoka went to Buddha's birthplace in person and performed worship, and not that he did the place the honour of going there in person, as Fleet has understood it.

Again, in Rock Edict VIII, Ashoka says that in the tenth year of his reign he repaired to Sambodhi. Whether Sambodhi here means ' supreme knowledge ' or something like it as scholars take it, or ' the place where Buddha obtained enlightenment ' as I and, following me, Hultzsch, understand it,, this much is admitted on all hands that it is a word technical to Buddhist scriptures, and cannot possibly be taken as equivalent to the ordinary Sanskrit word *sambodha* as proposed by Dr. Fleet. This rock edict thus proves that in the tenth year of his reign Ashoka was already a Buddhist.

There is, however, evidence that Ashoka was converted to Buddhism about one year earlier. This evidence is supplied by Minor Rock Edict I, copies of which have been found at no less than nine different places. He begins this edict by saying: "It is more than two years and a half that I am a lay worshipper, but did not exert myself for one year. But, indeed, for more than one year that I have been living with the Sangha. I have exerted myself strenuously." When, therefore, this edict was engraved, he had already been a Buddhist for just less than three years. This edict, again, describes his work as that of a zealot in such terms that it reminds us of his Rock Edict IV, as pointed out by Senart, and a little comparison is enough to convince any one that in both Ashoka gives an account of one and the same thing, namely, his achievements as a missionary. Now, it is worthy of note that Rock Edict IV, refers itself *to* the twelfth year of his reign. He therefore must have embraced Buddhism not more than three years before this date, that is, in the ninth year.

The principal events of this period of Ashoka's life may be thus briefly narrated. He became a Buddhist, as we have just seen, in the ninth regnal year. But for one year he was lukewarm and did little for the propagation of Buddhism. Then he lived with the Sangha for over a year and put forth such missionary activity that at the end of this period, that is, in the twelfth year of his reign, he could say in all good conscience that he achieved the progress of the people in Dhamma, such as never happened before.

Now, what does Ashoka mean by saying that he had been living with the Sangha for over a year? Senart thinks that this refers to the state visit of the King to the Sangha, in the midst of which he took his seat and made a public profession of his Buddhist faith, as the Sinhalese Chronicle Mahavamsa informs us. It was on this occasion that he showed the genuineness of his devotion by making his son and daughter enter the religious order. Recently Prof. B. M. Barua, and following him, Prof. Radhakumud Mukherji have attempted to revive Senart's theory, by expressing the opinion that Ashoka is here distinguishing between two stages of his life, of course, as *upasaka* that he was for his whole lifetime,—one, the stage of inaction for over two years and a half in which he was merely the personal admirer of an individual monk Nigrodha, and the other for over a year, the stage of exertion, when he visited the Sangha and became identified with its cause. In the first place, it is unfortunate that the interpretation of Hultzsch, though it is of such paramount importance for the religious history of Ashoka, has not been even so much as referred to by these scholars. Secondly, nowhere do the Pali Chronicles describe any part of Ashoka's life which was a stage of inaction. For even long before Ashoka paid a state visit to the Sangha', we find him bestowing alms on 60,000 Buddhist monks in his own palace and building 84,000 *viharas.* Thirdly, it was not during the second stage that he first visited the Sangha, as implied by them. As a matter of fact, his first visit came off immediately after his conversion by Nigrodha, as has been pointed out by Hultzsch himself. In fact, any scholar, who reads the Pali chronicles carefully and impartially, will find that no two stages in Ashoka's life after his conversion have been contrasted and that his career as a Buddhist is one of uniform unflagging zeal. Finally, what is here most important to remember is that the *samgham-upagatatva* of Ashoka had lasted the whole period of his second stage, namely for more than one year. We cannot therefore say that the King *visited* the Sangha for over a year, but rather *lived* with it for that period.

The second period of Ashoka's religious life began with a course of action which he thus describes in Rock Edict VIII:

> "For a long time past, Kings used to go out on tours of pleasure. Here there-were chase and similar diversions. Now, King Priyadarshin, Beloved of the gods, repaired to Sambodhi (Bodhi Tree) when he had been consecrated ten years. Hence, this touring for Dhamma."

Here Ashoka tells us that up till the tenth year of his reign, he, like the previous Kings, used to find his relaxation in tours of pleasure where he indulged in hunting and other sports. In that year, however, he gave up the idea of ever going on these pleasure tours, and started religious tours instead. What he actually did in these religious tours and how he was able to foster Dhamma not only in himself but also in his subjects. What we have to note in this place is that in the tenth year of his reign he paid a visit to the Bodhi Tree and that this was his first *Dhamma-yatra* or religious tour. And as this time coincides with that of his second period, it is difficult to avoid the inference that he began his career of strenuous exertion with a visit to the Bodhi Tree along with a Sangha of Bhikshus, and that the various spiritual benefits conferred upon him and also his people induced him to repeat this *Dhamma-yatra* so that it became a regular fixture with him. The reminiscence of a later *Dhamma-yatra* or pious tour certainly appears to be preserved in two pillar inscriptions found in the Tarai region of Nepal.

One of these is engraved on a column found at Rummindei, and the other at Nigliva, thirteen miles northwest of the former. The first of these records tells us that in the twentieth year of his reign Ashoka came in person to the locality where the inscribed pillar stands, did worship, and, as that was the place where Buddha, the sage of the Shakya family, was born, he constructed huge stone walls and set up the pillar there. The inscription further informs us that because the Blessed One was born there, the village of Lumbini was freed from all religious cess (bali) and was required to pay only one-eighth of the produce as land revenue *(bhaga).* What the epigraph means is that in his twentieth regnal year Ashoka visited the garden of Lumbini, where according to Buddhist tradition, Prince Siddhartha, the founder of Buddhism, was born, and that he did not rest contented with merely performing worship there, but put up a stone enclosure round the birth-spot of Buddha and erected a column there.

But this was not all. Even to this day we know pilgrims have to pay religious cesses at certain holy places, such, for instance, as Dwarka in Kathiawar. The village of Lumbini, just because it was the birthplace of the founder of Buddhism, must have become a sacred place and been visited by all sorts and conditions of Buddhists even before the time of Ashoka, and, must therefore have been saddled with a similar cess. Ashoka, being a Buddhist, naturally did not like the idea of his co-religionists being compelled to pay any kind of impost just at the place where the founder of their religion was born, and so abolished it. But that was not the only boon he conferred upon Lumbini. Every village of ancient

India had to pay one-fourth or one-sixth of its produce as revenue to the King in whose dominions it was comprised. The village of Lumbini, being subject to Ashoka's rule, had to pay some part of its produce as revenue to him. What portion of the produce he was actually receiving we do not know, but certainly it could never have been less than one-sixth. And what he did was that he reduced it to one-eighth. The other pillar of Ashoka in the Nepalese Tarai is at Nigliva. The inscription on the exact nature of this Dhamma was but rather such as has been recommended by Buddhism to its lay followers in general, as no doubt may be inferred from the fact that Ashoka preached it as a layman.

The first inscription that has to detain us here is the Bhabru Edict. This is really an epigraph discovered in the ruins of a hill monastery at Bairat in the northern part of the Jaipur State, Rajputana. It is a missive from Ashoka to the Buddhist Sangha, a copy of which must have been inscribed and deposited by him at every monastic establishment of importance, and the Bhabru Edict appears to be only one such copy at present discovered.

The epigraph opens with a declaration of Ashoka's faith in Buddha, Dhamma and Sangha according to the well-known Buddhist formula and of his conviction that the utterances of Buddha are gospel truth. No doubt can possibly be entertained in regard to the sectarian character of this record. The object of this missive is to enumerate certain *Dhammapariyayas* or canonical texts, which he earnestly wished to be listened to and retained in memory not only by monks and nuns but also by the lay people of both the sexes, in order that the Good Dhamma might long endure. The texts referred to by Ashoka are as follows:

- Vinaya-samukase
- Aliya-vasani = Ariya-vamsa.
- Anagata-bhayani.
- Muni-gatha = Muni-Sutra.
- Moneya-sute = Nalaka-Sutra.
- Upatisa-pasina = Rathavinita-Sutra.
- Laghulovada = Bahulovada-Sutra.

All these texts have been satisfactorily identified except the first. Buddhaghosha, in his *Visuddhimagga,* narrates a beautiful story of a young monk, who, although he ate for three months in the house of his mother, never said, ' I am thy son and thou art my mother,' showing clearly that to a conscientious monk mother and father are no hindrances. The young monk lived this exemplary life, because he lived up to the courses of conduct preached by Buddha in the Rathavinita-Sutra, the Nalaka, the Tuvataka, and the Maha-Ariyavamsa. The Sutras in which Buddha is represented to have preached to the Bhikshus are many, but as this story lays emphasis on only four, it appears that up till the time of Buddhaghosha the four Sutras just referred to were looked upon as of paramount importance to a Buddhist Bhikshu. That the Aliyavasani, Moneya-Sutra and Upatisapasina of Ashoka correspond to the Maha-Ariyavamsa, Nalaka-Sutra, and Rathavinita respectively of Buddhaghosha's story has now been accepted by most scholars. If three of the four Sutras referred to by Buddhaghosha have been identified with three of the *Dhamma-pariyayas* mentioned by Ashoka, it is very strange that the fourth, namely, the Tuvataka cannot be recognised in any one of the texts named by Ashoka. From verse 7 of this Sutra, however, it appears that Buddha is here expounding religious practices, precepts, and contemplation. And the words *patipada* and *patimokkha* used here lead to the surmise that in the Tuvataka Sutra we have Ashoka's *Vinaya-samukase,* Yinaya *par excellence.*

The *Moneya-sute* is but another name for the Sutra which is now known as the *Nalaka-sutra.* This was not, however, the peculiar feature of the canonical texts cited by the King. Several others are known, and have already been pointed out. The mention of these texts by Ashoka, again, does not prove anything against the existence of the whole body or any part of the Tipitaka in his time, for Ashoka is here recommending a few sacred texts only, and what he is here not citing or selecting from cannot be regarded as non-existent in his time.

The scriptural texts selected by Ashoka show what sort of Buddhist he was. His mind was ravished not by the ritualistic or metaphysical elements of Buddhism, but rather by the fundamentals of that religion, or for the matter of that, any religion.

He was fascinated not by any specification of rules and regulations to be observed externally and mechanically, but rather by what constitutes and conduces to real inner growth. Take for instance the *Ariyavamsa*, one of the texts cited by Ashoka. It lays down four courses of conduct for a monk. A monk, says the Sutra, should be (i) content with simple raiment, and (ii) with plain food, obtained in the proper way, (iii) should be satisfied with the humblest habitation, and (iv) should delight in meditation. The text thus tells us in a nutshell how a Bhikshu should be or ought to live. There are two or three other texts, such as Munigatha and Moneya-Sutra which tell us practically the same thing. And there is no sacred text referred to by Ashoka which is connected merely with the externals of a religion, with the mere disciplinary rules of a religious order, the observance of which may make a Bhikshu an outwardly perfect monk but not necessarily an inwardly good man. All the Sutras adduced by the King relate to the elevation of the soul and are applicable not only to the clergy but also to the laity. This is just the reason why he expressly that his Sutras should be listened to and pondered over not by monks and nuns alone but also by male and female lay-worshippers. Again, in the Sutras selected by Ashoka he is not content with including those which merely depict a higher mode of life or describe the constituents of lofty and sublime character, but he is careful enough to specify also those which are helps and guides in the path of spiritual elevation.

One such Sutra is *anagata-bhayani,* which depicts the 'fears and dangers of the future ' that may at any moment arise and frustrate the realisation of the goal of a man's religious strivings. It contains a series of admonitions to exercise all energies and lead a heedful and strenuous life in view of the adverse contingencies forthcoming, such as age, disease, famine, war and schism. Ashoka is thus not satisfied with merely adducing a text which describes the highest mode of living but also lays stress on a Sutra which warns a man against the dangers that threaten and tend to prevent the actualisation of this end if he is not always on the alert and watchful. But these dangers after all are of an external nature. It is true that we ought to be constantly on our guard and strive most assiduously to avoid them. Nevertheless, they are dependent on extraneous circumstances over which we have no control. But there are other dangers which are of an inner character and which with equal if not greater violence threaten the attainment of spiritual elevation. And the King has therefore done a most wise thing in drawing attention to a sacred text, Rahulovada-Sutra, a discourse where Buddha is represented to have exhorted one Ambalatthika Rahula and expatiated on the supreme necessity of rigorously scrutinising every act of the body, speech and mind both when and after it is initiated. A reading and contemplation of the religious texts recommended by Ashoka is sure to be edifying to any earnest soul that strives for a higher and nobler life, to whatever religion or creed he may belong.

The second document of a sectarian character which we have to note here is the *sasana* or order of Ashoka which we find engraved on pillars at three different places, namely, Sarnath, Sanchi and Allahabad. The pillars at the former two places are believed to be *in situ,* but that at present existing at Allahabad is rightly regarded as having originally been at Kaushambi. Through this *sasana* Ashoka aims at preserving the unity of the Buddhist Church by putting down all attempt at schism. " Whosoever," says he, " breaks up the church, be it monk or nun, shall be clad in white raiment, and compelled to live in what is not a residence. Thus should this order be respectfully communicated to the congregation of the monks and the congregation of the nuns." This order has been addressed to the Mahamatras, as is clear from two of these inscriptions.

One of these, again, shows, that in one case at least, these Mahamatras were those stationed at Kaushambi. And it is not at all improbable that in other cases too the Mahamatras addressed were those belonging to the Muffasil Districts, where the old Buddhistic clerical establishments now represented by the remains at Sarnath and Sanchi were originally situated. The prevention of schisms in the Buddhist Church was of extreme importance. It was not therefore enough that orders in that connection should merely be issued to the Mahamatras of the districts. He therefore further says as follows in the same edict: " One such document has been deposited in office in order that it may be accessible to you. And deposit just another such document so as to be accessible to the laity. And the laity should come every Fast day in order to assure themselves of that same order. And certainly on all Fast days as each Mahamatra comes in his turn for Fast, he should assure himself of that same order and understand it. And so far as your jurisdiction goes, you must set out on tour with this specification. So too in all fortified towns and the district subdivisions you must cause to go out on tour with this specification."

The contents of this edict are enough to convince anybody that Ashoka was bent upon eradicating all apostasy and division in the Buddhist Church. To gain this end he resorts to a threefold method. He of course issues the order that he who tries to create a schism shall be clad in white garments, that is, shall be dispossessed of his yellow robes—the monkish garb, and shall be transported to a place where monks do not reside. In other words, he is at once cut off from all intercourse with his fraternity. And as Ashoka's order is to be communicated to every Buddhist Sangha, that must naturally deter a bellicose monk from obtruding his heretic doctrines on the attention of his brethren. This dispels three-fourths of the danger of schism. But the heretic, though ostracised, may gain the ear of the lay people, and with their following create a split in the community. Ashoka is alive to this danger, and has therefore instructed the Mahamatras to post a copy of his order on this subject so as to be accessible to the laity. Where exactly this order was to be put up for their knowledge we are not told. But it is not unlikely that it was intended to be posted in the town hall of which we hear so much both in inscriptions and literature.

The Sarnath-Kaushambi-Sanchi edict leaves no doubt as to the firm determination of Ashoka to put down all attempt at creating a schism in the Buddhist Church. The earnest, almost severe tone of the edict and the fact that copies of it are found at places of important Buddhist monastic establishments presupposes that in his time the Buddhist Church was at least threatened with disruption, to prevent which he was straining every nerve. But were there, as a matter of fact, any divisions of the Buddhist Sangha obtaining in Ashoka's time? The edict was no doubt intended to arrest disruption, but that does not preclude us, it may be contended, from supposing that the Sangha had already broken up into a number of sections, and Ashoka's endeavour was directed against further division.

The Buddhist tradition, preserved in the Singhalese chronicles, which says that a Buddhist council was held at Pataliputra eighteen years after Ashoka's coronation, also says that at that time the Sangha was split up into the two main divisions: (i) Theravada and (ii) Mahasamghika and that the first division had branched off into two and the second into four sections. If we accept this tradition, we have to suppose that already in Ashoka's time there were not only divisions but also subdivisions in the Buddhist Church. What could then be the meaning of the edict which aimed at preventing schism? Are we to suppose that Ashoka intended to nip schism, not in the Buddhist Church as a whole but rather in that division or subdivision of it, to which he individually belonged? Of course, it is quite possible to contend that in this edict by Sangha Ashoka means only that sect of Buddhism of which he was a member.

But if we once countenance this view, we are compelled to hold that wherever Ashoka uses the word *sangha* he means by it that section of the Buddhist Church to which he pertained. This conclusion cannot, however, commend itself to us. For in Pillar Edict VII. where Ashoka speaks of the Dharma Mahamatras, he speaks of the Sangha side by side with the Ajivika and the Nirgranthas. And are we to suppose here that whereas these Dharma Mahamatras were to look to the welfare and progress of the Ajivikas and Nirgranthas without distinction of creed and division, in the case of the Buddhists only they were to confine their activities not to the Buddhist Church as a whole, but to that division of it of which the King was a follower, all the other divisions or subdivisions of the Sangha being consigned to neglect and indifference?

Similarly, in the Bhabru Edict, he refers, to certain scriptural texts which he recommends for perusal to the Sangha. These texts are so free from sectarian elements that they will bear recital even to those monks who are not Buddhists. And are we to suppose that in the case of the Buddhists alone they are to be recited not to the Buddhist monks and nuns in general but to those only who belonged to Ashoka's denomination? If we are not to land ourselves on such absurdities, it seems desirable to hold that in Ashoka's time the Buddhist Church was not divided and that wherever he uses the word *sangha,* he means the whole undivided Church. What then becomes of the Buddhist tradition? Scholars who have investigated these traditions about the Buddhist councils have lighted upon such downright absurdities and inconsistencies and detected so much of dogmatical and sectarian tendency that very little that is contained in these traditions may be accepted as historical truth.

Thus the Council of Pataliputra is not looked upon as any general council at all but a party meeting, and the Second General Council which was held at Vaishali came off, in all probability, not one century after Buddha but in the time of Ashoka, who is the real Kalashoka of the tradition, that is, Black Ashoka, as he is painted to be before his conversion to Buddhism. This inference is more in consonance with his edicts. For, at the time of the Second General Council, the Buddhist Church was still undivided, though it was threatened with a schism on account of the Ten Points about discipline raised by the Vrijian monks. The latter were defeated, and the split of the Sangha for the time averted. This is borne out also by the epigraphic records of Ashoka. Special attention may be drawn in this connection to the words *samghe samage kate,* ' the Sangha has been made whole and entire,' which occur about the beginning of the Sanchi and Allahabad Edicts. This no doubt shows that the Buddhist Church was then divided, but certainly not to such a serious extent as is implied by the Sinhalese tradition connected with the Council of Pataliputra. The differences were unquestionably of small importance, such as they were when the Council of Vaishali was convened. It seems that these differences were made up, that the whole Church was again united by Ashoka, and that it continued to be so till at least the 27th year of Ashoka's reign.

It is worthy of note that the Sarnath, Kaushambi and Sanchi Edicts contain a *sasana* or order to the Mahamatras of the districts concerned to expel a Bhikshu or Bhikshuni as soon as he or she is detected in the act of creating a schism. Many other Mahamatras must have been similarly instructed by the King. But the question arises: how were the Mahamatras to decide whether any particular Bhikshu or Bhikshuni was an apostate or not. Was the Sangha to decide this matter by a majority, and were the Mahamatras merely to carry out their decision? If this was so, it could be done by a general conference of Bhikshus for every such matter as would arise. The holding of such an unwieldy conference of Bhikshus from the different parts of India for every such occasion, especially at that time when there was no quick conveyance or communication, would be exceedingly cumbrous, nay impracticable. Are we then to presume that Ashoka had some Theras or seniormost Bhikshus at his capital to instruct him as to what constituted heresy in any particular case? But this sort of religious autocracy or oligarchy was utterly unknown to early Buddhism. What we might reasonably suppose is that, as a matter of fact, there was a council of Buddhist Bhikshus held at Pataliputra as is reported by the Singhalese tradition, and that the canonical literature was definitively and finally settled by them, so as to eliminate all disruptive tendencies. It is only on the supposition that such an authorised text of the canon was before the Mahamatras that we can understand how it was possible for them to detect, prove and punish apostasy.

That a Council of Buddhist Bhikshus was held in the time of Ashoka seems to be hinted at even in the Bhabru edict. This edict is a missive addressed by the King to the Sangha. The question arises: which Sangha is here intended? In one sense, the Sangha was spread over the whole of India. But it is impossible to despatch the missive to a Sangha which was not confined to any particular place at any particular time, but was spread over the whole of a country. Nor was any all-India Committee of this body known to which the missive could be addressed. There was a time when the third and fourth words of the edict were read as *Magadham Samgham,* and it was then possible to say that Ashoka had sent this epistle to the Sangha pertaining to the small province of Magadha. But the facsimile which Hultzsch has published leaves no doubt as to *Magadha Samgham* being the correct reading. *Magadha* has thus to be connected with *Piyadasi Raja* and not *Samgham.* Which was then the Sangha addressed by Ashoka? This question still remains unanswered. The only plausible reply is that the monarch had dispatched this missive to the Sangha of the Bhikshus who had gathered as representatives from the various parts of India to attend the Council that had been convened. This also receives confirmation from the fact that here Ashoka calls himself

King of Magadha.' In no inscription of his has this King been styled *Magadho.* Where was the necessity for this in the present instance? The reply is that to the Council must have come many Bhikshus who did not belong to his Empire, and to whom it was therefore necessary for Ashoka to introduce himself as King of Magadha.

Ashoka's Dhamma

Ashoka, no doubt, strove very hard for the temporal welfare of his subjects. But what has made Ashoka entitled to worldwide renown, and, in fact, the principal object, which he had invariably before his mind and on the realisation of which he prided himself, was the spiritual good of man, the dissemination of what he loved to call Dhamma, not only in his country but far beyond in the dominions of his independent neighbours.

It, therefore, behoves us, in the first place, to ascertain what exactly Ashoka understood by Dhamma. He is quite explicit on this point, and gives us not only the attributes that fall under the term but also specific practices thereof, which he is never wearied of asking his people again and again to bring into action. In Pillar Edicts II and VII, Ashoka specifies the qualities, which, in his opinion, constitute Dhamma.

With him Dhamma consists of (i) *sadhave* or *bahu-kayane,* much good, (ii) *ap-asinave,* freedom from depravity, (iii) *daya,* mercy, (iv) *dane,* liberality, (v) *sache,* truthfulness, (vi) *sachaye,* purity, and (vii) *madave,* gentleness. But how are these virtues to be put into practice? Ashoka makes several enumerations of duties in this connection, which vary but slightly in different inscriptions. These may be summed up as follows: *anarambho prananam,* non-slaughter of animate beings; *avihisa bhutanam,* non-injury to 'existing' creatures; *matari pitari susrusa,* hearkening to father and mother; *thaira susrusa,* hearkening to the elders; *gurunam apachiti,* reverence to teachers; *mita-samstuta-natikanam bahmana-samananam danam sampatipati,* liberality and seemly behaviour towards friends, acquaintances and relatives and towards Brahmana and Shramana ascetics; *dasa-bhatakamhi samyapratipati,* seemly behaviour to saves and servants; and, in one inscription only, *apa-vyayata* and *apa-bhandata,* small expense and small accumulation. This is part of Ashoka's message to the world for all climes and for all ages. It sounds almost a truism, and yet how lucid, simple and true! He does not rest satisfied by merely telling us to practise *daya, dana madava,* mercy, liberality, gentleness, and so forth, but also shows how these virtues are to be translated into action. Thus *daya,* mercy, means *anarambho prananam, avihisa bhutanam,* non-destruction and even non-injury to creatures; *dana,* liberality, means liberality towards friends, acquaintances and relatives and towards ascetics whether they belong to the Brahmana or Shramana sects; and *madava,* gentleness, is to be manifested by hearkening to the parents and the elders, and seemly behaviour not only towards relatives or Brahmana and Shramana recluses but also towards slaves and servants.

Ashoka is so fond of this part of his message that he takes delight in iterating it again and again in his edicts. In Rock Edict XIV, he frankly confesses that certain words have been repeated over and over again because of the sweetness of their import. The word Dhamma and its import are so sweet to him that he not only repeats the code of duties which constitute it, but also extols it by instituting a comparison between Dhamma and the ordinary practices of life and establishing the superiority of the former over the latter.

Thus in Rock Edict IX he speaks of Dhamma, or *Dhamma-mamgala* as he calls it, in contradistinction with the *mamgalas* or rites for inducing luck and averting calamities, which, in Ashoka's time as now, obtained in legion in Hindu society. "People perform," says he in that edict, " various (lucky) rites in sicknesses, at marriages, on the birth of sons, and on journey. In this matter, however, womankind performs much, manifold (but) trivial, useless rites. Rites should undoubtedly be performed. But a rite of this kind bears little fruit. That rite, however, bears great fruit which is *Dhamma-mamgala,*" that is, the rite which consists in the fulfilment of Dhamma. And after this he goes on inculcating the duties which form the practical character of his teaching and which have just been enumerated. Similarly, in Rock Edict XI he draws a contrast between dana or ordinary gift and *Dhamma-dana* or gift of Dhamma.

The latter, he tells us, is the highest form of *dana* and means making one acquainted with Dhamma, participate in Dhamma, and thus become a kinsman of Dhamma. And in order to explain this Dhamma he again enumerates his ethical practices, and winds up by saying that this *Dhamma-dana* or alms-giving of Dhamma can be conferred by anybody on anybody, by father on his son or *vice versa*, by brothers and relatives upon one another, and, in fact, by everybody upon his neighbour. Likewise, in Rock Edict XIII Ashoka compares *vijaya* or ordinary conquest with *Dhamma-vijaya* or conquest through Dhamma and in such a way as to conduce to the exaltation of the latter. In this connection he refers to his territorial conquest of Kalinga, and, with great heaviness of heart and even a little sense of shame, he speaks of the terrible massacre he inflicted on soldiers and the acute misery and grief of bereavement he caused to their relatives. These are the diabolical concomitants of a territorial conquest. But the conquest through Dhamma, says he, is *pritirasa* or flavoured with love, and can be accomplished anywhere, not only up to the outlying provinces of his Empire but also in the dominions of his independent neighbours, whether they are in India or far beyond its northwestern frontiers, where rule the Yavana or Greek Princes, Antiochus Theos, Ptolemy Philadelphos, and so forth.

We have thus seen what qualities and what practices go to make up Ashoka's Dhamma. But this is not all that we have to understand by his Dhamma. These qualities and practices form only its positive character. But Ashoka's Dhamma has also a negative side, which may be summed up in the one word, *apasinava*, that is, the negation of *asinava*. But what is a*sinava?* Ashoka gives a reply to this question in Pillar Edict III where he places it side by side with *papa*, and specifies the malevolent affections that lead to *asinava*. They are: *chamdiye*, violence; *nithuliye*, cruelty; *kodhe*, anger; *mane*, conceit; and *isya*, envy. Thus not only the performance of moral duties enumerated by Ashoka, but also freedom from these passions, is necessary for the full and adequate fulfilment of Dhamma.

It will be seen that Ashoka had thus a definite message to give to this world. And it is a pity that this has not yet been clearly perceived. In regard to the positive side of Dhamma, he specifies not only the attributes that constitute it but also the ethical practices in which they are to manifest themselves. As regards its negative character he has taken care to enumerate the malevolent affections which impel a man to sin and depravity *(asinava)* and to exhort us to keep ourselves as free from them as possible. But this is not all. Like a true prophet he has clearly apprehended what debars spiritual progress, and has suggested a remedy which enables us to pursue the evolution of piety unhampered.

This remedy is the self-examination which he inculcates on our minds as absolutely necessary for the real development of Dhamma. It is, however, worthy of note that Buddhaghosha in his *Visuddhimagga,* distinguishes between various forms of *pachchavekkhana,* which has been consecrated to the sense of ' examination of conscience,' ' self-examination.' And this idea of *pachchavekkhana* he has adopted from Buddha himself, who taught it to Ambalatthika-Rahula. Buddha's discourse to Rahula occurs in the Majjhima Nikaya, and is no doubt one of the texts referred to approvingly by Ashoka himself in the Bhabru Edict.

Therein Buddha exhorts Rahula to examine every act of the body, speech or mind before and also after it is initiated. Ashoka, however, is more human and teaches us to examine our character as a whole and thus take a broader outlook of our activities. " Man," says he, in Pillar Edict III, " seeth the good only, saying unto himself: ' this good have I performed.' In no wise doth he see (his) sin *(papa),* .nd say unto himself: ' this sin have I committed,' or ' this indeed is *asinava.'* This, however, is difficult to scrutinise. Nevertheless, man should see to this, and say unto himself:—' such and such (passions), indeed, lead to *asinava,* and by reason (of them) may I not cause my fall!' It is in this place that Ashoka enumerates the malevolent affections which conduce to *asinava,*— and we have already-seen what they are. Here Ashoka is evidently referring to the natural tendency of the human being to perceive and chuckle over the good he performs but not to see and regret the ill, the sinfulness, he is committing. Ashoka, therefore, very aptly remarks that it is very difficult for a person to conduct self-examination and see through the evil he has committed. He, however, insists upon self-scrutiny being carried on in order that man may not bring about his own fall. The idea, of self-examination is looked upon at present as essentially Christian both in origin and practice. But if Ashoka is not here preaching what the

Christians understand by ' self-examination,' it is; difficult to see what self-examination really is. What, again, is worthy of note here is the word which Ashoka uses for ' self-examination.' This word is *pativekha,* which, except for a little irregularity of form, is exactly the same as *pachchavekkhana* which, as we have seen, Buddha himself employs in the sense of ' examination of the conscience.' It is not, therefore, permissible to doubt that Ashoka taught ' self-examination ' to his people, and regarded it as essential to spiritual progress.

Any one who considers Ashoka's code of Dhamma cannot fail to be struck by the remarkably simple nature of his teaching. His Dhamma may be described as the common property of all religions. The virtues and practices which he tells us to follow are precisely those which all religions specify as worthy of our imitation. One is, therefore, almost tempted to say that there is nothing new or original in what he teaches. He himself admits as much in one of his edicts, Rock-Edict XIII, where he says "that" there is no country except that of the Yavanas where there are not the Brahmana and Shramana congregations and there is no place in any country where men have no faith in one sect or another," and that, in fact, " everywhere dwell these Brahmanic, Shramanic and other sects and householders among whom are established such practices as hearkening to the elders, hearkening to parents, hearkening to the preceptors, seemly behaviour and steadfast devotion to friends, acquaintances, companions and relatives, and to slaves and servants." Is it not tantamount to 13—1849 B Ashoka's admission that his Dhamma, which involves the performance of these duties, is something which all sects possess in common? This is just the reason why in another place he gives expression to his intense desire that " all sects may dwell at all places (in his kingdom), because they all desire self-restraint and purification of heart." "The people, however," he continues, are of various likings and various attachments. They will perform either the whole or a part (of their duty). But even the lavish liberality, (gratitude and firm attachment) of (a man) who has no self-restraint and purity of heart are quite worthless." What Ashoka means is that *samyama,* self-restraint, and *bhava-suddhi,* purification of heart, are virtues of such paramount excellence that every individual ought to develop them in himself. These virtues, again, are inculcated by every sect, and form the chief portion of its commandment. Whether the whole commandment will be put into practice by a member of a sect is doubtful. But it is supremely imperative on him to cultivate at least these two virtues, the negation of which can never be compensated by any degree of liberality, gratitude or devotion that he may show to his sect.

The same exhortation has been set forth by Ashoka in clearer language and at greater length in Book Edict XII. This edict is so important, as it faithfully portrays his attitude towards the different religions, that no excuse is needed for giving a full substance of it here. Ashoka says that he does not think of liberality and outward reverence *(puja)* to one's own religion so much as of the growth of its essential *(saravadhi)*. This growth of the essential is of various kinds, but at the root of it is restraint of speech.

In other words, a person must not make an exhibition of reverence to his own sect and condemn another's without any good reason. On the contrary, the other sects should be shown reverence for this and that reason. By so doing a person exalts his own sect, and does service to another's sect. By doing otherwise, he does harm to both. He who shows reverence to his own sect and condemns that of another because he is attached to his own sect and wants to illuminate it, inflicts, in reality, a severe injury on it. What course of action then is commendable in these circumstances? Ashoka replies: "people shall hear and desire to hear further one another's Dhamma." What will be the consequence of this? Ashoka describes it as follows. All sects, says he first, will thereby be possessed of much information and knowledge and will conduce to the performance of good deeds. There will thus arise, he also says, the exaltation of one's own sect and the illumination of Dhamma. This, in fact, is what Ashoka says in Rock Edict XII, and offers pabulum for reflection even to the present age. What he implies is that every religion, or Dhamma in its more extensive sense, has two sides: (i) doctrinal and (ii) ethical. The first concerns itself with questions of ritual and theology, and appeals to the intellect. The second is represented by Dhamma in its less extensive but proper sense, by what a man of sense, a man of right feeling, will naturally do; in other words, it appeals to the conscience as the modern people will say. So far as the doctrinal portion of a religion goes, there will always be diverse and mutually conflicting views not only in regard to the articles of belief but also in regard to the ritual we have to observe. This must be so, because the human intellect varies so widely. So far, however, as the ethical side of a religion in concerned, there is no divergence, no conflict, but perfect unanimity as regards the moral virtues and the moral practices we have to manifest in our conduct. This must be so, because the conscience, the sense of right and wrong, can never vary. What, therefore, the ethical side of a religion teaches cannot be something which is peculiar to that religion, but rather must be the common property of all religions.

It is really the essence of all religions and the Dhamma, which Ashoka teaches and which we have so far considered is really this essence. On the other hand, the moment we give a loose rein to our intellect, there is no end to the discussion we can carry on in matters connected with ritual and theology; and very often this discussion is nothing but acrimonious wrangling. It is this which tends the people to eulogise their sect even when no-occasion calls for it, or run down other sects without any good reason—a fanatic spirit, in fact, against which Ashoka, as we have seen, has so strongly protested. That there was this propensity to exalt one's own sect and revile that of another, that there were often hot and bitter debates between one sect and another probably over doctrinal points in Ashoka's time which put the essentials of a religion into the background seems to follow from the strong expostulations in which he has thought fit to indulge.

It is even possible to be more definite on this point and find out in what quarters exactly this animosity, this carping spirit, prevailed. For Ashoka distinctly tells us that the work of generating sympathy and concord between one sect and another was entrusted to the Dharma-Mahamatras, Stryadhyaksha-Mahamatras and Vachabhumikas. We know that the Dharma-Mahamatras were occupied with all sects, the most prominent of which were the Brahmanical Ajivikas, Nirgranthas and Buddhists. And as these officials have been instructed to attain this object, it is plain that there were friction and bitter spirit between those sects. This is clear also from a critical study of the early Buddhist literature which speaks of a number of schools, orders and sects, wrangling often bitterly with one another. Stryadhyaksha-Mahamatras were, of course, officers who were concerned with the welfare and happiness of women. And as they too have been ordered to attain the same object, it is evident that sectarian fervour and intolerant spirit were being displayed by women also. It is a pity we do not know yet definitely who the Vachabhumikas were and what their function was. But it is sufficiently clear that the tendency to eulogise one's sect and disparage that of another through religious frenzy was displayed by all the principal sects of the period and that women who are naturally more religious-minded, were by no means free from it. When, therefore, Ashoka lived and preached, theological disputation and sectarian spirit were rampant. And at a time when the people's attention is riveted not on the essential but on the non-essential element of a religion, it requires the penetrating insight and religious strength of a prophet to distinguish the essential from the non-essential and proclaim it to the world. As a matter of fact, this is what Ashoka has done. What constitutes his originality of mind as of all saints is his concentration on the essence of religion which all sects possess in common, specially at a time when they have lost sight of it.

It is interesting to note by what means he attempted to divert the mind of his people from the non-essential to the essential element of religion. He exhorts the people to hearken and desire to hearken still more to one another's Dhamma, by which he here means not only the ethics but also the ritual and theology of a sect. The effect of such a step must be at once to show to them that although one sect differed from another, they agreed in many important points. The attention of the people would thus be drawn to the points of agreement which, they must naturally conclude, constituted the essence of a religion. When the essential is thus selected and emphasised, the people would consider it to be their primary duty to put it into practice, and the result is that there is *dhammasa dipana,* illumination of Dhamma, and that the sects must thus contribute to benevolent activity (kalyan-agama). But like a true thinker Ashoka did not neglect the non-essential, that is, the sacerdotal, side of a religion which comprised ritual and theology and which appealed more to the intellect than to the moral or religious sense. By hearkening to one another's Dhamma, as proposed by Ashoka, people have to listen to and consider the doctrinal points also of the various sects. They will thus have for their reflection and judicious selection various forms of philosophy, nature lore and ceremonial developed by the various sects. They must consequently become *bahu-sruta,* that is, possessed of much knowledge and information, and be able to evolve their own system of ritual and theology in a satisfactory fashion. When the people in this manner hearken to one another's Dhamma, note the essence of religion, and emphasise it for conduct, and by a careful sifting of the different rituals and theologies of the different sects construct their own creed, they can thereby achieve the at *ma-pasamda-vadhi,* or the exaltation of their own sect, which was one of the uppermost thoughts in Ashoka's mind. The Dhamma of Ashoka is thus the essence of religion, and to perceive it in all religions and single it out for practice, and to study and weigh impartially and dispassionately their ritual and theology so as to enable us to frame our own theory in regard to the relation of man with nature is what the royal prophet of the third century B. C. teaches us. How grand and convincing this message, and how indispensable even to the present times!

No account of Ashoka's Dhamma can be complete unless we know with what ultimate end the Dhamma was to be practised. In other words, what is the *summum bonum* reserved for those who followed Dhamma? Did Ashoka believe in the future world? This question has, of course, to be answered in the positive. He often contrasts this with the next world. Thus in Pillar Edict IV. while speaking of the Rajukas, he says that he expects these officers to promote the *hidata* and pa*lata* of the provincial people, that is, their happiness in this world and the next. Similarly, in the Dhauli and Jaugada Separate Edict I, he tells us that the uppermost desire of his mind is that mankind should attain to welfare and happiness, *hida-lokika* and *pala-lokika,* that is, pertaining both to this and the other world. But what is it in the next world that a man secures by following Dhamma? Ashoka replies: *svarga,* heaven. There are at least three references to *svarga* in his edicts. In Rock Edict VI. Ashoka says that whatever effort he puts forth he puts forth in order to make his people happy and in order that they may attain to *svarga* in the next world. In Minor Rock Edict I, he insists upon all officers endeavouring strenuously to make his subjects obtain *svarga*. In Rock Edict IX, however, he tells us something more. It is this edict, which, we have seen, refers to his *Dhamma-mamgala,* that is, the auspicious rite which consists in the fulfilment of Dhamma.

The doctrine was essentially common to all Indian religions, although one sect or denomination might lay particular stress on one factor in it rather than on another." Prof. Radhakumud Mukherji follows in their footsteps. In another place Smith remarks: "The *dhamma* of the Edicts is that Hindu *dharma* with a difference, due to a Buddhist tinge, nay, rather due to saturation with the ethical thought which lies at the basis of Buddhism, but occupies a subordinate place in Hinduism." This is something like a contradiction, because at one time he admits that there was nothing distinctively Buddhistic in Ashoka's Dhamma, and at another he asserts that that Dhamma was saturated with Buddhist ethical thought. Similarly, in a third place, Smith says that the inducements of *svarga* held out by Ashoka were hardly consistent with the Buddhist philosophy of most books," and yet in a fourth place he remarks that very probably the monarch looked forward to *nirvana* although he did not express the hope. Prof. F. W. Thomas says: " there is no mention of the Four Grand Truths, the Eightfold Path, the chain of causation the word and idea of Nirvana fail to occur."

Thus there are some scholars like Smith and Thomas who have not been able to reconcile the apparently non-distinctive, non-sectarian, character of Ashoka's Dhamma with the fact of his being a Buddhist even at the time when he preached it. On the other hand, we have a scholar like Senart who has seen some points of contact between Ashoka's teaching and the Buddhist *Dhammapada,* and who considers Ashoka's inscriptions as representing such a whole and entire picture of Buddhism of that period as to justify the conclusion that up till the time of that monarch Buddhism was " a purely moral doctrine, paying little attention to particular dogmas or to abstract theories, little embarrassed with scholastic or monkish elements, and as yet without a regularly defined canon." The resemblances noticed by the French savant do not, however, appear to be of much importance except two. Besides, the Buddhist Dhammapada possesses many texts in common with such Brahmanical works as the Mahabharata, and it is doubtful whether the former can be regarded as an exclusively Buddhist work. And no scholar seems yet to have accepted the further statement of Senart based simply on the strength of the epigraphic records of Ashoka that up till the middle of the third century B. C, Buddhism was founded on the preference for the fulfilment of moral duties over the execution of the liturgical forms and practices.

It is a mistake to suppose that Ashoka's epigraphs portray the whole of Buddhism in his time. All these scholars have apparently forgotten that Buddhism has always consisted of two parts: (i) Dhamma for the monks and nuns, and (ii) Dhamma for the householders. Ashoka was a householder, at any rate he was so when he preached his Dhamma; and the people to whom he taught it were also householders, not men who had embraced the monastic life. If, therefore, it is desired to find out whether his Dhamma was at all inspired by Buddhism, it is necessary to ascertain what scriptural texts have been reserved by that religion for the lay people to read, contemplate, and practise.

The most important that has been prescribed for the Buddhist laity is the *sigalovada-Sutra* comprised in the Digha-Nikaya of the Buddhist scriptures. This is considered so important that it has been designated *gihi-vinaya*— 'Institute for the housemen,' as was first pointed out by Prof. B. M. Barua. "In this Sutra," says Buddhaghosha, " there is left nothing undescribed that constitutes the whole duty of a houseman. The Suttanta is, therefore, entitled *gihi-vinaya*—' Institute for the housemen.' Wherefore, if any person having hearkened to it, carries out what he is instructed therein, he may be expected not to decline, but to prosper." Such is the degree of importance attached to this Sutra, of course, from the laity's point of view. The gist of it is as follows: Buddha was once staying near Rajagriha in the Bamboo Wood; and, going out as usual for alms, observes Sigala, a householder's son, with wet hair and garments and with clasped hands uplifted, paying worship to the several quarters of earth and sky. On Buddha asking the reason why. Sigala says that he does this worship, holding sacred his father's word. Buddha, however, replies that in the religion of an Aryan, the six quarters should not be worshipped thus. And on being requested to explain how they should be worthy Buddhism for its laity. And it is impossible to resist the conclusion that it is this religion that is the basis and the source of inspiration in regard to Ashoka's Dhamma. We may proceed one step further and ask whether we cannot similarly trace in Buddhist scriptures the qualities which constitute Ashoka's Dhamma. We have seen that they are: (i) *daya,* (ii) *dane,* (iii) *sache,* (iv) *sochaye,* (v) *madave,* and (vi) *sadhave* or *kayane.* Now, in the *Lakkhana-suttanta* of the Digha-Nikaya we have verses which set forth certain virtues which, if practised, we are told, lead to ' Heaven to share in bliss and ravishment.'

It will be seen that *sachcha, socheyya* and *dana* are common to both the lists. And further there will be no difficulty at all in perceiving that *ahimsa (-asahasa),* and *(dama-) samyama* of the verses must correspond to *daya* and *madave* of Ashoka's inscriptions. And it is not impossible that *sila* of the verses stands for the *sadhave* or *kayane* of the epigraphs.

The Buddhist Sutra, which is next in importance to the Sigalovada-Sutra as regards lay conduct is the Mahamangala-Sutra contained in the Sutra-nipata. It recommends a certain, group of duties, the performance of which constitutes the greatest of *mamgalas* to a layman. This use of the word *mamgala* to denote righteous practices reminds us of the phrase—*Dhamma-mangala,* which Ashoka employs in Rock Edict IX to denote the *mamgala* consisting in the performance of the ethical practices specified by him as constituting Dhamma. And it leaves no doubt as to his being indebted for this idea and phraseology to the Buddhist canonical text just referred to. The Sutra commends, as the greatest of *mamgalas,* " waiting on father and mother, protecting wife and child, giving alms, taking care of relatives, abstaining from sin, intercourse with Shramanas, and religious conversations at due seasons." Here, again, is another enumeration of most of the qualities and practices referred to by Ashoka under Dhamma.

If it is once grasped that Ashoka was himself a lay follower of Buddhism and preached to the householders, and that his teaching was based on what that religion ordained for its laity, there is nothing surprising in the fact that he makes no mention of the Nirvana or the *ashtangikamarga* in his edicts, but, on the contrary, speaks of *svarga* and holds it up as the reward of Dhamma in the next life. According to Buddhism, the doctrine of heaven and hell is especially the layman's religion, the higher attainments and the goal of Nirvana being reserved for a Bhikshu. This was just the view of Buddha, who has more than once implied that a pious householder is' born in the next world as a god in one of the heavens. It is therefore no wonder at all, if Ashoka regards *svarga* as the *summum bonum* to be attained for leading a virtuous life on earth.

The belief in *svarga* is not something peculiar to Buddhism, but was shared by many religious sects. And the question that really arises is whether Ashoka believed in *svarga* such as that described in Buddhist works. In Rock Edict IV Ashoka says: " But now in consequence of the spread of Dhamma by King Priyadarshin, Beloved of the gods, the sound of the drum has become the sound of Dhamma, after his having shown to the people spectacles of aerial chariots, spectacles of elephants, masses of fire, and other divine representations." What he means is that with him the drum has become the proclaimer of Dhamma.

The sound of a drum invariably precedes either a battle, a public announcement, or the exhibition of a scene to the people. But since he entered on his career as a missionary it has ceased to be a summons to fight, but invites people to come and witness certain spectacles; and as these spectacles are of such a character as to generate and develop Dhamma, the drum has thus become the proclaimer of Dhamma. But what spectacles did Ashoka show to his subjects? Obviously they were the *vimanas, hastins, agni-skandhas,* and so forth.

The exact sense of these terms has been made clear by a work in the Pali literature called Vimanavatthu. It describes the various rewards which are in store for a virtuous man in his next life as he becomes one kind or another of *deva* according to the degree of his merit. One of these rewards is the *vimana* or column-supported palace which is a centre of supreme bliss and which could be moved at the will of its divine owner. Another kind of reward is the *hastin* or well-caparisoned, all-white, celestial elephant. The Vimanavatthu, again, describes most of the gods as possessed of a resplendent complexion, which is compared to lightning, star, or fire; and when therefore, Ashoka says that he exhibited *agni-skandhas* or *jyotih-skandhas* to his people, what he must have done is that he showed what kinds of lustre emitted from the bodies of virtuous men when they became gods in their next birth. The lives of the Devas in heavens according to Hindu belief then as now are limited, and depend upon the merit accruing from their good acts. What the Vimanavatthu, however, does is only to describe, according to the Buddhist notion, what celestial abodes and vehicles were reserved for the pious people, and lay particular stress on them, in order to induce readers and listeners to lead good unblemished lives on earth and be zealous in the performance of religious duties. Evidently, the mention by Ashoka not only of the *vimanas* but also of *hastins* and *agni* or *jyotih-skandhas* as being the cause of the development of righteousness among his people is a clear proof of the fact that the system of *svurga* in which he believed and to which he refers in his twelfth year is that known to and evolved by Buddhism.

These considerations are quite enough to convince anybody that Ashoka was a Buddhist, when he preached the Dhamma set forth in his Rock and Pillar Edicts and that there are clear traces of this Dhamma being inspired and inculcated by Buddhism. It may, however, be now asked: was he indebted for this solely to Buddhism? Did he borrow and assimilate anything from any other religion? Ashoka himself has advised his people to listen to one another's Dhamma in order that they may exalt their religion and themselves become *bahu-sruta,* 'well-informed.' What he has exhorted others to do he must have himself done. Are there any elements in his Dhamma or his own conduct, which were not Buddhistic and which were adopted from other faiths?

Anybody, who carefully considers the negative side of his Dhamma, cannot fail to be struck by the curious word a*sinava* and also the malaffections which he mentions as contributing to it. What is this word, a*sinava?* How is it to be derived? In Pillar Edict III, a*sinava* has been mentioned side by side with *papa,* 'sin,' and in Book Edict X, we meet with the word *palisave* in the sense of *apunya,* 'demerit.' It, therefore, seems at first sight that a*sinava* of Ashoka is the same as *asara* of Buddhism, which has precisely the same signification. But the Buddhists have three kinds of *asava:* (i) *kamasava,* 'sensual pleasure,' (ii) *bhavasava,* 'love of existence,' and (iii) *avijjasava,* 'defilement of ignorance.' Sometimes they add to this list a fourth one, namely, *ditthasava,* that is, 'heresy.' Ashoka, however, mentions five ways leading to *asinava,* which, again, are of an entirely different nature. They are, as we have seen, *chamdiye,* 'violence,' *nithuliye,* 'cruelty,' *kodhe,* 'anger,' *mane,* 'conceit,' and *isya,* 'envy.' The conclusion is irresistible that, curiously enough. Ashoka, although he was a Buddhist, did not adopt the *asava* of Buddhism, supposing *asava* is the same as *asinava.* From where could he then have borrowed his *asinavas*? Buhler notes that "the Jainas possess a term *anhaya,* which exactly corresponds to *asinava,* and is derived, like the latter, from *a-snu.*" *Anhaya* we find used, *e.g.*, in the well-known Jaina work *Ayaramga-Sutra* and translated as 'sins' by Prof. Jacobi. This suits here excellently, because in Pillar Edict III *asinava* has been placed side by side with *papa.* The former could not have been exactly identical with the latter in meaning, and we shall not be far from right if we take *asinava (anhaya)* to signify 'depravity, defilement.' This also seems to be the meaning of *parisava* used by Ashoka in Rock Edict X, where he equates it with *apunya* (demerit).

Now Jainism specifies eighteen kinds of *papa* or sin and forty-two kinds of *asravas.* These two lists have four malevolent affections in common, called *kashayas.* Two of these are *krodha* and *mana,* exactly two of the passions named by Ashoka. The *isya* of Ashoka, again, is to be found in the Jaina list of the *papas* as *irshya* or *dvesha. Chamdiye* and *nithuliye* are alone not traceable, though they are no doubt covered by the malaffection *himsa* mentioned under *asrava.* Thus the use of the term *asinava (anhaya),* distinction between it and *papa,* and the inclusion of at least three passions of the Jaina lists are enough to convince anybody that, in all likelihood, Ashoka has here adopted and assimilated some psychological concepts of Jainism. We thus see that although Ashoka was an ardent follower of Buddhism, he was yet Catholic enough to study other faiths such as Jainism, and adopt such features of the latter as commended themselves to him.

The same conclusion is pointed to by the terminology he employs when he speaks of the various kinds of life. He uses such words as *jiva, pana, bhuta* and *jata.* Does this not remind us of the phraseology, *pana bhuya jiva satta,* which is employed, for instance, in the Ayaranga Sutra of the Jainas? Of course, it is possible to contend that he never uses all of these words together, and may not have therefore, intended to distinguish between them. But it cannot be denied that at least *bhuta* Ashoka does contrast from *prana,* when he enumerates his ethical practices, as in *anarambho prananam, avihisa bhutanam.* Buddhist literature nowhere distinguishes between *prana* and *bhuta,* whereas Jaina scriptures not only distinguish them one from the other but also both from *jiva* and *satta.* This leads to the question: what was Ashoka's attitude towards other religious sects? We have seen that in Rock Edict VII he admits that all sects aim at self-restraint and purification of heart, and desires that they may dwell at any place in his Empire.

This point he has made clear in Rock Edict XIII by saying that the practices of Dhamma which he is preaching are practically the same as those inculcated by these sects. And he takes us one step further *by* remarking in Rock Edict XII that all people should love to listen to one another's Dhamma and thus augment its essence *(sara).* That Ashoka really meant what he has said is clear from the fact that his Dhamma, though it is Buddhism in the main, contains elements borrowed from other religions, such as Jainism, as we have just shown. When such is his mental attitude towards the various sects, one can well believe him when he tells us that he lavished gifts and honours on members of all sects, without any distinction, whether they were recluses or householders. And this belief is strengthened when we note that he regarded, as one of the constituents of Dhamma, respect and liberality towards Brahmans and Shramanas, that is, not only towards the non-Brahmanical sects other than Buddhism but also towards all Brahmanical sects. The Dharma-Mahamatras also were ordered to promote the temporal and spiritual weal of *all* sects, not only of the Buddhist Sangha but also of the Nirgranthas, Brahmanical Ajivikas, and so forth. The only action of his that is apparently inconsistent with his extremely tolerant attitude towards all religions is the prohibition of animal sacrifices to which he has referred in Rock Edict I. This, it is contended, was directed against the Brahmans and receives confirmation from a passage in Minor Rock Edict I.

The passage, however, is no longer interpreted by any scholar of repute as showing hostility to Brahmanism. And in regard to Rock Edict I, it is admitted that it does speak of Ashoka having prohibited sacrifices, but it is by no means clear that this prohibition was meant to be universal and not confined merely to his royal household. And even supposing for the moment that he prohibited sacrifices all over his kingdom, it does not necessarily imply any antagonism to Brahmanism as some of the Upanishads, which are *srutis* to a Brahman, have declared themselves in no uncertain terms against animal sacrifices and in favour of *ahimsa.*

Ashoka, as a Missionary

We have seen that Ashoka was a Buddhist and also that the Dhamma he preached was not simple piety common to all religions but the code of righteous practices laid down for a lay follower by Buddhism. Let us now find out what means he adopted for the promotion and propagation of Dhamma. Let us discuss what kind and degree of activity he displayed as a religious propagandist.

We have already seen that Ashoka embraced Buddhism in the ninth year of his reign. For one year, he did not show himself to be a zealot. But thereafter a change came over him, and about the middle of his tenth year he began to live with the Sangha and visited the Bodhi Tree. This was life turning a new leaf in the book of his life. He suddenly developed his missionary activity, and exerted himself to such an extent that although it was scarcely more than a year that he was with the Sangha, he felt himself justified in giving a glowing description of it.

This he has done in two places, once in Minor Rock Edict I, and another time in Rock Edict IV. In the first of these records which is addressed to his officers, Ashoka says: " During this period (that is, the period that he was with the Sangha), human beings who were unmixed were caused to be mixed with gods throughout Jambudvipa. This is the fruit of exertion. This is possible not only for the superior to achieve, but, indeed, it is possible for a subordinate one also, if he exerts himself, to cause people to attain to much heavenly bliss." In this edict Ashoka has described the result of his missionary work in a twofold mariner, first by saying that he has made gods and men one another's associates and next by saying that there was attainment of heavenly felicity. The commingling of men and gods must therefore be so explained as to show that it was tantamount to the achievement of heaven.

This is possible only if we say that by following Ashoka's Dhamma men became so virtuous that they attained to heaven and were associated with gods. The idea that in the days of yore men and gods lived together is known to Brahmanical literature also. Thus the Dharmasutra of the Apastamba has the following: " Formerly men and gods lived together in this world. Then the gods through *karman* went to heaven; men were left behind. Whosoever perform the *karman* of those (gods) in the same manner dwell (after death) with the gods and Brahma in the other world." From this it is clear that what Ashoka means is that he led men in the path of Dhamma and induced them to perform virtuous courses to such an extent that they became fit to be commingled with gods, not simply in the next, but rather in this, world. Instances are not wanting, in early Buddhist works, of men being worshipped by Brahma and his gods in this world as soon as their spiritual elevation was complete.

Knowing, as we do, how miracles come to spring into existence and cluster round the name of a saint in his life time even in India of the modern day, it is not unreasonable to suppose that in Ashoka's time those men from Jambudvipa who followed Dhamma and led a pure noble life came soon to be looked upon as saints and that they were believed to be associated with gods.

By what measures, it may now be asked, was Ashoka able to accomplish such a phenomenal result during the short space of a year or so? The reply is furnished by Rock Edict IV, where also the King gives a glowing account of his achievement. Ashoka informs us that he fostered and propagated Dhamma a ιong his subjects by showing them spectacles of the *vimanas, hastins,* and *agni* or *jyotih-skandhas.* These represent the kinds of heavenly bliss that are in store for the good virtuous people in their next birth when they become gods. We have thus to take note of this important fact, that is, of the first measure which Ashoka adopted for generating and developing his Dhamma. He showed to the people spectacles of the various classes of gods and of the various kinds of felicity they rolled in. He must have exhibited these spectacles in the Samajas, not the Samajas or feasts where the people were treated to meat and drink and which Ashoka condemned, but the Samajas or amphitheatres where the people were entertained with shows, music and dancing and which he looked upon favourably. Perhaps the first step then which Ashoka adopted when he started his missionary career was the exhibition of the different orders of gods, their resplendent complexions, their heavenly palaces, celestial elephants and so forth, which constituted their pomp and glory. How long he continued the exhibition of such spectacles we do not know. Probably he was showing them the whole period of his reign, as it most effectively served two purposes, namely, that of amusing the people and also of inducing them to live a life of piety. But certain it is that he persisted in it for over a year that he was with the Sangha, and that although this period was not a big one, Ashoka thought that by this means there was much growth of Dhamma, to such an extent, "indeed, that it had never been developed to this degree ever before.

We have already seen that the celestial booms referred to by Ashoka have been graphically described in a Pali work called *Vimanavatthu*. It is with much forethought that stress is laid upon their descriptions in this work, the object evidently being to induce the people to lead holy and pious lives. In this connection it is desirable to note a story narrated in Buddhist works about Moggalana, the right-hand disciple of Buddha, who was also a unique missionary. He succeeded in attracting such a number of followers to Buddhism that the preachers of other religions became jealous of him, and hired assassins to put him to death. But what was the secret of his missionary activity?

By means of his perfection in supernatural powers, we are told, he used to go to heavens, meet the gods, and interrogate every one of them as to how he contrived to rise to the position of a god. And they used to tell him by performing what acts they became what kind of gods. Similarly, he used to go to the world of Hell and ask its unfortunate inmates the story of their sufferings. Moggalana thereafter used to return to the earth and inform the people. This produced such a deep impression on the minds of the people that they used to flock to him in masses and get themselves converted to Buddhism. Most probably this story of Moggalana was known to Ashoka. But even supposing for the moment that it was not, it does not require much stretch of imagination on the part of a thoughtful and enthusiastic propagandist, such as Ashoka doubtless was, to bring into requisition the graphic descriptions of the various types of celestial felicity depicted in the *Vimanavatthu* and such works, and give it a practical turn by preparing actual representations of the *vimanas, hastins,* and so forth and exhibiting them to the people on such occasions as those of the Samajas where they must naturally gather in large masses. And if Moggalana could secure a large number of followers by merely intimating orally what virtue ensured what heaven and what unrighteousness what hell, in what terrific numbers must the people have rushed to the faith of Ashoka when not mere verbal descriptions but actual representations of the heavens and the varieties of supreme bliss to be enjoyed there were placed by him before them. There is nothing at all surprising if even in such a short space of time as one year or so, such a well-conceived, well-planned and well-carried-out propaganda work, as might be expected of Ashoka, gave him such wonderful results, —wonderful beyond all expectations.

There were other measures also which Ashoka adopted for the furtherance of his object. The beginning of his strenuous career, we have seen, synchronised with the formulation of another scheme, upon which he embarked. Rock Edict VIII says:

> For a long time past Kings used to go out on tours of pleasure *(vihara-yatra).* Here there were chase and other similar diversions. Now King Priyadarshin, Beloved of the gods, repaired to Sambodhi (Bodhi Tree), when he had been consecrated ten years. Hence these tourings for Dhamma. Here this happens, namely, visits and gifts to the Brahman and Shramana ascetics, visits and largesses of gold to the aged, and visits and instructions in and enquiries about Dhamma of the provincials."

Here Ashoka tells us that up till the tenth year of his reign he like the previous Kings used to find relaxation in *vihara-yatras* or tours of pleasure, where he indulged in hunting and other sports. In that year he gave up the idea of ever going on *vihara-yatras,* and started instead the *Dharma-yatras* where he now found his relaxation. The latter fulfilled the object that was uppermost in his mind, namely, the fostering of Dhamma. He developed

Dhamma in himself by visiting and giving gifts to the recluses and mendicants of both the Brahman and Shramana sects. During these visits he must have listened to and studied the Dhamma of every sect and assimilated its essential features, thus making himself *bahusruta.* As regards the people, he propagated Dhamma among them by coming into their personal contact, preaching righteousness, and enquiring about their spiritual progress. In other words, Ashoka turned a missionary in the real sense of the term. But when and how did the event happen? In the tenth year of his reign, when he paid a visit to the Bodhi Tree. In fact, his visit to the Bodhi Tree, as we have seen, was the first of his Dharmayatras, which he undertook along with a Sangha of Bhikshus, and the manifold spiritual benefits accruing not only to himself but also to his people induced him to repeat it so as to make it a permanent feature of his missionary programme. We may, therefore, safely say that side by side with the exhibition of the heavens and the blisses associated therewith, Ashoka undertook the work of personally preaching to his people, of course, with the same object in view, that is, for the dissemination of Dhamma.

The King actually taking upon himself the duty of preaching to his subjects must have produced a profound impression on their mind and must have been a most potent cause of the promotion of Dhamma all round. But the King, after all, was a single individual, and it was not possible for him to approach all people. Ashoka therefore thought it necessary to order his representatives, his officers, to follow in his footsteps and help him in the completion of the work personally started by him. This is clear from what he says in Pillar Edict VII, which, being a resume of the whole work achieved by him up till the twenty-seventh year of his reign, naturally describes the various measures devised and adopted by him for the realisation of his object. The edict itself begins with a vivid expression of his extreme and genuine solicitude for the spread of Dhamma among his subjects. The words he uses are so instinct with sincerity that they are worth quoting:

> "This occurred to me: In times past Kings had wished that men should grow with a befitting growth of Dhamma. But men did not grow with a befitting

> growth of Dhamma. How then may men be moved to conform (to Dhamma)? How may men grow with a befitting growth of Dhamma? How may I uplift some of them with a growth of Dhamma?"

It is quite clear that the question of the propagation of Dhamma Ashoka was for a long time revolving in his mind in all seriousness and with much careful thought. He is frank enough to admit that he was not the first King who thought of spreading Dhamma. But the efforts of the previous Kings were not crowned with any success worth mentioning. He, however, appears to have much pondered over the problem and finally hit upon a line of action which he now resolved to carry into effect for the attainment of his object. And most of the means he so adopted he mentions in this edict. " The same (object) being in view," says he in this edict, " I have set up Dharmastambhas, appointed Dharma-Mahamatras, and made Dharmasravanas." And he then proceeds to explain what he understood by each one of these measures.

The first of these, namely, Dharmastambhas do not denote any material pillars as one is apt to suppose, but rather his works of charity which he forthwith goes on to describe thus. On the roads I have planted the banyan trees. They will offer shade to man and beast. I have grown mango orchards. I have caused wells to be dug at every eight *hoses,* and I have had rest-houses. I have made many watering sheds at different places for the enjoyment of man and beast. This (provision) of enjoyment, however, is indeed a trifle, because mankind has been blessed with many blessings by the previous Kings as by me. *But I have done this with the intent that men may follow the practices of Dhamma.*" It is these works of public benevolence that are to be understood by the Dharmastambhas specified by him in Pillar Edict VII. Ashoka here candidly confesses that the provision of the various kinds of enjoyment which he has made for man and beast is not something which he alone has done, but is a duty which even Kings preceding him have performed.

Why then, it may be asked, does he notify his works of charity? He himself has given the reply to it. He says, he has done so, because others may follow his example. There can be no doubt that this was the real motive of Ashoka. For a little further on in the same edict he says precisely the same thing. " Whatever charitable works I have performed," says he, " these have been conformed to among men, and these they will perform (in future)." It looks singular that Ashoka should attach so much importance to the performance of charitable works. And it may naturally be asked whether Buddhism lays any stress on any works of public benevolence such as those referred to by Ashoka. The following text from the Samyutta-Nikaya will clear up the point:

Imperial Patron of Buddhism

The son and successor of Chandragupta is in Buddhist literature known as Bindusara, whereas the Puranas give the name Nandasara or Bhadrasara: in such a matter the Buddhist testimony would have superior authority. The Greeks use instead of the name a title, Amitrochates (Sanskrit *Amitraghkata)*, 'slayer of the foe', a form which is quoted, perhaps with reference to this King, in the grammatical work of Patanjali.

From Greek sources we learn concerning Bindusara only that he was in communication with Seleucus Nicator, from whom he received an envoy named Daimachus and solicited the purchase of sweet wine, figs, and a philosopher, the last named being refused on the ground that the sale of a sophist was not in accordance with Greek usage. The second Ptolemy, Philadelphus, also dispatched a representative, Dionysius, whose memoirs are unfortunately not preserved.

The Puranas attribute to Bindusara a reign of twenty-five years, the Pali books one of twenty-seven or twenty-eight. Whether he earned, or merely assumed, his soubriquet, we do not learn; but it is clear that he maintained intact the dominions inherited from Chandragupta. He had to deal with disaffection in Taxila, a city which was also to give trouble to his successor. It was allayed by the despatch of that destined successor, his son Ashoka.

The events and occurrences of the life of Ashoka, as we know them from the sole trustworthy source, namely his own inscriptions, are as follows. In the ninth year after his coronation he effected the conquest of the Kalinga country, i.e. Orissa with the Ganjam District of Madras. The slaughter and suffering which attended the conquest produced upon his mind such an impression that it proved the turning-point in his career. He joined the Buddhist order as a lay disciple, and thus subjected himself to the influence of ideas of which he was destined to be one of the greatest propagators. His active devotion to that faith began, however, two and a half years later, about the end of the eleventh year from his coronation, when he became a member of the *Sangha*, or order of monks, and in that capacity travelled from place to place, like the wandering Buddhist and Jain brothers, displaying energy, as he phrases it. This energy took the form of visits and gifts to Brahmans, ascetics, and old people, instructions and discussions relating to the Buddhist Dharma, or religious rules and principles. At the end of this tour, which he claims to have had important results, not however very clearly indicated, he issued the first of his religious proclamations, an exhortation to his officials to adopt the like principle of energetic action; and he also orders that his missive should everywhere be engraved upon rocks and on stone pillars, where such existed. The practice of carving Buddhist sentiments in this manner on conspicuous objects was afterwards to receive a very wide extension, as is still visible in Tibet, in Central Asia, in China, and throughout the Buddhist world.

During the following two years, the thirteenth and fourteenth, Ashoka's activity must have been at its height. He issued no fewer than sixteen missives, of which fourteen are found engraved, in one corpus, in places as far distant as the extremities of his Empire, at Girnar in Kathiawar, at Mansehra and Shahbazgarhi in the Punjab, and twelve of the same with two others at Dhauli and Jaugada in Orissa. In these records, which seem to have been engraved in his fourteenth year, Ashoka gives an account of the administrative and other measures which he had adopted. He had been active in causing wells to be dug by the roads, in providing medical aid for men and animals (perhaps a reference to animal hospitals, now known as *Panjroles*), and in propagating medical or useful plants; and this not only in his own dominions, but in those of the neighbouring, independent and quasi-independent, states of South India and the northwest frontier, nay, even as far as the Greek kingdom of Antiochus and beyond. Then he had made regulations restricting the slaughter of animals for food and especially on occasions of festivals and public shows. He had issued eloquent appeals for kindness and consideration in family relationships, in dealings with Brahmans and teachers, in the mutual attitudes of different sects; further, he had denounced what he regarded as excess of profitless (i.e. Brahman) ceremony in public and private life, and had inculcated economy, earnestness, and mutual exhortation. For the gay progresses of his predecessors on their hunting and holiday excursions he had substituted edifying spectacles and pious conferences; and he had arranged that he should himself always, even in his most private hours, be accessible to urgent calls a serious inroad upon the strict apportionment of the royal time.

Benevolent Institutions

Finally, in his thirteenth year he had instituted quinquennial circuits of the leading officials for the purpose of proclaiming the moral law as well as for the discharge of their normal functions. In the fourteenth year he appointed high officials, entitled *dharma-mahamatras,* with the duty of inculcating piety, redressing misfortune or wrong, organising charitable endowments and gifts. Some of these officers stood in special relation to the establishments, and benevolences, of his various relatives, and the operations of others extended even to the foreign countries.

The next objects of Ashoka's solicitude were the unsubdued frontier peoples, and persons in the provinces who had incurred penalties, concerning whom we have the two edicts addressed to his officers at Dhauli and Jaugada in the Kalinga country. Towards both classes he expresses a paternal regard: he is anxious to win the confidence of the borderers; and, as regards imprisoned persons, he solemnly exhorts his officials to make justice, patience, and forbearance the principles of their action. At the same time he gives instruction for the periodical public recitation of these admonitions, and repeats, for the benefit of the Kalinga officials, his intention of instituting quinquennial circuits. His sons, the Viceroys in Taxila and Ujjain, would follow a similar practice at intervals of three years.

The ensuing period of about twelve years has left little record in documents emanating from the Emperor himself. But we may plausibly conjecture that Ashoka now entered upon that course of religious foundations which has given him his unique reputation as a builder of Buddhist shrines. Eighty-four thousand religious edifices a conventional high number in India are ascribed to him, the chief sites being the places famed as having been visited by Buddha; and he is said to have redistributed among them the relics of Buddha, which were originally portioned between eight favoured cities. The actual records are not at variance with such a supposition. We know that in his thirteenth, and again in his twentieth, year he dedicated cave-dwellings in the Barabar hills for the use of monks of the Ajivika sect. In his fifteenth year he enlarged the *stupa* of the Buddha Kanakamuni, not far from Kapilavastu; and during the twenty-first year he personally visited this site and that of Buddha's own birthplace, the garden of Lumbini, setting up commemorative pillars and in the latter case granting a remission of taxation. In this period would also fall the inscriptions which attest his growing attachment to the Buddhist order and doctrine, that which ordains ecclesiastical penalties for schism, and the address to the community of monks, which among the sayings of Buddha, containing nothing that has not been well said, selects certain passages as pre-eminently suited for instruction and meditation.

At this point we should doubtless interpolate a series of events which were of high importance for the spread of Buddhism, and which, though not mentioned by the Emperor himself, are among all the legendary matter that has gathered round his name the portion best entitled to credence. It is in the nineteenth year from Ashoka's coronation, the twenty-first according to a proposed chronological emendation, that the Mahavamsa, the Pali history of Buddhism in India and Ceylon, places the Third Council, held under the Emperor's patronage in the Ashokarama at Pataliputra.

The Council, occasioned by sectarian differences among the Buddhist confession, of which as many as eighteen divisions are named, was held under the presidency of a famous monk, named Moggaliputra Tissa, to be distinguished from another Tissa mentioned in the same accounts as brother and viceroy of Ashoka: in the northern texts he is called Upagupta. It deliberated during a period of nine months; and its ultimate decision is stated to have been in favour of the school of the Sthaviras, which afterwards prevailed in Ceylon. This remarkable gathering, though ignored by the northern Buddhists, can hardly be a fiction: it represents the culmination of the earlier form of Buddhism, which with the ensuing expansion was destined to undergo a profound modification of spirit. The canon of authoritative scriptures is stated to have been on this occasion definitely closed; and in the Kathavatthu, composed at the time by Upagupta, we have a full record of the divergencies of opinion which led to its convention. Its dismissal was the signal for an organisation of the missionary activity which was already, as we have seen, included in the policy of Ashoka.

Missionary Activity

The names of the chief evangelisers of the different provinces are carefully preserved to us. To Kashmir and Gandhara was sent Madhyantika, and to the Yavana or Greek country (Bactria), Maharakshita; southern India, in its several provinces, claimed the apostles Mahadeva (Mahishamandala), Rakshita (Vanavasa), Dharmarakshita a Yavana (Aparantaka), and Mahadharmarakshita (Maharashtra); Majjhima proceeded to the Himalaya regions, and the fraternal pair Sona and Uttara, linked by the common vicissitudes of more than a single existence, to Suvarnabhumi, or a part of further India. That these are no mere legendary names we are permitted to know from some of the earliest surviving monuments of Buddhism, the stupas of Sanchi, dating from the second, or first, century BC, where relics of some of them have actually come to light. But their fame has been eclipsed by that of the saints entrusted with the conversion of Ceylon, who are said to have been no other than Ashoka's own children, his son the monk Mahendra and his daughter the nun Sanghamitra. Accompanied by the *sthaviras* Rishtriya, Utriya, Shambala, and Bhadrasara, they received a becoming welcome from the King of Ceylon, Devanampriya Tissa, who with his people was ultimately converted, and founded in honour of the evangelists the Great Vihara, thenceforward the headquarters of Singhalese Buddhism.

The special history of the island falls outside the scope of this chapter: the mission of the princely pair was treasured in the memory of Indian Buddhism; and its dispatch has been supposed to be depicted in a fresco on a wall in one of the caves of Ajanta.

We now return to Ashoka's own rescripts, the concluding group of seven edicts, which are found inscribed upon pillars, the whole number at Delhi and six of them also at other spots in the central regions of Hindustan. They belong to the twenty-seventh and following year from the coronation. In tenor they open out no new courses of action, but repeat and continue the earlier principles. One of them, however, which will be textually introduced below, has an especial interest, as a recapitulation of the aims and measures of the reign.

The whole duration of Ashoka's rule was, according to the concurrent testimony of the Brahman and Buddhist historians, 36-37 years, reckoned, no doubt, from his accession. He himself makes mention of his brothers and sisters, a sufficient refutation of the legend that at his accession he began his reign by putting to death all the hundred other sons of Bindusara. His elder brother, known hi northern literature as Susima, and in Pali books as Sumana, doubtless did incur the fate of a vanquished rival: and it is to the son of Susima, by name Nigrodha, that the King's conversion to Buddhism is ascribed. A full brother, Tissa, plays a considerable part in the Pali story. He is said to have been for a time viceroy, and to have joined the Buddhist order, along with Agni-Brahma, husband of Sanghamitra, in the fourth year after Ashoka's coronation. A Chief Queen and her sons, no doubt the Princes referred to as viceroys in Taxila and Ujjain, are mentioned in the edicts, as also are the second Queen Karuvaki and her son Tivara.

The Chief Queen, in the Ceylon records named Asandhimitra, may possibly have been the heroine of Ashoka's youthful romance as Viceroy of Ujjain, the lovely maiden named Devi, of Vedisa (Vidiga, the modern Bhilsa), mother of Mahendra and Sanghamitra. Another romance is connected with the name of Tishyarakshita, represented as an attendant upon Asandhimitra and Chief Queen of Ashoka's later years, who, enacting the part of Potiphar's wife, is stated to have occasioned the blinding of the Emperor's eldest son and heir, Kunala, Viceroy of Taxila, and in a still later legend founder of the Buddhist dynasty of Khotan in Chinese Turkestan. The jealousy of Tishyarakshita is said to have been aroused also by Ashoka's devotion to the sacred Banyan tree at Gaya, under which the son of Shuddhodana had attained to Perfect

Enlightenment. And thus on the Sanchi *stupa*, where we find carved the propitiatory procession to the tree, by which the threatened mischief was appeased, we have an actual first or second century representation in art, though by no means a portrait, of the great propagator of the Buddhist faith and morals and the imperially lavish founder of its shrines.

Foundation of Shrines and Cities

Ashoka's activity in this latter respect is not proportionally evidenced by existing monuments. When the Chinese pilgrims refer, as they constantly do, to a 'stupa of Ashoka', we cannot in strictness understand anything more than one of archaic style, such as are those still more or less intact at Sanchi or Bharhut or figured on their sculptures and elsewhere, nor are we allowed to ascribe *en bloc* to the Emperor himself the pillars at Delhi, Allahabad, Sarnath, Rampurva and in other places, on which his edicts are found inscribed: he himself forbids this, when he orders his edicts to be engraven on pillars, where such should be found. The only works of this nature particularised by him in the edicts relating to the places in question are the double enlargement of the *stupa* of Konagamana at Nigliva, the pillar erected at the same place and that at the Lumbini garden: the cave-dwellings assigned to the Ajivika monks in the Barabar hills are not expressly stated to have been constructed by Ashoka's orders. When we have added the stone railing round the Bodhi-tree, which seems to be figured on the stupa of Sanchi, we have completed the list of what can certainly be ascribed to him. But, no doubt, the remains of the palace, the Ashokarama, the Kukkutarama, and other erections at Pataliputra may be plausibly claimed for him; and we may also mention the completion on his behalf, by the Yavana King Tushaspha, of the Sudarshana tank in Junagarh, which had been begun by his grandfather Chandragupta. For the rest we must be content to believe that the great reputation which he enjoyed in this respect had a solid foundation.

Two famous cities in frontier countries have a traditional claim to Ashoka as founder. The former is Srinagar, the capital of Kashmir, embracing the site of the old Srinagari, which is connected with his name. In Nepal the ancient city of Deo-Patan (Deva-pattana) and the adjacent village of Chabahil are associated with a visit of Ashoka accompanied by a daughter Charumati and her Kshatriya husband Devapala. The two latter are said to have remained in the country and to have built respectively a nunnery and a monastery, the latter left unfinished by its founder. The legend for such it is derives some support from the archaic style of the four neighbouring stupas ascribed to Ashoka.

The name Ashoka occurs in only one of the known inscriptions. Elsewhere the Emperor employs (in conjunction with raja, 'king') the official titles *Devanampriya*, 'dear to the gods', and *priyadarshana*, 'of friendly mien'. The former style which in later ages the popular grumbling, so humorously common in India, as in other countries, diverted to the sense of 'fool' is known to have been employed by contemporary Kings in Ceylon, and by Ashoka's grandson (or still more remote descendant) Dasharatha, so that it was probably normal; indeed Ashoka himself once uses the plural in the sense practically of 'kings'. *Priyadarshin* also, which has been well rendered 'gracious', may represent a customary view that the King should wear 'a mild, pleasant, and composed aspect'. But it is certainly quite possible, as M. Senart suggests, that it was adopted by Ashoka as his ordination name.

Religion Defined: The degree of Ashoka's appreciation of Buddhism is not very easily definable; and it was even at one time contended that his early faith, which laid such special stress upon the doctrine of benevolence, was rather that of Jainism. He emphasises the principle of tolerance, wishes for the real prosperity of all sects, and, while not discouraging discussion, always a prominent feature of Indian religious life, earnestly preaches avoidance of offence. If he discountenances what he considers vain ceremonials and certain popular entertainments, which were occasions of animal slaughter, his attitude to the Brahman system in general is benevolent and respectful: he believes in the gods and would have his people strive for heaven. Nevertheless, Ashoka was undoubtedly a Buddhist: he became a lay disciple and then a monk; later he proclaims his regard for the religion and his personal faith; he addresses the church, naming certain passages from the scriptures as specially suitable for teaching and study; he denounces penalties for schism; he holds a council which defines the canon; and finally he stands out as by far the greatest author of the religious foundations of the sect. On the other hand we hear from him nothing concerning the deeper ideas or fundamental tenets of the faith; there is no mention of the Four Grand Truths, the Eightfold Path, the Chain of Causation, the supernatural quality of Buddha: the word and the idea of Nirvana fail to occur; and the innumerable points of difference which occupied the several sects are likewise ignored. Ashoka, therefore, is no theologian or philosopher; and only in the saying that the gift of dharma is above all other gifts, and in the preference of meditation to liberality, do we find any trace of such modes of thought.

Of Ashoka's personal action the most important features were his religious tours and progresses, which began at the end of the eleventh year. They were the occasion of personal intercourse with the people, including discussions and instructions in religious matters. In the course of these, and on other occasions, he was wont to issue religious proclamations, which were published by his officials and inscribed on rocks and pillars. He claims that in little more than a year he had brought the Brahman gods to the knowledge of those people in India, i.e. the wild tribes, who had formerly known nothing of them.

Further he organised shows and processions exhibiting figures of the gods in their celestial cars, of sacred elephants, and fires. The practice of earlier times, which made the King accessible to the public only at certain hours, he modified to the extent of being ready to transact business or see officials even in his most private seclusion. He subjected his household to supervision by special religious dignities: and finally he restricted the diet of the palace practically to the point of vegetarianism. His activity in causing trees to be planted by the roads, and wells for travellers to be constructed at every half-koss, also his provision of medical aid for men and animals, and his propagation of useful plants, need not be further dwelt upon: only in degree were they a new feature of royal beneficence in India.

Ashoka's relations with the Buddhist Sangha were, no doubt, friendly and cordial. He had himself been ordained, as had his brother, and by the surrender of his son and daughter also he had acquired a right to the title 'Kinsman of the Faith'. But no doubt the monkish chronicles go too far in representing his devotion as without bounds. Even his lavish expenditure upon religious edifices is exaggerated in the statement that he thrice gave away, and purchased back, Jambudvipa or the continent of India! It can hardly be that an Emperor so conscious of the responsibilities of his unique position should have been made more amenable to the authority of a religious order by himself joining it. Nor is there in his actual references to the Sangha any note of special deference; nor again do his ordinances accord to it any special regard, since the *parishads* whose affairs were to be supervised by the *dharma-mahamatras* included the managing committees of all sects.

On the other hand, we fail to detect even in the advice which Ashoka gives to the Sangha concerning specially applicable passages from the scriptures any note of the arrogance which might have betrayed an Emperor himself at home in the order. In fact such an attitude would be both un-Indian (as sanctity and learning in India excite a genuine respect) and anachronistic in what was still an age of faith. On the whole, easy as it would be to imagine flaws, one way or the other, in Ashoka's relations with the clergy, it would be hard to demonstrate them to a sound intelligence: by his grasp of the essential he rises superior to such personal suspicions.

Of the Buddhist leaders with whom he is said to have been in correspondence the most important is Upagupta or Moggaliputra Tissa. This divine is reckoned as fifth in the succession of Vinaya teachers from the time of Buddha, the series being Upali, Dasaka, Sonaka, Siggava and Chandavajji, Moggaliputra Tissa. Tissa was 60 years old at the time of Ashoka's coronation, and he died 26 years later, being succeeded by Mahendra. Apart from the Kathavatthu he is not known as an author, his great monument being the Third Council. A famous *stupa* was built in his honour at Mathura.

Moral Exhortations

Mention has already been made of the missionary leaders, whose activity is said to have followed upon the Third Council, and of Ashoka's several relatives who joined the order. The Pali books mention also a Mahavaruna, and the two sons of Kunti,

Tissa and Sumitta, who are said to have died after Ashoka's eighth year: they are not otherwise known.

The northern books mention a minister Radhagupta, who is said to have played an important part in Ashoka's attainment of sovereignty and his administration; and another minister, the Arhat Yashas, associated with the Khotan legend of Kustana. The existence of the minister Yashas seems deserving of credence as he is mentioned in the Sutralamkara of Ashvaghosha.

The moral exhortations which Ashoka most frequently addresses to his people refer to the practice of simple virtues, namely proper treatment of slaves and servants, obedience to father and mother, generosity and respect to friends, companions, relations, ascetics, and Brahmans, abstinence from cruelty to living creatures. For this imperial insistence upon such obvious duties we are right to demand some explanation; and we may perhaps find an explanation in his statement that there had been during a long period a deterioration in these respects.

Not to attribute to Ashoka the character merely of a retrospective pessimism, we may think of the social and other changes which might naturally accompany the growth of a great Empire, the succession of dynastic tragedies, the subjugation of small states, the Greek invasion, and the initiation of numerous sects. And, apart from the general responsibility of a paternal rule, he might have found even in the Arthashastra the principle that the royal authority should ensure the observance of proper discipline in the household, an obligation which even the modern state does not decline. As regards the aged and the poor, who are placed under the care of religious officials, we have seen that in the absence of a 'poor law' the care of such was a traditional obligation of royalty. These primary admonitions recur also in the latest of the edicts, as they had been prominent, along with the appeal for energy and mutual exhortation, in the earliest.

But we hear also from the beginning of piety friendship in piety, liberality in piety, kinship in piety concord and the growth of sects in essential matters, in a word of religion, dharma, as something more than shila, 'morality'. It was to be expected that with advancing years the religious feeling should acquire a stronger hold; whence we are not surprised to find in the later edicts a special exhortation to self-examination and the view that the chief thing is personal adherence to a man's adopted faith. In a country where during later ages the ecstatic, metaphysical, and fanciful aspects of religion have predominated, the sober Buddhist piety revealed in the edicts (and not uncommonly evidenced in the literature of Buddhism, both of the Great and Little Vehicles) deserves remark.

The measures, enactments, and institutions of Ashoka need not more than moderately detain us. His philanthropic activity in providing wells and trees along the roads, in propagating medicinal plants, and in founding hospitals for men and animals an activity not confined to his own dominions and further his great role as propagator of his religion and pious founder, also his regulations concerning the slaughter and treatment of animals, have already received due notice. To the same sphere belong his rules concerning prisoners, the reservation of capital punishment, and the respite of the condemned during three days with a view to their spiritual welfare and edifying works. The official system remained for the most part unchanged.

The presence of Ashoka's envoys even as far as the various Greek kingdoms is plainly contemplated. The general term denoting the superior officials is *mahamatra,* while the lower, especially the clerkly ranks, are entitled *yukta.*

The highest local officers 'set over many hundreds of thousands of people' corresponding no doubt to the *sthanikas* of the Arthashastra—are mentioned as *rajukas,* and with them are associated *pradeshikas,* perhaps the *pradeshtris* whose functions we have already defined. It is to these officers that a number of the edicts are addressed. They are exhorted to adopt towards the people under their charge the mild, patient, and benevolent principles of the Emperor himself: they are compared to nurses entrusted with the charge of children.

An institution several times referred to is the anusamyana, or periodical tour, still a feature of Indian administration. This was not an innovation on the part of Ashoka, but a part of the system which he inherited. However, he added to the duties of the touring officials, as early as his thirteenth year, that of following his own example in making their visitations the occasion of benevolent activity and religious propaganda.

For this purpose, however, he himself organised a special ecclesiastical hierarchy of religious officers (*dharma-mahamatra*), to whom these two functions were primarily assigned, and who moreover superintended the bounties of his own household, and those of his Queens, his sons, and other relatives, and organised the activities of the committees and councils (*parishad*) at the head of the Buddhist, Jain, Ajivika and other sects. The tolerance of all sects as regards liberty of residence in every district seems also to be a feature of Ashoka's own conception, as it is opposed to the rule of the Arthashastra.

7

Golden Words of Ashoka

- All men are my children.
- I am like a father to all people.
- As a father, I desire the good and happiness of all.
- I wish that all men should be happy, always.

8

Great Life at a Glance

304 BC: Ashoka was born at Patliputra.

286 BC: Marriage with Maharani Devi

284 BC: His son Mahindra's birth

281 BC: His daughter Sanghamitra's birth

275 BC: When Bindusara died, a year-long war for the succession erupted between Ashoka and his half-brothers. The Vedic sources vary on how many of Ashoka's brothers died; one says that he killed them all, while another states that he killed several of them. In either case, Ashoka prevailed and became the third ruler of the Mauryan Empire. Chandashok - Ashoka, the Terrible for the first several years of his reign, waged near-constant wars, for expanding his kingdom.

274 BC: Ashoka was anointed the new emperor. Immediately he began instituting his law of oppression by administering capital punishment for even the slightest infractions. His cruel heart showed mercy upon no one. His people spoke so poorly of the new king's antics, word went straight to the top by way of the spies Ashoka had created to investigate public concern.

272 BC: The Kalinga-Nippon-Buddha Sangha established a peace pagoda (Shanti Stupa) at Dhauli along with the construction of a monastery called Saddharma.

270 BC: Mauryan king, Ashoka was the first to formulate firm tenets for the governance of people. He had these tenets, the so called Edicts of Ashok inscribed on stone pillars, which were planted across his kingdom. The pillars were crowned with the statue of one or more lions sitting on top of a pedestal, which was inscribed with symbols of wheels.

266 BC: Eight Years after being crowned the king, Ashoka decided to annex Kalinga (Orissa) into his kingdom. This was the last battle that Ashoka fought. Though Ashoka won the battle, he was horrified by the loss of life and death of so many soldiers.

265 BC: The Mauryan Empire established unprecedented principles of civil rights under Ashoka, the Great. After his brutal conquest of Kalinga, he felt remorse for what he had done, and as a result, adopted Buddhism. From then, Ashoka, who had been described as "the cruel Ashoka" eventually came to be known as "the pious Ashoka".

262 BC: Ashoka established Buddhist pillars, rock-carved edicts, and stupas all over India. Ashoka's pillars and edicts can be seen in Delhi, Gujarat, Orissa, Sanchi (in Madhya Pradesh), near Varanasi at Sarnath, and in many other places. Just 8 km away from Bhubaneswar looking down on the plains that bore witness to the gruesome war waged on Kalinga by the Mauryan emperor Ashoka the Great, stand the rock edicts of Dhauli. It was here that Ashoka, full of remorse after the Kalinga War, renounced his blood-thirsty campaign and turned to Buddhism.

250 BC: In his Edicts, King Ashoka claimed to have sent Buddhist emissaries to the Hellenistic west.

245 BC: On the conclusion of the Buddhist convocation, Ashoka despatched a monk to Mahishamandala for the purpose of spreading Buddhism.

242 BC: The 2nd Buddhist Council held under the patronage of Emperor Ashoka, laid down the Buddhist orthodoxy. It spread rapidly in the South. It was almost atheistic.

— Emperor Ashoka's fifth pillar edict gave protection to fish, animals, and forests.

240 BC: An Ashokan Pillar was built at Bodhgaya by the Mauryan King.

234 BC: Buddha's teaching of love and compassion was further spread by emperor Ashoka.

232 BC: Ashoka died after ruling for 41 years.

Bibliography

A. L. Basham: *The Wonder that was India*, Director General of Archaeology, London, 1954.

A. Sen: *Asoka's Edicts*, Calcutta, 1956.

A. Seneviratna: *King Asoka and Buddhism*, New York, 1993.

A. Weigall: *Alexander the Great*, London, 1933.

Anderson, Norman: *The World's Religions*, InterVarsity, Downers Grove, 1991.

Avari, Burjor: *India: the Ancient Past*, Routledge, New York, 2007.

B. Subbarao: *The Personality of India*, M.S. University of Baroda, 1958.

Basham: *The Wonder that was India*, Sidgwick & Jackson, London, 1956.

Beer, Robert: *The Encyclopedia of Tibetan Symbols and Motifs*, Serindia Publications Inc., 2004.

Boa, Kenneth: *Cults, World Religions, and the Occult*, Victor Books, Wheaton, 1977.

Bongard-Levin, G. M.: *Mauryan India*, Advent Books Division, 1986.

Bornstein, David: *How to Change the World: Social Entrepreneurs and the Power of New Ideas*, Oxford University Press, New York, 2004.

C.B. Welles: *Alexander and the Hellenistic world*, Toronto, 1970.

Chand Chauhan, Gian: *Origin and Growth of Feudalism in Early India: From the Mauryas to AD 650,* Munshiram Manoharlal, 2004.

D. C. Sircar: *Inscriptions of Asoka,* Delhi, 1957.

D. H. Gordon: *The Prehistoric Background of Indian Culture,* Bhulabhai Memorial Institute, Bombay, 1958.

D. R. Bhandarkar: *Asoka,* Calcutta, 1955.

D.A. Scott: *Ashokan Missionary Expansion of Buddhism among the Greeks* NW India, 1985.

D.C. Vijayavardhana: *The Revolt in the Temple,* Sinha, Colombo, 1953.

E. Pargiter: *Ancient Indian Historical Tradition,* Banarsidass, Delhi, 1972.

E. Senart: *Buddhist India,* Banarsidass, Delhi, 1971.

Falk, Harry: *Asokan Sites and Artefacts,* Philipp von Zabern, Mainz, 2006.

Gard, Richard: *Buddhism,* George Braziller, New York, 1962.

Govind Gokhale, Balkrishna: *Asoka Maurya,* Irvington Publication, 1966.

H. van Thiel: *Leben und Taten Alexanders von Makedonien,* Darmstadt 1974.

H.G. Wells: *The Outline of History,* London, 1920.

Halverson, Dean: *The Compact Guide to World Religions,* Bethany House Publishers, Minneapolis, 1996.

Humphreys, Christmas: *The Buddhist Way,* Diamond Books, London, 1996.

Huntington, Susan: *The Art of Ancient India: Buddhist, Hindu, Jain,* Weatherhill, Boston, 1985.

J. Keay: *India: a History,* Grove Press, New York, 2001.

J. Seibert: *Alexander der Grosse,* Darmstadt, 1972.

J.W. Sedlar: *India and the Greek world: A Study in the Transmission of Culture,* Totowa, 1980.

John S.: *The Legend of King Asoka*, Jawaharlal Nehru University, New Delhi, 1983.

Joseph, Edkins: *Chinese Buddhism*, Kegan Paul, London, 1893.

K. A. Nilakanta Sastri: *Comprehensive History of India: The Mauryas & Satavahanas 325 B.C.-A.D. 300*, Bombay, 1957.

Keay, John: *India: A History*, Grove Press, 2001.

Martin, Walter: *The Kingdom of the Cults*, Bethany House, Minneapolis, 1985.

Maurice, Winternitz: *A History of Indian Literature*, Banarsidass, Delhi, 1983.

McDowell, Josh and Don Stewart: *Handbook of Today's Religions*, Here's Life, San Bernardino, 1982.

Mitra, D.: *Buddhist Monuments. Sahitya Samsad*, Calcutta, 1971.

N.A. Nikam and R. Mckeon: *Edicts of Asoka*, University of Chicago Press, Chicago, 1978.

Nilakanta, Sastri K. A.: *Age of the Nandas and Mauryas*, Motilal Banarsidass, Delhi, 1967.

Noss, John: *Man's Religions*, MacMillan Company, New York, 1968.

Parrinder, Geoffrey: *World Religions From Ancient History to the Present*, Facts on File, New York, 1971.

R. Mookerji: Asoka, Delhi, 1962.

R. Stoneman: *The Alexander Romance: From History to Fiction*, London 1994.

R. Thapar: *Asoka and the Decline of the Mauryas*, Oxford University Press, Oxford, 1998.

Radha, Kumud Mookerji: *Asoka*, Banarsidass, Delhi, 1972.

Renard, John: *Responses to 101 Questions on Buddhism*, Paulist Press, New York, 1999.

Romila, Thapar: *Asoka and the Decline of the Mauryas*, Jawaharlal Nehru University, in New Delhi, 1961

Sharma, S.P.: *History of Ancient India*, Mohit Publications, New Delhi, 1996.

Singh, M.V.: *Society Under the Mauryas*, Nav Bharat Press, Aurangabad, 1988.

Snelling, John: *The Buddhist Handbook*, Barnes and Nobles Books, New York, 1991.

Sukumar, Dutt: *The Buddha and Five After-Centuries*, Luzac, London, 1957.

Swearer, Donald: *Buddhism and Society in Southeast Asia*, Anima Books, Chambersburg, Pennsylvania, 1981.

Thapar, Romila: *Asoka and the Decline of the Mauryas*, Oxford University Press, New York, 1997.

U. Wilcken: *Alexander the Great*, New York, 1967.

V.R. Ramachandra Dikshitar: *The Mauryan Polity*, New Delhi, 1993.

Vincent, A. Smith: *Early History of India*, Banarsidass, Delhi, 1972.

W. Zwalf: *Buddhism: Art and Faith*, The British Museum Press, London, 1985.

W.W. Tarn: *Alexander the Great*, Cambridge, 1948.

Wolpert, Stanley: *A New History of India, Oxford University Press*, Oxford, 1982.

Yamamoto, Isamu: *Buddhism, Taoism and Other Eastern Religions*, Grand Zondervan Publishing, Rapids, MI., 1998.

Yardley and W. Heckel, Q. Curtius Rufus: *The History of Alexander*, Harmondsworth, 1984.

Index

A

Agnibrahma, 9, 10, 11, 12, 41, 43.

Ajivika, 5, 13, 18, 69, 319, 347, 350, 356.

Akbar, 3, 4, 159.

Alexander, 16, 19, 21, 24, 25, 119, 124, 148, 149, 152, 154, 155, 165, 179, 256, 277, 287, 288, 289, 295.

Aryan, 45, 72, 147, 150, 151, 172, 210, 219, 239, 257, 269, 272, 276, 280, 285, 287, 289, 293, 332.

Aryaputra, 12, 45, 50, 75, 85, 99.

Avanti, 40, 46, 64, 97, 99, 101, 103, 112, 117, 128, 129, 130, 132, 138, 139, 141, 144, 171, 196, 289.

B

Barhadratha Dynasty, 14.

Bhagavad Gita, 226, 250, 252, 256, 262, 263, 264, 268, 291.

Bhikhsus, 56.

Bindusara, 4, 5, 9, 11, 12, 13, 20, 22, 47, 63, 64, 65, 75, 84, 85, 87, 97, 151, 277, 295, 344, 349, 359.

Bodhisattva, 229.

Buddha Sangha, 359.

Buddhism, 2, 3, 14, 25, 34, 35, 36, 48, 55, 57, 68, 69, 167, 188, 201, 202, 203, 204, 205, 206, 207, 244, 246, 249, 268, 269, 270, 285, 289, 290, 291, 292, 295, 297, 300, 309, 310, 311, 313, 314, 315, 319, 320, 321, 331, 332, 333, 334, 335, 336, 337, 338, 340, 344, 347, 348, 349, 351, 355, 360.

Buddhist Church, 49, 87, 292, 301, 317, 318, 319, 320.

Buddhist Council, 15, 205, 206, 319, 360.

C

Cabinet, 87, 91, 182.

Chandragupta Maurya, 10, 18, 58, 63, 121, 134, 158, 160, 238, 277, 286, 303, 307.

Charaka, 110.

Christian, 3, 28, 189, 252, 258, 259, 284, 325.

Church, 49, 87, 201, 203, 204, 206, 292, 301, 317, 318, 319, 320, 351.

Civil Service, 26, 88.

D

Dharma, 5, 9, 13, 67, 82, 87, 88, 93, 96, 104, 187, 188, 191, 200, 202, 203, 204, 206, 207,

208, 209, 210, 211, 214, 215, 219, 226, 230, 235, 240, 241, 244, 245, 246, 249, 250, 253, 254, 256, 289, 292, 295, 296, 297, 298, 299, 300, 302, 319, 328, 337, 341, 343, 345.

Dipavamsa, 4, 12, 13, 20, 26, 28, 42, 48, 55, 101, 134, 181.

Divyavadana, 5, 6, 7, 9, 10, 76, 84, 85, 97, 109, 118, 119, 127, 135, 151, 171, 301.

E

Empire, 1, 2, 3, 4, 5, 17, 19, 24, 25, 26, 29, 32, 37, 38, 46, 50, 54, 57, 58, 59, 61, 63, 64, 65, 66, 67, 70, 71, 83, 84, 87, 90, 94, 104, 105, 112, 116, 117, 118, 124, 126, 128, 131, 132, 135, 136, 145, 148, 149, 151, 152, 155, 156, 157, 165, 166, 171, 172, 175, 177, 181, 188, 196, 203, 215, 219, 231, 262, 263, 268, 271, 276, 277, 289, 290, 295, 297, 299, 303, 304, 322, 324, 337, 345, 354, 359, 360.

Executive Council, 183.

F

Faith, 26, 55, 56, 57, 60, 104, 121, 201, 203, 204, 206, 207, 217, 219, 235, 240, 249, 250, 253, 266, 276, 292, 294, 309, 311, 314, 326, 341, 345, 350, 351, 352, 353, 355.

Freedom, 57, 66, 90, 155, 238, 291, 322, 324.

G

Gaya, 157, 177, 300, 349.

Government, 29, 39, 40, 45, 54, 59, 67, 71, 72, 78, 80, 81, 82, 83, 86, 87, 89, 96, 97, 99, 107, 113, 123, 124, 148, 182, 196, 198, 207, 213, 216, 217, 290, 301.

Great Vihara, 9, 348.

H

Heaven, 66, 86, 162, 225, 228, 237, 240, 241, 244, 263, 282, 330, 333, 338, 339, 341, 351.

Hindu, 1, 34, 82, 83, 125, 156, 245, 254, 257, 266, 267, 268, 269, 270, 307, 323, 331, 335.

Hindu Society, 323.

Hinduism, 244, 266, 270, 271, 331.

Hiuen Tsang, 70, 118, 119, 125, 130, 134, 145, 155, 166, 173, 269, 271, 293.

Home Provinces, 93, 102, 157, 161, 196.

Hultzsch, 95, 106, 132, 201, 207, 310, 312, 321.

I

Imperial Government, 161.

Independence, 46, 86.

Islam, 244, 274.

J

Jambudvipa, 6, 17, 72, 112, 116, 117, 125, 126, 135, 137, 155, 162, 163, 164, 165, 177, 180, 181, 182, 203, 241, 255, 257, 258, 276, 338, 339, 353.

K

Kalinga, 1, 2, 3, 7, 30, 35, 36, 37, 38, 50, 57, 59, 66, 84, 85, 88, 89, 97, 98, 112, 117, 124, 131, 132, 138, 139, 141, 157, 171, 196, 199, 200, 212, 232, 263, 276, 277, 296, 297, 298, 324, 344, 346, 359, 360.

Kalinga War, 2, 3, 66, 298, 360.

Kapilavastu, 23, 128, 153, 157, 177, 300, 347.

Karma, 77, 79, 91, 264.

karman, 339.

Karuvaki, 8, 9, 10, 31, 32, 349.

Kaushambi, 41, 42, 85, 87, 93, 112, 128, 129, 133, 157, 177, 201, 204, 317, 318, 320.

King, 3, 4, 6, 7, 8, 10, 11, 13, 15, 16, 17, 18, 20, 21, 22, 23, 24, 25, 26, 27, 28, 30, 32, 34, 35, 36, 38, 39, 43, 44, 45, 46, 47, 48, 49, 51, 52, 54, 56, 58, 60, 61, 65, 67, 70, 72, 73, 74, 75, 76, 77, 78, 79, 80, 81, 82, 83, 84, 85, 86, 88, 90, 91, 92, 93, 95, 97, 99, 102, 106, 107, 108, 109, 111, 114, 116, 118, 119, 120, 122, 123, 124, 138, 145, 150, 153, 154, 156, 158, 161, 163, 164, 167, 169, 170, 173, 174, 175, 179, 180, 182, 183, 184, 185, 186, 187, 189, 191, 192, 193, 194, 195, 196, 197, 198, 199, 200, 203, 204, 206, 208, 209, 211, 212, 214, 215, 216, 217, 222, 224, 225, 226, 227, 228, 229, 230, 231, 232, 233, 234, 235, 236, 241, 242, 243, 253, 254, 255, 256, 257, 259, 260, 268, 269, 273, 277, 278, 279, 280, 286, 287, 295, 300, 301, 303, 310, 311, 312, 314, 315, 316, 317, 319, 320, 321, 322, 334, 339, 341, 342, 343, 344, 348, 350, 351, 352, 359, 360.

Kshatriya, 5, 148, 279, 280, 285, 301, 351.

L

Literature, 9, 17, 20, 33, 35, 51, 92, 126, 134, 141, 150, 151, 163, 165, 166, 167, 170, 172, 176, 186, 223, 224, 228, 231, 236, 246, 264, 268, 278, 295, 307, 318, 321, 328, 334, 337, 339, 344, 349, 355.

Lord, 2, 20, 22, 49, 63, 66, 117, 158, 162, 195, 215, 255, 271, 281, 288, 289, 300, 301.

M

Magadha, 11, 14, 15, 17, 18, 24, 30, 46, 47, 64, 65, 66, 67, 70, 72, 79, 92, 112, 113, 116, 118, 120, 121, 127, 128, 154, 159, 172, 173, 177, 182, 194, 257, 258, 259, 277, 296, 321, 322.

Mahabharata, 33, 35, 105, 119, 121, 123, 130, 139, 142, 143, 154, 163, 168, 208, 226, 290, 331.

Mahavamsa, 4, 5, 8, 9, 10, 13, 16, 17, 18, 20, 21, 23, 40, 42, 48, 169, 302, 311, 347.

Mahavira, 15, 38, 223, 280.

Majjhima, 325, 348.

Maurya, 10, 12, 13, 14, 18, 19, 20, 22, 23, 24, 25, 26, 43, 44, 47, 49, 58, 59, 63, 69, 98, 113, 118, 119, 121, 124, 134, 156, 158, 160, 169, 170, 171, 173, 174, 179, 181, 182, 190, 194, 199, 226, 238, 256, 271, 277, 286, 303, 305, 307.

Mauryan Dynasty, 63.

Mauryan Empire, 37, 63, 359, 360.

Muslim, 3, 147, 253.

N

Nanda, 14, 16, 17, 18, 19, 21, 22, 118, 121, 199, 277.

Nirgranthas, 8, 118, 204, 218, 220, 285, 286, 319, 328, 337.

P

Pataliputra, 1, 5, 7, 8, 9, 11, 15, 17, 18, 19, 23, 24, 29, 31, 32, 37, 41, 42, 45, 46, 49,

57, 65, 66, 70, 75, 112, 117, 118, 119, 128, 129, 157, 172, 173, 174, 177, 195, 203, 205, 295, 297, 300, 302, 303, 305, 319, 320, 321, 347, 350.

Poetry, 195, 275.

Prime Minister, 17, 18, 20, 21, 73, 77, 78, 85.

Q

Queen, 5, 6, 8, 9, 13, 14, 15, 21, 23, 31, 41, 42, 45, 48, 52, 72, 73, 74, 75, 91, 193, 195, 212, 349.

R

Raja, 27, 28, 73, 84, 116, 127, 159, 176, 181, 182, 188, 191, 195, 210, 211, 216, 222, 226, 229, 302, 310, 321, 351.

Rajagriha, 14, 15, 128, 157, 173, 174, 284, 332.

Rajavachanikas, 93, 97, 103, 157, 196.

S

Sangha, 14, 49, 52, 55, 56, 57, 159, 192, 197, 202, 203, 205, 206, 219, 223, 224, 309, 310, 311, 312, 313, 314, 318, 319, 320, 321, 337, 338, 340, 342, 345, 352, 353, 359.

Sanskrit, 12, 14, 38, 41, 48, 138, 145, 150, 158, 231, 268, 310, 344.

Shakya, 8, 22, 23, 24, 40, 64, 201, 313.

Siddhartha, 313.

Suvanjagiri, 12.

T

Taxila, 5, 7, 57, 64, 65, 68, 84, 85, 89, 123, 145, 154, 305, 344, 346, 349.

Thomas, 99, 100, 123, 309, 331.

Tishyaraksha, 42, 48.

Tisya, 5, 6, 7, 8, 9, 84, 86.

U

Ujjaini, 7, 32, 40, 42, 84, 97, 98, 128, 129, 141, 157, 177, 196.

Upanishads, 14, 53, 124, 251, 264, 290, 338.

V

Vaishali, 15, 128, 157, 172, 206, 210, 300, 302, 303, 320.

W

Wilson, 309.

Wisdom, 1, 15, 39, 40, 64, 77, 78, 224, 229, 250, 253, 264, 278, 292, 299.

Y

Yavanas, 142, 143, 146, 148, 149, 150, 151, 152, 153, 155, 157, 231, 258, 293, 326.

Yuan Chwang, 6, 7, 9, 203, 301, 302, 305.

Yuvaraja, 6, 72, 73.

□□□